Metamorphoses of Helen

Metamorphoses of Helen

Authority, Difference, and the Epic

MIHOKO SUZUKI

Cornell University Press

Ithaca and London

Copyright © 1989 by Cornell University

All rights reserved. Except for brief quotations in a review, this book, or parts thereof, must not be reproduced in any form without permission in writing from the publisher. For information, address Cornell University Press, 124 Roberts Place, Ithaca, New York 14850.

First published 1989 by Cornell University Press.
First printing, Cornell Paperbacks, 1992.

International Standard Book Number 0-8014-2219-1 (cloth)
International Standard Book Number 0-8014-8080-9 (paper)
Library of Congress Catalog Card Number 89-764
Printed in the United States of America
Librarians: Library of Congress cataloging information
appears on the last page of the book.

⊗ The paper in this book meets the minimum requirements of the American National Standard for Information Sciences—Permanence of Paper for Printed Library Materials, ANSI Z39.48-1984.

For my parents

Contents

Acknowledgments

Metamorphoses of Helen has undergone its own metamorphoses, and I have the pleasure of thanking many people who have contributed to its making. First and foremost, I am grateful for the wise and kind guidance of Lowry Nelson, Jr., who also allowed me to use his translation of a poem by Osip Mandelshtam as one of my epigraphs. I also record my debt to the late Herbert Dieckmann, to Neil Hertz, W. R. Johnson, R. E. Kaske, and Pietro Pucci, who first taught me about reading literature, and to A. Bartlett Giamatti and Thomas M. Greene, who later shaped my study of Renaissance literature. Margaret W. Ferguson helped determine the focus of this study and made crucial suggestions at an early stage.

Michael Cadden, Ralph Hexter, Victoria Kahn, Ellen Peel, and Daniel Selden read and commented on the earliest versions. Thomas Fay—an exacting editor and a generous friend—encouraged me to rethink and clarify my ideas. Susanne L. Wofford cast a critical eye on various versions; she has also been a source of thought-provoking conversation and friendship over the years. At later stages, many friends and colleagues offered helpful comments, essential information, and welcome advice: Zack Bowen, James M. Cox, John Fitzgerald, Charles R. Forker, George Gilpin, Joseph Litvak, Patrick A. McCarthy, Mary Anne Mailloux, Steven Mailloux, Ross Murfin, Sheila Murnaghan, Frank Stringfellow, and Lindsey Tucker. Hermione de Almeida and Tassie Gwilliam contributed extensive and astute editorial comments, as well as friendship and support.

The editors of *English Literary Renaissance* and *Philological Quarterly* have kindly given me permission to use material of my own which first appeared in their journals: " 'Unfitly yokt together in one teeme': Vergil and Ovid in *Faerie Queene*, III, ix," *ELR*, 17 (1987), 172–85;

ix

"'Truth tired with iteration': Myth and Fiction in Shakespeare's *Troilus and Cressida*," PQ, 66 (1987), 153–74. Grateful acknowledgment is made also to the following publishers: Alfred A. Knopf, Inc., for permission to quote from Wallace Stevens, *The Palm at the End of the Mind* (copyright © 1967, 1969, 1971 by Holly Stevens); Harper and Row Publishers, Inc., for permission to quote from Richmond Lattimore's translation of *The Odyssey of Homer* (copyright © 1965, 1967 by Richmond Lattimore); New Directions Pub. Corp. for permission to quote from H.D., *Helen in Egypt* (copyright © 1961 by Norman Holmes Pearson); Oxford University Press for permission to quote from E. de Selincourt and J. C. Smith's edition of *Spenser Poetical Works* (1912) and Kenneth Muir's edition of Shakespeare's *Troilus and Cressida* (copyright © 1982); Random House, Inc., for permission to quote from Robert Fitzgerald's translation of *The Aeneid of Virgil* (copyright © 1981, 1982, 1983 by Robert Fitzgerald); University of Chicago Press for permission to quote from Richmond Lattimore's translations of *The Iliad of Homer* (copyright © 1951 by the University of Chicago) and *Greek Lyrics* (copyright © 1949, 1955, 1960 by Richmond Lattimore); the University of South Carolina Press for permission to quote from *The Older Sophists,* ed. Rosamond Kent Sprague (copyright © 1972); and Viking Penguin, Inc., and Georges Borchardt, Inc., for permission to quote from "Agamemnon," *The Oresteia* (copyright © 1966, 1967, 1975 by Robert Fagles; all rights reserved).

I acknowledge the generous support of the American Council of Learned Societies and the University of Miami Research Council, which gave me the released time to complete this book. Anonymous readers for Cornell University Press offered thoughtful and useful suggestions for improvement, and I feel especially privileged to have worked with Bernhard Kendler—an able, kind, exemplary editor. Frank Palmeri helped make the process of writing and revision a constantly challenging discovery. Finally, I dedicate *Metamorphoses of Helen* with love and gratitude to my parents.

Mihoko Suzuki

Coral Gables, Florida

Abbreviations

AJP	American Journal of Philology
CJ	Classical Journal
CL	Comparative Literature
CQ	Classical Quarterly
CSCA	California Studies in Classical Antiquity
ELH	English Literary History
ELR	English Literary Renaissance
HLQ	Huntington Library Quarterly
HSCP	Harvard Studies in Classical Philology
JHS	Journal of Hellenic Studies
PMLA	Publications of the Modern Language Association of America
SP	Studies in Philology
SEL	Studies in English Literature: 1500–1900
TAPA	Transactions and Proceedings of the American Philological Association
YCS	Yale Classical Studies

Metamorphoses of Helen

Introduction

What is becoming to a city is manpower, to a body beauty, to a soul wisdom, to an action virtue, to a speech truth, and the opposites of these are unbecoming. Man and woman and speech and deed and city and object should be honored with praise if praiseworthy and incur blame if unworthy, for it is an equal error and mistake to blame the praisable and to praise the blameable.
—Gorgias, "Encomium of Helen"

Epic has traditionally been considered a masculine genre, one that takes as its subject the founding, ordering, and defending of cities and the bequeathing of responsibility and prerogative from father to son. The *Iliad* can be described as at once the story of the Greek siege on Troy and of Achilles' rebellion against and acceptance of paternal authority. Yet at the heart of the *Iliad* we find a woman: Helen of Argos, the putative cause and object of the originary struggle between nations.

In *Metamorphoses of Helen*, I read the epic tradition "as a woman";[1] I examine the representation of woman by focusing on the metamorphoses of the figure of Helen, the prototypical woman in this tradition.[2] Given the importance of Helen and of other female figures

[1] On the woman reader as one who challenges the authority of patriarchal texts or interpretations, see Judith Fetterley, *The Resisting Reader: A Feminist Approach to American Fiction* (Bloomington: Indiana Univ. Press, 1978); and Annette Kolodny, "A Map for Rereading: Or, Gender and the Interpretation of Literary Texts," *New Literary History*, 11.3 (Spring 1980), 451–67. On the phrase "reading as a woman," see Jonathan Culler, *On Deconstruction: Theory and Criticism after Structuralism* (Ithaca: Cornell Univ. Press, 1982), pp. 43–63; and Mary Jacobus, "Reading Woman (Reading)," in *Reading Woman: Essays in Feminist Criticism* (New York: Columbia Univ. Press, 1986), pp. 3–26.

[2] For a complete account of the appearances of Helen of Troy in literature, see Helene Homeyer, *Die Spartanische Helene und der Trojanische Krieg: Wandlungen und Wanderungen eines Sagenkreisis vom Altertum bis zur Gegenwart* (Wiesbaden: Steiner, 1977). For the mythological background of Helen as a nature goddess, see Martin L. West's Inaugural Lecture at Bedford College, University of London, 30 April 1975,

in the epic tradition, I believe we can remedy a neglect of them by reading the epic from a feminist perspective. Already in the Homeric epics, the male poet inscribes not only a female subject but an audience that includes women. The Iliadic Helen knows her story will be the subject of future epics, and in the *Odyssey* the poet represents Helen as a storyteller of the Trojan war. Early in the *Odyssey*, Penelope asks the bard to choose a subject other than the Homecoming of the Achaians, a song whose silence about Odysseus implies that her husband has died. Despite Telemachus' rebuke that she should not involve herself with *mythos* that properly belongs to men, Penelope, by keeping Odysseus alive in her memory, does in fact succeed in choosing another song—Odysseus' own story of his wanderings which he recounts to her upon their reunion in Ithaca. In the *Aeneid*, Dido is the principal audience of Aeneas' narration of the fall of Troy and his wanderings before reaching Carthage, a narration that occupies two of the epic's twelve books. A focus on female subjects and readers will lead us not only to an understanding of the way woman functions as a figure of difference from patriarchal authority and institutions in these epics but also to a new appraisal of "the meshing of a definition of women and a definition of the world."[3] I will argue that the representation of woman, as the motivating force and stated goal of the epic narrative, becomes a crucial locus for the poet's assertion of difference from both literary and political authority.

Comparatist scholars of the Renaissance epic, including Thomas M. Greene, A. Bartlett Giamatti, Robert Durling, and Andrew Fichter, have preceded me in offering studies that map the trajectory of the genre.[4] Their works, like mine, focus on a particular aspect of the

"Immortal Helen." See also s.v. "Helene" in *Pauly-Wissowa Realencyclopaedie der Classische Altertumswissenschaft* (Stuttgart: J. B. Metzler, 1912), 7: 2823–37. On the anterior myth of Helen and her later appearances in literature, see Jack Lindsay, *Helen of Troy: Woman and Goddess* (London: Constable, 1974); John Pollard, *Helen of Troy* (New York: Roy Publishers, 1965); and Lilly B. Ghali-Kahil, *Les enlèvements et le retour d'Hélène dans les textes et les documents figurés* (Paris: Boccard, 1955).

[3]The phrase is Myra Jehlen's, from "Archimedes and the Paradox of Feminist Criticism," in *Feminist Theory: A Critique of Ideology*, ed. Nannerl O. Keohane, Michelle Z. Rosaldo, and Barbara C. Gelpi (Chicago: Univ. of Chicago Press, 1982), p. 200.

[4]Thomas M. Greene, *The Descent from Heaven: A Study in Epic Continuity* (New Haven: Yale Univ. Press, 1963); A. Bartlett Giamatti, *The Earthly Paradise and the Renaissance Epic* (Princeton: Princeton Univ. Press, 1966); Robert Durling, *The Figure of the Poet in the Renaissance Epic* (Cambridge: Harvard Univ. Press, 1965); and Andrew Fichter, *Poets Historical: The Dynastic Epic in the Renaissance* (New Haven: Yale Univ. Press, 1982).

epic—the convention of the divine messenger in Greene's *Descent from Heaven*, the enchanted garden in Giamatti's *Earthly Paradise and the Renaissance Epic*—in order to analyze each poem as an entity. More than these predecessors, however, I believe I stress discontinuity rather than continuity between the epics; this difference stems from my focus on the male poet's representation of woman as a figure that questions and at times subverts continuity, hierarchy, and order.[5] I share this focus on the representation of woman with Lillian S. Robinson, whose *Monstrous Regiment: The Lady Knight in Sixteenth-Century Epic* treats the figure of the androgyne as a site of the convergence of politics and gender in the epics of Virgil, Ariosto, Tasso, and Spenser. Robinson uses Marxist theory to elucidate "the contradiction between woman as an historical being and as a symbolic instrument";[6] I use theories of sacrifice and scapegoating in order to elucidate the contradictions *within* these texts—between the dominant patriarchal perspective and that of the female scapegoat.

I also share Robinson's conviction of the need to study the male-authored canonical literature "that makes up the great body of 'our' literary tradition."[7] I believe that a feminist perspective can make a

[5]Giamatti sees the ambiguously attractive and dangerous sorceresses who inhabit the enchanted gardens as synecdoches of the gardens and, ultimately, of the epics that contain them (p. 6).

[6]Lillian S. Robinson, *Monstrous Regiment: The Lady Knight in Sixteenth-Century Epic* (New York: Garland, 1985), p. 5. Less useful for my purposes is Stevie Davies, *The Feminine Reclaimed: The Idea of Woman in Spenser, Shakespeare and Milton* (Lexington: Univ. Press of Kentucky, 1986), which, as its title indicates, is interested in the Platonist "Idea, not just the idea, of woman" (p. ix).

[7]Lillian S. Robinson, "Dwelling in Decencies: Radical Criticism and the Feminist Perspective," in *Sex, Class, and Culture* (Bloomington: Indiana Univ. Press, 1978; rpt. New York: Methuen, 1986), p. 12. For similar views, see Jehlen, pp. 190–94, and Nina Auerbach, "Engorging the Patriarchy," in *Feminist Issues in Literary Scholarship*, ed. Shari Benstock (Bloomington: Indiana Univ. Press, 1987), p. 155. For examples of feminist criticism of canonical male writers that also reflect on their own practice, see Eve Kosofsky Sedgwick, *Between Men: English Literature and Male Homosocial Desire* (New York: Columbia Univ. Press, 1985); Christine Froula, "When Eve Reads Milton: Undoing the Canonical Economy," in *Canons*, ed. Robert von Hallberg (Chicago: Univ. of Chicago Press, 1984), pp. 149–75; and Adrienne Munich, "Notorious Signs, Feminist Criticism and Literary Tradition," in *Making a Difference: Feminist Literary Criticism*, ed. Gayle Greene and Coppélia Kahn (New York: Methuen, 1985), pp. 238–59. Elaine Showalter has seen this "feminist critique" of male-authored texts as less useful than "gynocriticism," the feminist analysis of woman's writing. "Feminist Criticism in the Wilderness," in *Writing and Sexual Difference*, ed. Elizabeth Abel (Chicago: Univ. of Chicago Press, 1982), pp. 9–35, esp. pp. 12–13. Yet Showalter appears to be moving away from this position in a recent essay, "The Other Bostonians: Gender and Literary Study," *Yale Journal of Criticism*, 1.2 (1988), 179–87.

difference in the way we read the epic, perhaps the foremost example of "man's writing," and the genre that purports to be universal in significance and value. Although it is crucial for feminist critics to recover women's writing, which has been excluded from a canon selected by male writers and critics, it is imperative that we subject that canon to renewed scrutiny. Despite recent efforts by feminist critics to conceive the canon anew, the texts of the established canon will continue to be read and taught;[8] thus we cannot forfeit these texts or forgo feminist readings of them simply because they are canonical and patriarchal. If we do, then these texts will continue to be read in ways that domesticate and obscure questions of gender. For example, Hector's farewell to Andromache, a section of the *Iliad* frequently anthologized for "masterpiece" surveys, is often read and taught as a sentimental affirmation of the separation of man's work from woman's and, moreover, as a celebration of man's patriotism built upon the sacrifice of family life. I would suggest that the *Iliad*, unlike the *Odyssey*, does indeed conceive of gender roles and spheres as distinct and separate; yet the meeting between Hector and Andromache and the later scene of Hector's death—Achilles slays Hector outside the walls of Troy while Andromache weaves his garments within—do not simply affirm such separation but demonstrate its consequences.

As exemplified by my reading of this scene between Hector and Andromache, my intention in this book is neither to reject these male-authored canonical texts as misogynist nor to reclaim them as protofeminist.[9] Allan Bloom oversimplifies matters in more ways than one when, in lamenting "the closing of the American mind," he asserts that "all literature up to today is sexist" and yet condemns feminism as "the latest enemy of the vitality of classic texts."[10] It is true that these texts cannot escape the conditions of their production in patriarchal culture; thus they inevitably participate in the encoding

---

[8]The pioneering study of women writers in the British tradition is, of course, Sandra M. Gilbert and Susan Gubar, *The Madwoman in the Attic: The Woman Writer and the Nineteenth-Century Literary Imagination* (New Haven: Yale Univ. Press, 1979). See also Margaret Homans, *Women Writers and Poetic Identity: Dorothy Wordsworth, Emily Bronte, and Emily Dickinson* (Princeton: Princeton Univ. Press, 1980); and Mary Poovey, *The Proper Lady and the Woman Writer: Ideology as Style in the Works of Mary Wollstonecraft, Mary Shelley, and Jane Austen* (Chicago: Univ. of Chicago Press, 1984).

[9]Jehlen, p. 192, expresses similar views: "We gain no benefit from either disclaiming the continuing value of the 'great tradition' or reclaiming it as after all an expression of our own viewpoint."

[10]Allan Bloom, *The Closing of the American Mind: How Higher Education Has Failed Democracy and Impoverished the Souls of Today's Students* (New York: Simon and Schuster, 1987), p. 65.

of woman as Other, assigning to woman the negative pole of any number of binary oppositions. But at the same time, I would suggest that they expose that very process of symbolic representation, and hence repression, of woman. To varying degrees, both these strands coexist in each epic text;[11] my task is to clarify the often self-divided motives (in the sense Kenneth Burke uses that term) in their representation of woman and, in the process, uncover the ideology of the text.[12]

In thinking about the complex motives of these texts and their often divided ideology, I have drawn on studies of sacrifice and scapegoating by Henri Hubert and Marcel Mauss, Victor Turner, Walter Burkert, and René Girard.[13] Burkert explains the relationship between sacrifice and scapegoating by reference to the ritual of Yom Kippur, the Day of Atonement, described in the Old Testament. Two goats are presented to the priest by the community; one is sacrificed to Jahve, and the other, destined for Azazel, is loaded with the sins of Israel and led away into the desert. Azazel stands for the "other" side in opposition to Jahve, as the desert is the opposite of man's fertile fields.[14] Thus sacrifice and scapegoating are complementary modes of protecting the community from situations of anxiety, whether caused by plague, enemies, or divisions within the community. The victim is selected on the basis of carrying marks of doubleness, of having contradictory traits: a repulsive person or a king (or both, such as Oedipus); a woman as an object of desire and yet less

---

[11]I am in agreement with Nicole Loraux, *Tragic Ways of Killing a Woman*, trans. Anthony Forster (Cambridge: Harvard Univ. Press, 1987), p. 62, who states that her study of "tragedy's very unusual orthodoxy" was conducted with only one preconception: "that at all costs the sterile opposition between feminism and misogyny should be avoided."

[12]See, for example, Kenneth Burke, *The Philosophy of Literary Form* (Berkeley: Univ. of California Press, 1973), p. 20: "*Situation* is but another word for *motives*. The motivation out of which [the writer] writes is synonymous with the structural way in which he puts events and values together when he writes. . . ."

[13]Henri Hubert and Marcel Mauss, *Sacrifice: Its Nature and Function* (1898), trans. W. D. Halls (Chicago: Univ. of Chicago Press, 1964); Victor Turner, *The Drums of Affliction: A Study of Religious Processes among the Ndembu of Zambia* (Oxford: Clarendon Press, 1968), pp. 269–83; Walter Burkert, *Structure and History in Greek Mythology and Ritual* (Berkeley: Univ. of California Press, 1979), pp. 59–77; idem, *Homo Necans: The Anthropology of Ancient Greek Sacrificial Ritual and Myth*, trans. Peter Bing (Berkeley: Univ. of California Press, 1983); René Girard, *Violence and the Sacred*, trans. Patrick Gregory (Baltimore: Johns Hopkins Univ. Press, 1977); idem, *Des choses cachées depuis la fondation du monde* (Paris: Grasset, 1978); and idem, *The Scapegoat*, trans. Yvonne Freccero (Baltimore: Johns Hopkins Univ. Press, 1986).

[14]Burkert, *Structure and History*, p. 64.

valuable than a man.[15] The community attempts to exorcize its own ambivalence by projecting it on a victim marked by weakness or difference and then either destroying the victim loaded with doubleness (in the case of a sacrifice) or expelling it from the community (in the case of scapegoating). The principle of substitution and displacement which underlies the mechanism of sacrifice and scapegoating explains the arbitrary choice of victim, the infinite substitutability of the victims, and the repeatability of the sacrifice and scapegoating. According to Claude Lévi-Strauss, women as signs were the first objects of exchange which made possible communities based on alliances between males.[16] Such exchanges parallel in intent the scapegoating or sacrificing of a female victim. In the texts I examine, woman as Other is consistently assigned the role of sacrificial victim or scapegoat so that epic community among men can be maintained and affirmed. Beginning with Iphigeneia, who was cast in the role of a sacrificial substitute for Helen—one tradition renders explicit this link between the two by making Iphigeneia the daughter of Helen and Theseus—the sacrifice or scapegoating of female characters recurs consistently in the texts I study here.[17] In fact, this book demonstrates that the substitution of sacrificial victims motivates the metamorphoses of Helen into other female figures.

René Girard, who among literary critics has written most extensively on theories of sacrifice, describes sacrifice in literature as an anthropologist describes ritual in society. I differ from him in believing that literary texts are not the equivalent of rituals; rather, texts contain rituals in their narrative framework, which functions to quali-

---

[15]Ibid., p. 66. On the marginality of the scapegoat, see Jan Bremmer, "Scapegoat Rituals in Ancient Greece," *HSCP*, 87 (1983), 303–5. He notes that although beautiful or important persons (kings, young men and women) were scapegoats in myth, in actuality the community sacrificed the least valuable persons, who were treated and represented as very valuable. On the ambivalence of the Greek *pharmakos*, see Jacques Derrida, "Plato's Pharmacy," in *Dissemination*, trans. Barbara Johnson (Chicago: Univ. of Chicago Press, 1981), esp. pp. 128–34.

[16]Claude Lévi-Strauss, *The Elementary Structures of Kinship*, trans. James Harle Bell, John Richard von Sturmer, and Rodney Needham (Boston: Beacon, 1969), p. 496. For a feminist critique of Lévi-Strauss, see Gayle Rubin, "The Traffic in Women: Notes on the 'Political Economy' of Sex," in *Toward an Anthropology of Women*, ed. Rayna R. Reiter (New York: Monthly Review Press, 1975), pp. 157–210.

[17]*Paulys Real-Encyclopaedie der Classischen Altertumswissenschaft* (Stuttgart: J. B. Metzler, 1914), 9:2599–2600. See also Hugh Lloyd-Jones, "Artemis and Iphigeneia," *JHS*, 103 (1983), 95. Seneca's *Trojan Women* links Helen and another sacrificial substitute, Polyxena: Helen prepares Polyxena for her sacrifice on the grave of Achilles under the pretext that Polyxena is to wed Achilles' son, Neoptolemus (and here we may recall that Iphigeneia was led to believe that she was to marry Achilles at Aulis).

fy or even subvert them. In his widely influential *Violence and the Sacred,* moreover, while describing sacrifice, Girard appears to align himself with those who perform the ritual. Here is an example:

> The rites of sacrifice serve to polarize the community's aggressive impulses and redirect them toward victims that may be actual or figurative, animate or inanimate, but that are always incapable of propagating further vengeance. The sacrificial process furnishes an outlet for those violent impulses that cannot be mastered by self-restraint; a partial outlet, to be sure, but always renewable, and one whose efficacy has been attested by an impressive number of reliable witnesses. The sacrificial process prevents the spread of violence by keeping vengeance in check.[18]

Not only does Girard affirm the efficacy of sacrifice to achieve social harmony, he also appears to justify the repeated sacrifice of new victims—a need that in effect calls attention to the inadequacy of sacrifice. Girard has more recently reiterated his belief in the beneficial and creative power of "generative scapegoating," his belief that it constitutes "the generative principle of mythology, ritual, primitive religion, even culture as a whole."[19] For he has repeatedly argued that society and culture originated in an actual collective murder of a human being and posits the corollary that such a murder was a necessary condition to the institution of human society as we know it.[20] In *Des choses cachées depuis la fondation du monde* and *The Scapegoat,* Girard maintains that texts depicting violence divide into two categories, according to whether they take the perspective of the persecutors or the victims. But even the exemplary text of victimage for Girard, Christ's Passion, affirms the benefits of scapegoating no less than do texts of persecution. Thus *all* texts, according to Girard, celebrate sacrifice. And by claiming that acts of sacrifice and scapegoating are the crucial "things hidden since the beginning of the world" and by purporting to reveal this secret, Girard's theory implicitly allies itself with religious revelation, at the same time privileging Christianity as the one religion aware of this secret.[21]

[18]*Violence and the Sacred,* p. 18.

[19]"Discussion," in *Violent Origins: Walter Burkert, René Girard, and Jonathan Z. Smith on Ritual Killing and Cultural Formation,* ed. Robert G. Hamerton-Kelly, (Stanford, Calif.: Stanford Univ. Press, 1987), p. 106.

[20]Jonathan Z. Smith, "The Domestication of Sacrifice," in *Violent Origins,* p. 195, calls for a detailed examination of elaborations which takes into account the diversity of the idioms and contexts of sacrifice rather than an insistent quest for origins.

[21]Burton Mack also notices "this curious correlation between the functions of the

Adorno and Horkheimer, on the other hand, claim that participants in sacrifice always already know it is a hoax (and here we may recall the representation of a lowly victim as an exalted person or the practice of spilling wine on the sacrificial animal's head so that it will "nod" its "assent").[22] Adorno and Horkheimer argue that the "priestly rationalization of death by means of an apotheosis of the predestined victim"—the deception in sacrifice—enacts the "antithesis of collective and individual" and marks the origin of the "history of domination," not the origin of culture, as Girard asserts.[23]

I seek to uncover not the *fact* of sacrifice, as a Girardian reading would do, but the ways in which literary texts narrate the "history of domination" while demystifying the deception involved in sacrifice and scapegoating. To this end, I offer a feminist revision of Girard's theory which approaches these texts consistently from the perspective of victims of scapegoating, which shows how the dominant group establishes and affirms community through the victimization of women and minorities.[24] In fact, Girard himself states that being a woman (along with being physically deformed, being foreign, being Jewish, etc.) is "the stereotypical victim's sign."[25] I am interested in elucidating how power and community are defined by their negations and opposites—power, by who is subordinated or victimized; community, by who is excluded or destroyed in its name.[26] It is my

---

biblical texts and the critic's task." "Introduction," in *Violent Origins*, p. 22. On this correlation, see also the revealing exchanges between Mack and Girard in "Discussion," pp. 144–45, and between Smith and Girard, pp. 185–87.

[22]Bremmer, p. 304.

[23]Max Horkheimer and Theodor W. Adorno, *Dialectic of Enlightenment* (1944), trans. John Cumming (New York: Continuum, 1972), pp. 50–51.

[24]Renato Rosaldo asks, "Whose perspective are we looking at as we're interpreting?" remarking that, "for the young men, a position very like Girard's is quite appropriate." He concludes, "One has to consider the social position of the people involved in the sacrificial enactment." "Anthropological Commentary," in *Violent Origins*, pp. 242–43. For trenchant feminist critiques of Girard's theory of mimetic desire, as presented in *Deceit, Desire, and the Novel*, trans. Yvonne Freccero (Baltimore: Johns Hopkins Univ. Press, 1965) and *Des choses cachées depuis la fondation du monde*, see Sarah Kofman, "The Narcissistic Woman: Freud and Girard," *Diacritics*, 10 (Fall 1980), 36–45, and Toril Moi, "The Missing Mother: The Oedipal Rivalries of René Girard," *Diacritics*, 12 (Summer 1982), 21–31. Sedgwick conceives of her work as a recasting of Girard's *Deceit, Desire, and the Novel* (p. 17).

[25]*Scapegoat*, p. 49.

[26]Hayden White finds troubling Girard's totalizing tendencies and his "reactionary perspective," asking whether for Girard Nazi Germany would not be a model solution for the problems of "modernity," as a society that meets his criteria of healthiness: "It was surely transcendent in its aspirations, distinguished in its own way between force and violence, possessed the scapegoat mechanism, and orchestrated

contention that the texts I consider here do not take solely the per-spective of the persecutors nor do they singlemindedly affirm sacri-fice. Showing interest in and awareness of the victim's subjectivity, these texts reveal the consequences of, and at times even contest the efficacy and justice of, scapegoating.[27]

Girard has also been criticized for failing to account for differ-ences—historical and literary—among texts, a danger inherent in using anthropological theories to study literary texts.[28] The theory of the dialectic between private and public spheres, formulated by femi-nist historian Joan Kelly, helps account for the ways texts can both scapegoat women and criticize that process. Kelly finds a correlation between the prevalence of patriarchy and the degree of separation of private and public spheres (with attendant devaluation of the pri-vate).[29] Using Kelly's theory, I discuss the differences between these texts not only in purely literary terms but also in terms of the differ-ent political and cultural contexts that produced them, though it is *through* the literary text that I concern myself with historical differ-ences.[30]

In elucidating literary difference, I have turned to Thomas M. Greene's work on humanist imitation, *The Light in Troy: Imitation and Discovery in Renaissance Poetry*, which has broken new ground in the

---

social action in terms of a hierarchical system of differentiation based on ritual sacri-fice." "Ethnological 'Lie' and Mythical 'Truth,'" *Diacritics*, 8 (Spring 1978), 8. Domin-ick LaCapra offers Bakhtin's carnivalesque as an alternative to what he calls Girard's "monologic" theory of culture, which is "marked both by an intolerance for ambiva-lence and by a desire for clarity and fullness of being that eventuate in an invidious distinction between Christianity and other cultural forms." *Rethinking Intellectual His-tory: Texts, Contexts, Language* (Ithaca: Cornell Univ. Press, 1983), p. 296n.

[27]Fetterley also discusses the female characters in her texts as scapegoats for the American male who fantasizes about eliminating his ills through the ritual of scape-goating. Yet the texts she considers perform the scapegoating of the woman without anxiety or guilt. The female reader is expected to dissociate herself from (and hence to accept) this position of victimage (pp. xiv–xv).

[28]See "An Interview with René Girard," in Girard, *"To Double Business Bound": Essays on Literature, Mimesis, and Anthropology* (Baltimore: Johns Hopkins Univ. Press, 1978), pp. 208–9,218,221,223. While affirming the usefulness of the "transhistorical clarity" of Girard's formulation in *Deceit, Desire, and the Novel*, Sedgwick argues that it "depends on *suppressing* the subjective and historically determined account of which feelings are or are not part of the body of 'sexuality'" (p. 22).

[29]Joan Kelly, "The Social Relation of the Sexes: Methodological Implications of Women's History," in *Women, History, and Theory: The Essays of Joan Kelly* (Chicago: Univ. of Chicago Press, 1984), p. 14.

[30]See Sedgwick, pp. 15,18, on the difficulty of balancing "synchronic and di-achronic formulations" and of focusing at once on the historical and literary.

study of the relationships between Renaissance texts and their antecedents. Going beyond a traditional study of "sources" or "influences," Greene insists on an understanding of an imitative literary work through its "subtext," which is not external to it but which constitutes an essential component of its verbal structure.[31] Gian Biagio Conte's *Rhetoric of Imitation: Genre and Poetic Memory in Virgil and Other Latin Poets* presents an understanding of imitation in classical texts which is remarkably similar to Greene's. For Conte, literary allusions are never simply passive repetitions but sites where differences between text and tradition become manifest.[32]

My concern with such theories of imitation has partially determined the texts I have chosen to discuss here. I conceive of this book as a diptych: the first half deals with the line of classical epic—the *Iliad,* the *Odyssey,* and Virgil's *Aeneid;* the second half treats two English Renaissance responses by Spenser and Shakespeare to these classical epics. During the middle ages, the Homeric epics were lost, and the medieval authors depended instead on the anti-Homeric accounts of Dares and Dictys.[33] For example, Benoît de Sainte-Maure, whose *Roman de Troie* (1155) first introduced the story of Troilus and Briseida, claims to follow the supposed eyewitness account of the Trojan Dares. Benoît's story effectively created an alternate tradition, forming the basis of Boccaccio's *Il Filostrato* (1336), Chaucer's *Troilus and Criseyde* (1385), and Henryson's *The Testament of Cresseid* (1475).[34] Studying the representation of woman in this medieval tradition,

[31]Thomas M. Greene, *The Light in Troy: Imitation and Discovery in Renaissance Poetry* (New Haven: Yale Univ. Press, 1982), pp. 36–37. See esp. chapter 3, "Imitation and Anachronism," pp. 28–53. See also G. W. Pigman III, "Versions of Imitation in the Renaissance," *Renaissance Quarterly,* 33 (1980), 1–32; Daniel Javitch, "The Imitation of Imitations in *Orlando Furioso,*" *Renaissance Quarterly,* 38 (1985), 215–39; and my "'Signiorie ouer the Pages': The Crisis of Authority in Nashe's *The Unfortunate Traveller,*" *SP,* 83 (1984), 348–71.

[32]Gian Biagio Conte, *The Rhetoric of Imitation: Genre and Poetic Memory in Virgil and Other Latin Poets,* trans. and ed. Charles Segal (Ithaca: Cornell Univ. Press, 1986), esp. pp. 23–31.

[33]These have been translated by R. M. Frazer, Jr., in *The Trojan War: The Chronicles of Dictys of Crete and Dares the Phrygian* (Bloomington: Indiana Univ. Press, 1966).

[34]Benoît's wide and lasting influence throughout the middle ages is attested to by various translations such as Guido delle Colonne's *Historia Destructionis Troiae* (1287) and John Lydgate's *Troy-Book* (1412–20). E. K. Gordon, *The Story of Troilus* (Toronto: Univ. of Toronto Press, 1978), gives excerpts from Benoît as well as the full texts of Boccaccio, Chaucer, and Henryson. But see Gretchen Mieszkowski, "E. K. Gordon and the Troilus and Criseyde Story," *Chaucer Review,* 15 (1980), 127–37, where she points out significant omissions, especially of Benoît's virulently antifeminist moralizing, in Gordon's excerpts.

Gretchen Mieszkowski has demonstrated that Criseyde, the preeminent female character in this tradition, functioned as the byword of inconstancy during this entire period.[35] I offer instead more detailed comparative readings of the classical and Renaissance texts, for the Renaissance poets conceived of themselves as the heirs of the classical epic, including the newly discovered Homer. For example, Shakespeare's *Troilus and Cressida* sets the newly available *Iliad* against the medieval versions of the story, exemplified most recently for Shakespeare in Henryson's poem.

In each of the texts I examine, "authority and difference" pertains to both the political and the literary; in the epic, political and poetic authority function as figures for each other. In the *Iliad*, political authority lies in the heroic code that motivates and underwrites the Trojan war, and difference in the poet's interrogation of the contradictions within it, by means of Achilles' wrath and Helen's victimage as pretext and scapegoat. The *Odyssey* identifies the heroic code with the *Iliad* and criticizes both its political and poetic authority by valuing wit (*metis*) over brawn (*bie*) and consequently by reevaluating Iliadic gender roles to allow Penelope to be recognized as Odysseus' equal and counterpart. Virgil bases the *Aeneid* on the two Homeric epics but criticizes both the Iliadic and Odyssean notions of heroism as inadequate for the more complex needs of the Roman Empire. More problematic for him is the authority of Augustus' *imperium* which his epic sets out to justify, but which he nevertheless interrogates through the tragedy of female victims who are sacrificed on the altar of Rome.

Both Spenser's *Faerie Queene* and Shakespeare's *Troilus and Cressida* were written during the 1590s, an anomalous period for patriarchy in that Elizabeth had been ruling England since 1558. Spenser chooses Virgil as his literary model, but his "Aeneas" is the female warrior, Britomart, ancestor of his queen and patron Elizabeth. His difference as male poet from the female monarch complicates by inverting the relationships between the sexes and between ruler and subjects in the *Faerie Queene*. In *Troilus and Cressida*, written at the end of Elizabeth's reign, Shakespeare not only dramatizes his position at the end of the

---

[35]Gretchen Mieszkowski, "The Reputation of Criseyde: 1155–1500," *Transactions of the Connecticut Academy of Arts and Sciences*, 43 (New Haven, 1971), 71–153. See also E. Talbot Donaldson, "Briseis, Briseida, Cresseid, Cressid: Progress of a Heroine," in *Chaucerian Problems and Perspectives: Essays Presented to Paul E. Beichner c.s.c.*, ed. Edward Vasta and Zacharias P. Thundy (Notre Dame: Univ. of Notre Dame Press, 1979), pp. 3–12.

line of a literary tradition by demystifying its authority, but also represents the persistence of patriarchy despite the long reign of a woman. My brief concluding discussion of *Antony and Cleopatra* argues that the Jacobean play nostalgically represents Elizabeth in the powerful figure of Cleopatra. Through his portrait of defiant Cleopatra, Shakespeare achieves a renewal of tradition by transvaluing the received history that affirmed the Augustan achievement.

Metamorphoses of Helen

> Like a wedge of cranes toward barbarous lands
> (a divine foam upon the heads of kings),
> where do you sail? If it were not for Helen
> would Troy alone, Achaean men, suffice?
> —Osip Mandelshtam

> Was it Apollo's snare
> so that poets forever,
> should be caught in the maze of the Walls

> of a Troy that never fell? . . .

> a suspect stranger from Greece,
> is she a slave or a queen?
> —H.D.

In these lines, Osip Mandelshtam and H.D. give testimony to the West's continuing fascination with the legend of Troy and Helen's role in that city's fall. Jean Lemaire de Belges, in *Illustrations de Gaule et singularités de Troie* (1509–12), expressed this universal longing for Troy by distributing the names of various Trojan heroes, like spoils of war, among the nations of Western Europe.[36] The fall of Troy,

---

[36]See Jean Seznec, *The Survival of the Pagan Gods: The Mythological Tradition and Its Place in Renaissance Humanism and Art,* trans. Barbara F. Sessions (New York: Pantheon, 1953), pp. 24–25: "Only the Germans and French could boast undisputed descent from Hector himself, but others—Bretons, Flemings, Scandinavians, Normans, Italians, and Spaniards—also found ways of asserting their own relationship with him, to justify either their pride or their ambition. . . . the Bretons were said to be descendents of Brutus, first king of Brittany; the Spaniards of Hesperus, the Italians of Italus, the men of Brabant of Brabo, the Tuscans of Tuscus, and the Burgundians of Hercules the Great of Libya."

then, as the myth of national origins for Western Europe, became a secular Fall; accordingly, Helen attained the status of a secular Eve. Like Eve and Pandora, Helen became a type of all women who bring woe to man.[37] Although Eve has been blamed for man's expulsion from Eden, and Pandora for bringing manifold troubles and evils, Helen was exonerated of the responsibility for bringing about the originary war in an alternate tradition that tells she never went to Troy. This alternate tradition makes explicit Helen's status as a figure of difference.

In the *Phaedrus* Plato alludes to Stesichorus' *Palinodia,* in which the poet begs Helen's pardon for singing of her elopement with Paris.

> For those who have sinned in matters of mythology there is an ancient purification, unknown to Homer, but known to Stesichorus. For when he was stricken with blindness for speaking ill of Helen, he was not, like Homer, ignorant of the reason, but since he was educated, he knew it and straightway he writes the poem: "That saying is not true; thou didst not go within the well-oared ships, nor didst thou come to the walls of Troy"; and when he had written all the poem, which is called the recantation, he saw again at once.[38]

Helen contests the literary tradition about her, imposing this difference from Homeric authority on Stesichorus, thereby instituting an alternate tradition, another authority.[39] Yet the ambivalence in

[37]For discussions of Eve as a Jungian "archetype," see Maud Bodkin, *Archetypal Patterns in Poetry: Psychological Studies of Imagination* (London: Oxford Univ. Press, 1934), pp. 165–74. Joan Ferrante, *Woman as Image in Medieval Literature* (New York: Columbia Univ. Press, 1975), discusses the "Eve-Mary" antithesis as well as female allegorical figures such as *Fortuna* and *Natura*. On the iconography of Pandora, see Erwin Panofsky and Dora Panofsky's study, *Pandora's Box: The Changing Aspects of a Mythical Symbol* (New York: Pantheon, 1956). Pietro Pucci's *Hesiod and the Language of Poetry* (Baltimore: Johns Hopkins Univ. Press, 1977) discusses the creation of Pandora as the "figure" of the origin and the origin of the rhetorical "figure." Pandora is the paradoxical "gift-bane" which allows the establishment of various oppositions (pp. 100–101).

[38]Plato, *Phaedrus,* ed. and trans. Harold North Fowler, Loeb Classical Library (Cambridge: Harvard Univ. Press, 1914), 243a-b. See also *Republic* 9.586c, for an allusion to Stesichorus' claim that the Trojan War was fought over a phantom Helen through the men's ignorance of the truth.

[39]See Ann L. T. Bergren, "Language and the Female in Early Greek Thought," *Arethusa,* 16 (1983), 82:" [Stesichorus] . . . attempt[s] to divide the sexual and ethical ambivalence of Helen into two figures, assign them two *logoi,* label one true and the other false, and assign the false one to his older poetic rivals, while arrogating the true one to himself." Bergren also notes Helen's doubleness as "the distinguishing mark of her entire tradition" (p. 81). Froma Zeitlin, "Travesties of Gender and Genre in Aristophanes' *Thesmophoriazousae,*" in *Writing and Sexual Difference,* p. 149, observes

Stesichorus' transformation from sight to blindness and back again (especially in light of the purported blindness of Homer himself as well as of poets and prophets such as the *Odyssey*'s Demodocus and Teiresias) makes it uncertain whether blindness is a mark of insight or a punishment, whether it signifies false or true speech.[40] By blaming Helen, the poet follows the authoritative tradition, is blinded, and hence becomes like other poets. By making him renounce the tradition and then restoring his sight, Helen makes him different from these other poets. Of the two competing authorities, then, Helen appears to have won the poet's allegiance. The question remains: does Helen or the tradition speak the truth? Is the poet's ambivalent relationship with her a privilege or a curse? The palinode itself remains double-voiced, for in recanting the tradition, it contains and repeats it.

Herodotus, like Stesichorus, first stated, in Book 1 of the *Histories*, that Helen was indeed abducted by Paris (following a series of other abductions of women), and then later, in Book 2, maintained that she never went to Troy. In fact, he states that Homer was familiar with the story but suppressed it as unsuitable for epic poetry.[41] Here again, Herodotus couches his revisionary account concerning Helen as a challenge to the authority of Homer. He claims in Book 1 that Helen was not abducted by Paris but eloped with him willingly, and that the Greeks should not have launched a war to reclaim her: a woman would not be carried away unless she wished to be.[42] Here Herodotus addresses the question of Helen's motivation and responsibility— Was she a subject or an object?—a question raised but never explicitly answered in the *Iliad*. Herodotus' account in Book 2 of Helen's sojourn in Egypt, however, was not meant to exonerate her. He believes that Helen never went to Troy, because if she had gone she would have been handed back to the Greeks with or without Paris' consent. He claims that the Trojans told Menelaus that neither Helen

---

that Stesichorus "raises the notion of fictionality as a possible attribute of mythic texts in order to account for his own innovations, and in the process, he invents a new generic form—the palinode."

[40]In the *Odyssey*, the Muse blinded Demodocus in return for poetic powers she granted him (7.62–65), and Teiresias' blindness is a mark of his prophetic insight. According to Ovid, Juno struck Teiresias blind when he told the truth—that women enjoy sex more than men (*Metamorphoses* 3.332–38).

[41]Herodotus, *Histories*, trans. A. D. Godley, Loeb Classical Library (London: William Heinemann, 1920), 2.116.

[42]Ibid. 1.4.

nor the treasure was in their possession, but the Greeks nevertheless laid siege.[43]

Euripides, in *The Trojan Women* and *Helen,* dramatizes both traditions. In *The Trojan Women,* the trial of Helen after Troy's fall, with Hecuba as chief accuser, finds her guilty. In *Helen,* on the other hand, he tells that chaste Helen remained with Proteus in Egypt, though beset by an importunate suitor, Proteus' son Theoclymenus—much like the *Odyssey*'s Penelope—while an *eidolon,* a phantom created by Hera, went to Troy. The *eidolon* taunts the warriors:

> Wretched men of Troy and all you Achaeans who, day after day, went on dying for me beside Scamander, by Hera's craft, you thought Paris had Helen, when he never did. . . .
> All for nothing Tyndareus' daughter has heard evil things said of her, who did nothing wrong.[609-11,614-15][44]

This version of the origin of the Trojan war explicitly addresses the question of Helen's role as *casus belli* by separating Helen from her name in the form of an *eidolon,* thus making evident that "Helen" was a construct for the warriors to justify the war, as Herodotus had already implied.

Gorgias' *Encomium* exonerates Helen in yet another manner.[45] He claims that his power to tell the truth will set her free from the bondage of the "univocal and unanimous" (and lying) testimony of inspired poets. Thus he explicitly marks his difference from tradition as bondage, conceiving not a new Helen but a new way of understanding Helen's actions as a means of that empowerment. Diverging from even those who claimed that she never went to Troy, Gorgias assumes that she indeed went but excuses her because she acted for one of three reasons: she was coerced, she was persuaded, or she was in love. In no case was she responsible, for persuasion and love are both forms of coercion. But Gorgias' defense of Helen is itself double-edged: it makes Helen innocent only because it considers her not as a subject who willed her own actions but as a passive object—not least of his own rhetorical exercise.[46]

---

[43]Ibid. 2.118.

[44]*Euripides II,* trans. Richmond Lattimore (Chicago: Univ. of Chicago Press, 1956).

[45]*The Older Sophists,* ed. Rosamond Kent Sprague (Columbia: Univ. of South Carolina Press, 1972), pp. 50–54.

[46]Zeitlin sees Gorgias' encomium to be "a defense of his art of the *logos*" (p. 154). She further states: "Thus if Helen is the subject of the discourse, she is also the object within it," for "she is reseduced (and exonerated) by the rhetoric of Gorgias" (p. 156).

The germ of these revisions is already present in Homer, for in the *Iliad,* Helen serves as a pretext for the war, a pretext that inevitably proves inadequate for the nine years of protracted fighting. The warriors in a sense fight over Helen's phantom, for they have transformed her into an emblem, a construct of their own minds: on Helen, goddesslike beauty and scourge of war, they project their ambivalence toward the apparently self-generating and self-sustaining war that brings both glory and death. Homer thus reveals the process through which men make sense of the divisions of experience and affirm community among themselves (even across battlelines) by scapegoating Helen, the female Other, and by reducing her to an emblem to which they assign a double meaning.[47] To Helen as a static emblem of doubleness, however, Homer opposes his own complex and nuanced representation of her, which implicitly addresses the question of her culpability and innocence, the subject of Gorgias' *Encomium.*

Homer's juxtaposition of Helen as a mystified emblem and as a fictive character is consistently reenacted in post-Iliadic accounts.[48] It is only the poet of the *Iliad,* however, who endows Helen with subjectivity and an inwardness that makes her akin to Achilles, the fore-

---

Bergren also states that Gorgias appropriates Helen's *logos* and demonstrates his power of *logos* over her (pp. 82–83), but she is "'raped,' as it were, by a *logos/phallos* with the character of female language." She concludes: "a female is endowed with a degree of knowledge, especially sexual knowledge, that gives her a *metis*-like power over the utterance of both truth and imitation, a power that every male from Zeus to Gorgias must make his own" (p. 85).

[47]The *locus classicus* is Freud's "The Antithetical Sense of Primal Words": "In Latin *altus* means 'high' and 'deep,' and *sacer,* both 'sacred' and 'accursed'." *Collected Papers,* trans. Joan Riviere (New York: Basic Books, 1959) 4: 184–91. The second example he gives is especially pertinent to my concerns here.

[48]See Claude Lévi-Strauss's statement on myth and mystification in Georges Charbonnier, *Conversations with Claude Lévi-Strauss,* trans. John Weightman and Doreen Weightman (London: Jonathan Cape, 1969), p. 55: "Myth is the most fundamental form of inauthenticity. I defined authenticity as the concrete nature of the knowledge people have of each other, and contrary to what might seem to be the case there is nothing more abstract than myths. Myths depend on propositions which, when we try to analyse them, force us to resort to symbolic logic. It is not absolutely without reason . . . that 'myth' and 'mystification' have a great deal in common." See also Frank Kermode's statement on myth and fiction in *The Sense of an Ending: Studies in the Theory of Fiction* (Oxford: Oxford Univ. Press, 1967), p. 39: "Myth operates within the diagrams of ritual, which presupposes total and adequate explanations of things as they are and were; it is a sequence of radically unchangeable gestures. Fictions are for finding things out, and they change as the needs of sense-making change. Myths call for absolute, fictions for conditional assent. Myths make sense in terms of a lost order of time . . . fictions, if successful, make sense of the here and now."

most male warrior of the epic. From the *Odyssey* on, Helen is always present in the texts to be studied, but as a myth—either an emblem of doubleness or of duplicity on the one hand, or a trivial cardboard figure on the other—to be scapegoated and repudiated. As the figure of Helen becomes thus reduced, the poets create surrogate figures whom they endow with complexity and subjectivity as characters. This mystification of Helen, and hence of the anterior epic tradition, constitutes a necessary condition for the new poet's representation of the fiction of Helen's "daughters," enabling him to signal his difference from the authority of epic tradition. For the poet constantly faces the threat to be written and mastered as woman—like the poets (such as Demodocus) and prophets (such as Teiresias) who were blinded or castrated in return for their powers—just as the warriors expose themselves to the danger of defeat and humiliation as woman (Hector ponders how Achilles will "kill me naked . . . *as if I were a woman*" [21.124; emphasis added]).

The poets, like the prophets, occupy the woman's position in yet another important sense: in their apartness from the world of deeds. The prophets speak of the future, the poets of the past; both are excluded from the arena where events are shaped. Thus they describe the world of action from its margins, not only spatially but temporally. Epic heroes such as Achilles and Aeneas act as poets in reflective moments, removed from epic action. Their decentered position proves to be a source of visionary power as well as of anxiety concerning their impotence. The myth of the woman prophet Cassandra explicitly links this double-edged gift-bane to female sexuality: Apollo granted her prophetic powers to win her love but cursed her with the disbelief of her countrymen when she refused him. [49]

The poets thus stand in an ambivalent relation to woman as both the Other and the Same: although they strive to avoid occupying the position of woman as Other, their desire to assert their difference from the paternal authority of previous male poets and their apartness from political authority induce them to represent woman, no longer as the Other to be shunned and feared but identified with as the Same.

---

[49]In the final canto of *Orlando Furioso* (46.80–85), Ariosto figures Cassandra's tapestry as an analogue to his own poem.

I *The Iliad*

she, who surpassed in beauty
all mortality, Helen, once forsaking
her lordly husband,

fled away to Troy-land across the water.
Not the thought of child nor beloved parents
was remembered, after the Queen of Cyprus
won her at first sight.

—Sappho

Helen the wild, maddening Helen,
one for the many, the thousand lives
you murdered under Troy. Now you are crowned
with this consummate wreath, the blood
that lives in memory, glistens age to age.
Once in the halls she walked and she was war,
angel of war, angel of agony, lighting men to death.

—Aeschylus

In the *Iliad,* at the beginning of her literary tradition, the figure of
Helen is marked by radical undecidability. The warriors claim to
fight over her possession—but is Helen, in fact, the object of the
struggle? It is said that she eloped with Paris—but did Aphrodite
compel her? As wife of both Menelaus and Paris, is she Greek or is
she Trojan?

The poet of the *Iliad* represents this undecidability of Helen's function and significance through her liminality, her crossing of various
boundaries. Victor Turner describes the ambiguous and indeterminate attributes of liminality: "This condition and these persons elude
or slip through the network of classifications that normally locate
states and positions in cultural space. Liminal entities are neither here
nor there; they are betwixt and between the positions assigned and

18

arrayed by law, custom, convention, and ceremonial."[1] In the *Iliad,* not only does Helen cross the boundary between nations, she crosses a more absolute boundary, that between the world of women and the world of men. As Hector bids Andromache farewell at the Scaean gates, he directs her to woman's work within, to spin and weave among her handmaidens; then he proceeds to man's work, the battle outside the walls of Troy (6.490–93).[2] Like Andromache, Helen properly belongs to the domestic world of peace which the warriors have left behind—a world evoked in many of the epic similes—but she also presides over scenes of combat as she catalogues the Greek warriors for Priam.

Through Helen's liminal position in this society, which divides her loyalties but also gives her a perspective that comprehends such divisions, the poet represents her complex inwardness and subjectivity— much as he does in representing Achilles, a warrior withdrawn from combat. At the same time, her undecidability makes her a perfectly ambiguous sign; the warriors read her as an emblem with antithetical meanings—beautiful as an immortal goddess but a baneful bringer of death. For these warriors, Helen as *casus belli* reflects their ambivalence toward the inextricable duality of glory and death that marks the heroic code.

In a famous statement on the heroic code, Sarpedon explains that the warriors are honored with pride of place as well as with tangible rewards for braving the battle; yet he expresses his ambivalence toward a code that necessarily entails the glory of one and the shame and death of the other, musing that were he to escape this battle, he would forgo glory to live on (12.310–328). Achilles himself confronts a similar choice between eternal glory and a life cut off in its prime on the Trojan battlefield on the one hand, and obscurity and longevity in his homeland on the other (9.410–16). Like Sarpedon, he expresses his ambivalence toward that glory and its price, stating that all the wealth of Ilion cannot outweigh a man's life, fragile and fleeting (9.400–409). Hector, too, expresses the contradictions in the heroic code in the *homilia* with Andromache, to which I have already re-

---

[1] Victor Turner, *The Ritual Process: Structure and Anti-Structure* (Chicago: Aldine, 1969), p. 95.

[2] On this scene, the *homilia* between Hector and Andromache, see Marylin B. Arthur, "The Divided World of *Iliad* VI," in *Reflections of Women in Antiquity,* ed. Helene P. Foley (New York: Gordon and Breach Science Publishers, 1981), pp. 19–44. Arthur argues that there is an interpenetration of spheres between Hector and Andromache.

ferred. For Hector is compelled to give up his life with Andromache and Astyanax, not so much for their sake as for the sake of *kleos:*[3]

> yet I would feel deep shame
> before the Trojans, and the Trojan women with trailing garments,
> if like a coward I were to shrink aside from the fighting;
> and the spirit will not let me, since I have learned to be valiant
> and to fight always among the foremost ranks of the Trojans,
> winning for my own self great glory, and for my father.
> For I know this thing well in my heart, and my mind knows it:
> there will come a day when sacred Ilion shall perish,
> and Priam, and the people of Priam of the strong ash spear.
>
> [6.441–49][4]

Significantly, the *Iliad* is interested in Achilles and Hector, who experience these fissures in the heroic code, not Diomedes, the warrior who performs comfortably within it.[5] For the *Iliad* does not, in my view, simply affirm the heroic code and celebrate the warriors according to its dictates but rather questions the authority of the prevailing ethos among the aristocratic warriors on both sides.

The warriors project their ambivalence toward this authority—their simultaneous desire for glory and fear of death—on the putative

[3]On the contradictions in the heroic code, see Seth L. Schein, *The Mortal Hero: An Introduction to Homer's Iliad* (Berkeley: Univ. of California Press, 1975), pp. 70–71. Schein sees Hector and Troy as the focus of these contradictions (pp. 169,179). James Redfield, *Nature and Culture in the Iliad: The Tragedy of Hector* (Chicago: Univ. of Chicago Press, 1975), p. 85, states that the *Iliad* accepts the heroic ethic and yet inquires into its limits and contradictions, concluding that it is a more profound work than the *Odyssey*, which proposes an alternative to the ethic. See also his discussion of the tensions in Hector between obligations to household and city (p. 123). Arthur argues that the heroic code is inconsistent with an emphasis on the nuclear family, and that Hector as both a warrior and family man embodies the clash between heroic society and the newly emerging pre-polis society. "Early Greece: The Origin of the Western Attitude Toward Women," in *Women in the Ancient World: The Arethusa Papers*, ed. John Peradotto and J. P. Sullivan (Albany: State Univ. of New York Press, 1984), p. 10.

[4]All quotations are from *The Iliad of Homer*, trans. Richmond Lattimore (Chicago: Univ. of Chicago Press, 1951). Line numbers are Lattimore's, which follow closely those in the original Greek. In my text, I have used Latinized spellings of proper names.

[5]Cedric Whitman calls Diomedes the "fully satisfactory offspring of the heroic ideal." *Homer and the Heroic Tradition* (Cambridge: Harvard Univ. Press, 1959), p. 167. For a more detailed discussion of Diomedes as a normative warrior-hero whose wife and children are irrelevant to his martial activity, see Arthur, "Divided World," pp. 21–23.

object of the war, Helen, the terrible beauty.[6] Despite Helen's apparent centrality to the war effort, then, she in fact serves as a scapegoat who allows the warriors to affirm their community with one another.[7] Yet as we shall see, the *Iliad* shows this scapegoating mechanism to be ineffectual as well as inhumane. Aeschylus' chorus in the *Agamemnon* speaks of Helen as "one for the many," an "angel of war . . . lighting men to death," thereby perpetuating the scapegoating of Helen as instigator of the war. Yet Gorgias demystifies this scapegoating: "Her one body was the cause of bringing together many bodies of men thinking great thoughts for great goals. . . . And all came because of a passion which loved to conquer and a love of honor which was unconquered."[8] The poet of the *Iliad* already gives an anatomy of this scapegoating not only of Helen but also of her surrogate, Briseis.

Briseis: The Second Helen

The *Iliad* relates not the complete story of the Trojan War from its inception to the fall of Troy but only the events of the tenth and final year of the siege. The principal subject of the epic, as Homer announces in the invocation to Book 1, is "the anger of Peleus' son Achilleus / and its devastation" (1.1–2): the vicissitudes of the war occasioned by Achilles' quarrel with Agamemnon, his decision to withdraw from combat, and his subsequent reentry into battle upon Patroclus' death.[9] Since the doom of Troy becomes inevitable once

[6]Jean-Pierre Vernant says of Helen: "She who is 'most beautiful' also incarnates horrible Erinys, the savage and murderous Ker. In her desire and death are joined and intimately mixed." "Feminine Figures of Death in Greece," *Diacritics,* 16 (Summer 1986), 59. Linda Lee Clader, *Helen: The Evolution from Divine to Heroic in Greek Epic Tradition* (Leiden: Brill, 1976), pp. 17–23, points out that the diction surrounding Helen strongly suggests violence and death.

[7]Walter Burkert, *Structure and History in Greek Mythology and Ritual* (Berkeley: Univ. of California Press, 1979), pp. 73–74, sees Helen's story as following the scapegoat pattern in yet another way, in that she brings destruction to the Trojans who accepted her.

[8]"Encomium of Helen," in *The Older Sophists,* ed. Rosamond Kent Sprague (Columbia: Univ. of South Carolina Press, 1972), p. 51.

[9]On the "Homeric Question," see Adam Parry's introduction to Milman Parry's collected papers, *The Making of Homeric Verse* (Oxford: Oxford Univ. Press, 1971), pp. ix–lxii, and Schein's succinct and lucid exposition on the implications of M. Parry's theory of oral composition (pp. 2–13). Adam Parry departed from his father's theory in "Have We Homer's *Iliad*?," *YCS,* 20 (1966), 190: "So much was he con-

Achilles slays the foremost Trojan warrior, Hector, a crucial causal link connects the "Achilleid" to the "Iliad." But perhaps a more important structural analogy links the wrath of Achilles to the story of Troy: the dispute between Achilles and Agamemnon reenacts the Trojan war in miniature.[10]

The epic begins with the division between Agamemnon and Achilles (1.6–7), just as the war itself had its origin in an essentially private dispute between Menelaus and Paris. The analogy can be pressed even further: the Greeks and the Trojans battle for the possession of Helen, while Achilles and Agamemnon find themselves divided over another woman, the slave girl Briseis. The Greek army discovers that the plague decimating its ranks has as its cause Agamemnon's refusal to return Chryseis to her father, Chryses, a priest of Apollo. Upon Achilles' intervention, Agamemnon finally relents but insists on being compensated for his loss by taking from Achilles his prize, Briseis. Agamemnon thus unwittingly plays the role of a second Paris: like Paris, who abducted Helen from her husband Menelaus, Agamemnon robs Achilles of his rightful prize, Briseis. The two acts of violation are parallel, especially since we later learn that Patroclus had promised to formalize Achilles' marriage to Briseis (19.297–99). They are parallel but not identical: whereas Agamemnon, as general, has authority over Achilles, Paris has flouted the *xenos* (guest/host) relation,[11] and hence his crime is more heinous.

Achilles himself displays his understanding of the analogy between his quarrel with Agamemnon and the war when he speaks to the em-

---

cerned to establish the tradition, and Homer's participation in it, that he consistently underplayed the uniqueness of the creator (or creators) of the *Iliad* and the *Odyssey*." Schein argues that "traditional formulas are manipulated in the *Iliad* to produce meanings beyond what Parry . . . seems to have considered possible" (pp. 8–9). Similarly, both Michael N. Nagler and Gregory Nagy accept Parry's theory of the oral formula, while arguing for creativity and freedom within the tradition, even allowing for irony (Nagler) and meaningful inconsistencies (Nagy). Michael N. Nagler, *Spontaneity and Tradition: A Study in the Oral Art of Homer* (Berkeley: Univ. of California Press, 1974), esp. pp. 201–209; Gregory Nagy, *The Best of the Achaeans: Concepts of the Hero in Archaic Greek Poetry* (Baltimore: Johns Hopkins Univ. Press, 1979), pp. 1–5. For a detailed exposition of the significant (and not simply utilitarian) use of Homeric formulas, see Norman Austin, *Archery at the Dark of the Moon: Poetic Problems in Homer's Odyssey* (Berkeley: Univ. of California Press, 1975), pp. 11–80.

[10]Kenneth John Atchity, *Homer's Iliad: The Shield of Memory* (Carbondale: Southern Illinois Univ. Press, 1978), p. 29, makes a similar observation: "The wrath is a microcosm of the war itself specifically by reference to marriage."

[11]The importance of this bond becomes evident when Diomedes and Glaucus refrain from fighting one another and instead exchange armor in honor of an old *xenos* relationship (6.212–36).

issaries from the Greek camp who approach him to effect a reconciliation:

> Yet why must the Argives fight with the Trojans?
> And why was it the son of Atreus assembled and led here
> these people? Was it not for the sake of lovely-haired Helen?
> Are the sons of Atreus alone among mortal men the ones
> who love their wives? Since any who is a good man, and careful,
> loves her who is his own and cares for her, even as I now
> loved this one from my heart, though it was my spear that won her.
> Now that he has deceived me and taken from my hands my prize of
>   honour,
> let him try me no more.
>
> [9.337–45]

Achilles' perception of this parallel leads him to a bitter appraisal of the paradox of Agamemnon's position. Despite his responsibility as general of the Greek army, Agamemnon repeats against Achilles an offense disquietingly similar to the one that originated the war and justifies his selfish action by his superior rank: "but I shall take the fair-cheeked Briseis, / your prize . . . that you may learn well / how much greater I am than you" (1.184–86).[12] Achilles' understanding is motivated by an utterly personal sense of grievance and indignation, but the ramifications of this analogy between Agamemnon and Paris, implicit in Achilles' speech, are far-reaching. Agamemnon himself acknowledges that "I and Achilleus fought together for a girl's sake / in words' violent encounter" (2.377–78). The Greeks' claim to fight the Trojans over the theft of Helen is therefore undermined, since a quarrel analogous to the one that caused the war is reproduced *within* the Greek camp. The dispute over Briseis thus works to demystify the scapegoat mechanism: Helen as scapegoat proves to be inadequate in uniting the Greek army, and Briseis, who has temporarily superseded Helen as the object of contention, brings division, rather than unity, within the army. The quarrel between Agamemnon and Achilles over Briseis, then, raises questions crucial for the epic: it calls

---

[12]Commenting on these lines, Walter Donlan, "The Structure of Authority in the *Iliad*," *Arethusa*, 12 (1979), 58, states that the Quarrel brings to the fore the opposing claims between Agamemnon's position-authority and Achilles' standing-authority. He argues that the poem ultimately resolves the conflict (in Books 19 and 23) in favor of position-authority, though the solution proves to be a tenuous one because of "the inherently ambiguous and conflictual nature of the relationship between position and standing" (pp. 65–66).

into question not only Agamemnon's authority as general but also the logic behind the Greek war against Troy, and even the heroic code that underwrites the lives of the warriors, both Trojan and Greek. The fluctuating value of a woman such as Helen or Briseis serves as a mere pretext for divisions between nations as well as between men such as Achilles and Agamemnon, who regard having such women as signs of prestige.

Like Helen, Briseis is assigned a status and significance that are decidedly double. Achilles expressed his double-edged relationship with her: "I . . . / loved this one from my heart, though it was my spear that won her" (9.342–43). Briseis was awarded to Achilles as *geras,* a prize of honor, but she is more important to him than a piece of armor or a tripod (the word Lattimore translates as "love" is *philein,* and Achilles refers to Briseis as a wife, *alochos* [9.340]). Agamemnon apparently expresses the same sentiment when he declares that he values Chryseis higher than his wife Clytemnestra; but at the same time, he refuses to go without his *geras* (1.118–19). In fact, he appears able and willing to replace Chryseis with Briseis without much ado, for either woman would satisfy his need for a signifier of prestige.[13] At the very beginning of the epic, then, the poet presents two contrasting but overlapping ways in which men ascribe value to women—as wife and as *geras,* signifier of prestige.[14]

But in Book 19, once Agamemnon and Achilles effect a reconciliation, Briseis' importance—as either wife or signifier—suddenly pales:

[13]Ovid mocks Agamemnon by having him baldly state that, but for the first syllable, the two women have the same name: "'Est' ait Atrides 'illius proxima forma, / Et, si prima sinat syllaba, nomen idem" (*Remedia,* 475–76). It is an interesting development in literary history that Agamemnon's conflation and substitution of Chryseis and Briseis is enacted in the medieval transformation of Benoît de Sainte-Maure's Briseida to Chaucer's Criseyde.

[14]But see M. I. Finley, "Marriage, Sale and Gift in the Homeric world," in *Economy and Society in Ancient Greece* (New York: Viking, 1982), p. 231, who states, "Marriage is never confused with the purchase of a slave woman. In the language of Homer, a wife might be called a 'wooed bedmate,' *mneste alochos,* never an *onete alochos,* a 'purchased bedmate.'" On the value placed on women in Homer, see also W. Thomas MacCary, *Childlike Achilles: Ontogeny and Phylogeny in the Iliad* (New York: Columbia Univ. Press, 1982), pp. 100–108. MacCary states that "all women are always potentially prizes in conflicts between men" (p. 100), though "they are never really what men fight about or really what men desire" (p. 108). MacCary's analysis intersects at several points with my own, but his perspective is an essentially "masculinist" one that sees the *Iliad* as representing without criticism a male-centered social order and narcissistic relationships between male warriors.

Son of Atreus, was this after all the better way for
both, for you and me, that we, for all our hearts' sorrow,
quarrelled together for the sake of a girl in soul-perishing hatred?
I wish Artemis had killed her beside the ships with an arrow
on that day when I destroyed Lyrnessos and took her.

[19.56–60]

Although Achilles had earlier "sorrow[ed] in his heart for the sake of
the fair-girdled woman" (1.429), he now claims that she should have
died rather than create strife between the two men. Significantly, he
refers to Artemis, who earlier demanded the sacrifice of Iphigeneia
"beside the ships," in return for winds that would enable the Greeks
to sail from Aulis to Troy. In fact, Briseis plays the role of a second
Iphigeneia, for just as the sacrifice of Iphigeneia supposedly promoted
the Greek war effort, so the death of Briseis, according to Achilles,
would have preserved the alliance between himself and Agamemnon.
Moreover, both Iphigeneia and Briseis are sacrificial substitutes:
Iphigeneia was substituted and sacrificed for Helen, and Briseis is
substituted for Chryseis. Even Chryseis plays the role of a scapegoat,
for her return to her father, Chryses, is meant to dispel the plague
from the Greek camp. In Agamemnon's mind, the return of Chryseis
recalls the sacrifice of Iphigeneia as he denounces Calchas, who called
for both sacrifices:

Seer of evil: never yet have you told me a good thing.
Always the evil things are dear to your heart to prophesy,
but nothing excellent have you said nor ever accomplished.
Now once more you make divination to the Danaans.

[1.106–9]

In that earlier instance, Agamemnon lured Iphigeneia and Clytemnestra to Aulis by promising to marry his daughter to Achilles. Thus
when the embassy in Book 9 relays to Achilles Agamemnon's offer of
his daughter in marriage, it is not the first time that such an alliance
has been discussed. Agamemnon's substitution of Iphigeneia with
another daughter (as a gift to reestablish his male bond with Achilles)
recalls his willingness to substitute Briseis for Chryseis, again casting
an ironic light on the Greek general.

Agamemnon answers Achilles' scapegoating of Briseis by blaming
Ate for their rupture:

> I am not responsible
> but Zeus is, and Destiny, and Erinys the mist-walking
> who in assembly caught my heart in the savage delusion
> on that day I myself stripped from him the prize of Achilleus.
> Yet what could I do? It is the god who accomplishes all things.
> Delusion is the elder daughter of Zeus, the accursed
> who deludes all; her feet are delicate and they step not
> on the firm earth, but she walks the air above men's heads
> and leads them astray.
>
> [19.86–94]

He relates how *Ate* succeeded in tricking even Zeus, when Hera "female . . . in her craftiness" (19.97) intervened in the birth of Hercules. The two men thus effect a reconciliation by devaluing Briseis and by blaming *Ate;* neither is willing to take responsibility for the initial contention and rupture. Moreover, Agamemnon projects what he perceives to be irrational, undesirable, and perhaps incomprehensible in himself on the female *Ate,* whose power is such that even Zeus cannot escape it.[15] Achilles seems quite willing to accept Agamemnon's explanation:

> Father Zeus, great are the delusions with which you visit men.
> Without you, the son of Atreus could never have stirred so
> the heart inside my breast, nor taken the girl away from me
> against my will, and be in helplessness.
>
> [19.270–73]

In order to reaffirm their male community, both Achilles and Agamemnon scapegoat the female Other: for Achilles, Briseis is the Other, and for Agamemnon, *Ate.* Finally, Odysseus asks Agamemnon to swear that he never laid a hand on Briseis (19.175–76);

[15]But Redfield claims that "both times [Agamemnon] refers to *ate* he is taking full responsibility and restitution. He is not trying to deny his wrongdoing but rather to describe its quality." He concludes that Agamemnon fell into *hamartia* (p. 97). See also E. R. Dodds's famous discussion of this passage as an example of what he calls psychic intervention: "The notion of *ate* enabled Homeric man in all good faith to project on to an external power his unbearable feelings of shame." *The Greeks and the Irrational* (1951; rpt. Berkeley: Univ. of California Press, 1966), p. 17. On this scene, see also A.W.H. Adkins, *From the Many to the One: A Study of Personality and Views of Human Nature in the Context of Ancient Greek Society, Values, and Beliefs* (Ithaca: Cornell Univ. Press, 1970), pp. 25–27, who concludes that "Agamemnon's different statements are not harmonised with one another."

Agamemnon duly complies (19.258–65), thereby effectively objectifying her as a pawn of Achilles' honor.

In *The Elementary Structures of Kinship*, Lévi-Strauss traces such objectification to the use of woman as word or sign:

> The emergence of symbolic thought must have required that women, like words, should be things that were exchanged. In this new case, indeed, this was the only means of overcoming the contradiction by which the same woman was seen under two incompatible aspects: on the one hand, as the object of personal desire, thus exciting sexual and proprietorial instincts; and, on the other, as the subject of the desire of others, and seen as such, i.e., as the means of binding others through alliance with them.[16]

This passage explains the movement in the Homeric text that I have been describing. The contradictory value of woman that Lévi-Strauss speaks of here corresponds to the fluctuating value ascribed to Briseis by Achilles and Agamemnon; when such disparate meanings prove dangerously divisive, the men reconcile differences and bind the alliance between them by blaming and even scapegoating Briseis. When Agamemnon and Achilles both ascribe their loss of control to the female (*Ate* and Briseis), they move to reassert mastery—over the self rendered helpless by desire, over the object of that desire, and over the male rival—by fixing the meaning of the unruly female signifier. This objectification and then exchange of woman as signifier transforms male rivals into allies; such exchanges of women are analogous to the scapegoating of women, which also seeks to establish community among males. In the Homeric text, the scapegoating of Briseis by Agamemnon and Achilles lays the groundwork for her exchange from one to the other. The circulation of signifiers, such as women or words, and the performance of rituals, such as scapegoating, all work to constitute and define the male community.

Yet Lévi-Strauss qualifies his exposition of woman as sign: "Woman could never become just a sign and nothing more, since even in a man's world she is still a person, and since in so far as she is defined as a sign she must be recognized as a generator of signs."[17] The poet of the *Iliad* shares this insight; he subtly criticizes Achilles' and Aga-

[16]Claude Lévi-Strauss, *The Elementary Structures of Kinship*, trans. James Harle Bell, John Richard von Sturmer, and Rodney Needham (Boston: Beacon, 1969), p. 496.
[17]Ibid.

memnon's objectification of Briseis as scapegoat by endowing her with subjectivity and a voice. In his attention to the victims of the war and their palpable grief and suffering, the poet reveals the underside of the heroic code. Immediately after the reconciliation scene between Agamemnon and Achilles, Homer introduces Briseis into the poem; significantly, she does not express joy for her impending reunion with Achilles, but sorrow for Patroclus' death:

> Patroklos, far most pleasing to my heart in its sorrows,
> I left you here alive when I went away from the shelter,
> but now I come back, lord of the people, to find you have fallen.
> So evil in my life takes over from evil forever.
> The husband on whom my father and honoured mother bestowed
>   me
> I saw before my city lying torn with the sharp bronze,
> and my three brothers, whom a single mother bore with me
> and who were close to me, all went on one day to destruction.
> And yet you would not let me, when swift Achilleus had cut down
> my husband, and sacked the city of godlike Mynes, you would not
> let me sorrow, but said you would make me godlike Achilleus'
> wedded lawful wife, that you would take me back in the ships
> to Phthia, and formalize my marriage among the Myrmidons.
> Therefore I weep your death without ceasing. You were kind always.
>   [19.287–300]

This speech is hauntingly echoed by Helen when she laments the death of Hector at the epic's close. Both women, likened by the poet to Aphrodite, perceive of themselves as victims, as pawns to be shuttled back and forth between men. Yet Patroclus appears to have assuaged Briseis' sense of loss and vulnerability in a new and alien environment, as Hector had done for Helen. It is fitting that Patroclus, who played a woman's role in relation to Achilles and whom Achilles compared to a young girl as he wept for Achaian losses (16.6–11), diverged from the warriors' scapegoating of Briseis.[18]

---

[18]Charles Rowan Beye, in "Male and Female in the Homeric Poems," *Ramus*, 3 (1974), 88–89, asks, "Is Patroklos modeled on a woman?" and argues that Patroclus, acting as an alter ego to Achilles, "supports and reinforces his masculinity." Nagler sees Patroclus as playing the role of a female suppliant to Achilles, a role corresponding to that of Cleopatra in the Meleager story told by Phoenix in Book 9 (pp. 135, 138n.). Ann Bergren, "Helen's Web: Time and Tableau in the *Iliad*," *Helios*, 7.1. (1980), 30, points out an intriguing connection between Helen and Patroclus. The poet describes Patroclus entertaining Eurypylus with stories and sprinkling healing

Briseis' lament expresses her sense of utter helplessness upon Patroclus' death, even though she is to be reunited with Achilles; she
belongs to Achilles precisely because he had killed her husband and
brothers.

Briseis' past before she was enslaved by the Greeks recalls Andromache's past and prefigures her future: Achilles killed Andromache's father and brothers (6.414–24), and he will kill her husband, Hector, in the course of the poem. In fact, the fate Hector
envisions for Andromache after his death, that she will be enslaved by
another man, is precisely the fate Briseis laments here. This surprising
link between Briseis, a captive slave in the Greek camp, and Andromache, the wife of the foremost Trojan warrior, not only underscores Achilles' terrible prowess as a warrior but also reveals the
universality of Briseis' fate as woman's fate in the *Iliad*. Briseis thus
functions as a typical female in the poem, related to all the other
young female figures: as we have seen, she is substituted for Chryseis
as Agamemnon's *geras*, and she is cast in the role of a second Helen in
the quarrel between Achilles and Agamemnon. Briseis' name, like
Chryseis' a patronymic, signals her position vis-à-vis the men who
claim her; she is a cipher whose identity or meaning is determined by
the dominant males to whom she is attached. Yet the poet endows
her with a voice that expresses her subjecthood and suffering, which
calls attention to the inhumaneness of the heroic code toward those
designated as signifiers of *kleos*. He also questions the seemingly absolute separation of genders by having "feminine" Patroclus, not Briseis, die as a means to bring Achilles back into the battle; even so,
Patroclus' sacrifice does not succeed in reintegrating Achilles with his
community of Greek warriors.

Helen: *Casus Belli?*

Briseis' varying significance among her male captors finds its parallel in Helen's uncertain value as object of the war. The poet demystifies Helen's role as a scapegoat, as he did in the case of Briseis:
the recovery of the abducted Helen ultimately proves inadequate to
justify or explain such a protracted war. In fact, the poet underscores

---

drugs on the wound (15.393–94) with the same language that he uses to describe
Helen's weaving.

this inadequacy of Helen as a symbol of the war effort by juxtaposing her abstraction to the concreteness of wives, children, and homeland the warriors have left behind, as well as their tangible suffering for nine years. Although the Greek warriors supposedly lay siege to Troy in order to recover Helen, they also perceive the paradox in carrying on a war to restore Menelaus' wife at a time when they are exiled from their own homes, perhaps never to return to them again. Achilles makes this very point to Agamemnon:

> I for my part did not come here for the sake of the Trojan
> spearmen to fight against them, since to me they have done nothing.
> Never yet have they driven away my cattle or my horses,
> never in Phthia where the soil is rich and men grow great did they
> spoil my harvest, since indeed there is much that lies between us,
> the shadowy mountains and the echoing sea; but for your sake,
> o great shamelessness, we followed, to do you favour,
> you with the dog's eyes, to win your honour and Menelaos' from the
> Trojans.
>
> [1.152–60]

Achilles moves from debunking the idea of a common cause behind the war to a poignant evocation of the countryside he left behind and the distance that now separates him from it—in much the same way that the poet, in the epic similes, juxtaposes these scenes of peace to those on the battlefield. On the Trojan side, Sarpedon echoes Achilles in stating that he has no personal stake in the war, and in evoking his life back home in faraway Lykia: "by the whirling waters of Xanthos; / there I left behind my own wife and my baby son, there / I left my many possessions which the needy man eyes longingly" (5.479–81). Sarpedon and Achilles express their misgivings about both the war and the heroic code in general, as we have already seen.[19]

Once the quarrel between Achilles and Agamemnon is established, the poem picks up and generalizes Achilles' questioning of the war effort in Book 1 and focuses its attention on the problematic value of Helen as the object of the war by turning to the demoralized Greek

[19]Though most frequently considered a typical warrior-hero, Sarpedon, in echoing Achilles' sentiments, can be seen as Achilles' Trojan counterpart. Like Achilles, Sarpedon is favored by Zeus (who is his father), and upon his death, Zeus weeps tears of blood. This incident shows the inexorability of death even for those thus favored, and so serves as a proleptic representation of Achilles' death, which lies beyond the conclusion of the poem.

army and its leaders. Near the beginning of Book 2, Agamemnon, having been told in a false dream sent by Zeus that his position favors an immediate assault on Troy, decides to test his troops first by suggesting that they abandon the war. He strikes a responsive chord in his men when he evokes the passing of nine years and the families they left behind:

> And now nine years of mighty Zeus have gone by, and the timbers
> of our ships have rotted away and the cables are broken
> and far away our own wives and our young children
> are sitting within our halls and wait for us, while still our work here
> stays forever unfinished as it is, for whose sake we came hither.
> Come then, do as I say, let us all be won over; let us
> run away with our ships to the beloved land of our fathers
> since no longer now shall we capture Troy of the wide ways.
> So he spoke, and stirred up the passion in the breast of all.
> [2.134–42]

It becomes clear from the great joy evinced by the Greek soldiers at the prospect of returning home that they have not fought the war with enthusiasm. Memories of their wives and children compel them more strongly than the idea of the abducted Helen.

Although Agamemnon does not mention Helen by name in his speech to the troops, Hera invokes her as the goal of the war when she sends Athena to exhort the Greek troops not to abandon battle:

> As things are, the Argives will take flight homeward over
> the wide ridges of the sea to the land of their fathers,
> and thus they would leave to Priam and to the Trojans Helen
> of Argos, to glory over, for whose sake many Achaians
> lost their lives in Troy far from their own native country.
> [2.158–62]

It is significant that immortal Hera, speaking from above the battlefield, untouched by the suffering of the warriors, evokes Helen as the object of the war. Yet even she understands that the idea of Helen can no longer rally the troops' sagging spirits, and so she argues that whatever the validity of the original conflict, the enormity of the Achaian losses makes it unacceptable to stop now. Hera thus attempts to shift the ground of her argument for continuing the war from the heroic recovery of legendary Helen to the concrete and real sacrifice of the common soldiers, a more tangible and acutely felt motivation for continued combat. This reason, however, can just as well be used to support the argument for abandoning the effort, as Agamemnon had done. The poet elsewhere insists upon the compelling affection between comrades: Achilles will reenter battle solely to avenge Patroclus' death. For grief-stricken Achilles, Helen is not a prize but one abhorred and accursed, unworthy of his efforts to regain her (19.325).

Hera's reasoning, that it is impermissible to give up after so many have been sacrificed, undercuts the supposed value of Helen. Instead, and conversely, the enormous sacrifice of lives is precisely what confers value on the war's goal, whatever that goal may be. Moreover, the irony in Hera's invocation of Helen lies in a fact Homer alludes to in the final book of the epic: Hera's hatred of Troy stems from the Judgment of Paris, in which he bestowed the coveted apple on Aphrodite rather than on herself or Athena (24.25–30). Of course, Helen, as the most beautiful woman, was Aphrodite's reward to Paris for choosing the goddess of love over the other two goddesses. Hera wishes the war to continue because she and Athena desire to punish the Trojans for Paris' slight.

Homer then presents alternate accounts of the war's goal through the speeches of cynical Thersites and pragmatic Odysseus. In his only appearance in the *Iliad*, Thersites the debunker—whose character Shakespeare develops in *Troilus and Cressida* as a biting critic of the war—berates Agamemnon for his selfishness and, in the process, exposes the general's ambiguous motives for perpetrating war:

> Son of Atreus, what thing further do you want, or find fault with
> now? Your shelters are filled with bronze, there are plenty of the choicest
> women for you within your shelter, whom we Achaians
> give to you first of all whenever we capture some stronghold.
> Or is it still more gold you will be wanting, that some son
> of the Trojans, breakers of horses, brings as ransom out of Ilion,
> one that I, or some other Achaian, capture and bring in?
> Is it some young woman to lie with in love and keep her
> all to yourself apart from the others? It is not right for
> you, their leader, to lead in sorrow the sons of the Achaians.
>
> [2.225–34]

Here, Thersites voices the resentment felt by the common soldiers against those in power who use their subordinates as agents to satisfy their sexual and material greed. According to Gregory Nagy, Thersites fulfills the role of a scapegoat;[20] and so it is fitting that he, like Briseis, articulates the victim's perspective on the heroic code. Yet in exposing the contradiction in the heroic code, he also echoes the epic's hero, Achilles, deconstructing the seemingly unbridgeable opposition between the "best" and the "worst" of the Achaians. The poet appears ambivalent about this surprising analogy: despite Thersites' championing of Achilles over Agamemnon, the poet has Achilles dissociate himself from the ugly and deformed malcontent: "Beyond all others Achilleus hated him, and Odysseus" (2.220). Although Achilles cannot be forced to obey Agamemnon, Thersites can be cudgeled into silence; but even so, Thersites has already spoken, exposing not only Agamemnon's deficiency as a leader but the problematic authority of the heroic code itself. For Achilles, too, his grievance against Agamemnon will lead to a questioning of the heroic code. And it is significant that the repeated disputes over the value of two women, Helen and Briseis, occasion this interrogation of the authority of the heroic code, the authority that underwrites the warriors' coming together on the Trojan battlefield.

At this point, Odysseus, perhaps aware of the justice of Thersites' accusations, intervenes and succeeds in silencing and discrediting the "fluent orator" (2.246). He then proceeds to correct the balance temporarily upset by Thersites; he persuades the troops to stay and continue fighting by echoing Agamemnon's speech. First he appeals to their sense of honor and shame: "For as if they were young children or widowed women / they cry out and complain to each other about going homeward" (2.289–90). Warriors are manlike, and so men who refuse to fight and yearn for home negate manliness: they are like children and women. Odysseus attempts to dismiss the argument for abandoning the war effort by appealing to prevailing notions about the opposition between genders—and between the "best" and the "worst" of the Achaians—which will allow him to discredit Thersites' claims. But then he, like Agamemnon, voices an understanding of the strong yearning for home and hearth:

[20]Nagy, p. 279. Nagy associates the baseness, boldness, and ugliness of Thersites with blame poetry—the institutional opposite of praise poetry—concluding that "it is Epos that gets the last laugh on the blame poet, rather than the other way around" (pp. 259–63). But Peter W. Rose, "Thersites and the Plural Voices of Homer," *Arethusa*, 21 (1988), 5–25, after showing the aristocratic bias of critical opinion on Thersites, argues that the text is more open to ambiguity and irony, more expressive of class tensions, than previous readings have allowed.

In truth, it is a hard thing, to be grieved with desire for going.
Any man who stays away one month from his own wife
with his intricate ship is impatient, one whom the storm winds
of winter and the sea rising keep back. And for us now
this is the ninth of the circling years that we wait here.

[2.291–95]

In the end, however, Odysseus repeats Hera's argument that "yet
always it is disgraceful / to wait long and at the end go home empty-
handed" (2.297–98). While appealing to the soldiers' sense of duty to
their chieftain—thus undercutting Thersites' contention that the soldiers are fools to follow Agamemnon—Odysseus shrewdly acknowledges the most compelling reason for giving up the war: the soldiers'
longing for their own wives. His final argument, however, is identical to Hera's: that the war, in its protraction, has become self-
perpetuating. Both Hera, who invoked Helen as the war's goal, and
Odysseus, who does not even mention her, offer the same argument
for continuing the war. Already at this point in the *Iliad,* the poet has
demystified Helen's role as an inadequate pretext for the war. According to Thersites, the motives of the leaders are sexual and material greed, and Odysseus implies that the war is self-generating and
self-perpetuating.

Menelaus and Nestor, the old counselor who voices the values of
tradition, claim Helen to be still the issue. But Nestor's exhortation,
coming after the speeches of Thersites and Odysseus, seems some-
how beside the point: "Therefore let no man be urgent to take the
way homeward / until after he has lain in bed with the wife of a
Trojan / to avenge Helen's longing to escape and her lamentations"
(2.354–56). Nestor justifies the prevailing practice of taking conquered women as slaves—already evident in the enslaving of
Chryseis and Briseis—as revenge for the wrongs done to Helen.
Nestor again exemplifies what Thersites exposed: the disguising of
concrete and material goals by abstractions—be it the achievement of
kleos or the recovery of Helen. Menelaus' desire to recover his own
wife may be understandable, but for the soldiers, the wives they left
behind are more compelling than the myth of the abducted Helen.

Having demystified the status of Helen as scapegoat and sign, the
poet brings her into the poem in Book 3. The difficulty of interpreting Helen, however, becomes more rather than less acute when
she actually enters the poem. The poet does not give a clearly com-
prehensible portrait of her; instead, he succeeds in conveying her

elusiveness, both as an indeterminate sign and as a woman with an unknowable inner subjectivity.

The Greeks have not seen Helen for twenty years,[21] and consequently, for them, she has become an abstraction, almost a phantom. The Trojans have accepted Helen into their world, but her presence seems to make her even more enigmatic than her absence. As an alien (and adulterous) woman, Helen proves to be, for most Trojans, an unassimilable presence, doubly Other. The poet conveys a radical ambivalence in the Trojan counselors toward her:

> Surely there is no blame on Trojans and strong-greaved Achaians
> if for long time they suffer hardship for a woman like this one.
> Terrible is the likeness of her face to immortal goddesses.
> Still, though she be such, let her go away in the ships, lest
> she be left behind, a grief to us and our children.
>
> [3.156–60]

For some, Helen is like a goddess, for others a grief; she is never a mere woman but one exalted or sinister, beyond the ordinary, the real. Victor Turner claims that extremes meet in the scapegoat who is considered at once innocent and guilty: "innocent because the conflicts that have gone before are not the victim's fault, but guilty because a scapegoat is required to atone for those conflicts."[22] Helen's doubleness renders her the perfect scapegoat, for the counselors believe the war would cease if she were to be banished from their midst. This doubleness in the Trojan counselors' view of Helen recalls the analogous double valuation of Briseis by the Greeks Achilles and Agamemnon. Helen, however, is a much more prominent and potent emblem than Briseis; hence, the two poles between which her meaning oscillates—encapsulated in the terror of her goddesslike beauty— are much more violently and uneasily opposed.

---

[21]See 24.765–66: "and here now is the twentieth year upon me since I came / from the place I was, forsaking the land of my fathers." A. T. Murray, in his Loeb edition (Cambridge: Harvard Univ. Press, 1924), appends this note to these lines: "This astonishing statement is perhaps to be explained by the legend that the Greeks shortly after Helen's abduction had made an abortive expedition against Troy, but had landed by mistake in Mysia. Thence they returned to Greece, and it was only after ten years that their forces were reassembled. . . . The whole suggests, however, an elaborate parallelism which arouses suspicion: nine years of preparation, the fleet sails in the tenth; nine years of siege, Troy falls in the tenth; nine years of wandering, Odysseus reaches home in the tenth."

[22]Victor Turner, *The Drums of Affliction: A Study of Religious Processes among the Ndembu of Zambia* (Oxford: Clarendon Press, 1968), p. 276.

As in the case of Briseis, the poet juxtaposes his own nuanced portrayal of Helen as a character to the counselors' scapegoating of her as an emblem of doubleness. Although the counselors consider her a stranger, Priam and Hector treat her as one of their own and do not regard her with hatred for causing the siege of their city. For Helen's ambiguous status, as wife of both Menelaus and Paris, involves her in a double network of legitimate alliances. The poet represents this ambiguity not only in terms of the opposing ways others perceive Helen but also from Helen's own perspective, in terms of her own divided loyalties. Although it is said that Aphrodite "left in her heart sweet longing / after her husband of time before, and her city and parents" (3.139–40), her affectionate relationship with Hector reveals that if Paris had been more like his brother, she might not have had so many regrets. She explicitly compares the two brothers, allying herself with Hector against Paris:

> I wish I had been the wife of a better man than this is,
> one who knew modesty and all things of shame that men say.
>
> . . .
>
> But come now, come in and rest on this chair, my brother,
> since it is on your heart beyond all that the hard work has fallen
> for the sake of dishonoured me and the blind act of Alexandros.
>
> [6.350–51, 354–56]

Helen's judgment of Paris is supported by the poet, for even Hector repeatedly shows scorn for his brother (3.39–57; 6.280–85). Moreover, the poet reports that Paris was hated among the Trojans as much as death, and that they would have willingly turned him over to the Greeks (3.451–54). Helen's allegiance is thus drawn along personal, rather than national, lines; her ability to recognize personal worth implicitly criticizes the arbitrary divisions of war in which Agamemnon unwittingly plays the role of a second Paris. Achilles will reveal the same capacity for overcoming national divisions when he accords the Trojan king, Priam, the respect due his own father.

Yet another uncertainty characterizes the relationship between Helen's past and her present predicament, between Helen who eloped with Paris and Helen who regrets her transgression, scorns her second husband, and longs for what she left behind. The poet only portrays the present Helen and leaves her past self a mystery. He represents Helen as an almost disembodied consciousness passively living out the effects of her fatal act. Despite the uncertainty and ambiguity of her identity and nature, Helen, paradoxically, is over-determined by that one act in her life. And even her role in that event is not entirely clear: Menelaus conceives of her as a victim, and even Priam exonerates her by blaming the gods (3.164).

Helen, on the other hand, blames herself by cursing her birth (6.344–48) and wishes she had died when she betrayed Menelaus (3.173–75). Her relationship with her protectress Aphrodite reveals further complications of motive and responsibility.[23] When Aphrodite bids Helen to go and join Paris in his bed—after the goddess removed him from combat with Menelaus—Helen counters by implying that her abduction was Aphrodite's doing and scornfully tells the goddess to join him herself:

> Strange divinity! Why are you still so stubborn to beguile me?
> Will you carry me further yet somewhere among cities
> fairly settled? In Phrygia or in lovely Maionia?
> Is there some mortal man there also who is dear to you?
>
>   . . .
>
> Go yourself and sit beside him, abandon the gods' way,
> turn your feet back never again to the path of Olympos
> but stay with him forever, and suffer for him, and look after him
> until he makes you his wedded wife, or makes you his slave girl.
>
>   [3.399–402, 406–9]

The question of human responsibility in the face of divine interference arises again in Book 4 when Athena encourages Pandarus to shoot the arrow that breaks the truce between the two armies (4.93–103) and the Greeks blame the Trojans for deception (4.168). Are Helen, and perhaps Paris, to be exonerated if Aphrodite is found responsible for the abduction of Helen and the removal of Paris from the battlefield? But if Aphrodite is seen not as a character or a personal agent but rather as the abstract embodiment of erotic passion, then Paris' abandonment of battle to take his pleasure with Helen and Helen's desire for him when she eloped with him become acts motivated by passions.[24] Gorgias will later exonerate her on these very

---

[23]On Helen as a "faded" Aphrodite, see Paul Friedrich, *The Meaning of Aphrodite* (Chicago: Univ. of Chicago Press, 1978), pp. 46–47. See also his discussion of this scene of confrontation between Helen and Aphrodite, pp. 59–61.

[24]Euripides gives an "allegorical" interpretation of the gods in *The Trojan Women*, where Hecuba refutes Helen's self-defense that she was compelled by Aphrodite (989–90). Whitman argues that the gods are to be read in poetic, not theological terms: "The gods of Homer are symbolic predicates of action, character, and circumstance"

grounds, for being compelled either by a god or by love. But even so, the exact degree of Helen's personal responsibility is difficult to ascertain.

Whatever her role or responsibility in her elopement with Paris, Helen now is powerless to act with consequence. Although she no longer loves Paris, the initial passion having turned into scorn and disgust, her more accurate appraisal of him can have no consequences. She cannot undo her act of twenty years before, and she cannot even refuse Aphrodite's behest to join Paris in the bedroom, for Aphrodite threatens to make hatred for her grow among both the Trojans and the Greeks (3.413–17). Helen is afraid, and rightly so, because she knows the extent of her dependence on others' valuation of her. Many Greeks and Trojans already scorn her, but she is protected by those who still prize her. For Helen, the good will of Hector and Priam is essential, since Paris would not be able to defend her alone if the others were to turn against her. When Aphrodite cows Helen into submission, after her brief assertion of independence, Helen's collapse reveals her essential passivity. To define Helen as passive may seem paradoxical, for her actions ostensibly brought about the war; but it is precisely her passivity as a woman that allows her to become an emblem, a scapegoat. As Rachel Bespaloff suggests, "She is the prisoner of the passions her beauty excited, and her passivity is, so to speak, their underside."[25] Conversely, it is her emblematic status that enforces her passivity, so that the significance of the emblem may be perpetuated.

Yet the male warriors cannot entirely control Helen's significance; just as the poet represented Helen's uncertainty and undecidability through her liminal position as Trojan and Greek, he shows how she crosses other boundaries. Like her protectoress Aphrodite, Helen participates in both the worlds of love, associated with women, and of war, associated with men.[26] Diomedes perhaps best expresses the

---

(p. 223). See also his discussion of Helen's "guilty nobility" in her confrontation with Aphrodite, "the predicative image of all Helen's deeds, attitudes, and circumstances" (p. 225).

[25]Rachel Bespaloff, On the Iliad, trans. Mary McCarthy (New York: Pantheon, 1947), p. 61.

[26]See Friedrich's discussion of the liminality of Aphrodite (pp. 132–48), in particular, of the dual nature of love as at once integrative and divisive (pp. 145–46). On the analogy of sex and battle, see Emily Vermeule, Aspects of Death in Early Greek Art and Poetry (Berkeley: Univ. of California Press, 1979), pp. 101–3, 157–59; and MacCary, pp. 137–48, who concludes: "Men 'mix' in love and war . . . violence seems originary, and sex only one of its expressive modes" (p. 148).

dichotomy in chiding Aphrodite, after wounding her: "Give way, daughter of Zeus, from the fighting and the terror. It is / not then enough that you lead astray women without warcraft?" (5.348–49). Her father, Zeus, concurs: "No, my child, not for you are the works of warfare. Rather / concern yourself only with the lovely secrets of marriage" (5.428–29). The opposition between the two worlds is again exemplified in Book 14 when Hera lures Zeus away from his supervision of the war by seducing him. While Hector resists Andromache's attempt to detain him from the battlefield, Paris, an accomplished lover but an ineffectual warrior, is swept away by Aphrodite in the midst of his duel with Menelaus, to join Helen in the bedroom. Thus, despite Diomedes' and Zeus' exhortations, Aphrodite does indeed involve herself in battle. Like Aphrodite, and as her human surrogate, Helen cannot be contained in the properly feminine sphere of love; projecting their own unruly desires on Helen as a dangerously unstable female, the males interpret and blame her as a figure of division and conflict.

The poet, however, represents Helen's liminal position as integrative rather than divisive, enabling her to participate imaginatively in both the worlds of masculine war and feminine domesticity. As a woman, and like Andromache, Helen properly belongs to the world of peace and domesticity (and here we may recall Hector rebuking Andromache for advising him on battle strategies), but like the Greek warriors, she is exiled from her homeland. Homer represents her involvement in the activity on the battlefield in the *teichoskopia,* the View from the Wall, where she catalogues the Greek warriors for Priam:[27]

> And I see them
> all now, all the rest of the glancing-eyed Achaians,
> all whom I would know well by sight, whose names I could tell you,
> yet nowhere can I see those two, the marshals of the people,
> Kastor, breaker of horses, and the strong boxer, Polydeukes,
> my own brothers, born with me of a single mother.
> Perhaps these came not with the rest from Lakedaimon the lovely,

[27]See Adam Parry's interpretation of the *teichoskopia* in terms of the poet's creative use of oral formula, in "Have We Homer's *Iliad?*," pp. 197–99. Clader points out that Helen knows the warriors because they were her suitors, and the *teichoskopia* functions as a reminder that the Trojan War is a second contest for the possession of Helen (p. 10). See also Bergren, pp. 21–22, who argues that in pointing to its own formulaic method of composition, the *teichoskopia* transcends linear time and achieves the *kleos* of the epic medium itself.

or else they did come here in their sea-wandering ships, yet
now they are reluctant to go with the men into battle
dreading the words of shame and all the reproach that is on me.
  So she spoke, but the teeming earth lay already upon them
away in Lakedaimon, the beloved land of their fathers.

[3.233–44]

In Helen's lament over her brothers, who she doesn't know are dead,
the poet sympathetically represents the gap in her knowledge and
underscores her human limitations—as he does again in her confrontation with the divine power of Aphrodite. Like the warrior-heroes,
then, Helen ranks above ordinary mortals, but the gods' (and the
poet's) superior power and knowledge repeatedly call attention to her
human limits.

  Not only does Helen resemble male warriors, she occupies a position akin to that of the male poet, a position she shares with the hero
of the poem, Achilles. Helen's catalogue of the Greek warriors for
Priam (3.177–242) follows the poet's own catalogue of the ships.[28]
Unlike Andromache, whose domestic weaving contrasts with Hector's martial deeds, Helen weaves the story of the war (3.125–28).[29]
In fact, a commentary in the Scholia of Venice states that Homer took
the greater part of his history of the Trojan war from the scenes
embroidered on her tapestry. Helen possesses not only a spatial, but
also a temporal perspective, for she knows about her literary afterlife,
knows that she will become a character in poems such as the *Iliad*
(6.358–59).

  Achilles, whose abilities parallel Helen's, also participates in the
worlds of war and peace, since he withdraws from battle to nurse his
wrath.[30] Like Helen, Achilles reveals a consciousness of his participation in poetic tradition: when the embassy from Agamemnon comes
to seek him, they find him singing to a lyre *klea andron,* the fame of
men (9.189), just as the bards to come will sing of his own fame.

---

[28]Clader, p. 9. She also suggests that it was traditional for the informant to be an
exile or renegade, like Sinon in *Aeneid* 2 (p. 10n.).

[29]On Helen's weaving as a symbol of poetic composition, see Clader, pp. 7–8.
Whitman, pp. 117–18, characterizes her weaving as "the symbol of her self-conscious
greatness and guilt."

[30]Atchity also sees Helen and Achilles to be alike in their apartness from other
characters in the epic. Achilles' shield, moreover, is complemented by Helen's weaving (p. 22). For a similar view, see Redfield, p. 36. Schein also notices the parallel
between the two characters but argues that Helen is not affected by the war as is
Achilles, who can never "escape the consequences of the war and of his own actions"
(p. 23).

Later poets made explicit Homer's representation of Helen and
Achilles as poet figures by having their ghosts, now married to one
another, declaim Homer's verses to the poem's heroes on the island of
Leuke.[31] In the *Iliad*, however, the poet represents the link between
the two more subtly in his comparison of Achilles to a woman:
Achilles himself invokes female Niobe as a prototype of a mourner
like himself (24.602–617). This subtle acknowledgment of Achilles'
understanding of feminine experience becomes in later tradition a
quite explicit opposition and tension between Achilles as an effemi-
nate lover and masculine warrior, much like in the myth of Hercules.
This tension is encapsulated in the story of Achilles' falling in love
with the Amazon Penthesilea the same moment that he slays her on
the battlefield.[32] Later traditions emphasize his effeminacy: Statius'
Achilleid tells how Achilles disguised himself as a woman in order to
seduce Deidameia before coming to Troy.[33] Dares and Dictys recount Achilles' traitorous (and fatal) love for the Trojan princess
Polyxena, and in Shakespeare's *Troilus and Cressida,* Achilles withdraws from the war because of his love for her. These later traditions
caricature and debase Achilles' link with the feminine, a link that in
the *Iliad* likens him to the bard and gives him access to a complex and
inclusive vision.

Homer repeatedly presents the inclusive vision, which embraces
both war and peace, in the similes that compare a martial act of
violence to events in the natural and domestic world and in the evocation of the warriors' peaceful childhood at the moments they meet
their gruesome deaths.[34] The most comprehensive embodiment of
both realms can be seen on the shield that Hephaestus forges for
Achilles.[35] Under the cosmic order, under "the tireless sun, and the

---

[31]Robert Graves, *The Greek Myths* (Baltimore: Penguin, 1955), 1: 121, citing
Pausanias, 3. 19.11 and Philostratus, *Heroica,* 10.32–40. *Pauly-Wissowa Real En-
cyclopaedie der Classischen Altertumswissenschaft* (Stuttgart: J. B. Metzler, 1912), 7: 2828.
According to Proclus, the *Cypria* told that Achilles desired to see Helen and that
Aphrodite and Thetis arranged a meeting between them upon his arrival to Troy. Of
this tradition, *Pauly* says, "Homer weiss nichts davon." Katherine Callen King,
Achilles: Paradigms of the War Hero from Homer to the Middle Ages (Berkeley: Univ. of
California Press, 1987), p. 174, notes that Lycophron lists Achilles as the last of
Helen's five husbands (*Alex.* 146, 171–79).

[32]Vermeule, p. 158.

[33]See King, pp. 180–83.

[34]On Homer's similes, see Carroll Moulton, *Similes in the Homeric Poems* (Got-
tingen: Vandenhoeck and Ruprecht, 1977), and Susanne L. Wofford's forthcoming
The Choice of Achilles: Action and Figure in Epic Narrative from Homer to Milton.

[35]On the shield, see Atchity's discussion, pp. 172–87. He also sees the shield as

moon waxing into her fullness, / . . . the constellations that festoon
the heavens" (18.484–85), Hephaestus portrays two cities, one at
peace, one at war. In the city at peace, there is a wedding, the basic
unit of community and harmony, whose disintegration is the cause of
the Trojan war. In the same city, there already exists a scene of
altercation, a dispute over property, like that over Briseis or Helen.
The presence of an arbiter assures a peaceful settlement of the dispute,
but the seeds of war are present even in the city of peace. The struggle
in the city at war also concerns property. The war engulfs and de-
stroys the shepherds and their flocks, just as the Trojan war annihilates warriors with their pastoral childhoods.

Thus the Trojan war is demystified as a self-perpetuating and om-
nipresent counterpart to precarious peace; the reasons given for wag-
ing it are merely pretexts so men can come together on the battlefield.
Homer reveals how irrelevant Helen has become even to the warriors
themselves when, in Book 7, Diomedes—a thoroughly representative warrior-hero—urges the Greeks not to accept any offer of rep-
aration from the Trojans: "Now let none accept the possessions of
Alexandros, / nor take back Helen . . . / . . . the terms of death
hang over the Trojans" (7.400–402). Although the Trojan messenger,
Idaius, had come to offer only the treasure, Diomedes advocates the
refusal not only of the treasure but of Helen as well, were she to be
returned. The troops enthusiastically endorse Diomedes' position,
and Agamemnon sanctions it: "Idaios, you hear for yourself the word
of the Achaians, / how they are answering you; and such is my pleasure also" (7.406–7).

Yet Homer is not content to present Helen as merely an object to
be exchanged back and forth between the two armies, as the female
sign that Lévi-Strauss described; he criticizes the warriors' reification
of her by showing how she, like Achilles and the poet himself, is a
generator of signs possessing an imaginative capacity. This capacity
derives partly from her dual identity as both Greek and Trojan, as
participant in the otherwise mutually exclusive realms of masculine
war and feminine domesticity; like the poet, she is privileged with an
inclusive vision that allows her to rise above the seemingly endless
struggle between the nations. She knows that peace will eventually
come, when her story will be recounted by poems such as the *Iliad*. In

reflecting "the all-encompassing scope of Homer's poetic perspective," which includes actions of both peace and war (p. 173). See also Redfield's discussion of the
relationship between the shield and the poem's similes (pp. 186–89).

depicting Helen as a subject, the poet endows her with an inwardness that she shares with Achilles, an inwardness that proves for both to be a source of imaginative power. Yet unlike Helen, Achilles acts as a subject throughout the epic and is never cast in the role of scapegoat or sign: though he too occupies the liminal position of a scapegoat and carries double meanings as at once the champion and destroyer of his people, the poem makes clear that the death of Hector, not the death of Achilles, makes inevitable the city's fall. Helen as woman, on the other hand, is objectified and hence contained by the male warriors as signifier: they read her as an emblem of doubleness, whose dual significance as a goddesslike beauty and a scourge of war reflects their ambivalence toward the war which brings them both glory and death. Thus, the significance of Helen as "primal word" in the *Iliad* fluctuates between two antithetical poles.[36] As a pretext for the war, Helen necessarily proves an inadequate word to explain the ensuing deed.

Achilles: "Feminine" Word / "Masculine" Deed

Considering female Helen as signifier for the signified of the male war-effort reveals the disjunction and opposition between signifier and signified, between words and deeds, that pervades the *Iliad*.[37] Nestor, the man of counsel, laments that he can no longer trust in covenants:[38]

Where then shall our covenants go, and the oaths we have taken?
Let counsels and the meditations of men be given to the flames then,
with the unmixed wine poured and the right hands we trusted.

[2.339–41]

Covenants, which would bind men together if kept, are persistently broken, and strife rather than harmony reigns in the aftermath: Paris

[36]I refer, of course, to Freud's influential essay "The Antithetical Sense of Primal Words" (1910), *Collected Papers,* trans. Joan Riviere (New York: Basic Books, 1959), 4: 184–91.

[37]On the association between language, duplicity, weaving, and the female, see Ann L. T. Bergren, "Language and the Female in Early Greek Thought," *Arethusa,* 16 (1983), 6–95.

[38]MacCary, p. 208, identifies a parallel continuum in the *Iliad* between youth and old age on the one hand and words and deeds on the other: "Young men in the *Iliad* despise old men almost as much as they despise women: old men are no longer action, but have become words" (p. 245).

has broken his important pact as a guest of Menelaus, Agamemnon has robbed Achilles of his rightful prize, Briseis, and Pandarus breaks the truce between the Trojans and the Greeks with a single arrow. Words are not matched by deeds, and the heroic society's valuation of warlike deeds as masculine and the consequent devaluation of words as feminine fosters divisions between men and nations. The disjunction between word and deed becomes especially prominent in the latter part of the epic, where the violence of the war increases and deeds outstrip the capacity of words to denote them.[39]

These references to words and deeds cluster around Achilles, who experiences most acutely the tragic disjunction between them. Adam Parry has suggested that Phoenix's advice to Achilles to be a "speaker of words and doer of deeds" (9.442–43) exemplifies "the complementary halves of a hero's abilities, and the obverse and reverse of his great purpose: to acquire prestige among his fellows."[40] During his withdrawal from battle, Achilles' words replace his deeds as he criticizes the heroic code. Even after he reenters battle, at the beginning of his *aristeia* his words continue to take precedence over deeds, as his encounter with Aeneas will show. By the time he confronts Lycaon and Hector, however, Achilles has forgone words in favor of violent deeds on the battlefield. He finds that he cannot balance these complementary halves until his interview with Priam. Simone Weil has observed that "the true hero, the true subject, the center of the *Iliad* is force," and that Achilles is the hero of the poem because of his superhuman might.[41] I suggest, rather, that the poem interrogates heroic society's exaltation of force as masculine; Achilles is the hero of the poem not because of his terrible *aristeia* but because of the understand-

---

[39]Charles Segal, *The Theme of the Mutilation of the Corpse in the Iliad* (Leiden: Brill, 1971), sees the brutality toward the bodies of the slain to build up in rapid crescendo after Book 16, climaxing in the death of Hector.

[40]Adam Parry, "The Language of Achilles," *TAPA*, 87 (1956), 4. Parry argues that Achilles' "misusing of conventional language" in his speech to the embassy signals his apartness from the heroic code. Whitman also sees Achilles' wrath as a sign of his withdrawal from the standards as well as from the society of his peers (p. 183). Extending and elaborating Parry, Schein describes Achilles' tragedy as his inability to posit an alternative to honor and glory, which he has become unable to accept (pp. 108–9). Other critics consider Achilles' wrath to be an error or tragic *hamartia*. For example, C. M. Bowra thinks that Achilles falls into sin when he refuses to accept the offer of reconciliation brought by the embassy and, for his refusal, is punished by the death of Patroclus. *Tradition and Design in the Iliad* (Oxford: Oxford Univ. Press, 1930), pp. 19–20. For Redfield, Achilles' wrath stems from his vivid vision of a "partial truth" (p. 17).

[41]Simone Weil, "The *Iliad* or the Poem of Force," trans. Mary McCarthy (1940; Wallingford, Penn.: Pendle Hill, n.d.) pp. 3–4.

ing of the power of "feminine" words that he attains at the end of the epic.

When Achilles encounters Aeneas upon his reentry into battle, Achilles speaks at length, explaining why he will not fight Aeneas (20.178–98). Here Achilles uses words to avoid combat with Aeneas, invoking an earlier encounter in a pastoral setting on the hills of Ida; at that time, Aeneas succeeded in fleeing from Achilles' spear. He also implies that since Aeneas is not a son of Priam, he is too insignificant a match for Achilles. Aeneas, however, refuses to take Achilles' advice that he retreat:

> Son of Peleus, never hope by words to frighten me
> as if I were a baby. I myself understand well enough
> how to speak in vituperation and how to make insults.
>   .   .   .
>   Since I believe we will not in mere words, like children,
> meet, and separate and go home again out of the fighting.
>   .   .   .
> But what have you and I to do with the need for squabbling
> and hurling insults at each other, as if we were two wives
> who when they have fallen upon a a heart-perishing quarrel
> go out in the street and say abusive things to each other,
> much true, and much that is not, and it is their rage that drives
>   them.
> You will not by talking turn me back from the strain of my
>   warcraft,
> not till you have fought to my face with the bronze.
>
> [20.200–202, 211–12, 251–57]

Although Aeneas himself speaks for nearly sixty lines, giving a lengthy account of the genealogy that Achilles insulted, he nevertheless perspicaciously recognizes the use to which Achilles has put his rhetoric: by insinuating that his victory is a foregone conclusion, Achilles substitutes words for spears. Aeneas repeatedly associates words with children and women (and here we may recall Odysseus' association of men who refuse to fight with women and children), thereby underscoring the opposition between "masculine" deeds and "feminine" words. Achilles prevails over Aeneas, after a fashion, for Poseidon whisks Aeneas away. This victory of "feminine" words over deadly deeds allows Aeneas to live on to continue the Trojan line after the fall of the city (20.302–8).[42]

---

[42]See Nagy, pp. 265–75, for a discussion of an "independent *Aeneid* tradition within

Yet after his encounter with Aeneas, Achilles begins to give and exact deeds instead of words. Accordingly, he brutally slays the next warrior he encounters, and this time his words follow the deed:

> Great Achilleus struck him with the spear as he came in fury,
> in the middle of the head, and all the head broke into two pieces.
> He fell, thunderously. Great Achilleus vaunted above him:
> Lie there, Otrynteus' son, most terrifying of all men.
> Here is your death, but your generation was by the lake waters
> of Gyge, where is the allotted land of your fathers
> by fish-swarming Hyllos and the whirling waters of Hermos.
>
> [20.386–92]

Despite his exultation, Achilles' speech is peculiarly elegiac; he names the dead warrior's birthplace and describes the landscape around it, pointing to the great disparity between that idyllic birthplace and this gruesome place of death, as the poet himself often does in describing deaths on the battlefield. Achilles had spoken similarly of Patroclus' and his own eventual deaths: "And now, far away from the land of his fathers, / he has perished" (18.99–100); "Thus it is destiny for us both to stain the same soil / here in Troy; since I shall never come home . . . / . . . in this place the earth will receive me" (18.329–32). Not only does Achilles single out this obscure warrior by acknowledging his origins—as he had done with the more high-born Aeneas—his words allow him to express his sense of kinship with and tribute to the slain warrior because he knows that he will meet a similar fate.

From here on, Achilles has no words. Instead, he kills silently and brutally:

> Achilleus
> stabbed [Demoleon] in the temple through the brazen sides of the
>   helmet,
> and the brazen helmet could not hold, but the bronze spearhead
> driven on through smashed the bone apart, and the inward
> brain was all spattered forth. So he beat him down in his fury.
>
> [20.396–400]

The transformation of Achilles into a machine that kills can most

---

the *Iliad*." Aeneas himself is a master of the poetic skills in the language of praise and blame.

clearly be seen in his slaying of Polydorus, Priam's youngest son, whom he spears in the back as the boy runs by (20.413–14). At the end of Book 20, he cold-bloodedly kills Tros, who begs for mercy, cutting off the supplicant's words with a single swordstroke (20.463–72).

This last encounter sets the stage for his confrontation with Lycaon at the beginning of Book 21. Lycaon, like Tros, begs for mercy, embracing Achilles' knees in the position of a supplicant (21.70–96). Lycaon's plea echoes Achilles' speech to Aeneas; Achilles attempted to avoid combat with Aeneas, citing Aeneas' genealogy and referring to an earlier encounter in a pastoral setting. Now Lycaon adduces similar reasons why Achilles should spare him: that Achilles had once captured him in an orchard but had allowed him to be ransomed, and that, though Priam's son, he was not born from the same womb as Hector. But this time, Achilles is deaf to his pleas. By remaining silent, Achilles refuses to acknowledge the common humanity and past that he shares with his adversary. Simone Weil describes Achilles' predicament well: "Deliverance appears in the extreme and tragic aspect of destruction—a more moderate or reasonable solution would expose the mind to suffering so naked, so violent, that it could not be borne. . . . The intoxication of force intervenes to drown terror, grief, exhaustion.[43] Achilles therefore forgoes words in favor of deeds, though in the end, indiscriminate slaughter of the Trojans and even the death of Hector will not assuage his sorrow.

These incidents culminate in Achilles' climactic encounter with Hector. Before the fatal confrontation, Hector considers offering peace to Achilles but realizes the futility of such overtures:

> Or if again I set down my shield massive in the middle
> and my ponderous helm, and lean my spear up against the rampart
> and go out as I am to meet Achilleus the blameless
> and promise to give back Helen, and with her all her possessions,
> all those things that once in the hollow ships Alexandros
> brought back to Troy, and these were the beginning of the quarrel;
>   . . .
>   yet still, why does the heart within me debate on these things?
> I might go up to him, and he take no pity upon me
> nor respect my position, but kill me naked so, as if I were
> a woman, once I stripped my armour from me. There is no
> way any more from a tree or a rock to talk to him gently

---

[43]Weil, pp. 18–19.

whispering like a young man and a young girl, in the way
a young man and a young maiden whisper together.
Better to bring on the fight with him as soon as it may be.
We shall see to which one the Olympian grants the glory.

[22.111–16, 122–30]

Hector correctly recognizes that at this point words are irrelevant and
impotent, although in an idyllic peacetime setting, words exchanged
between a young man and a girl—like those Helen and Paris exchanged twenty years before—could enchant and beguile. Hector's
musings reveal his consciousness of a radical opposition between
words and deeds: words are the proper medium of exchange in peacetime between men and women, not on the battlefield between male
warriors. The exchange of deeds between male warriors will inevitably result in the victory of one and the other's humiliation "as a
woman."

When the two warriors actually confront each other, Hector promises Achilles honorable treatment of his corpse if he is victorious and
asks for reciprocal treatment. Achilles refuses:

Hektor, argue me no agreements. I cannot forgive you.
As there are no trustworthy oaths between men and lions,
nor wolves and lambs have spirit that can be brought to agreement
but forever these hold feelings of hate for each other,
so there can be no love between you and me, nor shall there be
oaths between us, but one or the other must fall before then
to glut with his blood Ares the god who fights under the shield's
    guard.

[22.261–68]

Achilles' refusal is ostensibly motivated by his perception of an enormous and unbridgeable difference between himself and Hector. Hector as the slayer of Patroclus is incontrovertibly Other, since Achilles
always perceived his comrade to be a second self: "Patroklos, whom I
loved beyond all other companions, / as well as my own life" (18.81–
82). Of Patroclus' death, Achilles had said that no greater ill could
come to him, not even the death of his father or his son (19.321–27).
Moreover, Patroclus had entered the war on Achilles' behalf and had
been wearing Achilles' armor when he met his death.

Yet Achilles must also recognize that he and Hector are more alike
than different. As I have already suggested, they share the burden of
fighting in service of a heroic code about which they feel ambivalent.
The foremost warriors of their armies, they also bring deaths to their

comrades: Achilles' pride required a great sacrifice from his comrades which included the death of Patroclus, and Hector admits that his pride cost his own troops their lives (22.104–7). Finally, Hector wears Achilles' armor as they meet in battle. Achilles, however, chooses to emphasize the difference between himself and Hector by comparing them to "men and lions," "wolves and lambs"; he denies any common ground, any shared humanity between them. He specifically denies the possibility of a shared language, which distinguishes humans from animals;⁴⁴ instead, he affirms only force, animalistic and inhuman. The poet thus criticizes heroic society's valuation of deeds over words by revealing that "masculine" force is indeed bestial, whereas "feminine" words define what is human and humane. Hector exposes Achilles' ambivalence by pointing out that although Achilles dismisses language, he nevertheless speaks at great length:

> You missed; and it was not, o Achilleus like the immortals,
> from Zeus that you knew my destiny; but you thought so; or rather
> you are someone clever in speech and spoke to swindle me,
> to make me afraid of you and forget my valour and war strength.
> [22.279–82]

Hector also seems to realize that Achilles' insistence on their difference masks a recognition of their affinity with one another, for he reiterates yet again his request for burial, only to be refused anew. Achilles again insists on the difference, this time between Patroclus and Hector: "On you the dogs and the vultures / shall feed and foully rip you; the Achaians will bury Patroklos" (22.335–36). By denying Hector burial, Achilles again allies himself with the bestial—with the dogs and vultures that he predicts will disfigure Hector's body. Yet Hector reminds him of their common destiny as he dies: "Be careful now; for I might be made into the gods' curse / upon you, on that day when Paris and Phoibos Apollo / destroy you in the Skaian gates, for all your valour" (22.358–60). Achilles seems finally to accept, if with bitterness, Hector's last words: "Die: and I will take my own death at whatever time / Zeus and the rest of the immortals choose to accomplish it" (22.365–66).

Heroic mores require revenge for the death of Patroclus, and that

---

⁴⁴But Hera allows Peleus' horses to prophesy Achilles' death at the end of Book 19, though the Furies intervene to silence them. Redfield points out that horses, like heroes and unlike dogs, have names, can have divine parents, and even be immortal (p. 195).

revenge is the acceptable outlet for Achilles' sorrow. Yet he also knows that killing Hector and other Trojans will not assuage his sorrow, since they are ultimately not responsible for his comrade's death. Achilles, however, persists in excess, dragging Hector's body around the walls of Troy (thus replacing the dogs and vultures that the gods keep away from Hector's corpse) and even sacrificing twelve Trojan youths on Patroclus' funeral pyre.[45] It is therefore ironic that when the spirit of Patroclus appears to Achilles, he chides Achilles for forgetting him; Patroclus requests a burial but does not ask to be avenged (23.69–71). The gods also criticize Achilles' excess. Apollo faults him for his lack of justice, pity, and shame, comparing him in his prideful strength to a wild lion (24.39–45), as Achilles had spoken of himself in his speech to Hector.

Achilles finally listens to his mother, Thetis, whose words convey Zeus' command to return Hector's body to Priam. When Priam kneels before Achilles in supplication, unlike in Lycaon's case, Achilles heeds Priam's words, which evoke Achilles' own father in asking for mercy (24.503–6). Here, as elsewhere, words bring the recognition of common ground; in this case, of common suffering.[46] Priam and Achilles, the aged Trojan king and the youthful Greek hero, can weep together despite their differences, because Achilles' father will experience Priam's sorrow upon Achilles' death. Although the two weep for their own losses—"the two remembered, as Priam sat huddled / at the feet of Achilleus and wept close for manslaughtering Hektor / and Achilleus wept now for his own father, now again / for Patroklos" (24.509–12)—Achilles' imagination enables him to go beyond his own grief for the death of Patroclus and to extend his compassion toward Priam's grief. The recognition of links with others which he had been trying to deny during his frenzied *aristeia* brings about the inevitable acknowledgement of human helplessness in the face of fate and the gods:

> Such is the way the gods spun life for unfortunate mortals,
> that we live in unhappiness, but the gods themselves have no
> sorrows.

---

[45]Nagler, pp. 165–66, noting the paratactic juxtaposition of Achilles' failure to treat Hector's corpse properly with his similar failure to ignite Patroclus' pyre, points out Achilles' "selfish attachment to his friend which mirrors, in Homer's brilliant psychology, his attachment to his enemy."

[46]See Thomas M. Greene, *The Descent from Heaven: A Study in Epic Continuity* (New Haven: Yale Univ. Press, 1963), pp. 44–47, for a discussion of this scene as a "recognition scene peculiar to epic." Nagler, pp. 185–98, sees this scene as a mutual

There are two urns that stand on the door-sill of Zeus. They are unlike
for the gifts they bestow: an urn of evils, an urn of blessings.

    . . .

Such were the shining gifts given by the gods to Peleus.

    . . .

Thereto
the gods bestowed an immortal wife on him, who was mortal.
But even on him the gods piled evil also. There was not
any generation of strong sons born to him in his great house
but a single all-untimely child he had, and I give him
no care as he grows old, since far from the land of my fathers
I sit here in Troy, and bring nothing but sorrow to you and your children.
And you, old sir, we are told you prospered once. . . .

    . . .

But now the Uranian gods brought us, an affliction upon you,
forever there is fighting about your city, and men killed.
But bear up, nor mourn endlessly in your heart, for there is not
anything to be gained from grief for your son; you will never
bring him back; sooner you must go through yet another sorrow.

[24.525–28, 534, 536–43, 547–51]

In the striking emblem of the two urns of good and evil gifts, Achilles offers an alternative to Helen as an emblem for the doubleness of experience as governed by the heroic code, which promises immortal fame in return for death on the battlefield. For Priam and his own father, Peleus, the fame of their sons will not console them for their untimely deaths. Achilles understands his own predicament to be double: Zeus honored Achilles' wish that the Greeks suffer for his wrath against Agamemnon, but the setback also entailed Patroclus' death, which ultimately renders the honor accorded him meaningless and trivial. The acute self-consciousness that makes Achilles the hero of the poem is itself a mixed gift, for this very awareness has proven to be a source of great pain and anguish. Like his own emblem of the two urns, Achilles himself carries double meanings: a murdering machine and yet also a compassionate man capable of moving beyond national identities; the fighter who most advances the Greek effort but who also indirectly causes multitudes of Greek deaths.[47] He

---

consolatio. For other discussions, see Bespaloff, pp. 97–106; Redfield, pp. 216–18; and Whitman, pp. 218–19.

[47]Segal also sees Achilles as "unit[ing] in himself the extreme polarities of Homer's heroic world . . . of all Greek culture: immense capacities for love and for hatred,

knows he is the best of the Achaians, but he also knows that, even so, he will not be able to escape death, the ultimate "evil gift" of which he speaks.

Achilles' speech reverberates beyond its immediate context to encompass virtually all the other oppositions and divisions that Homer presents in the *Iliad*. By reconciling himself with Priam, Achilles establishes a separate peace—however temporary—between Hellas and Troy. This, the only peaceful meeting between men from the two nations, paradoxically recalls all the violent encounters in which one warrior's glory by necessity entails the other's shame and death. In this reconciliation with Priam, Achilles returns to the use of "feminine" words and regains his humanity without feeling shame about being cowardly. Significantly, he compares himself to Niobe, a proud mother devastated by the gods' destruction of her children (24.602–17).[48]

In braving the journey through the enemy camp to arrive at Achilles' tent—a journey figured as one to Hades with Hermes as guide—Priam shows courage and a heroism that does not find its expression in force. In Priam, Achilles seems finally to have come to terms with a father figure, after rebelling against Agamemnon and dismissing the advice of his surrogate father, Phoenix, during the embassy visit in Book 9. The acceptance of paternal authority entails a recognition of the limit to one's freedom, and that limit is represented in the poem by the gods, whose immortality constantly reminds humans of their mortality.[49] Apollo compares mortals to leaves, which flourish momentarily but soon fade away to die (21.463–66). In this speech Achilles concerns himself almost exclusively with his mortal parent, Peleus, and only alludes to his divine mother, Thetis, in a way that underscores Peleus' mortality. Although Peleus never actually appears in the poem—in fact it is Thetis who repeatedly intervenes between Achilles and Zeus—Achilles here allies him-

---

social responsibility and self-centered recklessness, devotion to personal ties and tragic isolation" (p. ix). On the doubleness of Achilles as benefactor and destroyer, and his character as "inconsistent and morally opaque," see Nagler, p. 161.

[48]See Nagler, pp. 194–95, for a different emphasis on the relevance of the story of Niobe: "The image of rock and water becomes a focus for the themes of unyielding strength and compassion, immortality and the cyclical flow of birth and death."

[49]Both Schein, *passim,* and Jasper Griffin, *Homer on Life and Death* (Oxford: Clarendon Press, 1980), esp. pp. 81–143, focus on the importance of mortality in the *Iliad*. Wofford sees death as the central fact that the figural dimension of the *Iliad* seeks to hide.

self with his mortal father, thereby insisting on his own humanity and mortality.[50]

Death marks the ultimate limit, as the final gift from the urn of evil gifts. After rebelling so insistently against the death of Patroclus, Achilles finally confronts his mortality by alluding calmly and without anger to his own impending death. Finally, he heals the split between word and deeds which marked his *aristeia* by matching the word to the deed, by offering Priam this very speech, together with Hector's body. In the moment of reconciliation between Achilles and Priam, Achilles demonstrates his hard-won acceptance of the divisions of experience, a vision that comprehends and embraces all the oppositions that Homer had dramatized in the *Iliad*.

This moment of reconciliation is preceded and followed by two funerals: Patroclus' among the Greeks and Hector's among the Trojans. Funerals are society's way of healing, of coming to terms with the final and most terrible evil gift. The poem itself is a funeral, an elegy to the civilization that was destroyed, a heroic society that passed away, as well as to the individual men and women who were caught in the process. Homer's poem, like his hero's speech on the two urns, encompasses these various oppositions in a comprehensive vision.[51] The poet's valuation of words over deeds stems from a recognition of the human ability to attain and articulate a complex awareness through language, an awareness the poem achieves and, among its characters, Achilles and Helen achieve. At the beginning of Book 12, the poet gives a proleptic view of the destruction worked by the rivers after Troy's fall:

> So long as Hektor was still alive, and Achilleus was angry,
> so long as the citadel of lord Priam was a city untaken,
> for this time the great wall of the Achaians stood firm. But afterwards
> when all the bravest among the Trojans had died in the fighting,
> and many of the Argives had been beaten down, and some left,
> when in the tenth year the city of Priam was taken
> and the Argives gone in their ships to the beloved land of their fathers,

[50]See, however, Nagy's discussion of post-Homeric accounts that accorded Achilles immortality on the Isles of the Blessed (pp. 165–72).

[51]Redfield, p. 220, gives a similar view of the poet's craft: "As the forming of art is a further forming of forms already present in nature and culture, so it follows that artistic form is inclusive of culture and nature."

then at last Poseidon and Apollo took counsel
to wreck the wall, letting loose the strength of rivers upon it,
                                . . .
   And the shaker of the earth himself holding in his hands the trident
guided them, and hurled into the waves all the bastions'
    strengthening
of logs and stones the toiling Achaians had set in position
and made all smooth again by the hard-running passage of Helle
and once again piled the great beach under sand, having wrecked
the wall, and turned the rivers again to make their way down
the same channel where before they had run the bright stream of
    their water.

[12.10–18, 27–33]

Here Homer takes us beyond the poem's limits and presents the
events that follow the death of Hector: Achilles' death, Troy's fall,
and the general destruction by the rivers. It takes only nine days for
nature to obliterate the work of man; the war itself has already lasted
for nine years. Nature, like the poet, does not discriminate between
the victors and the vanquished: despite Dares and Dictys' claim that
Homer favored the Greeks, the Achaeans' bastion meets the same fate
as Troy's walls. Thus Homer presents the same inclusive vision,
comprehending and embracing oppositions, that Achilles achieves.

Unique among the *Iliad*'s characters, Helen shares with the poet
this proleptic vision. To Hector she speaks of herself and Paris: "Us
two, on whom Zeus set a vile destiny, so that hereafter /
we shall be
made into things of song for the men of the future" (6.357–58).
Helen's understanding concerning Zeus' ambiguous gifts—a vile destiny and immortality in poetry—prefigures Achilles' hard-won acceptance of Zeus' gifts from his two urns. Despite her superior
awareness, Helen cannot escape being reduced to an emblem like the
two urns by men who attempt to explain their own ambivalence
toward the war and the heroic code, which brings them good and evil
gifts.

Hector stood apart from this society's way of making sense of these
troubling disjunctions; rather than project his ambivalence toward the
war on Helen as scapegoat, he treated her with kindness and generosity. It is a measure at once of Helen's close relationship with Hector
and of her status as a captive stranger in Troy that she laments for
Hector at his funeral.[52] By following Hecuba and Andromache in

---

[52]Margaret Alexiou has pointed out that, traditionally, funeral laments were per-

singing her lament, Helen signals her status as a kinswoman of Hector, but at the same time, her lament echoes that of Briseis—a captive woman among the Trojans—for Patroclus:

> Hektor, of all my lord's brothers dearest by far to my spirit:
> my husband is Alexandros, like an immortal, who brought me
> here to Troy; and I should have died before I came with him;
> and here now is the twentieth year upon me since I came
> from the place where I was, forsaking the land of my fathers. In this time
> I have never heard a harsh saying from you, nor an insult.
> No, but when another, one of my lord's brothers or sisters, a fair-robed
> wife of some brother, would say a harsh word to me in the palace,
> or my lord's mother—but his father was gentle always, a father
> indeed—then you would speak and put them off and restrain them
> by your own gentleness of heart and your gentle words. Therefore
> I mourn for you in sorrow of heart and mourn myself also
> and my ill luck. There was no other in all the wide Troad
> who was kind to me, and my friend; all others shrank when they saw me.
>
> [24.762–75]

Helen's lament for Hector not only enacts the ambiguity of her own status as kinswoman and stranger but also functions as a lament for herself. She mourns the loss of her former self before she was cursed with the "ill luck" that brought her to Troy, thus giving voice to a self-conscious subjecthood that understands divisions within the self. Now, after Hector's death, with no one else to protect her, she knows that she will be treated solely as a stranger and no longer as a kinswoman. Her lament thus accurately predicts her literary afterlife, for in the *Odyssey,* having returned to Sparta with Menelaus, she is represented as an unassimilable and sinister presence in her own house.

Helen's lament for Hector parallels the poet's elegy for Troy and for the heroic age. In marking the loss and absence not only of Hector but also of her former self, her lament, like all elegies, enacts the disjunction between word and deed, between language and what it

---

formed by kinswomen and strangers, often slaves. She notes that in the *Iliad,* Trojan women, captives in the Greek camp, are forced to lament for Patroclus (18.339). *The Ritual Lament in Greek Tradition* (Cambridge: Cambridge Univ. Press, 1974), p. 10. See Clader, p. 11, on Helen's role in the lament as the Cause of the War.

describes. Unlike Sappho's Helen, who never regretted her love for Paris, Homer's Helen, in this final expression of remorse and self-hatred, again poses the question of her responsibility—a question that remains unanswered in the *Iliad*.[53] Achilles' reconciliation with Priam, which accomplishes a bridging of important divisions and oppositions in the poem, is momentary and passing; ultimately it gives way to a renewed perception of the tragic disjunctions of heroic society which mark its passing. Helen of Argos, the poem's primary figure of difference, embodies and voices this perception by closing the poem with a funeral lament for Hector, the best of the Trojans.

[53]On Sappho's critique of Homer, see Page duBois, "Sappho and Helen," in *Women in Classical Antiquity*, pp. 95–105; and Jack Winkler, "Gardens of Nymphs: Public and Private in Sappho's Lyrics," in *Reflections of Women in Antiquity*, pp. 63–89.

2   The Odyssey

> She has composed, so long, a self with which to welcome him,
> Companion to his self for her, which she imagined,
> Two in a deep-founded sheltering, friend and dear friend.
>   · · ·
>
> But was it Ulysses? Or was it only the warmth of the sun
> On her pillow? The thought kept beating in her like her heart.
> The two kept beating together. It was only day.
>
> It was Ulysses and it was not.
> —Wallace Stevens, "The World as Meditation"

The *Odyssey*, though acutely conscious of the *Iliad*, does not mourn for a heroic past as the *Iliad* did but rather appears to represent the origins of the poet's own culture[1]—like Aeschylus' *Oresteia*, which purports to recount the origins of the Athenian law courts.[2] The *Odyssey*'s interest in continuity—the quality that makes it a comedy rather than a tragedy like the *Iliad*—is perhaps most evident in its

---

[1]The *Odyssey* differs from the *Iliad*, which approximates more closely Mikhail Bakhtin's definition of epic in taking as its subject the absolute past: "The epic world is an utterly finished thing, not only as an authentic event of the distant past but also on its own terms and by its own standards; it is impossible to change, to re-think, to re-evaluate anything in it. It is completed, conclusive and immutable, as a fact, an idea and a value. This defines absolute epic distance. One can only accept the epic world with reverence; it is impossible to really touch it, for it is beyond the realm of human activity, the realm in which everything humans touch is altered and re-thought." "Epic and Novel," in *The Dialogic Imagination*, ed. Michael Holquist, trans. Caryl Emerson and Michael Holquist (Austin: Univ. of Texas Press, 1981), p. 17. Concerning the transition from epic to the Hellenistic romances, Bakhtin says: "In the era of Hellenism a closer contact with the heroes of the Trojan epic cycle began to be felt; epic is already transformed into novel" (p. 15). In the *Odyssey*, this transformation seems already to have begun to take place. On Odysseus as a romance hero, see Pietro Pucci, *Odysseus Polutropos: Intertextual Readings in the Odyssey and the Iliad* (Ithaca: Cornell Univ. Press, 1987), p. 56.

[2]Indeed, in both the *Odyssey* and the *Oresteia*, Athena's rather abrupt intervention makes possible at once narrative closure and the continuity of civilization.

subject matter: the poem depicts the period of peace after the cataclysmic war.

At many points the *Odyssey* critically interrogates its epic pre-decessor.[3] Perhaps the most striking instance occurs when the shade of Achilles, speaking to Odysseus in the underworld, implicitly re-pudiates the choice he perforce made in the *Iliad* of a short and glori-ous life over a long and obscure one:[4]

> O shining Odysseus, never try to console me for dying.
> I would rather follow the plow as thrall to another
> man, one with no land allotted him and not much to live on,
> than be a king over all the perished dead.
>
> [11.488–91][5]

Odysseus is alive; Achilles is not. The *Odyssey* reverses Achilles' crit-icism of Odysseus in the *Iliad* for saying one thing while meaning another (9.312–13)—a characteristic of Odysseus which the *Odyssey* celebrates—by having the Iliadic hero concede Odysseus' superiority.

[3]I am assuming separate authorship for the poems. M. I. Finley states that the *Odyssey* came a generation or two after the *Iliad*. *The World of Odysseus* (1954; rev. ed. New York: Viking, 1978), pp. 15,31. Denys Page, in *The Homeric Odyssey* (Oxford: Oxford Univ. Press, 1955), p. 149, notes the difference in vocabulary between the two poems and concludes: "Not only the extent but also the nature of the differences indicates that these two vocabularies could not have existed in the mind of a single poet. . . . there is no possibility that so great a change might have occurred within the lifetime of one man." He thinks, however, that since the *Odyssey* never repeats or refers to any incident related in the *Iliad,* the poet of the *Odyssey* did not know the *Iliad* (pp. 157–58). But see James Redfield, "The Making of the *Odyssey,*" in *Parnassus Revisited,* ed. Anthony C. Yu (Chicago: American Library Association, 1973), p. 145: "The poet of the *Odyssey* was self-consciously an epigonid; he thought of the *Iliad* much as we do, as The Poem." Gregory Nagy and Pietro Pucci hold that the two texts developed simultaneously, each aware of the other. See Nagy, *The Best of the Achaeans: Concepts of the Hero in Archaic Greek Poetry* (Baltimore: Johns Hopkins Univ. Press, 1979), p. 41, and his rejoinder to Page, pp. 20–21; and Pucci, p. 18. See also Seth L. Schein's exposition of arguments for both single and separate authorship in *The Mortal Hero: An Introduction to Homer's Iliad* (Berkeley: Univ. of California Press, 1984), pp. 37–38. Schein himself assumes that the poems are complementary works of one poet.

[4]See Nagy, pp. 42–58, for a discussion of the competition between Achilles and Odysseus—alluded to in one of Demodocus' lays—for the title *aristoi Akhaion* (best of the Achaeans). The two qualities at stake are Achilles' *bie* (might) and Odysseus' *metis* (strategem). See also W. B. Stanford's commentary on 8.76ff., in his edition, *The Odyssey of Homer,* 2 vols. (1947–48; sec. ed. London: Macmillan, 1958–59), 1:333.

[5]All quotations are from the translation of Richmond Lattimore, *The Odyssey of Homer* (New York: Harper and Row, 1965). Line numbers are Lattimore's, which follow closely those in the original Greek. In my text I have used Latinized spellings of proper names.

The *Odyssey* thus explicitly criticizes the heroic code by asserting that a long life need not be an obscure one and that its hero can gain *kleos* *and* a return home. The poet of the *Odyssey* identifies the heroic code with the Iliadic hero Achilles, as he does here, and the *Iliad* itself with its heroine Helen, as we shall see, mythologizing (and mystifying) them in order to mark his difference from his predecessor.

Yet the *Odyssey* also acknowledges that having survived the Trojan war, Odysseus is older and no longer commands his former strength. At the court of the Phaeacians, Odysseus admits to a youthful challenger:

> I am not such a new hand
> at games as you say, but always, as I think, I have been
> among the best when I still had trust in youth and hand's strength.
>
> [8.179–81]

Here the two temporal concerns of the poem come together: the passage of historical time, from the Trojan war to its aftermath, and of human time, from youth to maturity. If the *Iliad* dramatized the death of youthful warriors on the Trojan battlefield, the *Odyssey* concerns itself with an older hero's reunion with the family he left behind twenty years before.

The *Odyssey*'s affirmation of continuity, as embodied in its hero's family, explains the new prominence of female characters and domestic concerns, which prompted Samuel Butler to posit a female author for the poem.[6] Even if we reject this idea as fanciful, the contrast between the two poems is striking. Unlike in the *Iliad,* where Hector was compelled to leave behind Andromache in order to defend his city, the *Odyssey,* as the poem of *nostos,* of homecoming, conceives as the hero's goal his wife, Penelope. Accordingly, many of Odysseus' temptations along the way are female: Circe, Calypso, the Sirens, and Nausicaa.[7] It is Penelope who sets the standard by which these female

---

[6]Samuel Butler, *The Authoress of the Odyssey* (1897; 2d ed. 1922; rpt. Chicago: Univ. of Chicago Press, 1967). Robert Graves's novel *Homer's Daughter* (Garden City, New York: Doubleday, 1955), is narrated in the voice of Nausicaa: "The *Iliad,* which I admire, is devised by a man for men; this epic, *The Odyssey,* will be devised by a woman for women" (p. 278).

[7]See Charles H. Taylor, Jr., "Obstacles to Odysseus' Return," *Yale Review,* 50 (1961), rpt. in *Essays on the Odyssey: Selected Modern Criticism,* ed. Charles H. Taylor, Jr. (Bloomington: Indiana Univ. Press, 1963), p. 98: "Odysseus' quest for identity is in fact profoundly involved with the feminine. In seeking the wholeness of his being, he passes through intimate experience with various embodiments of archetypal woman, each reflecting some aspect of what he as masculine hero lacks." W. B. Stanford,

figures must inevitably be judged. Just as the poet defines Odysseus
by juxtaposing him to the warriors of the *Iliad,* such as Achilles and
Agamemnon, so he sets his own heroine Penelope against Helen, the
heroine of the earlier epic. Athena implicitly contrasts the significance
of the two women for Odysseus when she exhorts him to take heart
in his battle against the suitors.

> No longer, Odysseus, are the strength and valor still steady
> within you, as when, for the sake of white-armed, illustrious
> Helen, you fought nine years with the Trojans, ever relentless;
> and many men you killed there in the dreaded encounter,
> and by your counsel the wide-wayed city of Priam was taken.
> How is it now, when you have come back to your own possessions
> and house, you complain, instead of standing up to the suitors?
>
> [22.226–32]

Odysseus fights the suitors to win back his property and to reestablish order in his hall. It is noteworthy that Athena does not
explicitly refer to Penelope, for she is understood to be part of his
"possessions and house." We shall see, however, that Penelope does
not act as though she were mere property: she will not welcome her
husband back simply because he has slain the suitors. Although
Helen, "white-armed and illustrious," may have been a prize to be
fought over (Pietro Pucci points out that this epithet is Iliadic and thus
associates Helen with the *Iliad*), Penelope avoids Helen's example and
forges a complex identity of her own.[8] Yet the presence of Helen, the
heroine of the anterior epic, nevertheless haunts the *Odyssey* and provides a standard for both the new epic poet and his heroine.

Helen's *Pharmakon*

Helen appears along with her husband, Menelaus, in Book 4 and
again in Book 15 at the endpoint of Telemachus' miniature odyssey,
the *Telemachia.* The poet gives this episode in Sparta structural prominence, for the two parts in which it is told flank Odysseus' wander-

---

The Ulysses Theme: A Study in the Adaptability of a Traditional Hero (Oxford: Basil
Blackwell, 1954), p. 65, notes the "closer temperamental affinity between Odysseus
and women of the Heroic Age than between him and the more conventional warrior-
heroes who felt uneasy and distrustful in his company."

[8]Pucci, p. 35n.

ings: in Book 5 Odysseus, stranded on Calypso's isle, enters the poem, and in Book 14 he finally returns to Ithaca. Moreover, within Book 4 the poet abruptly leaves Sparta to return to Ithaca, thus juxtaposing Helen and Penelope, since Penelope would not otherwise reappear until Book 17. Butler has even suggested that the purpose of the *Telemachia* is to bring Helen into the poem.[9] According to Athena, however, the purpose of the journey is to allow Telemachus to gather news of his long absent father through his comrades from the Trojan expedition (1.280–86) and, at the same time, to gain *kleos,* fame and renown, in his own right (3.77–78; 13.421–24). Like Athena, who in the guise of Mentes and Mentor served as a surrogate father for Telemachus in Ithaca, Nestor and Menelaus act as paternal figures for Telemachus by recounting to the son his father's *kleos* and by recognizing him as Odysseus' son in his likeness to his father.

Perhaps equally important, Telemachus learns the essential features of Odysseus' adventures after leaving Troy through Menelaus' tale of his journey to Egypt before reaching Sparta. Just as Agamemnon's ignominious slaughter at the hands of Aegisthus is constantly alluded to as the antitype of Odysseus' successful homecoming and victorious battle with Penelope's suitors, so Menelaus' journey to Egypt and homecoming to Sparta function as analogues to Odysseus' more extended wandering and eventual return to Ithaca. Significantly, Odysseus, in his lying tales to Eumaeus and others in Ithaca, will speak of journeying to Egypt, as Menelaus had actually done. Beyond this, the parallels between the experiences of the two men are detailed and striking: Eidothea advises Menelaus on how to obtain prophecy from her father, Proteus, just as the Phaeacian princess Nausicaa will instruct Odysseus on how to win favor with her parents, Alcinous and Arete, and just as Circe, Calypso, and Ino will give crucial information to Odysseus at various points in his journey. Further, Menelaus' disguise under a sealskin in order to trick Proteus parallels Odysseus' similar ruse of hiding under Polyphemus' sheep to elude the blinded Cyclops. Both men receive prophecies and warnings concerning their homecoming—Menelaus from Proteus and Odysseus from Teiresias.

---

[9]Butler, p. 141. Howard W. Clarke, *The Art of the Odyssey* (Englewood Cliffs, N.J.: Prentice-Hall, 1967), p. 34, sees the function of the *Telemachia* as the introduction of Telemachus to the heroic life, "to commune with its leaders, and to be confirmed in its values" in order to become a fit successor to his father. But see also the recent discussion by Sheila Murnaghan, *Disguise and Recognition in the Odyssey* (Princeton: Princeton Univ. Press, 1987), pp. 158–66, who argues that the *Telemachia* works at cross purposes with the larger poem that contains it; for in preparing Telemachus to take his father's place, it assumes that Odysseus will not return.

Proteus, immediately after describing Odysseus' sojourn in Ogygia as Calypso's prisoner, prophesies semidivine Helen's gift to Menelaus of immortal life in Elysium; he implicitly associates Odysseus' with Menelaus' future by portraying Elysium in ways that anticipate the features of Calypso's isle.[10] Finally, the figure of shape-shifting Proteus, whose essential identity under many guises Menelaus uncovers through persistence, becomes an emblem for both *polytropos* Odysseus, the man of many turnings, and for the various sufferings inflicted upon him by Poseidon before he is allowed to reach home.[11]

If Menelaus' journey to Egypt parallels Odysseus' wanderings, then Menelaus' life at Sparta with Helen might also be compared to Odysseus' sojourn with Calypso in Ogygia and to his eventual reunion with Penelope in Ithaca. Just as the divine nymph Calypso promises immortality to Odysseus, so Helen will grant Menelaus that privilege: Proteus tells Menelaus, "This, because Helen is yours and you are son-in-law therefore / to Zeus" (4.569–70). In Book 5, however, Odysseus forgoes the opportunity to live forever with the immortal nymph, choosing instead to return to his mortal wife, Penelope:

> Goddess and queen, do not be angry with me. I myself know
> that all you say is true and that circumspect Penelope
> can never match the impression you make for beauty and stature.
> She is mortal after all, and you are immortal and ageless.
> But even so, what I want and all my days I pine for
> is to go back to my house and see my day of homecoming.
> And if some god batters me far out on the wine-blue water,
> I will endure it, keeping a stubborn spirit inside me,
> for already I have suffered much and done much hard work
> on the waves and in the fighting. So let this adventure follow.
>
> [5.215–24]

[10]See William S. Anderson, "Calypso and Elysium," *CJ*, 54 (1958), rpt. in Taylor, *Essays on the Odyssey*, pp. 73–86, for a discussion of "the structural and semantic relation between Ogygia and Elysium." On the *Odyssey*'s diction that links Calypso and the Iliadic Helen, see Pucci, pp. 35–36.

[11]A. Bartlett Giamatti, "Proteus Unbound: Some Versions of the Sea God in the Renaissance," in *Exile and Change in Renaissance Literature* (New Haven: Yale Univ. Press, 1984), p. 115, cites a passage from Sir Thomas Elyot's *Bibliotheca Eliotae* (1559): "Proteus . . . whom Homere nameth to be the herde man of the fisshes called Phocae, and also a prophete, notwithstandyinge he would not geue aunswere but beyng costrained by *Ulisses*. . . . He also tourned himselfe into sundrie figures. Sometime like a bull, an other time like a terrible serpente. . . . Of him came the proverbe, PROTEO MUTABILIOR, more changeable than Proteus, applied to him that in his acts or words is unstable." This latter-day substitution of Ulysses for Menelaus significantly makes explicit the implicit association between Odysseus and Proteus in the *Odyssey*.

Odysseus' decision entails his reentry into the world of temporality with its attendant hardships, for as Proteus tells Menelaus, immortal existence is a dream of ease.[12] The poet exemplifies with pathos the gulf between immortal and mortal in Calypso and Odysseus' final meal together: Calypso serves him food for mortals while her hand-maidens set before her nectar and ambrosia (5.194–99). In the *Iliad,* Achilles and the other warriors perceived their eventual deaths as the tragic corollary of the heroic code, but the *Odyssey* celebrates mortality in Odysseus' departure from Ogygia to Ithaca and in the conti-nuity promised through the succession from fathers to sons—from Laertes to Odysseus to Telemachus. In this poem, even the immortals seem envious of mortal existence, for both Calypso and Circe seek to detain Odysseus, and Calypso complains to Hermes that the gods are jealous when goddesses take mortal men for husbands (5.118–20). Odysseus' preference for mortality, together with the poet's por-trayal of Menelaus' melancholy life with Helen, qualify the attractive-ness of Menelaus' promised immortality; the eternal continuation of his present existence would be less than unequivocally blissful.

Upon Telemachus' arrival at Sparta, the poet already introduces a note of melancholy to the apparently festive activities of the double wedding of Menelaus' daughter and son.[13] The gods have sanctioned the marriage of Hermione, Helen and Menelaus' daughter, to Neop-tolemus, Achilles' son—an alliance that fulfills the affinity between Helen and Achilles in the *Iliad.* Yet the poet adds that Megapenthes was born to Menelaus by a slave woman, for "the gods gave no more children to Helen / once she had borne her first and only child" (4.12–13). We are told that Laertes refrained from sleeping with his slave Eurycleia out of respect for his wife (1.430–33); Menelaus' relation-ship with the mother of Megapenthes (whose name means "great sorrow") points to the disruption of conjugal ties brought about by Helen's elopement with Paris.

This note of melancholy is confirmed when Menelaus intimates that all the splendor of his palace—which Telemachus marvels at and praises by likening it to Zeus' hall in Olympus—cannot assuage his painful memories of the past: the deaths of his comrades at Troy, the murder of his brother Agamemenon, and the absence of his friend

---

[12]Norman Austin, *Archery at the Dark of the Moon: Poetic Problems in Homer's Odyssey* (Berkeley: Univ. of California Press, 1975), p. 87, also sees the poem's central concern to be temporality, but in the sense of *hora,* "season," "timing."

[13]Clarke, p. 36, however, considers Sparta to be marked by "prosperity, security, and family intimacy"; the union of the family here contrasts with its disruption in Ithaca.

Odysseus. But the most painful memory of all must be of Helen's elopement, the cause of all his other losses. To this, he refers only obliquely:

> You will have heard all this from your fathers, whoever your fathers
> are, for I have suffered much, and destroyed a household
> that was very strongly settled and held many goods within it.
>
> [4.94–96]

Although Menelaus does not explicitly refer to Helen as the cause of his anguish and desolation, only two lines earlier he had referred to Agamemnon's tragedy brought about through "his cursed wife's treachery," a periphrasis that could apply as well to Clytemnestra's sister, Helen. Here Menelaus suggests that the most important event of his life was his betrayal by Helen; his identity is solely that of a betrayed husband. Despite the Achaean victory and Helen's return, despite the riches gained in his seven years of wandering before returning to Sparta, Menelaus cannot be content, since he is unable to refrain from looking backward to the traumatic disruption of his domestic peace and to the war that came in its wake. Incapable of living in the present or looking forward to the future, Menelaus instead derives a certain pleasure in mourning and dwelling on the past: "Still and again lamenting all these men and sorrowing / many a time when I am sitting here in our palace / I will indulge my heart in sorrow" (4.100–102).

At this point, after the poet has set an atmosphere of uneasy peace, Helen enters to greet Telemachus, who has not yet revealed his identity. In the *Iliad,* she was always linked to Aphrodite and portrayed in intimate, if somewhat ambivalent, association with the goddess of love; here she is compared instead to Artemis, the goddess of chastity: "Helen came out of her fragrant high-roofed bedchamber, / looking like Artemis of the golden distaff" (4.121–22). This shift in association from Aphrodite to Artemis seems to signal Helen's transformation from a woman of passion to a chaste wife. Whereas in the *Iliad* she wove the story of the Trojan war, here she appears with her spinning. Helen does not engage in ordinary spinning, however, but with "a golden distaff and a basket, silver, / . . . and the edges were done in gold" (4.131–32). In Book 15 she gives a robe she has woven to Telemachus for his future wife, to be guarded by Penelope until his wedding. Through this gift, a link is established between Helen and Penelope, who replaces the Iliadic Helen as the most prominent weaver in the poem.

Immediately upon her entrance, Helen recognizes Telemachus as Odysseus' son with her uncanny intuitive powers. She does not hesitate to make known her superior insight:

> Shall I be wrong, or am I speaking the truth? My heart tells me
> to speak, for I think I never saw such a likeness, neither
> in man nor woman, and wonder takes me as I look on him,
> as this man has a likeness to the son of great-hearted Odysseus,
> Telemachos, who was left behind in his house, a young child
> by that man when, for the sake of shameless me, the Achaians
> went beneath Troy, their hearts intent upon reckless warfare.
>
> [4.140–46]

Menelaus had already recognized Telemachus when the boy wept upon hearing his father mentioned, but he had hesitated to identify him. Helen reveals an intuitive ability, superior to her husband's, to read outward signs. In Book 15 this superiority is again dramatized when she immediately and accurately reads the omen of the eagle preying on a goose as a forecast of Odysseus' homecoming; Menelaus again hesitates to speak. Her gift of recognition links her to Arete, Circe, and Calypso, but also to Argos the dog, the only member of Odysseus' household who immediately recognizes his master, disguised as a beggar. In fact, the word translated as "shameless," *kynopidos*—an epithet that Redfield notes is used for adulterous women[14]—literally means "dog-faced" and perhaps associates Helen of Argos with Argos the dog. In her impetuosity, she is also like Penelope's suitors, Odysseus' crew, Agamemnon, and Aegisthus. Penelope's suitors were foolishly audacious in their ravaging of their lord's hall in his absence, without paying heed to the consequences of their actions; as was Odysseus' crew in opening the windbags of Aeolus in search of hidden treasure and eating the kine of Helios; so too was Agamemnon in his over-hasty and unvigilant homecoming; so was Aegisthus in acting against Hermes' warning. Heeding Teiresias' counsel to act with restraint, Odysseus forestalls disaster by his cautious homecoming. Penelope will decline to recognize her husband until she has him undergo the test of the olive bed to reestablish his identity as her husband. Thus Helen is endowed with an uncanny sixth sense; yet she lacks restraint and regard for consequences—the very qualities that led her to the fateful elopement with Paris, of which she speaks with regret in this very passage.

[14]James Redfield, *Nature and Culture in the Iliad: The Tragedy of Hector* (Chicago: Univ. of Chicago Press, 1975), p. 195.

Helen yet again displays her disquieting abilities when she drops the *pharmakon* Nepenthe in the wine, as Menelaus and Telemachus, remembering the past, weep together:

> Now Helen, who was descended of Zeus, thought of the next thing.
> Into the wine of which they were drinking she cast a medicine
> of heartsease, free of gall, to make one forget all sorrows,
> and whoever had drunk it down once it had been mixed in the wine
>   bowl,
> for the day that he drank it would have no tear roll down his face,
> not if his mother died and his father died, not if men
> murdered a brother or a beloved son in his presence
> with the bronze, and he with his own eyes saw it. Such were
> the subtle medicines Zeus' daughter had in her possessions,
> good things, and given to her by the wife of Thon, Polydamna
> of Egypt, where the fertile earth produces the greatest number
> of medicines, many good in mixture, many malignant.
>
> [4.219–30]

Helen's *pharmakon* brings forgetfulness and eases the pain of memory. In light of Menelaus' perpetual melancholy, she must have had to administer many a dose of this drug to her husband in order to efface his nightmarish memories of her infidelity and the ensuing war. Like the other Egyptian medicines of Polydamna, Helen's *pharmakon* is both "good and malignant":[15] salutary, in that it ensures rest from constant awareness, just as the sleep Athena repeatedly brings to Penelope eases her longing for absent Odysseus; baneful, in that it dulls consciousness—even of the loss of parents or the butchery of one's brother or child before one's very eyes. In a similar moment, Circe turns Odysseus' men into swine with her magic wand, replacing the memory of home and the desire to return with bestial oblivion. This subhuman lack of consciousness has attractions; the men

[15]Ann L. T. Bergren, "Helen's 'Good Drug': *Odyssey* IV 1–305," in *Contemporary Literary Hermeneutics and the Interpretation of Classical Texts,* ed. S. Kresic (Ottawa: Ottawa Univ. Press, 1981), pp. 201–14, places the good and bad drugs within the context of polarities that mark the world of Sparta. She argues that Helen's "good" drug is analogous to the poetry of *kleos* in that it acts as an antidote to "grief" and a "forgetfulness of cares" (p. 207). By the end of the storytelling, however, "the good drug of Helen's speech has become the 'good-wretched drug' of its non-identical twin" (p. 211). My reading differs from Bergren's in that I see the drug as already problematic from the very beginning. For I take the erasure of memory, painful though the memory may be, to be the fundamentally dangerous temptation in the *Odyssey*. And *kleos* can and does bring pain, as made evident in Penelope's request to Phemios to desist from singing the homecoming of the Achaians and Odysseus' tears upon hearing Demodocus' lays.

weep when transformed back into their human forms, and Circe pities them. The *pharmakon,* in its ability to obliterate time, moreover, carries associations with Elysium and Calypso's isle, both of which offer immortality. It is therefore appropriate that the drug effects forgetfulness of one's kin, for human time is unfolded in the succession of generations. Just as Helen in the *Iliad* mediated between various opposing realms—Troy and Greece, the world of masculine combat and feminine domesticity—so here in the *Odyssey,* as the daughter of Zeus, she mediates between the human and the divine. Yet just as the *pharmakon* even in its doubleness is more baneful than salutary, Helen's supernatural abilities and Menelaus' promised immortality as her husband place her beyond the realm of the human.

Helen's doubleness—"good and malignant" as her *pharmakon* was said to be—is again played out in the two stories, told by herself and Menelaus, which ostensibly inform Telemachus about his father's exploits at Troy but which in fact inform us about Helen. Through these stories, the poet revises the portrait of the Iliadic Helen in order to blame and hence to scapegoat her as the evil wife. To that end, he represents Helen in Troy as sinister, destructive, and culpable and robs Helen in Sparta of any power to act with consequence, thereby relegating her to the margins of his narrative. The poet associates Helen with the *Iliad* through these Iliadic stories told by and about her; by representing Helen as at once evil and inconsequential, he thereby subverts the authority of the *Iliad.*

Helen begins her story by echoing Achilles' speech to Priam in *Iliad* 24 on the two urns of good and evil gifts:

> Son of Atreus, dear to Zeus, Menelaos: and you who
> are here, children of noble fathers; yet divine Zeus sometimes
> gives out good, or sometimes evil; he can do anything.
> Sit here now in the palace and take your dinner and listen
> to me and be entertained.
>
> [4.235–39]

Although Helen in the *Iliad,* like Achilles, voiced a hard-won understanding of the divisions of experience, here the statement of that same awareness sounds platitudinous. This is especially so since her preamble accurately characterizes the two stories about to be told; it is Helen who brings both good and bad luck—but mostly bad luck.[16]

---

[16]Linda Lee Clader, *Helen: The Evolution from Divine to Heroic in Greek Epic Tradition* (Leiden: Brill, 1976), p. 35, suggests that Homer may be using materials from two different traditions on Helen; in one she is loyal to the Greeks, in the other to the

Thus the poet diverges from the Iliadic poet who declined from scapegoating Helen and reinscribes the scapegoating of Helen by the Iliadic warriors. Just as the import of the two stories proves to be double, so her storytelling, which serves to cheer the time as the *pharmakon* did, is also double-edged. In her narrative powers, Helen approximates the role of the poet as she did in the *Iliad,* where she wove the story of the Trojan war; but here, while ostensibly telling Telemachus about his father's exploits, in effect she relates a story that she intends to be self-congratulatory.

Helen tells of how she recognized Odysseus during his clandestine mission to Troy despite his disguise as a beggar (a disguise that he will reassume upon his arrival on Ithaca), just as she intuited Telemachus' identity on sight. On the former occasion, however, she refrained from identifying and hence betraying Odysseus to the Trojans. She insists upon her loyalty to the Greeks by describing her joy when Odysseus slaughtered the Trojans during the mission:[17]

> The rest of the Trojan women cried out shrill, but my heart
> was happy, my heart had changed by now and was for going back
> home again, and I grieved for the madness that Aphrodite
> bestowed when she led me there away from my own dear country,
> forsaking my own daughter, my bedchamber, and my husband,
> a man who lacked no endowment either of brains or beauty.
>
> [4.259–64]

Helen is Greek, but as Paris' wife she has allegiances to Troy, for in the *Iliad* she was treated with kindness by Priam and Hector, and she acted as Hector's kin in singing the final lament at his funeral. Her loyalty to the Greeks, therefore, entails a problematic betrayal of the Trojans: her rejoicing over the deaths of Trojan warriors in the midst of bewildered and grieving Trojan women casts a sinister light on her loyalty, the very quality that she intends to illustrate by her story. Finally, Helen echoes her former self in the *Iliad* by blaming *ate* for her elopement with Paris and by voicing the longing she felt for what

---

Trojans. She states that though Homer tells the two versions without comment, he places the disloyal Helen in the second, stronger narrative position.

[17]Bergren, pp. 208–9, notes that "Helen's recollection is oddly elliptical" and asks many provocative questions of her story: "What was Helen doing bathing a naked beggar? . . . what in Helen's story would be *lugros* without the "good drug" and for whom? . . . Would Helen's intimacy with Odysseus be painful to Menelaus? And if so, why does she include it? Is she trying . . . to seduce her young guest with glimpses of a sexual scene with his father?"

she left behind. But like her other lines from the *Iliad*—the reference to herself as "dog-faced" (*kynopidos*) and the sententia about good and bad luck—this speech does not carry the deeply felt force it did in the anterior poem.[18] Through creative repetition of the *Iliad*, the *Odyssey* parodies the Iliadic Helen. Her praise of Menelaus as "a man who lacked no endowment in either brains or beauty" seems ironic in light of her past preference for Paris over him and her present insistence on asserting her superiority over him at every opportunity. In fact, though she has returned to Sparta, she lives exiled from her more compelling past at Troy and in the *Iliad*.

At this point, Menelaus tells his side of the story. Although he does not explicitly contradict her, starting his narrative with "Yes, my wife, all this that you said is fair and orderly" (4.266), the import of his tale is clear. While walking by the Wooden Horse with Deiphobus, her husband after Paris' death, Helen imitated the voices of the wives of the Greeks hidden within and almost caused them to betray themselves. Odysseus, typically intrepid, restrained them from crying out. This story shows Helen in her full "malignant" colors: her infidelity to Menelaus is exacerbated by her marriage to Paris' brother after his death, and her sinister prank demonstrates her almost supernatural ability to enchant and beguile—as her *pharmakon* allows her to do. Her allure, coupled with her impersonation of the warriors' wives, links her to Calypso and Circe, who through similar means attempt to divert Odysseus from his true wife. Since Helen is in fact Menelaus' true wife, his inability to be reunited with her here is a measure of the violation of conjugal ties she has brought about. By foiling Helen's trick, Odysseus proleptically evinces his ability to resist the temptation of the other false wives, such as Calypso and Circe, whom he will encounter on his wanderings after leaving Troy. Helen's seduction, moreover, parallels that of the Sirens; for just as Helen's evocation of the memory of their wives tempts the warriors to abandon their military plan, so the Sirens' singing of Odysseus' past deeds at Troy invites him to forgo his journey home.[19] By this association to the Sirens, and to Calypso and Circe who sing as they

---

[18]Clader, p. 17, points out that Helen characterizes herself as "bitch" (*kynopidos*) four times in Homer, always in contexts where she refers to the shame of having brought about the war.

[19]Pietro Pucci, "The Song of the Sirens," *Arethusa*, 12 (1979), 121–32, notes the Sirens' exclusively Iliadic diction which "invite[s] [Odysseus] to change poet and poem, and to return to be the character in the *Iliad*" (p. 125). He also discusses the connection between the Sirens and the Iliadic Muses (p. 126). In his more recent discussion in *Odysseus Polutropos*, Pucci argues that the *Odyssey* displaces and replaces

weave, Helen is again cast in the role of a poet, for all these women tempt Odysseus to turn aside from the mindfulness of the present to seek oblivion in the past or in timeless immortality.

Thus Helen's various activities—her use of the *pharmakon*, her storytelling, and her temptation of the Greeks—associate her with poetry. In the *Iliad*, Helen was also portrayed as a poet figure, in her weaving of the story of the Trojan war that paralleled the activity of the narrating poet and in her awareness that she and Paris would gain immortality in future songs in return for the woes they suffered in life. But the poet of the *Odyssey* is more ambivalent about poetry, as he is about immortality, than is the poet of the *Iliad;* this ambivalence finds expression in his representation of Helen.

The *Odyssey's* ambivalence toward poetry paradoxically arises from its very centrality in the epic. Early in the poem, Penelope asks Phemios to choose a song other than one about the Achaians' bitter homecoming from Troy, which painfully reminds her of her absent husband. Telemachus' exoneration of Phemios ("It is not the singers / who are to blame, it must be Zeus is to blame" [1.347–48]) and his recommendation of aesthetic distance ("So let your heart and let your spirit be hardened to listen" [1.353]) offer an alternative "literary theory" of both the production and reception of song. Telemachus asserts the authority of his theory, rebuking his mother for involving herself with *mythos:*

> Go therefore back in the house, and take up your own work,
> the loom and the distaff, and see to it that your handmaidens
> ply their work also; but the men must see to discussion,
> all men, but I most of all. For mine is the power in this household.
>
> [1.356–59]

These lines, which echo Hector's speech to Andromache in the *Iliad,* underscore the *Odyssey's* divergence from its predecessor in conceiving poetry, not war, as the privileged activity that Telemachus wants to claim as his male prerogative. In the *Iliad,* the only explicit portrayal of poetic activity occurred when Achilles sang *klea andron* to a lyre while withdrawn from battle; in the anterior poem, poetry marked the reflective moments away from the heat of military action, where glory, later to be celebrated by poetry, was gained. The *Odys-*

---

the Sirens' sublime song by incorporating in its own song the Sirens' unsung poem (pp. 209–13).

sey, however, not only accords prominence to professional bards—
Phemios in Ithaca and Demodocus in Phaeacia—it associates, indeed
almost equates, poetry with heroism.

The most explicit instance of this convergence of poetry and heroic
activity occurs when the poet compares Odysseus, as he strings the
bow before the battle with the suitors, to a bard:

> but now resourceful Odysseus,
> once he had taken up the great bow and looked it all over,
> as when a man, who well understands the lyre and singing,
> easily, holding it on either side, pulls the strongly twisted
> cord of sheep's gut, so as to slip it over a new peg,
> so, without any strain, Odysseus strung the great bow.
> Then plucking it in his right hand he tested the bowstring,
> and it gave him back an excellent sound like the voice of a swallow.
>
> [21.404–11]

Heroism is here redefined, for in the same way that the bow—in the
Iliad a weapon for cowards such as Paris and Pandarus—becomes a
worthy weapon for Odysseus, so poetic performance—in the earlier
epic a signal of Achilles' removal from the battlefield—is here closely
associated with heroic deeds.[20] *Polymetis* Odysseus earns his epithet
through not only his heroic excellence but also his poetic competence,
as evidenced in the various tales designed to conceal his true identity
in Ithaca.[21] Alcinous praises Odysseus by comparing him to a poet:

> You have
> a grace upon your words, and there is sound sense within them,
> and expertly, as a singer would do, you have told the story
> of the dismal sorrows befallen yourself and all of the Argives.
>
> [11.366–69]

And so Eumaeus:

> But as when a man looks to a singer, who has been given
> from the gods the skill with which he sings for delight of mortals,

---

[20]For a different reading of this passage, see Page, p. 158: "Picture the scorn and
indignation of a poet brought up in the tradition of the *Iliad:* is this fellow so profoundly ignorant as to be unaware that no first-class hero in the *Iliad* ever deigned to
use the bow in warfare?"

[21]For a discussion of the underlying unity of these tales, see Redfield, "The Making
of the *Odyssey*," pp. 148–50.

and they are impassioned and strain to hear it when he sings to them,
so he enchanted me in the halls as he sat beside me.

[17.518–21]

Unlike Achilles, who was unable to balance his words and deeds,
Odysseus is able to harness them to one another; the hero of the later
epic is to be known by his words as well as his deeds, for his words
are, in a very important sense, his deeds.

Although the *Odyssey* heals the split between words and deeds,
words themselves, and hence poetry, can be problematic: Odysseus'
pseudonym, "Nobody," and his lying stories in service of his disguise
are enabling assertions of his power; at the same time, as the phantom
of Penelope's sister says to her in a dream and as Odysseus tells
Agamemnon in the underworld, "It is bad to babble emptily" (4.837
= 11.464). Like Helen herself, then, poetry can be either salutary or
baneful. As the repository of memory and the past, it is salutary,
preserving tradition, and hence identity and morality. Odysseus' *kleos*
is known afar, as Demodocus' two lays about him show. The poet
tells that Agamemnon left a minstrel to be the guardian of Clytemnestra and that she was faithful to her husband until Aegisthus murdered him (3.267–72). The privileged position of minstrels again
emerges when Odysseus spares Phemios and Medon the herald after
the general slaughter of the suitors. But poetry has its baneful aspects,
not only for its listeners who may be seduced or deceived but also for
the poets themselves: both Demodocus and Teiresias won their
powers at the cost of their sight. Demodocus' relationship with the
Muse curiously recalls Menelaus' marriage with Helen:

> the excellent singer
> whom the Muse had loved greatly, and gave him both good and
>   evil.
> She reft him of his eyes, but she gave him the sweet singing
>   art.

[8.62–65]

The Muse brought her bard both good and evil, as Helen, a daughter
of Zeus like the Muse, did to Menelaus.[22] More specifically, the Muse
unmanned her favorite in depriving him of sight, just as Helen emas-

[22]On the ambivalent relationship between the poet and his proper god, in particular
Apollo, see Nagy, pp. 301–8.

culated her husband by her past elopement and by her present assertion of superiority over him, and just as Calypso and Circe sought to
detain Odysseus in their power.

Thus, in her various associations with poetry and in her duplicity,
Helen becomes the emblem for poetry's doubleness, "good and malignant," and represents the poet's ambivalence toward the power of
poetic inspiration and its effect on its listeners: like poetry, Helen is
both beautiful and dangerous.[23] For the poet of the *Odyssey*, then,
Helen plays the role of the *pharmakos*—a magician and poisoner—
which Jacques Derrida compares to a scapegoat:

> The *evil* and the *outside*, the expulsion of the evil, its exclusion out of
> the body (and out) of the city—these are the two major senses of the
> character and the ritual. . . . The origin of difference and division, the
> *pharmakos* represents evil both introjected and projected. Beneficial in-
> sofar as he cures—and for that, venerated and cared for—harmful inso-
> far as he incarnates the powers of evil—and for that, feared and treated
> with caution.[24]

Whereas the poet of the *Iliad* portrayed Helen as a character endowed
with subjectivity, at the same time showing how she was reduced to
an emblem for the doubleness of the heroic code and scapegoated by
the men around her, in the *Odyssey* she is conceived of as an emblem
for the doubleness of poetry and a scapegoat by the poet himself.
Through this shift in the representation of Helen, then, we discern a
shift in the values of the two epics. In the earlier poem, Helen, like
Achilles and the poet, possessed an imaginative power that encom-
passed various divisions, but in the later poem, her doubleness verges
on duplicity. By loading on Helen the doubleness of the *Iliad* and of
poetry itself, the poet clears a space for his own poem and his heroine.
The poet transfers the subjectivity of Helen in the *Iliad* to her cousin,
Penelope, and sets his heroine against Helen, whom he reduces to a
static emblem with antithetical meanings, relegated to inconsequen-
tiality in the epic's subplot. The *Iliad* was Helen's poem; the *Odyssey*
is Penelope's.

[23]Nagy suggests another aspect of poetry that makes it double: the poet in praising
man, raises him to the level of a demigod; in blaming man he lowers him to the level
of a beast (pp. 222ff.) The two stories about Helen enact this split between praise and
blame; she is, moreover, at once the daughter of Zeus and "dog-faced."
[24]Jacques Derrida, "Plato's Pharmacy," in *Dissemination*, trans. Barbara Johnson
(Chicago: Univ. of Chicago Press, 1981), pp. 130,133.

Penelope's Choice and the Poetics of the *Odyssey*

Penelope in the *Odyssey* is more complex than the traditional image of a housewife, "bloodless, tearful, incompetent, occupied in endless complainings and everlasting needlework."[25] Like Helen before her marriage to Menelaus, Penelope is beset by numerous suitors in her husband's absence. But unlike Helen, who succumbed to Paris during her husband's much shorter absence, Penelope succeeds in fending off her suitors. The shade of Agamemnon compares Penelope to Helen's sister, Clytemnestra, on this very point of marital fidelity:

> O fortunate son of Laertes, Odysseus of many devices,
> surely you won yourself a wife endowed with great virtue.
> How good was proved the heart that is in blameless Penelope,
> Ikarios' daughter, and how well she remembered Odysseus,
> her wedded husband. Thereby the fame of her virtue shall never
> die away, but the immortals will make for the people
> of earth a thing of grace in the song for prudent Penelope.
> Not so did the daughter of Tyndareos fashion her evil
> deeds, when she killed her wedded lord, and a song of loathing
> will be hers among men, to make evil the reputation
> of womankind, even for one whose acts are virtuous.
>
> [24.192–202]

Agamemnon here accurately predicts how Penelope and Clytemnestra will become subjects of the poetry of praise and of blame. Thus Clytemnestra, like her sister Helen, is also cast in the role of the scapegoat so that Penelope's loyalty to Odysseus can be affirmed. But as Clytemnestra is not as "evil" in the *Odyssey* as later accounts will claim she was, Penelope herself intimates upon her long-delayed recognition of Odysseus that she is not very different from Helen:

> For always the spirit deep in my very heart was fearful
> that some one of mortal men would come my way and deceive me
> with words. For there are many who scheme for wicked advantage.
> For neither would the daughter born to Zeus, Helen of Argos,
> have lain in love with an outlander from another country,
> if she had known that the warlike sons of the Achaians would bring
>   her
> home again to the beloved land of her fathers.

[25]J. W. Mackail, "Penelope in the *Odyssey*," *Classical Studies* (London: John Murray, 1925), p. 55.

It was a god who stirred her to do the shameful thing she
did, and never before had she had in her heart this terrible
wildness, out of which came suffering to us also.

[23.215–24][26]

Penelope justifies her caution, her delay in recognizing Odysseus, by
citing Helen's example: Helen was taken in by deceptive words, as
Penelope might have been. By comparing herself to Helen without
blaming Helen's infidelity or boasting of her own virtuous behavior,
Penelope's speech unmasks the poem's earlier scapegoating of Helen.
Penelope implies that Helen's fate could very well have been her own,
if she, like Helen, had succumbed to *ate,* which erases the human
sense of time, the remembrance of past ties, and heed for future
consequences. What sustained Penelope was precisely her vigilant
consciousness of the passage of time, her ability to live out the unbearable present by harnessing to it the memory of the past, and
hope, however tenuous, for the future.

Despite her acute and ever-present awareness of temporality, Penelope's strategy for survival in Odysseus' absence, her delaying tactics
against the suitors, paradoxically has involved a concerted effort to
freeze time. The poet appropriately compares Penelope's tears to a
spring thaw upon her encounter with Odysseus disguised as a beggar:

As she listened her tears ran and her body was melted,
as the snow melts along the high places of the mountains
when the West Wind has piled it there, but the South Wind melts it,
and as it melts the rivers run full flood. It was even
so that her beautiful cheeks were streaming tears, as Penelope
wept for her man, who was sitting there by her side.

[19.204–9]

Determined to resist erosion in her fidelity to the absent Odysseus
and to arrest change in the people and events around her, Penelope
engages in her weaving of Laertes' shroud by day and unraveling it by
night—an apt emblem for her effort to make time stand still. The
shroud itself, intended for the eventual death of Odysseus' father,
represents not only Penelope's loyalty to Odysseus' household but
also her effort to conjoin the past and the future in the service of the
seemingly endless present. But as the suitors' discovery of her ruse

---

[26]See Stanford, 2:401, for a defense of this passage condemned by Aristarchus as an
interpolation.

shows, time cannot be stopped, however strongly Penelope may will it. She must listen with distress to the minstrel sing of the "Homecoming of the Achaeans," although knowing that the return from Troy of Odysseus' comrades has become the stuff of song must bring to her the painful awareness that ten years have passed since the fall of Troy. Telemachus is no longer the infant that Odysseus left behind but a youth who chafes under his mother's authority. His coming of age also serves as a signal for Penelope to cede to him his patrimony by choosing one of the suitors, as Odysseus had decreed. The inexorable passage of time makes Penelope's situation truly desperate, but it brings her long-awaited husband home as well. Therefore, her previous strategy of suspending the passage of time in her husband's absence now requires her to make some effort to reconcile the middle-aged beggar before her eyes with the image in her dream of the young warrior who left for Troy twenty years before (20.88–90).

This necessity for temporal realignment provides a key to Penelope's delayed recognition. Not only must Penelope herself adjust the past to the present but she asks that Odysseus prove himself her husband now as he was then, that he reaffirm his relationship to her after twenty years of separation. The test of the olive bed, a secret sign known only to the two of them, accomplishes just that: Odysseus' description of how he built his bedroom and then his house around the rooted trunk of the olive tree reveals that the steadfastness of their bond—specifically, Penelope's fidelity to her marriage bed— served as the foundation for the survival of Odysseus' household in his absence. Unlike Helen, claimed by Paris and then reclaimed by Menelaus, Penelope successfully defends herself against becoming an object of exchange: she not only foils the suitors' attempt to win her but also insists on her right to accept Odysseus back to their marriage bed.

But the crucial question still remains: When exactly does Penelope recognize Odysseus? Penelope's opaqueness and elusiveness, especially after Odysseus returns to Ithaca, has elicited much critical comment. Denys L. Page, for example, explains the "inconsistencies" in Penelope's behavior as deriving from the poem's conflation of multiple versions of the legend, the earliest of which placed the recognition at the beginning of the couple's encounter rather than at the end.[27] Philip Harsh has contributed to an understanding of the complexity of Penelope's character by suggesting that she recognizes the beggar

[27]Page, pp. 92–98.

as Odysseus in their conversation in Book 19 and that, accordingly, she obliquely asks him about his intentions to slay the suitors on the morrow.[28]

It can be argued, however, that Penelope suspects the identity of the beggar in Book 17, even before she has seen him. In Book 2, Mastor had interpreted the omen of the eagles as signaling Odysseus' immediate return and had referred to his earlier prophecy:

> I said that after much suffering, with all his companions
> lost, in the twentieth year, not recognized by any,
> he would come home.
>
> [2.174–76]

Even if Penelope were not present at the council where the omen was read, she would certainly have known about the prophecy made at the time of Odysseus' departure. It therefore seems reasonable to expect that Penelope would eagerly await her husband's return during the twentieth year, especially after Theoclymenus states with confidence that Odysseus is already in Ithaca (17.152–61).

The heretofore desolate Penelope laughs for the first time when she takes Telemachus' sneeze to be a confirming omen of her wish: "But if Odysseus could come, and return to the land of his fathers, / soon, with his son, he could punish the violence of these people" (17.539–40). Moreover, Penelope's sympathetic interest toward the newly arrived beggar and her repeated expression of eagerness verging on impatience to meet him (17.508–11, 529, 544–50, 576–78) may suggest that she has already intuited the beggar's secret. Might not she be indicating an awareness of his disguise when she promises him new clothes in exchange for his rags (17.549–50)?

---

[28]Philip W. Harsh, "Penelope and Odysseus in *Odyssey* XIX," *AJP*, 71 (1950), 1–21. Stanford, *Ulysses Theme*, p. 253 n.25, states that this interpretation was already known in antiquity (Seneca, *Ep.* 88, 8). See also Robert Fitzgerald's "Postscript" to his translation of the *Odyssey* (New York: Doubleday, 1963), pp. 499–503, where he elaborates Harsh's thesis. Similarly, Anne Amory, in "The Reunion of Odysseus and Penelope," in Taylor, *Essays on the Odyssey*, pp. 100–121, holds that Penelope begins to suspect the truth during her conversation with her husband. She thinks, however, that Penelope "looks at things only intermittently and thinks intuitively rather than rationally. . . . [Her] knowledge is often unconscious" (p. 104). Murnaghan points out that "this view tends to involve . . . the construction of a portrait of Penelope as innately irrational, impulsive and passive, a portrait that is often identified as typically feminine" (p. 138). She holds that Penelope is assigned the role of an outsider to the plot and that "she fosters Odysseus' return without knowing that she is doing it" (p. 118).

Odysseus sends back a message to her to be patient, so that they may speak undisturbed by the suitors (17.564–70). His insistence on the danger posed by the suitors and their need for privacy from them might confirm her intuition that it is indeed Odysseus who counsels caution. More important, though Penelope requires no lesson in patience, by invoking a quality they share Odysseus sends a verbal token of recognition—much like that of the olive bed—which reaffirms their likemindedness (*homophrosyne*). The poet does not give Penelope the epithet "wise" (*periphron*) without reason:[29] upon receiving the beggar's message, she comments on his wisdom, "The stranger's thought is not without good sense (*aphron*)" (17.586).[30] Again, in this invocation of a shared quality, Odysseus' earlier description to Nausicaa of a perfect marriage is confirmed:

> and then may the gods give you everything that your heart longs for;
> may they grant you a husband and a house and sweet agreement
> in all things, for nothing is better than this, more steadfast
> than when two people, a man and his wife, keep a harmonious
> household; a thing that brings much distress to the people who hate
>   them
> and pleasure to their well-wishers, and for them the best reputation.
>
>   [6.180–85]

This likemindedness between husband and wife is dramatized in Book 18, when Penelope displays herself to the suitors in order to obtain gifts. Some critics have found her behavior in this incident mysterious, if not unseemly, especially if she has not yet recognized Odysseus and therefore intends to marry one of the suitors.[31] But Penelope's action does make complete sense if she has guessed the

---

[29]Through a study of name-epithet formulas in the *Odyssey*, Austin argues that "there is more than metrical convenience at work in Homer's selection of formulas. . . . Their selection is governed by various contextual forces" (p. 24).

[30]Owen C. Cramer, in discussing Odysseus' "deliberately incomplete and misleading presentation of himself" in the *Iliad*, notes Antenor's description of Odysseus as appearing to be unknowledgeable, sullen and stupid (*aphron*) before he begins to speak to the assembly in Book 3. He further notes that Odysseus is characteristically *polyphron*. "Speech and Silence in the *Iliad*," *CJ*, 71 (1976), 303. Given the unusual nature of the Iliadic epithet, *aphron*, it is striking that Penelope describes the beggar, who again is giving a "deliberately incomplete and misleading presentation of himself," by its negation: here is another instance of the *Odyssey* alluding to the *Iliad* while subverting its authority.

[31]For example, W. J. Woodhouse, *The Composition of Homer's Odyssey* (Oxford: Oxford Univ. Press, 1930), p. 89, maintains that Penelope's unexplained collapse of resistance against the suitors strains the logic of her character.

identity of the beggar in the previous book. The poet explains that Athena put this strategy in Penelope's head:

> But now the goddess, gray-eyed Athene, put it in the mind
> of the daughter of Ikarios, circumspect Penelope,
> to show herself to the suitors, so that she might all the more
> open their hearts, and so that she might seem all the more precious
> in the eyes of her husband and son even than she had been before
> this.
>
> [18.158–62]

This "divine intervention" is entirely explicable in psychological terms, for Athena's agency on behalf of Odysseus and his family proves consistently to be a metaphor for their mental acumen.[32] In preparation for Odysseus' reclaiming of his hall, "circumspect" (*periphron*) Penelope shrewdly manages to replenish her husband's coffers, depleted by years of conspicuous consumption by the suitors. This time, her ruse proves more successful than that of her weaving Laertes' shroud. Like Odysseus and Telemachus, who brought back gifts from their travels abroad, Penelope shows herself quite capable of contributing her share to Odysseus' property.

Odysseus seems perfectly aware of her intentions, for instead of being offended by what on the surface may appear to be infidelity, he rejoices at his wife's canniness:

> and much-enduring great Odysseus was happy
> because she beguiled gifts out of them, and enchanted their spirits
> with blandishing words, while her own mind had other intentions.
>
> [18.281–83]

In addition to being a strategic move, Penelope's display of her beauty celebrates the homecoming of her husband and son. Her repeated protests that her beauty has faded in her husband's absence (18.180–81, 251–53) underscore the fact that her enjoyment of her own attractiveness signifies her knowledge that Odysseus is present to witness it. For the first time, the justness of the poet's comparison of Penelope to Aphrodite as well as to Artemis (17.36–37), becomes apparent.

In Book 19, the oft-discussed conversation between Penelope and the beggar again turns on the equivalence between husband and wife

[32]Austin, p. 108, suggests that the gods in the *Odyssey* are the "projection outwards of the human community, of the individual characteristics and social intercourse."

and on the couple's secret exchange of further tokens of recognition. Instead of answering the queen's questions about his identity, the beggar begins the conversation by praising her *kleos,* likening it to that of a wise and just king:

> Lady, no mortal man on the endless earth could have cause
> to find fault with you; your fame goes up into the wide heaven,
> as of some king who, as a blameless man and god-fearing,
> and ruling as lord over many powerful people,
> upholds the way of good government, and the black earth yields him
> barley and wheat, his trees are heavy with fruit, his sheepflocks
> continue to bear young, the sea gives him fish, because of
> his good leadership, and his people prosper under him.
>
> [19.107–14]

In effect, Odysseus obliquely pays a compliment to his wife for managing his estate during his absence. Although the real threat the suitors posed Penelope and her attendant sense of desperation must not be minimized, she had in a sense domesticated them, just as Circe, albeit through more sinister means, had tamed Odysseus' crew. It is neither the whim of the poet nor of Penelope's unconscious that the suitors appear in her dream in the guise of her pet geese. In fact, it was not only Penelope's conjugal fidelity that made Odysseus' successful homecoming possible; she protected her household during her husband's absence by having the suitors attend her, rendering the suitors—preoccupied with feasting and entertainment—unfit for martial activity upon Odysseus' return. The suitors, though much younger than Odysseus, are no match for the veteran from Troy, and once they are decimated only their fathers remain as obstacles to Odysseus' reinstatement as king of Ithaca. In the absence of a male ruler, Ithaca may appear disorderly and chaotic, but Penelope's effective rule over the suitors lays the groundwork for Odysseus' restoration of order.

Through Odysseus' praise of Penelope's *kleos* as that of a wise and successful king, the *Odyssey* reevaluates the roles apportioned to the sexes in the *Iliad,* where Hector admonished Andromache to attend to domestic duties while he engaged in battle (6.490–93). Although Penelope does indeed attend to her domestic duties faithfully while Odysseus fights at Troy, the *Odyssey* does not consider the two activities to be opposed, but analogous. The *Odyssey*'s most explicit revision of the opposition between gender roles in the *Iliad* occurs in the striking simile in Book 8, where the poet compares Odysseus, weeping over Demodocus' portrait of his own exploits at Troy, to a Trojan woman:[33]

> So the famous singer sang his tale, but Odysseus
> melted, and from under his eyes the tears ran down, drenching
> his cheeks. As a woman weeps, lying over the body
> of her dear husband, who fell fighting for her city and people
> as he tried to beat off the pitiless day from city and children;
> she sees him dying and gasping for breath, and winding her body
> about him she cries high and shrill, while the men behind her,
> hitting her with their spear butts on the back and the shoulders,
> force her up and lead her away into slavery, to have
> hard work and sorrow, and her cheeks are wracked with pitiful
>   weeping.
> Such were the pitiful tears Odysseus shed.
>
> [8.521–31]

In this astonishing comparison of the Greek hero, architect of the fall of Troy, to a Trojan woman widowed and about to be taken into slavery, the poet alludes to Hector's portrayal of Andromache's unhappy fate after his death and the fall of Ilium:

> But it is not so much the pain to come of the Trojans
> that troubles me . . .
> as troubles me the thought of you, when some bronze-armoured
> Achaian leads you off, taking away your day of liberty,
> in tears; and in Argos you must work at the loom of another,
> and carry water from the spring Messeis or Hypereia,
> all unwilling, but strong will be the necessity upon you;
> and some day seeing you shedding tears a man will say of you:
> "This is the wife of Hektor, who was ever the bravest fighter
> of the Trojans, breakers of horses, in the days when they fought
>   about Ilion."
> So will one speak of you; and for you it will be yet a fresh grief,
> to be widowed of such a man who could fight off the day of your
>   slavery.
>
> [6.450–51, 454–63]

[33]See Helene P. Foley, "'Reverse Similes' and Sex Roles in the *Odyssey*," in *Women in the Ancient World: The Arethusa Papers,* ed. John Peradotto and J. C. Sullivan (Albany: State Univ. of New York Press, 1984), pp. 59–78, for a discussion of this and other "reverse similes," such as the poet's comparison of Penelope to a ship-wrecked sailor (23.233–40) which recalls Odysseus' landing in Phaeacia (5.394–98), and to a beleaguered lion (10.791–92), an image usually associated with warriors.

The *Odyssey* thus questions the commonly accepted opposition between man and woman as well as that between victor and vanquished, and posits instead a congruence between them.

This convergence of victor and vanquished, of giving and receiving pain, marks the four tokens of recognition, or signs (*semata*), exchanged between Penelope and Odysseus in Book 19: Odysseus' description of his brooch, Eurycleia's recognition of her master by the famous scar, Penelope's recounting of her dream, and her proposal of the contest of stringing the bow.[34] Even before the exchange of the first of these signs, Penelope's surrender to the disguised Odysseus is suggested by the simile, cited earlier, which compares her tears, shed upon the beggar's evocation of Odysseus, to a spring thaw. Seeing Penelope weep, Odysseus conceals his own tears as he had done earlier when he heard Demodocus sing about himself: in this, as in the earlier instance, Odysseus gives as well as receives pain. Moreover, the beggar responds to Penelope's repeated questioning of his identity by speaking of his pain:

Question me now here in your house about all other
matters, but do not ask who I am, the name of my country,
for fear you may increase in my heart its burden of sorrow
as I think back; I am full of grief, and I should not
sit in the house of somebody else with my lamentation
and wailing. It is not good to go on mourning forever.

[19.115–20]

and:

O respected wife of Odysseus, son of Laertes,
you will not stop asking me about my origin?
Then I will tell you; but you will give me over to sorrows
even more than I have; but such is the way of it, when one
strays away from his own country as long as I have,
wandering many cities of men and suffering hardships.

[19.165–70]

It is significant that the beggar speaks of pain in connection with his

[34]Gregory Nagy, "*Sema* and *Noesis*: Some Illustrations," *Arethusa*, 16 (1983), 35–55, points out that these *semata*, tokens of recognition, require an act of interpretation "as code[s] bearing distinct messages that are to be interpreted by both the witnesses and the narrative itself" (p. 36).

identity, for the etymological meaning of Odysseus' name, as George Dimock has argued, is "to cause pain" (from the verb *odyne*).[35]

If giving and receiving pain is Odysseus' mark of distinction, then the appropriateness of the four tokens of recognition exchanged by husband and wife becomes evident. The first exchange of signs occurs when the beggar describes Odysseus' clothing and in particular the brooch that depicts a hunting dog preying on a fawn—an apt emblem for giving and receiving pain. This description serves as a sign known and remembered only by the couple, for its every detail answers to the brooch Penelope fixed on her husband's clothes when he departed from Ithaca.

Next, Eurycleia, Odysseus' nurse, recognizes her master by the scar on his thigh which he received as a child on a boar hunt[36]—a sign whose origin recalls the predatory activity depicted on the brooch. In hunting the boar, Odysseus both gave and received pain; appropriately, therefore, the poet recounts the naming of Odysseus in the lengthy narrative of the scar's origin. It is Penelope who specifically calls on Eurycleia to bathe the beggar; moreover, she virtually ensures the old woman's recognition of her master by pointedly noting that Odysseus would be about the beggar's age and would look like him after the hardships he surely has suffered. The poet relates that

---

[35]George Dimock, "The Name of Odysseus," *Hudson Review*, 9 (1956), rpt. in Taylor, *Essays on the Odyssey*, p. 55. Stanford, *Ulysses Theme*, p. 12, etymologizes the name as "Man of Odium." See also Jenny Strauss Clay, *The Wrath of Athena: Gods and Men in the Odyssey* (Princeton: Princeton Univ. Press, 1983), pp. 54–68, who suggests that the doubleness of Odysseus' name corresponds to the doubleness in *polytropos* (p. 64).

[36]The most noted discussion of the passage is Erich Auerbach's "Odysseus' Scar," in *Mimesis: The Representation of Reality in Western Literature*, trans. Willard R. Trask (Princeton: Princeton Univ. Press, 1953), pp. 3–23. Auerbach distinguishes between Homeric narrative, which he characterizes as "externalized" and "foregrounded," and biblical narrative, which he characterizes as "mysterious" and "fraught with background." My interpretation of the character of Penelope takes issue with Auerbach's claim that in Homer, "wholly expressed, orderly even in their ardor—are the feelings and thoughts of the persons involved" (p. 3); in fact, my reading approximates more closely his view of biblical characters, in whom there exist simultaneously "various layers of consciousness and conflict between them" (p. 13). Bakhtin, "Forms of Time and Chronotope in the Novel," in *Dialogic Imagination,* pp. 133–34, makes an observation similar to Auerbach's, that "Homer's heroes express their feelings vividly and noisily," and attributes this feature to the fact that "for the classical Greek, every aspect of existence could be *seen* and *heard*." But Austin, pp. 6–7, states: "That Homer knows nothing of the ego, the superego, and the id, which occupy so much of our attention, is not in itself proof that Homer was ignorant of psychological motive and complexity of motive."

Athena bemused Penelope so that she took no notice of the havoc—
Eurycleia dropping the beggar's leg in the basin when she recognizes
him as Odysseus. But here, as in the case of Penelope's earlier ruse to
obtain gifts from the suitors, Athena serves as a figure for *metis,* and
her appearance calls attention to Penelope's wiliness in orchestrating
the recognition scene.

Penelope then asks the beggar to interpret the dream in which an
eagle preys upon her pet geese—a dream that recalls in its detail the
omen Helen read for Telemachus as signifying Odysseus' successful
return. But since the eagle, identifying himself as Odysseus within
the dream, had explained its meaning, Penelope is in effect asking the
beggar to confirm the eagle's prophetic statement, that Odysseus'
slaughter of the suitors will indeed come to pass. Having secured the
beggar's affirmation, Penelope proposes to set a contest for the suitors: she will marry the man who is able to string Odysseus' bow.
These two signs—Penelope's dream and her attendant proposal of the
contest—not only figure Odysseus as the dealer of pain but also allow
the couple to formulate a common strategy against the suitors without incurring either their suspicion or that of the maids who attend
Penelope—maids whose loyalties are suspect since they have taken
the suitors as their lovers. Through these signs, Penelope confirms
Odysseus' intention to slay the suitors and places the requisite weapon in his hands. Although Amphimedon, one of the slaughtered
suitors, tells Agamemnon in the second *Nekya* that Odysseus assigned Penelope her part in their destruction, it is indeed Penelope
who contrives the strategy by proposing the contest. In fact, Odysseus sends only the first sign, the description of the brooch, and
Penelope initiates the exchange of the rest, including the final sign of
the olive bed. Just as this proliferation of signs culminates in the final
recognition, so in these last books omens pointing to the doom of the
suitors multiply: Telemachus' sneeze, Zeus' thunder and the old ser-
vantwoman's prayer, Theoclymenus' bloody vision.

These four signs in Book 19 thus confirm to Penelope the beggar's
identity as her husband by reiterating Odysseus' intrinsic association
with pain. In his ten years of wandering, Odysseus has borne pain
and he has also given pain: to the Trojans he vanquished by means of
the Wooden Horse, to his adversaries, such as Polyphemus, during
his wandering, to his crew who perished before reaching Ithaca, and
most important, to his family during his prolonged absence. These
signs of Odysseus as pain dealer dramatize the pain Odysseus inflicted

on his own wife; Clytemnestra in the *Agamemnon* describes the desolation of a wife left behind for many years—in Clytemnestra's case ten; in Penelope's, twenty. Upon her recognition of Odysseus, Penelope blames the gods for their separation; yet during her conversation with the disguised Odysseus in Book 19, she mourns her faded beauty and expresses the pain she suffered in her husband's absence. Her narration of her dream and subsequent commentary on it crystallize her ambivalence toward Odysseus' return: her expression of terror and distress at the eagle's violent destruction of her pet geese calls attention to the way in which Odysseus' return is cataclysmic and disruptive to her as well as to the suitors.[37] In her oft-discussed musings about the twin gates of horn and ivory through which true and false dreams are said to issue, she expresses uncertainty concerning the validity of the dream, even after the eagle within the dream and the beggar outside it have pronounced it true.[38] Penelope's ambivalence about Odysseus' return would also explain her expression of a desire to die, which she surprisingly pronounces in Book 20 after her conversation with the beggar. Moreover, Penelope weeps as she handles the bow before the contest, perhaps expressing anxiety for her husband's success, but perhaps also expressing distress over the slaughter that will ensue if he succeeds.

Penelope's ambivalence emerges clearly in her hesitation after Eurycleia tells her of Odysseus' successful battle against the suitors. First she displays disbelief, then joy, then again disbelief: it must be some god who killed the suitors, not Odysseus. The poet makes clear, however, that Penelope entertains no doubt about the identity of the man downstairs, as he reports her musings:[39]

---

[37]Anne V. Rankin, "Penelope's Dreams in Books XIX and XX of the *Odyssey*," *Helikon*, 2 (1962), 618, suggests that "there is something equivocal about [Penelope's] relations with the suitors." Penelope's relief in finding her pet geese alive and feeding leads Rankin to argue that Penelope is secretly inclined to remarry (p. 622). For a similar interpretation, see George Devereux, "Penelope's Character," *Psychoanalytic Quarterly*, 26 (1957), 382. John H. Finley refutes this type of "subtle but unHomeric" reading: "The geese express what a well-bred lady wants as least denominator, not as happiness but minimal order" *Homer's Odyssey* (Cambridge: Harvard Univ. Press, 1978), pp. 19n, 20.

[38]On this motif, see Ann Amory, "The Gates of Horn and Ivory," *YCS*, 20 (1966), 55, who suggests that horn is associated with Odysseus and ivory with Penelope, who "looks at things only intermittently; she is always holding a veil in front of her face, or looking away from things."

[39]But see Stanford, 2:394, who states "it is not easy to decide whether Homer is simply referring to the fact already well known to his audience that the stranger is

She . . . came down from the chamber, her heart pondering
much, whether to keep away and question her dear husband,
or to go up to him and kiss his head, taking his hands.

[23.85–87]

Penelope's uncertainty lies not in the stranger's identity but in her
own feelings about her returned husband. Then she sees him:

She sat a long time in silence, and her heart was wondering.
Sometimes she would look at him, with her eyes full upon him,
and again would fail to know him in the foul clothing he wore.

[23.93–95]

Here Penelope's ambivalence is encapsulated in her double vision of
the bloody old beggar and the Odysseus she once knew. Her testing
of Odysseus by the final token of recognition of the olive bed is
motivated by the need to reconcile the two visions and to accept the
pain he has caused her together with the joy of their reunion. The sign
of the olive trunk, as their marriage bed long vacated by the absent
Odysseus, is an apt emblem for this mixed pain and joy. At their
mutual recognition, Penelope expresses the bittersweetness of their
reunion:

The gods granted us misery,
in jealousy over the thought that we two, always together,
should enjoy our youth, and then come to the threshold of old age.
Then do not now be angry with me nor blame me, because
I did not greet you, as I do now, at first when I saw you.

[23.210–14]

Although she accepts Odysseus, Penelope nevertheless evokes her
desolation during their twenty years' separation. Moreover, through
this final token of recognition, she manages to match her husband's
caution and, by tricking the great trickster, deals him momentary
pain, just as Odysseus had attempted to trick Athena, the goddess of
metis, upon his return to Ithaca. As Athena and Odysseus, the goddess and her favorite mortal,[40] stand as equals in that earlier scene, so

---

Odysseus, or else wishes to imply that Penelope despite her recent doubts has inwardly decided that the avenger must be her husband after all."

[40]Clay, pp. 51–53, makes the interesting suggestion that the *Odyssey* begins at the
point where Athena forgoes her wrath against Odysseus. The poem attempts to
suppress this wrath, along with other unflattering characteristics of Odysseus, espe-

here Penelope demonstrates her likemindedness to her husband in her corresponding caution and wiliness, and by her insistence upon accepting him on her terms as well as his.

Thus, Penelope's delayed recognition serves as a counterpart to Helen's immediate recognition of both Odysseus at Troy and Telemachus at Sparta, just as Odysseus' delay in revealing his identity— he actually arrives in Ithaca in Book 13, so half of the poem is concerned with this problem—is set off against Agamemnon's hasty, violent, and unsuccessful return. Moreover, if Helen recognized Odysseus in his beggar's guise, it is highly unlikely that Penelope would not have recognized her husband in the same disguise.[41] Penelope also accomplishes much through her delay, as she did in stalling the suitors with her weaving, whereas Helen's acts are shown to be of little consequence; for example, it does not matter whether Telemachus is recognized earlier or later. The poet considers Helen's one act of heedlessness, her elopement with Paris, to have transformed her into an object to be fought over, robbing her of any further power to act with consequence. Now that she has been won back by Menelaus, she seems consigned to live in the shadow of that one traumatic act and to pass her time in gratuitous acts.

Unlike Helen and Menelaus, who will be placed outside human time in Elysium, Penelope and Odysseus forge a reunion that necessarily entails aging and death. Penelope wistfully calls attention to the fact that after twenty years of separation they are no longer young; but the passage of time must be accepted, not overcome. Odysseus chose to forgo the immortal existence and perpetual youth offered by both Calypso and Circe in order to take his place beside his mortal wife Penelope, his son, and his father. As Odysseus, Telemachus, and Laertes stand side by side in combat in the final book of the poem, the *Odyssey* insists upon the importance of the succession of generations through which human time unfolds. This affirmation carries its corollary, the injunction against crossing the generations: Odysseus will not marry Nausicaa who is young enough to be his daughter; he has

---

cially those in connection with Autolycus (pp. 68–74). She further argues that Athena's wrath stems from Odysseus' almost superhuman *metis* that calls into question her superiority as a god of *metis* (p. 209).

[41]Stanford, *Ulysses Theme*, p. 65, notes that Odysseus had been among the suitors of Helen. Seen in this light, Helen's recognition of the beggar as Odysseus and his subsequent slaughter of the Trojans prefigures Penelope's recognition of her husband in the same disguise and his subsequent slaughter of the suitors. Penelope, unlike Helen, does not rejoice over the carnage, however.

instructed Penelope to remarry when Telemachus grows up to be a younger version of Odysseus;[42] the suitors err by courting the wife of Odysseus, who acted as a father to them. The last of the cyclic epics, the *Telegonia,* perversely violates this Odyssean injunction against crossing the generations by having Telemachus marry his father's lover Circe and Penelope marry Telegonus, Odysseus' son by Circe.[43] Indeed, this willful inversion of the original text's intent also characterizes postclassical versions of the story of Odysseus. In *Inferno* 26, Dante—who of course had no direct knowledge of Homer— equates Ulysses' classical heroism with an insatiable desire to see and know by journeying perpetually rather than with his persistence in reaching home and his acceptance of his identity as husband, father, and son.

The *Odyssey* affirms human time with its attendant mortality, unlike the *Iliad,* which mourned the death of its heroes and in which the immortals' carefree existence made the limitations placed on men all the more tragic. The later poem offers ways of becoming old, of using the past to serve the present, of being aware of the past without letting that knowledge be crippling. In the unfolding of time, prophecies are fulfilled, dreams come true, and word matches deed: Odysseus does not experience the tragic disjuncton between word and deed that Achilles did in the *Iliad*.

This insistence on the importance of the unfolding of time lies at the heart of the poetics of the *Odyssey*. Just as Penelope heeded Helen's example in forging her own distinct identity, so the poet makes use of the *Iliad* but diverges from it. Refusing to become an object of exchange between a suitor and either her son Telemachus or her father Icarius, Penelope avoids Helen's fate as a sign that is exchanged among men; instead, she insists upon her status as a subject, a generator of signs. Similarly, the poet reduces Helen, the heroine of the *Iliad,* to an emblem for the doubleness of poetry in order to set against her his own Penelope, who in her weaving represents a poet figure and in her delayed recognition an ideal audience as well. Unlike Helen, who insists on the immediate reading of signs to ascertain

---

[42]Not only is Telemachus recognized by Helen and others through his resemblance to his father, he is the only one among the suitors nearly to succeed in stringing the bow; Odysseus stiffens at this Oedipal moment.

[43]Stanford, *Ulysses Theme,* p. 86. See also Marie-Madeleine Mactoux, *Pénélope: Légende et mythe,* Centre de recherches d'histoire ancien, vol. 16 (Paris: Belles Lettres, 1975), p. 33.

identity, Penelope, conscious of the complexity of identity, reads them in context, against one another.[44] She also reveals her awareness of the multivalency of signs in her use of the same sign as confirmation of Odysseus' identity, as indication of their common strategy against the suitors and also as an expression of the pain she suffered in his absence. Her use of signs and her interpretation of them are teleological and thus mirror the unfolding of the poem itself. Penelope's reading of signs serves as a model for the interpretation of this endstriving, teleological narrative; an interpretation that places her recognition in Book 23 and no earlier would follow Helen's model in requiring only one sign.

There is no denying, however, that the poet's representation of Penelope remains elusive and enigmatic; he never, as it were, lifts the veil that covers her face when she first appears. Various characters state repeatedly that "her mind has other intentions" (Antinous— 2.92; Athena—13.381; Odysseus—18.283). Penelope's opaqueness causes Telemachus and some critics of the poem to be suspicious of her behavior toward the suitors and Odysseus.[45] Indeed, it is not an accident that the question repeatedly raised by male characters and critics proves to be, as was the case with the Iliadic Helen, a question about her loyalty to her husband and her unspoken intentions, for the poet has endowed Penelope with the inwardness that marked the Iliadic Helen. Another question asked of the Iliadic Helen—Is she a subject or an object?—critics now ask of the *Odyssey*'s Penelope: does Penelope propel the poem's plot or is she its victim?[46] Within the

[44]See Austin, p. 128: Homer demands from his readers "the sensitivity of the Homeric seers, which can detect the invisible canvas from a single visible brushstroke." He notes the contrast between those who notice tokens and put together meanings and those who do not: "Better the perspicacity of Theoclymenus than the myopia of the suitors." Austin, however, does not distinguish between Helen's perspicacity and Penelope's.

[45]For example, Mactoux, pp. 7–10, argues for Penelope's "fidelité équivoque," citing her four appearances before the suitors and the psychological absurdity of the test of the bow following the series of encouraging signs. On Telemachus' ambivalence toward Penelope, see Austin, pp. 163–64. Eva Cantarella, *Pandora's Daughters: The Role and Status of Women in Greek and Roman Antiquity* (Baltimore: Johns Hopkins Univ. Press, 1986), p. 29, considers Penelope's ambiguity to arise from, on the one hand, the need for epic poetry to propose a model of virtuous woman, and on the other, a misogynist ideology that mistrusted women.

[46]J. Finley, pp. 2–3, holds that Penelope's various decisions make Odysseus' homecoming possible, but it is through "desperate instinct" that she, for example, sets the test of the bow. Chris Emlyn-Jones, "The Reunion of Penelope and Odysseus," *Greece & Rome*, 12 (1984), 12, sees Penelope as a victim, due to the social situation in which she is placed.

poem itself, Amphimedon's conjecture about Penelope's role in Odysseus' victory in effect calls attention to the uncertainty about her role.

In order to exorcize anxiety-producing qualities from his own heroine, Penelope, the poet of the *Odyssey* loads them on the Iliadic Helen as scapegoat; to that end, he refashions Helen as clearly duplicitous and disloyal, yet marginal and inconsequential. This preoccupation with woman's sexual fidelity is also evident not only in his multiple references to Clytemnestra but also in his inclusion and punishment of other adulterous and promiscuous women in his narrative: Demodocus sings of Aphrodite and Ares caught in Hephaestos' net and ridiculed by the other gods; the poet compares Odysseus' disloyal maids hanging from a noose to birds caught in a net.[47] Here again, Penelope's weaving and unweaving marks her difference as subject from other females who make themselves objects to be ensnared. Eumaeus' maid, who kidnapped him and stole gold from his father's household after being seduced by a Phoenician trader, exemplifies the threat to property and genealogy that woman's unregulated sexuality brings. Inevitably, swift punishment follows:

> Artemis of the showering arrows struck down the woman,
> and she dropped with a splash, like a diving tern, in the hull's bilge.
> They then
> threw her overboard to be the spoil of fishes and seals.
>
> [15.478–81]

Despite the *Odyssey*'s palpable anxiety concerning female sexuality, it escapes being a univocally misogynistic text. Penelope's opacity is not exclusively feminine, for what Achilles so deplored in the *Iliad*— hiding one thought while speaking another—is an identifying trait of her likeminded husband as well. Hence the *Odyssey* as the poem of *metis* (as opposed to *bie*) can allow Penelope to be the hero's equal. As Marcel Détienne and Jean-Pierre Vernant state in their study of the place of *metis* in Greek culture, "[*metis*] is, in a sense, the absolute weapon, the only one that has the power to ensure victory and domination over others, whatever the circumstances, whatever the condi-

---

[47]Theodor Adorno and Max Horkheimer, *Dialectic of Enlightenment* (1944), trans. John Cumming (New York: Continuum, 1972), pp. 79–80, commenting on the line "kicked for a short while, but not for long," suggest that Homer "prevents us from forgetting the victims, and reveals the unutterable eternal agony of the few seconds in which the women struggle with death."

tions of the conflict."[48] We might add to this statement, "whatever the gender of the protagonist." The reigning goddess of the poem, Athena, thus represents the likemindedness between husband and wife in their shared *metis*. But unlike Odysseus, Penelope is portrayed from without, and the poet, while according her subjectivity, does not seek to represent it; he sees her through the eyes of the male characters around her—Odysseus, Telemachus, and the suitors—and conveys their uncertainty about her.

It is curiously appropriate that the *Odyssey*'s Penelope follows the fate of the Iliadic Helen in her later literary incarnations. Just as Helen's ambiguity is reduced to doubleness and duplicity in the *Odyssey*, so the questions concerning Penelope will no longer be held in delicate suspension but will be split and reified: she becomes in later tradition either the chaste and patient wife or the mother of Pan, fathered by all the suitors.[49] As mother of Pan, the divine patron of poets, Penelope, like Helen, also becomes a figure associated with the disquieting promiscuity of poetry.

---

[48]Marcel Détienne and Jean-Pierre Vernant, *Cunning Intelligence in Greek Culture and Society*, trans. Janet Lloyd (Atlantic Highlands, N.J.: Humanities Press, 1978), p. 13. Although they take *Iliad* 23, Antilochus' race, as the exemplary text of *metis* (pp. 12–17), they also discuss Odysseus as the embodiment of cunning (pp. 18, 22–23, 226–28).

[49]See Mactoux, pp. 97–102. During the Hellenistic and early Roman period, Penelope became reduced to a clichéd virtuous wife in popular literature. Lycophron, however, portrays her as a shameless prostitute who dissipates Odysseus' goods with her suitors and enjoys the spectacle of his humiliation, while Douris of Amos and Theocritus both make her the mother of Pan. Concerning these two traditions that coexist, Mactoux concludes: "ils traduisent la méfiance d'une époque qui n'a pas voulu choisir" (p. 102).

3 Virgil's *Aeneid*

alter habendus amor tibi restat et altera Dido;
  quamque iterum fallas altera danda fides.
quando erit, ut condas instar Carthaginis urbem
  et videas populos altus ab arce tuos?
omnia ut eveniant, nec te tua vota morentur,
  unde tibi, quae te sic amet, uxor erit?
                                        —Ovid, *Heroides*

Another love remains for you to win, another Dido; another pledge
to give, and another time to play false. When will it be your fortune
to found a city like Carthage, and from the citadel look down upon
your own people? Should your every wish be granted, even should
you meet with no delay in the answering of your prayers, whence
will come the wife to love you as I?

In the *Aeneid,* epic of Augustan Rome, Virgil transmutes the figure
of Helen as he does so much else from the Homeric epics.[1] In the first
half of the *Aeneid,* he casts Dido in the role of a sacrificial substitute
for Helen, and in the second half, his characters call Lavinia the second Helen. Yet these two women are diametrically opposed to each
other, both in their relationships to Aeneas and their significance for
him, as well as in Virgil's modes of representing them. Virgil divides
the doubleness of Helen in the *Odyssey* and assigns Dido and Lavinia
to each pole of the binary opposition.

---

[1]The first six books, which tell of Aeneas' wanderings from Troy to Italy, follow
the *Odyssey;* the last six books, in their concern with the Italian wars, model them-
selves on the *Iliad.* On the relationship between Virgil and Homer, see, for example,
Viktor Pöschl, *The Art of Vergil: Image and Symbol in the Aeneid,* trans. Gerda Seligson
(Ann Arbor: Univ. of Michigan Press, 1962), pp. 24–33; and Brooks Otis, *Virgil: A
Study in Civilized Poetry* (Oxford: Oxford Univ. Press, 1964), chapters 6 and 7, "The
Odyssean *Aeneid*" and "The Iliadic *Aeneid.*" See also his "The Originality of the
Aeneid," in *Virgil,* ed. D. R. Dudley (London: Routledge and Kegan Paul, 1969), pp.
27–66.

In the first half of the poem, Virgil represents Dido's passion as the most dangerous force opposing Aeneas' *fatum* to found Rome. Her destruction as a sacrificial victim thus aims to exorcize the threats of irrationality and disorder against Jupiter's (and Aeneas') rational, orderly, and masculine *fatum*.[2] Calypso and Circe, who represent similar obstacles for Odysseus' return home, need not be destroyed, because in the *Odyssey* the opposition between the sexes is not as strict as that between mortals and immortals; Odysseus' temptation to remain with the two goddesses is not simply sexual but more fundamentally involves the promise of immortality. In the second half of the poem, Virgil again exorcizes the dangers of female sexuality by rendering Lavinia passive and silent—qualities befitting her role as vessel for Aeneas' *fatum*. Nevertheless, the threat of the female cannot be entirely contained: consequently, Lavinia appears to splinter into various surrogates—Amata, Camilla, and Juturna—who act and then are sacrificed on her behalf. Unlike Dido, Amata, and Camilla, however, Lavinia will survive the conclusion of the poem so that she may serve to unite the Italian and Trojan peoples; yet she is in effect sacrificed as a person to form the foundation of the patriarchal order of Rome. Here again, Lavinia, who approximates the role of Penelope in the *Odyssey* as goal of the epic quest, diverges from her prototype in that she functions solely as an object to be exchanged rather than as a subject who wills her own actions. Like Lavinia, the nymph Juturna cannot be destroyed because she is immortal. But in effect she is doubly sacrificed: by Jupiter's exercise of patriarchal prerogative in raping her and then granting her immortality and by his decree that her brother Turnus die for the sake of Aeneas' *fatum*. She survives the conclusion of the poem, only to mourn eternally.

Yet Virgil follows the *Odyssey* in the strategy of juxtaposing the myth of the anterior epic heroine Helen with the fiction of his own female characters: the question of Dido's culpability and innocence in her passion for Aeneas and her subsequent suicide is an interpretive crux of the poem, and even the silent Lavinia is far from innocuous, for a double-edged omen foretold that her fame would be gained at

---

[2]See Lillian S. Robinson, *Monstrous Regiment: The Lady Knight in Sixteenth-Century Epic* (New York: Garland, 1985), pp. 12–13, on the conflict between the masculine and feminine elements in the *Aeneid*. She points out that Aeneas rescues from Troy the masculine element as embodied in the household gods of the patriarchal family and his father and son—his dynasty represented in patriarchal terms; he never identifies with the feminine "Oriental" luxury that caused its fall. Robinson sees the root of the female threat in the *Aeneid* to be female sexuality.

the cost of destruction to her people. Virgil sacrifices these women, including Amata, Camilla, and Juturna, on the altar of Jupiter's—and hence Aeneas'— *fatum* to found the new Troy, the Roman Empire; but at the same time, Virgil questions the justice and even efficacy of such sacrifice through the doubleness of *fatum* itself and of his poem that imitates its unfolding.

Helen: *Tyndaris* and *Lacaena*

Helen, it must be remembered, is inextricably linked to Aeneas' trials on his journey to Italy: Juno's implacable wrath toward Aeneas and the Trojans that compels the poet to ask, "Can anger / Black as this prey on the minds of heaven?" (1.11 [F:18–19]) stems from the Judgment of Paris.[3] In the *Aeneid,* Helen appears twice: in Aeneas' story of the night Troy fell in Book 2 and in Deiphobus' tale of the same night in Book 6. The first passage is of disputed authenticity since it is only preserved in Servius' *Vita Vergilii,* and scholars have questioned it for its verbal repetitions, extravagance of expression, and contradiction of Deiphobus' tale in Book 6.[4] If we accept the passage as Virgil's, as R. G. Austin and, more recently, Gian Biagio Conte have done, then we can perhaps explain these textual problems as Virgil's attempt to dramatize the violence of an earlier heroic model, as exemplified by the *Iliad.*[5]

[3]The translation I use is Robert Fitzgerald's (New York: Random House, 1983). The Latin quotations are taken from the edition of R. D. Williams, *The Aeneid of Virgil* (London: Macmillan, 1972), 2 vols. Since Fitzgerald's line numbers do not match the Latin, I mark them with an "F."

[4]For recent restatements of the skeptical position, see G. P. Goold, "Servius and the Helen Episode," *HSCP,* 74 (1970), 101–68. C. E. Murgia, "More on the Helen Episode," *CSCA,* 4 (1971), 203–17, concludes that in seeking to produce a Virgilian passage, the poet has gone too far: "He has been able to imitate the anomalies of Virgilian style, but has been unable to duplicate Virgilian restraint. The result is super-Virgil." See also Gordon Williams, *Technique and Ideas in the Aeneid* (New Haven: Yale Univ. Press, 1983), pp. 283–84.

[5]R. G. Austin, "Virgil, *Aeneid* 2.567–88," *CQ,* n.s. 11 (1961), 185–98. See also the commentary on and bibliography for these lines in his edition *P. Vergili Maronis Aeneidos Liber Secundus* (Oxford: Oxford Univ. Press, 1964), pp. 217–18. Michael C. J. Putnam, *The Poetry of the Aeneid: Four Studies in Imaginative Unity and Design* (Cambridge: Harvard Univ. Press, 1966), p. 225n, states: "The need to retain the Helen passage, with Servius and against the manuscript authority, has now been thoroughly established." The most recent, and perhaps most authoritative, defense of this passage comes from Gian Biagio Conte, "The Helen Episode in the Second Book of the *Aeneid:* Structural Models and a Question of Authenticity," in *The Rhetoric of Imitation: Genre and Poetic Memory in Virgil and Other Latin Poets,* trans. and ed. Charles

On the last night of Troy, Aeneas confronts Helen immediately after witnessing Pyrrhus' horrible slaughter of Priam on his own altar. This murder of the defenseless king stands as a synecdoche for Troy taken by a ruse. More immediately for Aeneas, the image of the old king's mutilated corpse calls forth anxiety for his own aged father as well as for his wife and son (2.559–63). In accordance with Augustus' establishment of his authority as emperor on the model of the *pater familias,* Virgil signals the fall of Troy not only by the death of its *pater* and king Priam but also by the destruction and dispersal of the family.

Virgil juxtaposes Pyrrhus' murder of Priam with the appearance of Helen:

> And then I saw
> Lurking beyond the doorsill of the Vesta,
> In hiding, silent, in that place reserved,
> The daughter of Tyndareus. Glare of fires
> Lighted my steps this way and that, my eyes
> Glancing over the whole scene, everywhere.
> That woman, terrified of the Trojans' hate
> For the city overthrown, terrified too
> Of Danaan vengeance, her abandoned husband's
> Anger after years—Helen, that Fury
> Both to her own homeland and Troy, had gone
> To earth, a hated thing, before the altars.
>
> [2.567–74 (F:742–53)]

Aeneas' vision of Helen is illuminated only by the light that burns the sacked city. Aeneas does not describe her—he does not even allude to her famous beauty—except to stress repeatedly how she lurks and crouches in an attempt to hide herself from view. Although she does nothing else and remains silent, this image of her is portentous and sinister. Aeneas interprets Helen's posture as signifying fear of reprisal, but from Deiphobus' account in Book 6, she could very well be waiting for the moment to spring forth, just as the Greek soldiers in the Wooden Horse, another Greek gift to Troy, had done.

Helen's seeking of sanctuary on the altars of Vesta—the household

---

Segal (Ithaca: Cornell Univ. Press, 1986), pp. 196–208. Conte bases his defense of the passage on Virgil's imitation of an Iliadic model, Achilles' wrath against Agamemnon and Athena's intervention: "The underlying Homeric structure . . . straddles the two dividing lines between the challenged and unchallenged parts of the text" (p. 204).

deity of the hearth whose sacred fire was tended by the Vestal Virgins—is a subtle but nevertheless unmistakable example of the desecration of altars announcing the fall of Troy.[6] In the scene immediately preceding, Pyrrhus had desecrated Priam's altar with the blood of both the king and his son, and Hecuba and her daughters sought sanctuary there in vain. Helen's position on the threshold ("limina" [567]) suggests how she straddles boundaries, here as the common Fury for both the Greeks and the Trojans ("Troiae et patriae communis Erinys" [573]);[7] her ability in the *Iliad* to go beyond national divisions has degenerated into a curse. Although Priam and Hector in that earlier epic had treated Helen as one of their own, here for Aeneas she is unequivocally hateful, referred to with contempt only by her patronymic, *Tyndaris* (569). Aeneas represents her as a Fury who instigated sexual lust in Paris and destructive warlust in both the Greeks and the Trojans. This image of Helen as a Fury, moreover, recalls the various instances in which serpents desecrated altars in Book 2: the grim sacrifice of the prophet Laocoon on his own altar by twin serpents and the simile likening Pyrrhus, about to murder Priam on his own altar, to a snake.[8] Despite their sinister associations, these serpents, including Helen, signal the unfolding of *fatum,* as Venus will show Aeneas.

Aeneas himself is not exempt from the effect of this Fury, and he seeks to sacrifice Helen on Vesta's altars:

> Now fires blazed up in my own spirit—
> A passion to avenge my fallen town
> And punish Helen's whorishness.
> > "Shall this one
> Look untouched on Sparta and Mycenae
> After her triumph, going like a queen,
> And see her home and husband, kin and children,
> With Trojan girls for escort, Phrygian slaves?
> Must Priam perish by the sword for this?
> Troy burn, for this? Dardania's littoral

[6]On Vesta and Vestal Virgins, see Cyril Bailey, *Religion in Virgil* (Oxford: Oxford Univ. Press, 1935), p. 95. Austin, ad 2.572, p. 221, notes that, according to Ibycus, Helen took refuge in the temple of Aphrodite, and that this tradition provided the motif for this scene. Virgil's substitution of Vesta for Aphrodite, however, contributes masterfully to Aeneas' bitter portrait of Helen.

[7]Note other Furies on thresholds; for example, the Eumenides ("in limine" [6.279]) and Tisiphone, who guards the gates of Dis (6.554–56).

[8]On this motif, see Bernard M. W. Knox, "The Serpent and the Flame: The Imagery of the Second Book of the *Aeneid*," *AJP,* 71 (1950), 379–400.

Be soaked in blood, so many times, for this?
Not by my leave. I know
No glory comes of punishing a woman,
The feat can bring no honor. Still, I'll be
Approved for snuffing out a monstrous life,
For a just sentence carried out. My heart
Will teem with joy in this avenging fire,
And the ashes of my kin will be appeased."

[2.575–87 (F:754–71)]

The fire that envelops the ruins of the city and reveals Helen to
Aeneas by its light now enters his breast as he contemplates her.
Helen does not arouse desire in him, as she had done in Paris, but a
lust for revenge, akin to that felt by the Greek sackers of Troy.[9] Here,
and later in the character of Turnus, Virgil conceives of sexual and
martial fury as inextricably linked, for both subvert the rational ordering of *fatum*.

The series of rhetorical questions and the obsessive repetition of
"poena" (572, 576, 584, 586) led R. G. Austin to regard this passage as
an unfinished draft; but the repetition effectively expresses the tumult
in Aeneas' mind—also figured in his wavering eyes (570)—as he
convinces himself of the justice of punishing Helen. The image of her
homecoming to Sparta in Aeneas' mind's eye leads him to contrast
her triumph with Troy's devastation. She will be reunited with her
family, whereas Aeneas had imagined the worst about his own; the
train of slaves that Helen takes home with her may plausibly even
include Creusa and Ascanius. These scenarios may contradict Aeneas'
earlier sense that Helen was hiding from the Greeks as well as from
the Trojans; but the ambiguity is justified, for although she was
reunited with Menelaus in the *Odyssey,* in an alternate tradition he
drew his sword against her but sheathed it at the sight of her breast.
Now when the merit and dishonor of executing Helen finally stand in
the balance, Aeneas' overwhelming desire to sate his lust for revenge
tips the scales.

But as Aeneas rushes toward Helen, his mother Venus intervenes:

I turned wildly upon her,
But at that moment, clear, before my eyes—
Never before so clear—in a pure light

---

[9]Kenneth J. Reckford, "Helen in *Aeneid* 2 and 6," *Arethusa,* 14 (1981), 86, suggests
that Aeneas in this passage plays the role of Euripides' mad Orestes.

Stepping before me, radiant through the night,
My loving mother came: immortal, tall,
And lovely as the lords of heaven know her.
Catching me by the hand, she held me back,
Then with her rose-red mouth reproved me:
                                        'Son,
Why let such suffering goad you on to fury
Past control? . . .'

[2.588–94 (F:772–82)]

Contrasting with the murky light that pervaded the scene up to this point, Venus' brilliance illuminates the import of Aeneas' fury driving him to revenge. His insistence on Venus' beauty makes his refusal to mention Helen's beauty even more pointed. Venus reminds her son of the special relationship between Helen and herself, but more important, she reproaches him for giving way to uncontrolled anger and *furia*. In this episode, Venus directs Aeneas away from the example of the Iliadic Achilles who acted to satisfy vengeful desires; Aeneas must learn to forgo gratification of emotions, for unlike Achilles, whose goal was personal glory, he will need to act for the community as founder of Rome. Venus thus redirects his attention to Ascanius, Anchises, and Creusa (596–98), and admonishes him to look to the future rather than to the past. Moreover, she points out Aeneas' error in desiring to sacrifice Helen on the altar of Vesta by revealing to him the apocalyptic vision of the gods fighting against and destroying Troy; she thus demonstrates that the cruelty of the gods ("divum inclementia" [602]) and the great power of Jupiter ("numina magna deum" [623]), not Helen and Paris, are responsible for the city's fall. Finally, in the Gorgon on Athena's shield (616), Virgil again signals the doubleness of serpents as agents of destruction that nevertheless promote *fatum*.

In this episode, Aeneas confronts his first test in subordinating his private desires to *fatum*. Like the poet of the *Odyssey,* Virgil deploys the figure of Helen as a synecdoche for the authority of the *Iliad* and mystifies both Helen and the *Iliad* in order to overgo it: through Helen's first appearance in the text, he marks Aeneas' divergence from a simplified version of the Iliadic hero Achilles.

This story should perhaps have served as a warning to Dido, that Aeneas must follow a *fatum* that is larger than himself. When Aeneas recounts this story of Helen to Dido, he had already given her the mantle and veil that Helen brought with her when she eloped to Troy with Paris (1.647–52). In fact, although Helen escaped Aeneas, Dido replaces her as his unwitting victim and sacrificial substitute, for she, not Helen, meets her death by Aeneas' sword.

Helen appears for the second time in the poem during Aeneas' tour of the underworld, almost immediately after his encounter with Dido in the *Lugentes Campi,* the Mourning Fields. As in Book 2, Helen enters Book 6 indirectly, through the narrative of Deiphobus, her Trojan husband after Paris' death. In both instances, Helen is the subject of stories told about her; no longer a character within the poem, she has become a myth. Like the image of Hector who appeared to Aeneas in a dream to warn him of the impending fall of Troy (2.268–97), Deiphobus' form is severely disfigured:

> Mutilated from head to foot, his face
> And both hands cruelly torn, ears shorn away,
> Nose to the noseholes lopped by a shameful stroke.
> Barely knowing the shade who quailed before him
> Covering up his tortured face, Aeneas
> Spoke out to him.
>
> [6.494–99 (F:665–70)]

This vision of Deiphobus elicits from Aeneas a cry of disbelief: "Who chose this brutal punishment, who had / So much the upper hand of you?" (6.501–2 [F-673–74]). Through the analogy between the two episodes, Virgil insists upon Aeneas' imperative to confront in the dead brothers the destruction of Troy in order to found the future Rome. But the two episodes also point to a fundamental difference between the two brothers, dramatized in the widely divergent manner of their deaths. Hector died valiantly in combat with Achilles, and although his corpse suffered defacement (2.272), he was accorded full funeral honors. But Deiphobus, despite Aeneas' address to him as "armipotens" (6.500), acquired his wounds not from a heroic stand but as the disgraceful memorial ("monimenta" [6.512]) of Helen, and his tomb remains empty (6.505). Hence the brothers embody two aspects of Troy that Aeneas left behind: Hector's heroism in service of a doomed city and Deiphobus' decadence in succumbing to a woman.

Deiphobus' story of Helen directly evokes the Night of Troy, as portrayed by Aeneas in Book 2. Aeneas again testifies to the confusion of that night by his assumption, based on notoriously unreliable *fama,* that Deiphobus had died fighting the Greeks (6.502–4). De-

iphobus' account of the falseness of Helen recalls Aeneas' story of
how Sinon's deception allowed the Wooden Horse to enter Troy:

> When the tall deadly horse came at one bound,
> With troops crammed in its paunch, above our towers,
> She made a show of choral dance and led
> Our Phrygian women crying out on Bacchus
> Here and there—but held a torch amid them,
> Signalling to Danaans from the Height.
>
> [6.515–19 (F:692–97)]

Here Deiphobus links Helen's treacherous assistance to the enemy in
entering Troy to the Greek ruse of the Wooden Horse ("fatalis equus"
515). Moreover, his descriptions of Helen feigning ("simulans" [517])
Bacchic rites—a form of subversive madness associated with
women—and the Wooden Horse carrying the Greek soldiers in its
belly/womb (*alvus* [516]) allow him to characterize the Greek deception as a feminine one. Helen's Bacchic torch ("flammam" [518])
brings the flames consuming Troy in Book 2 into the bridal chamber
she shared with Deiphobus. There, Menelaus and Odysseus—the
arch-deceiver who played a major role in Sinon's lying story—kill the
defenseless Deiphobus in his unvigilant sleep, exhausted after a night
of deluding joys ("falsa . . . gaudia" [513]). If Helen's appearance in
Book 2 gave Virgil occasion to criticize the authority of the *Iliad*
through Aeneas' divergence from Achilles, her appearance here allows Virgil to criticize the *Odyssey* through an explicit reference to the
deadly guile of its hero. Virgil more subtly alludes to both stories told
about Odysseus and Helen in *Odyssey* 4: Helen's story recounted how
she aided Odysseus in his infiltration of Troy and rejoiced at his
slaughter of the Trojans; here we hear a similar story from a Trojan
victim's point of view. Menelaus' story, which linked Helen with
Odysseus, Deiphobus, and the Wooden Horse, as does Deiphobus'
story here, praised Odysseus' *metis* for preventing the slaughter of the
Greeks hidden in the Wooden Horse; Deiphobus' story (which includes Menelaus, the teller of the Odyssean story) indicts Odysseus'
guile turned against a defenseless victim slaughtered in his sleep.

Deiphobus' wounds serve as a testimony to his ignominious
slaughter, abetted by Helen, to whom he refers with contempt only
as *Lacaena* (511), the Laconian woman. Yet he minimizes his own
guilt by calling Menelaus the "lover" ("amanti" [526]), as though
Menelaus were the adulterer instead of the wronged husband, and by

asking the gods for retributive justice: "di, talia Grais / instaurate, pio si poenas ore reposco" (529–30), "O gods, / If with pure lips I pray, requite the Greeks / With equal suffering!" (F-710–12). Deiphobus' desire for punishment ("poenas") is undercut by Aeneas' reference to his wounds by the same word ("quis tam crudelis optavit sumere poenas?" [6.501]), which reveals Aeneas' understanding of Deiphobus' guilt. William S. Anderson points out that the cutting off of nose, ears, and genitals was the usual vengeance of an outraged husband;[10] Deiphobus' wounds therefore would have served as unmistakable signifiers of his crime. Deiphobus' story, framed by the word "poenas," thus exemplifies the endless cycle of crime and punishment from which Aeneas extricated himself when he refrained from exacting vengeance on Helen. Deiphobus himself implicitly admits his moral confusion by referring to his allotted place in Hades as a sad and sunless land of disorder, "tristis sine sole domos, loca turbida" (6.534), for his story itself is a dark tale of chaos. The difference between the two Trojan men was already implicit in Aeneas' judgment of Deiphobus' guilt even before he heard the tale, but Deiphobus makes explicit the wide gulf that separates them in his parting words to Aeneas: "i decus, i, nostrum; melioribus utere fatis" (6.546), "Go on, sir, glory of us all! Go on, / Enjoy a better destiny" (F:733–34).[11] Deiphobus remains behind and turns his back on Aeneas as the Sibyl directs him to the right, the way to Elysium, the land of eternal sunshine where Anchises will show his son the orderly procession of unborn souls into Roman history.

Aeneas' fate is "happier," because by leaving Dido he avoided Deiphobus' mistake; Deiphobus' story of Helen exemplifies the danger that Dido posed for Aeneas' epic mission. Aeneas' encounter with Dido's shade precedes by only twenty lines his meeting here with Deiphobus, so when Deiphobus enjoins Aeneas to remember, "nimium meminisse necesse est" (514), the memories evoked are not only of the night that Troy fell but also of Aeneas' love affair with Dido. Deiphobus' tale thus functions to justify for Aeneas his abandonment of Dido, by dramatizing the consequences of succumbing to sexual passion and of allowing oneself to be overpowered by a woman. Like Helen, who simulated Bacchic rites, Dido in her madness is com-

---

[10]William S. Anderson, *The Art of the Aeneid* (Englewood Cliffs, N.J.: Prentice-Hall, 1969), p. 60.

[11]Reckford, p. 93, suggests that the contrast between Aeneas and Deiphobus reenacts that between Odysseus and Agamemnon in the *Odyssey*.

pared to a Bacchante (4.300–303), and the flame on Helen's torch
anticipates the fires on Dido's funeral pyre. Just as Helen hid Deiphobus' weapons (6.523–24), so Dido appropriates Aeneas' sword as
the instrument of her suicide; both heroes are unmanned by their loss
of weapons to women. These associative links, however, also point
to important differences between the two women: unlike Helen,
Dido directed her destructive and violent impulses toward herself
rather than toward her husband/lover. Similarly, Dido's *monimentum*
of her love for Aeneas was the horse she gave Ascanius (5.570–72),
more benign than the Wooden Horse or Helen's *monimenta*—
Deiphobus' disfiguring wounds—or Pasiphae's memorial of abomin-
able love—the Minotaur ("Veneris monimenta nefandae" [6.26]).
Each love affair has left traces and consequences, and Aeneas cannot
ignore them, despite Mercury's command to leave Dido behind. His
encounters with both Dido and Deiphobus in the underworld are
reminders that Dido has left an even more powerful and compelling
monimentum in Aeneas' mind than her actual gift of the Sidonian horse
and that Helen's *monimentum* is even greater than Deiphobus'
wounds, horrible as they may be.

The two portraits of Helen in Books 2 and 6, then, may appear to
contradict one another, in that Aeneas describes her as cowering and
helpless and Deiphobus represents her as a dangerous agent of destruction.[12] In fact, the contradictory portraits encapsulate the doubleness of Helen—as did the two stories told about her in *Odyssey* 4.
But Virgil demystifies Helen's role as a scapegoat in these stories: in
Book 2, Venus reveals to Aeneas that Helen is not responsible for
Troy's fall, although she offers instead another mystification, that the
gods are fighting against Troy. In Book 6, Aeneas shows that he
understands Deiphobus' guilt and his projection of that guilt on
Helen as scapegoat. Yet Aeneas is not exempt from similar mystifica-
tions when he himself confronts Helen's legacy in various women he
encounters after leaving Troy. Although Virgil demystifies the process of scapegoating Helen as *casus belli,* he remystifies her as a scapegoat representing the authority of the Homeric epics: her two appearances in the poem occasion his assertion of Aeneas' superiority over
simplified versions of Achilles and Odysseus. Yet Virgil and Aeneas
find it more difficult to go beyond Dido, Helen's sacrifical substitute,
whose presence dominates the first half of Virgil's epic.

---

[12]Reckford, p. 96, says of the "discrepancy between Helen's acts in *Aeneid* 2 and 6":
"Virgil may have thought of doing something about it; but there is much traditional
material and meaning in both versions." He links it to the "two contrasting 'Helen and
Odysseus' stories" in the *Odyssey.*

Infelix Dido

Aeneas' love affair with Dido and his subsequent abandonment of her is perhaps the most problematic episode in the *Aeneid*, analogous to the later books of the *Odyssey* which were marked by uncertainty concerning Penelope's role and motivation, and equaled in its ambiguity within the *Aeneid* only by its final episode, Aeneas' killing of Turnus. It is also a crucial episode for Virgil's narrative of the Roman Empire's origins, for he represents the love affair as having disastrous epic repercussions: not only does Dido's detention of Aeneas threaten his mission to found Rome; when Aeneas leaves Dido, Carthage loses its queen, and her curse will bring about the future enmity between Carthage and Rome—the Punic Wars. Moreover, since Dido's historical type is Cleopatra, Aeneas approximates Julius Caesar and avoids Antony's fate by leaving the foreign queen behind.[13]

Along with Aeneas' sinister gift of Helen's robes to Dido, Helen's two appearances in the poem suggest an unmistakable link between the epic heroines of the *Iliad* and the *Aeneid:* in Book 2, Aeneas speaks of Helen within his narration to Dido, and in Book 6, he hears Deiphobus' story of Helen immediately after encountering Dido's shade in the *Lugentes Campi*. In fact, Iarbas, Dido's principal suitor, refers to Aeneas as another Paris (4.215), thereby implying that Dido is the second Helen. Aeneas is a second Paris for Dido in that she has pledged her troth to her first husband, Sychaeus.[14] The uncertainty of the Iliadic Helen's role in her elopement with Paris resurfaces in the ambiguity of Dido's passion for Aeneas and her subsequent suicide. The central issue of the Dido episode, then, becomes the question of Aeneas' and Dido's responsibility as ethical agents in the face of *fatum*, unfolded through various interventions by the gods.

Early in the poem, Jupiter, having reassured Venus of the fulfillment of Aeneas' *fatum* in the establishment of the Roman Empire, sends Mercury to Dido so that she will receive Aeneas with kindness (1.303–304). Upon Dido's first mention in the poem, Virgil already suggests her eventual victimization by Jupiter's—and hence Aeneas'—*fatum* when he describes her as "fati nescia" (1.299), igno-

---

[13]On the multiple historical correlations of episodes in the *Aeneid*, see Kenneth Quinn, *Virgil's Aeneid: A Critical Description* (London: Routledge & Kegan Paul, 1968), p. 55.

[14]See *Heroides*, 7.97: "Exige, laese pudor, poenas! violate Sychaei . . ." Gordon Williams, *Tradition and Originality in Roman Poetry* (Oxford: Oxford Univ. Press, 1968), p. 378, explains the honorific title of *univira* given to women who were faithful to their first husband; there can be no question of a second marriage.

rant of fate. Her tragedy will arise precisely because she is not privy to Jupiter's *fatum*—his pronouncements to Venus, which immediately precede this scene. Moreover, Jupiter's concluding image of *Furor* bound within Janus' gates (1.294–96) foretells not only the Augustan peace but also the fulfillment of Aeneas' *fatum,* through projecting *furor* on Dido and then sacrificing her.

Immediately following Mercury's descent from heaven, Venus appears to Aeneas, who has spent a night of anxiety shipwrecked on strange shores and separated from most of his men. Venus' primary purpose is to direct Aeneas toward Carthage, and to this end she informs him of Dido, the ruler of the realm: "imperium Dido . . . regit" (1.340). Dido, though a female ruler ("dux femina" 1.364), is, like Aeneas, a leader of exiles, who was compelled to flee Tyre to establish a *nova Karthago*. It is later revealed that the Phoenicians, like the Trojans, were storm-tossed before reaching Carthage (1.442). Moreover, Dido's former life in Tyre strikingly resembles Aeneas' experiences in Troy, as described in Book 2: Dido's husband Sychaeus was butchered by her brother Pygmalion before his very altars ("impius ante aras" [1.349]), in a manner that recalls Priam's murder; the dead Sychaeus came to Dido in a dream and instructed her to take flight, just as Hector's and Creusa's shades had come to Aeneas.

In Book 2, Aeneas tells how Creusa was left behind in the confusion of the Night of Troy (2.736–95).[15] As Aeneas' Trojan wife, and thus a part of the old Troy that fell, she must give way to the "regia coniunx" (2.783) who will fulfill the necessary condition for his founding of the new Troy. Aeneas, however, is not unaffected by this loss: he rushes back into the burning city only to be stopped by Creusa's shade, who tells him that he must not look behind but rather move on. In relating this story to Dido, Aeneas perhaps gives two conflicting messages: that he was a loving husband (Creusa calls him "o dulcis coniunx" [2.777]), but that his wife was sacrificed to his *fatum* in Italy, as Creusa's shade herself informs him (777–78). In fact, Aeneas will experience another separation from a woman associated with a city he must leave behind, though Dido will prove to be not as placable as Creusa was in deferring to his Roman *fatum*.

Dido, too, repeats with Aeneas her love for her first husband Sychaeus, who was "magno miserae dilectus amore" (1.344), greatly

---

[15]See Putnam, *Poetry of the Aeneid,* pp. 41–45, for an analysis of Aeneas' loss of Creusa in terms of Virgil's earlier treatment of Orpheus and Euridyce in the fourth *Georgic* (Austin, ad 2.795, p. 287, notes that Virgil changed the traditional name of Aeneas' wife, Euridyca, to Creusa).

loved by a wretched woman. The analogies between Dido and Aeneas as exiled leaders bereft of their spouses point to the similarity of their circumstances and their susceptibility to each other when they actually meet. Yet by contrast with the *Odyssey,* where Penelope's ability as a ruler and her likemindedness with Odysseus in this respect made possible their reunion, here Dido's and Aeneas' analogous duties as rulers of separate realms make a lasting union between them impossible and the tragic outcome inevitable.

Aeneas' exchange with his mother Venus further contributes to his susceptibility to Dido. Venus appears to him in disguise as a Tyrian maid, and Virgil compares her to a Thracian Amazon, Harpalyce (1.316–17). This disguise links Venus to Dido, for when Aeneas first sees Dido, Virgil will juxtapose her portrait to an image of the Amazon queen, Penthesilea. Accordingly, Venus carries the gear of a huntress ("venatrix" 319), a bow on her shoulder, which leads Aeneas to cry out: "o dea certe! / (an Phoebi soror?)" (328–29), "O, Goddess, beyond doubt! Apollo's sister" (F:446). Dido, too, will be compared to Diana, and this additional link between Venus and Dido not only reinforces the connection between Aeneas' mother and his lover, but the goddess of love's masquerade as the goddess of virginity will find an ironic corollary in Dido's transformation from a chaste queen to an impassioned lover. Moreover, Venus' gear introduces the important motif of the hunt, a motif which Virgil will exploit to suggest the predatory and sinister aspects of the relationship between the two lovers: Dido in her wounded passion will be compared to a hunted hind, and they will be finally united in a cave while on an actual hunt.

Befitting her gear as a huntress, Venus' attitude toward Aeneas verges on the predatory. After she has accomplished the purpose of the interview, Venus abruptly cuts short her son's tale of his sufferings to reiterate her command to go forward: "perge modo" (389, 401). The mother finally reveals her identity to her son only as she leaves him, compelling him to cry out:

> You! cruel, too!
> Why tease your son so often with disguises?
> Why may we not join hands and speak and hear
> The simple truth?
> [1.407–9 (F:558–61)]

Aeneas' frustrating inability to touch those closest to him recalls his unsatisfying leavetaking with Creusa's shade: "Three times / I tried to put my arms around her neck, / Three times enfolded nothing, as the wraith / Slipped through my fingers, bodiless as wind, / Or like a flitting dream" (2.792–94 [F:1028–32]). Yet unlike the shade of Creusa who spoke tenderly to Aeneas, his own mother, Venus, speaks to him only as the agent of impersonal *fatum,* even more so than in her earlier appearance to him in Book 2—where she came to him undisguised ("confessa deam" [2:591]). The juxtaposition of this episode to its Odyssean subtext, the reunion of Athena and Odysseus upon his landing on Ithaca, makes Venus' distant treatment of her son even more striking in its contrast with Athena's affectionate interchange with her favorite mortal. Aeneas thus understandably feels comforted by the almost maternal sympathy shown him by Dido, whom Virgil links to Aeneas' unavailable mother by associating both women to the Amazons and Diana. Since Venus refuses to listen to his chronicle of *Troia antiqua* (375) and of his identity as *pius Aeneas* (378), he will recount to Dido instead the lengthy tale—extending through Books 2 and 3—cut short by his mother.

Before he meets Dido, however, Aeneas has occasion to marvel at the vital signs of civilization being built—walls, citadels, dwellings, even a theater (421–29). The sight of the fruitful industry of the Carthaginian workers, compared by Virgil to that of bees in a famous simile (430–36), moves Aeneas to apostrophize in envy: "o fortunati, quorum iam moenia surgunt!" (437), "How fortunate these are / Whose city walls are rising here and now!" (F:595–96). For Aeneas, who left the ashes of fallen Troy only to found wrongheaded and pathetic replicas of his once magnificent city, such as Aeneadae (3.18) and Pergamum (3.133), and to stumble upon Helenus' and Andromache's *parva Troia* (3.349) with its dried up counterfeit of Xanthus, the potential splendor of Carthage holds an understandably irresistible attraction.[16]

In the temple of Juno, where he takes shelter and sanctuary, Aeneas finds the ultimate sign of civilization that bespeaks its people's reverence for the gods. The scenes on the temple's walls depicting scenes from Troy, moreover, exemplify the builders' knowledge of other and past civilizations, in particular Aeneas' own. Aeneas does not

---

[16]See Lowry Nelson, Jr., "Baudelaire and Virgil: A Reading of 'Le Cygne,'" *CL,* 13 (1961), 332–45, for a discussion of Andromache and Helenus, "whose lives are over and who can only live them out in repetition and stasis" (p. 333). Of the "Troy of the mind" he states: "Memory . . . is both liberation from the present and at the same time, ironically, bondage to the past. . . . The human condition is one of inescapable exile" (p. 345).

know, however, that the temple is dedicated to Juno, the tutelary goddess of Carthage and Aeneas' most determined enemy; in fact, the pictures on its walls celebrate the destruction of the city she hated. His obsession with his Trojan past, as evidenced in his uncompleted tale to Venus, resurfaces here in his rapt and teary absorption in the empty imaging, "pictura . . . inani" (1.464).

Virgil masterfully connects Aeneas' past to his present by juxtaposing the final scene on the temple walls—portraits of Aeneas and the *bellatrix* Penthesilea—and Aeneas' first glimpse of Dido. The pairing of Aeneas and Penthesilea prefigures that of Aeneas and Dido: just as Penthesilea in her fiery furor ("furens . . . ardet" [491]) battled against male warriors, so Dido will set herself in passionate opposition against Aeneas. But perhaps more important is the disjunction between the past and the present, between the figures painted on the temple's walls and those outside it: Aeneas can no longer be the hero on the plains of Troy, and his coming to Carthage will end Dido's career as a warrior queen similar to the Amazon Penthesilea. Dido later explains that Carthage's defensive strategy, which barred from her shores Aeneas' comrades separated from their leader, had been necessitated by the hostility of surrounding states and the precariousness of a newly founded city (562–64). Accepting, however, Ilioneus' supplication that they come with peaceful intent (527–29) and that they hail as their king the *pius*, just, and glorious Aeneas whom Dido would not regret receiving (544–49), the queen sets aside these defensive measures to embrace, as it were, the enemy:

> The city I build is yours; haul up your ships;
> Trojan and Tyrian will be all one to me.
> If only he were here, your king himself,
> Caught by the same easterly, Aeneas!
>
> [1.573–76 (F:778–81)]

The dramatic irony in Ilioneus' supplication—signaled also by his portentous name—and in Dido's acceptance of his request underscores Dido's ignorance of the consequences of her actions and prepares the way for Virgil's portrayal of her as a tragic heroine.

Dido's fatal reception of the Trojans within her city's walls, which repeats Troy's acceptance of the Wooden Horse, leads to the slackening of her defensive chastity. At Dido's first appearance in the poem, Virgil compares the Carthaginian queen to Diana:

As on Eurotas bank or Cynthus ridge
Diana trains her dancers, and behind her
On every hand the mountain nymphs appear,
A myriad converging; with her quiver
Slung on her shoulders, in her stride she seems
The tallest, taller by a head than any,
And joy pervades Latona's quiet heart:
So Dido seemed, in such delight she moved
Amid her people, cheering on the toil
Of a kingdom in the making. At the door
Of the goddess' shrine, under the temple dome,
All hedged about with guards on her high throne,
She took her seat. Then she began to give them
Judgments and rulings, to apportion work
With fairness, or assign some task by lot.

[1.498–508 (F:678–92)]

As in Venus' earlier appearance to Aeneas, the huntress' gear ("pharetram" [500]) and arms ("saepta armis" [506]) link Dido to both Penthesilea and Diana. Through this simile Virgil insists upon the necessary connection between Dido's chastity and her success as ruler of her city. As in the case of the Italian warrior-maiden Camilla, Virgil believes that the strict boundary between masculine and feminine spheres can only be crossed by a woman if she forgoes her female sexuality. Dido's all-consuming passion for Aeneas will therefore prove fatal to her role as queen of Carthage.

The meeting between Dido and Aeneas, which has been so carefully prepared, is beset by further dramatic ironies. Perhaps the best example can be found in Aeneas' praise of Dido for her generosity:

May the gods—
And surely there are powers that care for goodness,
Surely somewhere justice counts—may they
And your own consciousness of acting well
Reward you as they should. What age so happy
Brought you to birth? How splendid were your parents
To have conceived a being like yourself!
So long as brooks flow seaward, and the shadows
Play over mountain slopes, and highest heaven
Feeds the stars, your name and your distinction
Go with me, whatever lands may call me.

[1.603–10 (F:821–31)]

Dido's fate resulting from her acceptance of Aeneas will indeed question the *iustitia* (604) of the gods. His promise to her of everlasting fame ("honos nomenque . . . laudesque" [609]) will be fulfilled not for her generosity to him but for her sacrifice to Aeneas' *fatum* that calls him to another land. In addition, his praise of Dido's parentage will find an ironic echo in her later accusation that he could not be the descendant of Dardanus but must have been sired by Caucasus' rocks (4.365–67). Finally, Dido's compassionate reply to Aeneas, "non ignara mali miseris succurrere disco" (1.630), that having experienced pain she has learned to help the suffering, reveals the pathos of her ignorance: the *malum* she has suffered will prove insignificant compared to that which Aeneas brings. These ironies dramatize Dido's victimization by Aeneas, however unintended, and her sacrifice, through the manipulations of Venus and Juno, to Jupiter's *fatum*.

The scene is thus set for the fateful banquet where Aeneas will recite his seductive story to Dido and where she will be inflamed to passion by Cupid masquerading as Ascanius.[17] Just as Odysseus required the civilized setting of Phaeacia to tell his story, so Aeneas finds an appropriate milieu in Dido's opulent palace:

> Now the queen's household made her great hall glow
> As they prepared a banquet in the kitchens.
> Embroidered table cloths, proud crimson-dyed,
> Were spread, and set with massive silver plate,
> Or gold, engraved with brave deeds of her fathers,
> A sequence carried down through many captains
> In a long line from the founding of the race.
>
> [1.637–42 (F:870–76)]

Dido, like Aeneas, enjoys a long and distinguished line, and Aeneas' tale of his own origins will complement Dido's genealogy figured on the tables. Aeneas will be speaking to an audience already familiar with and sympathetic to his story, as evidenced in the scenes from Troy on the temple of Juno and in Dido's admiring words: "Who has not heard / Of the people of Aeneas, of Troy city, / Her valors and her heroes?" (565–66 [F:767–69]).

---

[17]Virgil takes this incident from Book 3 of Apollonius Rhodius' *Argonautica*, where Medea is wounded by Eros' arrow and falls in love with Jason, her father's enemy. See Williams, *Tradition and Originality*, pp. 374–87, for a discussion of how Virgil diverges from Apollonius in his treatment of Dido.

The presence of the bard Iopas, like that of Demodocus among the Phaeacians, signals civilized life in Carthage; following his song of the origins of things, Aeneas tells of his own origins ("prima . . . origine" [753]) and of the originary fall of civilization—which prefigures the destruction he will bring to Carthage. Aeneas' story is ambiguous, for it carries two contradictory messages: that he is compelled by *fatum* to move on regardless of his personal desires and happiness, but also that he is strongly attached to his Trojan past and finds it difficult to go beyond it. Dido, who already admires his reputation as a Trojan hero, falls irretrievably in love with his past without regard for his *fatum* that calls him elsewhere. It is ironic that Aeneas' telling of his past seems necessary for him to come to terms with it and hence to go beyond it. Aeneas' seduction of Dido by his narrative repeats Sinon's deception of the Trojans by his tale: this time, however, the victim becomes the unwitting aggressor. Moreover, along with the story, Aeneas bestows upon Dido Helen's robes and the scepter of Priam's daughter, presents snatched from the ruins of Ilium ("munera praeterea, Iliacis erepta ruinis" [647]), thus bequeathing Troy's fate to Carthage.

Virgil, however, gives an additional explanation for Dido's passion for Aeneas: through Venus' agency, through her new wiles and schemes ("novas artis, nova . . . / consilia" [657–58]), Dido is inflamed by Cupid in the guise of Ascanius. The injection of fire ("ignem" [660]) and poison ("veneno" [688]) signals the onslaught of mad passion. These metaphorical flames are part of Troy's legacy (679) and prefigure the actual flames on Dido's funeral pyre. It is ironic, moreover, that Venus is said to fear Tyrian deception ("domum . . . ambiguam Tyriosque bilinguis" [661]) when it is actually Aeneas who will turn out to be double-tongued in his story and his later desertion of Dido.

What are we to make of this "divine intervention"?[18] Dido's pas-

---

[18]For a discussion of the various roles played by the gods in the poem and a survey of critical opinions on the problem, see W. R. Johnson, *Darkness Visible: A Study of Vergil's Aeneid* (Berkeley: Univ. of California Press, 1976), pp. 161–63n. In the case of Dido, Johnson holds that "Virgil chooses to create a baffling design in which the supernatural and the natural, the physical and the psychological, divine intervention and psychological realism, are merged together implausibly" (p. 44). In comparing the "mimesis of erotic complusion" in the *Iliad* and the *Aeneid,* Johnson finds that Homer's representation of Helen's confrontation with Aphrodite is "dramatic and externalized," whereas Virgil's representation of Dido's passion for Aeneas is blurred and uncertain. He sees this contrast to be paradigmatic of the difference between Homer and Virgil. On the gods, see also Williams, *Technique and Ideas,* pp. 17–39; and

sion is entirely explicable in human and natural terms: she is aware of Aeneas' fame as a Trojan hero and is touched by his affecting story. Even Virgil's representation of her attraction to Ascanius, verging on the grotesque, can be explained by her childlessness, for when Aeneas is about to depart, she laments that he did not at least leave her with his child (4.327–30). Similarly, Andromache, in her protracted mourning for her husband, expressed her own attachment to Ascanius, who reminded her of Hector's son (3.489). Moreover, Venus had told Aeneas that Dido passionately loved her first husband, Sychaeus, and Dido herself says of her love for Aeneas: "agnosco veteris vestigia flammae" (4.23) "I recognize / The signs of the old flame" (F:31–32). Thus it is perfectly plausible that Dido, a widow who had pledged her troth to her dead husband and had spurned so many suitors until now, would succumb completely and fatally because her feelings had for so long been repressed.

At the same time, the "divine intervention" by Venus in setting off Dido's passion and that by Venus and Juno in planning the "marriage" between Dido and Aeneas provides another explanation for her unhappy love affair: in seeking either to promote *fatum* or to hinder it, the gods victimize Dido as their instrument. In fact, Venus and Juno agree on a common strategy although their purposes are diametrically opposed: Venus intends to prevent the building of the fortresses of Carthage which will threaten Rome, and Juno wishes to detain Aeneas so that the new Troy will never be founded. The unscrupulous manipulation of Dido by the two goddesses shows how little they regard human lives in exploiting them for their own ends.

Thus, as in so many Greek tragedies, the "divine" and personal responsibilities seem evenly weighed. In fact, Virgil likens Dido in her plight to tragic heroes:

> as Pentheus gone mad
> Sees the oncoming Eumenides and sees
> A double sun and double Thebes appear,
> Or as when, hounded on the stage, Orestes
> Runs from a mother armed with burning brands,
> With serpents hellish black,
> And in the doorway squat the Avenging Ones.
>
> [4.469–73 (F:649–55)]

Susanne L. Wofford's forthcoming *The Choice of Achilles: Action and Figure in Epic Narrative from Homer to Milton,* for a discussion of the gods as providing a narrative dimension to the figurative scheme of the poem.

Pentheus' character contained his fate, despite Dionysus' agency in bringing it about; Orestes was held responsible for his murder of Clytemnestra, despite Apollo's command to avenge his father. Dido, too, shares with these heroes an uneasy and problematic balance between culpability and innocence, and the pervasive dramatic ironies in her first meeting with Aeneas announce the representation of her as a tragic heroine.[19] These allusions to tragedy bespeak Virgil's own ambivalence toward tragedy itself: whereas these links between Dido and tragic heroes grant her a stature beyond that of a disposable instrument of Aeneas' *fatum,* at the same time the references to tragedy suggest irrationality, violence, and excess—associated with the feminine and, more specifically, with maternal power—as they do here. Under the overarching patriarchal order, Virgil's epic narrative subsumes tragedy's interest in the subjectivity of Dido.

At the beginning of Book 4, Dido's condition seems already beyond remedy: "At regina gravi iamdudum saucia cura / vulnus alit venis et caeco carpitur igni" (4.1–2), "The queen, for her part, all that evening ached / With longing that her heart's blood fed, a wound / Or inward fire eating her away" (F:1–3). The oscillation between the passive ("gravi," "carpitur") and the active ("alit") suggests the undecidability of whether she is a subject or an object. Even as she confides in Anna the frenzy of her passion, she still invokes her former self in her concern with *Pudor* and her pledged troth to Sychaeus. Anna, as typical confidante, encourages Dido's passion by pointing out the pragmatic advantage of joining Carthage to Troy: "With Trojan soldiers as companions in arms / By what exploits will Punic glory grow!" (48–49 [F:69–70]). The wrongheaded advice proves to be just sufficient to push Dido over the edge: "This counsel fanned the flame, already kindled, / Giving her hesitant sister hope, and set her / Free of scruple" (54–55 [F:76–78]).

Dido's furious wandering, compelled by this "flamma" (66) and "vulnus" (67), is compared to that of a hunted and wounded hind:

> Unlucky Dido, burning, in her madness
> Roamed through all the city, like a doe
> Hit by an arrow shot from far away
> By a shepherd hunting in the Cretan woods—
> Hit by surprise, nor could the hunter see

[19]Many critics have discussed Virgil's use of the tragic mode. See, especially, Quinn, pp. 323–49.

His flying steel had fixed itself in her;
But though she runs for life through copse and glade
The fatal shaft clings to her side.

[4.68–73 (F:95–102)]

This simile dramatizes Dido's pathetic victimization by Venus and by
her own passion, which overtakes her unawares, as the hind was so
struck. The figurative hunt in the simile becomes literal in the actual
hunt planned by Juno for the purpose of snaring Dido into a marriage
with Aeneas (117–18). By means of a storm, Juno drives the two into
a cave while the hunters gird the glades with nets (121), and so
transforms the hunters into the hunted. Although Virgil earlier compared Dido to Diana, here he likens Aeneas to Apollo, the god of the
hunt (143–50); if Aeneas is the hunter here, Dido is the prey, as she
was in the simile comparing her to a hunted hind. The simile's natural
landscape where the wounded hind roamed becomes literal in the
hunting scenes, and the violence of Juno's storm mirrors the untamed
wildness of the lovers' passion:

Primal Earth herself and Nuptial Juno
Opened the ritual, torches of lightning blazed,
High Heaven became witness to the marriage,
And nymphs cried out wild hymns from a mountain top.

[4.166–68 (F:229–32)]

The shrieking of the Nymphs ("ulul04arunt" [168]), like the comparison of Dido to a wounded hind roaming the woods, anticipates
the onslaught of Dido's Bacchic madness upon her discovery of
Aeneas' intention to leave her.[20] Already at this moment of their
union, Virgil foreshadows the ending, for the Carthaginian women
will also cry out ("ululatu" [667]) upon Dido's death. He also makes
explicit this tragic outcome: "ille dies primus leti primusque
malorum / causa fuit" (169–70), "That day was the first cause of
death, and first / Of sorrow" (F:233–34). The ambiguity of the "marriage" sanctioned by Earth and *pronuba* Juno (166), but not by human
witnesses, allows Dido to call it marriage ("coniugium vocat" [172])
and Aeneas to repudiate it: "I never held the torches of a bride-
groom, / Never entered upon the pact of marriage" (338–39 [F:467–

---

[20]Compare with *Heroides* 7.95–96: "audieram vocem; nymphas ululasse putavi—/
Eumenides fatis signa dedere meis!"

68]).[21] Moreover, it is "Dido" and the "dux . . . Troianus" (165) who enter the cave together; Virgil's use of this periphrasis already suggests that Aeneas' role as the leader of his people will compel him to leave her.

On one level, Dido herself sets in motion the sequence of events leading to her tragic end. Assuming her marriage to Aeneas, she no longer shows concern for her *fama* (170), and *Fama* accordingly brings the news to Iarbas, her principal suitor. Iarbas obviously feels that even though Dido rules Carthage, she has no right openly to defy patriarchal prerogatives by refusing him and then accepting Aeneas. Inflamed ("accensus" [203]) by what he hears, Iarbas invokes Jupiter, the god of patriarchy, who in turn sends Mercury to Aeneas reminding him of his *fatum*. But that Mercury comes to Aeneas and not to Dido—unlike in the Odyssean subtext where Hermes came to Calypso on a similar errand—again points to the gods' victimization of Dido, who is kept in the dark until the end. It is not only the gods who do not honor her with an explanation; Aeneas himself seeks to deceive Dido concerning his departure: "they were to keep it secret, / Seeing the excellent Dido had no notion" (290–92 [F:397–98]).

The same *Fama* that was instrumental in this crisis now sets off Dido's Bacchic madness by bringing to her the news of Aeneas' departure:

> Furious, at her wits' end,
> She traversed the whole city, all aflame
> With rage, like a Bacchante driven wild
> By emblems shaken, when the mountain revels
> Of the odd year possess her, when the cry
> Of Bacchus rises and Cithaeron calls
> All through the shouting night.
>
> [4.300–303 (F:409–15)]

This simile links Dido to the other Bacchic women in the poem—Helen in Book 6 and Amata in Book 7—but Virgil distinguishes between Helen and Amata, who feign Bacchic rites for subversive purposes, and Dido, whom he only compares to a Bacchante. Nevertheless, the simile insists upon the grotesqueness of Dido's hysteria,

[21]Williams, *Tradition and Originality*, pp. 379–80, sees this marriage as a formal Roman wedding translated into supernatural terms; moreover, the ceremony was not necessary, for what distinguished marriage from cohabitation was consent and *affectio maritalis*. Johnson, however, discusses this as "an extreme and crucial example of deliberately confused and confusing impressionism" (p. 163n).

thereby justifying Aeneas' abandonment of her. Virgil also compares Dido to Pentheus, a male ruler who becomes seduced by Dionysus and the power of his repressed femininity, sexuality, and irrationality, and who meets his horrible end at the hands of his mother. By comparing Dido to a Bacchante, Virgil has her embody the threat of female sexuality and the threat of the violent mother against which Aeneas must defend himself.

Since she continues to roam the city and not the wilds, Dido still attempts to persuade Aeneas to reconsider his departure in two lengthy speeches that enclose his much shorter reply: "pro re pauca loquar" (337), "As to the event, a few words" (F:465). Dido punctuates her speeches with "perfide" (305, 366), emphasizing the betrayal of their personal relationship, but Aeneas invokes Italy as his love, "hic amor, haec patria est" (347), and their duties as rulers:

> If, as a Phoenician,
> You are so given to the charms of Carthage,
> Libyan city that it is, then tell me,
> Why begrudge the Teucrians new lands
> For homesteads in Ausonia?
>
> [4.347–50 (F:479–83)]

Dido's Bacchic frenzy prepares for this confrontation between what Virgil represents as feminine and masculine concerns, between the private and the public, the emotional and the rational.[22] Mercury's taunting Aeneas for being "uxorius" (266) and his subsequent warning in the dream concerning woman's mutability, "varium et mutabile semper / femina" (569–70), dramatizes this radical opposition between the sexes. Aeneas must avoid the fate of Pentheus and keep his male self intact from the threat of the feminine—the irrational and the violent. Mercury's sententia ostensibly refers to the danger posed by Dido's emotional outburst upon learning of Aeneas' plans to embark; but from Dido's point of view, it is Aeneas who has proven to be "varium et mutabile" in his dealings with her.

Aeneas' realization, perhaps externalized by Mercury's "intervention," that he should be building his own city rather than Dido's,

---

[22]See Charles Segal, *Dionysiac Poetics and Euripides' Bacchae* (Princeton: Princeton Univ. Press, 1982), chapter 6, "Arms and the Man: Sex Roles and Rites of Passage." He argues that the *Bacchae* reinforces, rather than eliminates, sexual differentiation, and that it gives "not the solution to these tensions but their dramatic representation in the most extreme and uncompromising terms" (p. 213).

does not leave him free of conflicts, however. Although Aeneas is terrified by this reminder of his duty to *fatum* (280), which precludes his giving ear to Dido's pleas, he feels pain that he must nevertheless suppress: "The man by Jove's command held fast his eyes / And fought down the emotion in his heart" (331–32 [F:456–57]).

> Duty-bound,
> Aeneas, though he struggled with desire
> To calm and comfort her in all her pain,
> To speak to her and turn her mind from grief,
> And though he sighed his heart out, shaken still
> With love of her, yet took the course heaven gave him
> And went back to the fleet.
>
> [4.393–96 (F:545–51)]

This final confrontation between the two lovers, then, is beset by uncertainties concerning their blame and innocence: Dido is victimized by Aeneas' *fatum* as well as by her own passions, but Virgil justifies Aeneas' abandonment of Dido by his imperative to heed Jupiter's *fatum*.

Dido's suicide, though on one level a logical conclusion to her mad passion in literalizing the figurative flames consuming her, is also ambiguous in import. She prepares her tragic exit in stealth, just as Aeneas sought to hide his proposed departure from her. Her staging of her death verges on grotesque melodrama: having invoked various possible endings to her own tragedy, such as Pentheus' dismemberment and Atreus' serving to Thyestes of his own son (600–602), Dido writes her own. It is a dramatic scene laden with eroticism, with apposite props: a death self-inflicted by her lover's sword, surrounded by his garments, on the bed they once shared.[23] This tragic death, however, is also epic in its import, for it is likened to the fall of Carthage:

[23]Nicole Loraux, *Tragic Ways of Killing a Woman,* trans. Anthony Forster (Cambridge: Harvard Univ. Press, 1987), pp. 14–15, notes that death by the sword was considered male and virile, as opposed to hanging, which was considered a female mode of death. But she also goes on to note that "a suicide that shed blood was associated with maternity, through which a wife, in her 'heroic' pains of childbirth, found complete fulfillment" (p. 17). She concludes that the woman in tragedy is more entitled to play the man in her death than vice versa: "For women there is liberty in tragedy—liberty in death."

as wails and sobs
With women's outcry echoed in the palace
And heaven's high air gave back the beating din,
As though all Carthage or old Tyre fell
To storming enemies, and out of hand,
Flames billowed on the roofs of men and gods.

[4.667–71 (F:924–29)]

The unmistakable echoes from the Night of Troy, as well as from the very first day of their union, point to the fact that the epic subsumes the tragic, as Aeneas' *fatum* did Dido's passion and her successful sovereignty over Carthage. The final ambiguity of her death is summed up in the terseness of "nec fato merita nec morte peribat" (696), "not at her fated span / Nor as she merited" (F:963–94), and in the tension between "misera ante diem," unhappy before her time, and "subitoque accensa furore" (697), inflamed and driven mad: her death is at once a sacrifice and an act of self-destruction.[24]

Venus' introduction to Dido's story, "longa est iniuria, longae / ambages" (1.341–42), long is the tale of wrong, long its winding course—the final word meaning both "windings" as in a labyrinth and ambiguity—describes Virgil's own story of Dido.[25] The tensions between Dido's chastity and her passion, her success as a ruler and her self-destruction as a lover, her sympathetic nurturing of Aeneas and her later threat to overwhelm him, cannot be easily resolved. Despite his oft-noted sympathy for Dido, however, Virgil does not entirely demystify her role as a sacrificial victim for Aeneas' Roman *fatum*. For example, Virgil represents Dido's love for her husband as diseased— she is called "aegram / . . . amantem" (351–52)—thus preparing the way for a similarly negative representation of her passion for Aeneas. He also has Dido embody first Aeneas' need for the nurturing moth- er, then his fear of the engulfing, destructive (and sexual) mother, by linking her with Aeneas' mother, Venus, and by representing her as a woman frustrated in her maternal instincts. In this, Virgil inverts the

---

[24]This ambiguity is also present in Dido's own epitaph (which parallels Dido's staging of her suicide) in *Heroides* 7.195–96: "PRAEBUIT AENEAS ET CAUSAM MORTIS ET ENSEM; / IPSA SUA DIDO CONCIDIT USA MANU." Austin, ed., *P. Vergili Maronis Aeneidos Liber Quartus* (Oxford: Oxford Univ. Press, 1955), ad 696, p. 200, however, thinks that "Virgil's judgment here is explicit" and that Dido is exonerated in "merita nec morte."

[25]On the symbolic import of labyrinths in the poem, see W. F. Jackson Knight, *Cumaean Gates* (Oxford: Oxford Univ. Press, 1936).

Odyssey's transformation of Circe from a sinister witch to a helpful counselor and renders more explicit Telemachus' anxieties about achieving independence from his mother, as well as his suspicions about her sexuality. Virgil explains Aeneas' vulnerability to maternal influence by the absence of the father, for Aeneas speaks of Anchises' death as "labor extremus" (3.714), his last ordeal before arriving in Carthage. Thus the Dido episode represents Aeneas' passage from a dependence on a maternal figure to a position of leadership in a society of male comrades.[26] It is telling that after leaving Dido behind, Aeneas lands in Sicily near the tomb of Anchises, which allows him to honor his dead father by sacrificing at his tomb and by celebrating funeral games—an athletic competition among males. Virgil marks Aeneas' assumption of patriarchal responsibility by repeatedly referring to him as *pater* during the funeral games (e.g., 348, 358, 424, 461).

Thus Virgil does not show, as he did in the stories about Helen, the process through which Dido is loaded with qualities inimical to the fulfillment of Aeneas' *fatum*, so that she can be sacrificed. A more extreme example of this mystification can be found in Aeneas' description to Dido of the Harpies and Scylla with virgin faces and disgusting nether parts: "With young girls' faces, but foul ooze below, / Talons for hands, pale famished nightmare mouths" (3.216–18 [F:300–301]); "First she looks human—a fair-breasted girl / Down to the groin; but then, below, a monster / Creature of the sea, a wolvish belly / Merging in dolphins' tails" (3.426–28 [F:573–76]). In fact, such mystification will continue in the Italian section of the poem, where the anxiety-producing doubleness of female passion or sexuality—emblematized in the Harpies and Scylla—will be divided between the silent and passive virgin, Lavinia, and the grotesquely hysterical mother, Amata. But before Aeneas reaches Italy, he will have to come to terms with Dido's death: her threat that her shade will haunt him (4.384–87) will indeed come true.

In the underworld in Book 6, Aeneas briefly encounters the shade of Dido in the *Lugentes Campi*, the Mourning Fields, where reside "those whom pitiless love consumed / With cruel wasting" (6.442

---

[26]Segal, *Dionysiac Poetics*, pp. 160–61, sees the *Bacchae* as dramatizing a failed rite of passage, which, if successful, would entail separation from women and initiation into the father's world. He also notes that both Pentheus and Dionysus have remote and obscure father figures—Echion in the one case and Zeus in the other.

[F:595–96]). As in Dante's *Inferno*, the shades are fixed in their condition while alive, unrelieved of their sorrow: "In death itself, pain will not let them be" (444 [F:599]). In a significant recapitulation of Odysseus' encounter with the shade of his mother Antiklea in the company of famous heroines in the *Nekya*, Aeneas finds Dido among women such as Phaedra and Pasiphae, who were consumed by monstrous love, a passion for inappropriate objects. But Dido is also among loyal wives who died for love of their husbands: Evadne, wife of Capaneus, who killed herself on her husband's funeral pyre, and Laodamia, who committed suicide after the gods allowed her husband, Protesilaus, to return to her from the dead for three hours. Among these women who experienced opposing forms of consuming passion, unlawful and lawful, are wives such as Procris, who foolishly suspected her husband Cephalus' fidelity and was accidentally killed by him, and Eryphyle, who, bribed by a necklace, treacherously induced her husband to fight for the Seven Against Thebes, thereby causing his death. Dido's love for Aeneas, like that of Procris and Eryphyle, occupies the middle ground between monstrous and exemplary love, but unlike them she was neither foolish nor treacherous. Rather, her passion oscillates between the two diametrically opposed poles of unlawful and lawful love: it was inappropriate for her to love Aeneas, who was intended for a different end, but on the other hand, like both Evadne and Laodamia, Dido committed suicide, having believed for a time that, like them, she was a lawfully wedded wife. Finally, the indeterminate sexuality of Caeneus, who was born a woman but changed by Poseidon to a man—dramatized by the coupling of feminine *revoluta* with the masculine name (449–50)—anticipates the reversals of roles between Aeneas and Dido in the scene to follow.

Virgil makes evident this reversal immediately upon Dido's first appearance:

> Among them, with her fatal wound still fresh,
> Phoenician Dido wandered the deep wood.
> The Trojan captain paused nearby and knew
> Her dim form in the dark, as one who sees,
> Early in the month, or thinks to have seen, the moon
> Rising through cloud, all dim.
>
> [6.450–54 (F:606–11])]

When they first met in Book 1, Aeneas was the wanderer, wounded

figuratively by the loss of his native city and by Juno's trials. But here
it is Dido who wanders, carrying the literal wound self-inflicted with
Aeneas' sword and the figurative one of her abandonment by Aeneas.
Virgil here alludes to the simile in Book 4 which likened Dido to a
hunted and wounded deer; in both instances, he calls attention to the
predatory aspect of Aeneas' search for empire, while exorcizing as an
obstacle to Aeneas' mission what Virgil represents as Dido's misplaced and excessive love.

The density of the forest is illumined only by the light of the moon:
the final line of the brief naturalistic simile, "aut videt, aut vidisse
putat . . ." (454), expresses the obscurity of Aeneas' vision of Dido,
which recalls Aeneas' dimly lit vision of Helen and which contrasts
with the sunlit clarity of his later vision of the future Roman kings in
the Elysian Fields. The uncertainty extends beyond the visual, for
Aeneas punctuates his speech to follow with various questions—left
unanswered by Dido. Aeneas' attempt to understand retrospectively
the tragedy of Dido parallels that of the reader, and the central undecidability of the episode, as well as that of the earlier story of Dido
and Aeneas, resides in the difficulty of ascertaining ethical responsibility. The mediated vision here also dramatizes the unbridgeable
distance between the living Aeneas and Dido's shade, who refuses to
speak to him or hear his excuses. Moreover, the image of the moon
recalls Virgil's earlier comparison of Dido to Diana and her invocation of Hecate upon her suicide: no longer inflamed by Venus and
Cupid, she is now reunited with Sychaeus in the underworld and has
returned to her former self before she loved Aeneas.

Although it is to their public identities that Virgil refers, "Phoe-
nissa . . . Dido" (450) and "Troius . . . heros" (451), thereby suggesting the decisive reason behind the tragic impossibility of their love,
Aeneas initially appeals to Dido as a former lover, shedding tears and
speaking to her with tender love (455):

> Dido, so forlorn,
> The story then that came to me was true,
> That you were out of life, had met your end
> By your own hand. Was I, was I the cause?
> I swear by heaven's stars, by the high gods,
> By any certainty below the earth,
> I left your land against my will, my queen.
> The gods' commands drove me to do their will,
> As now they drive me through this world of shades,

These mouldy waste lands and these depths of night.
And I could not believe that I would hurt you
So terribly by going. Wait a little.
Do not leave my sight.
Am I someone to flee from? The last word
Destiny lets me say to you is this.

[6.456–66 (F:613–28)]

Aeneas' address, "infelix Dido" (456), and the lines that follow under-score his personal relationship to her and his realization of culpability in her suicide. By echoing the poet ("infelix Dido"—[e.g., 4.450]), Aeneas evinces a more complete understanding of the consequences of his actions that he did not possess when he left Dido in Book 4. Aeneas' supplication, however, moves from the personal to the pub-lic as he addresses Dido as "regina" (460); although the "invitus" ("unwilling") in the same line dramatizes the tension between the public and the private, Aeneas defends his actions by emphasizing the public responsibilities ("iussa deum" [461]) that constrained him to leave her. In the final line of the speech, however, the tension be-tween the two concerns again resurfaces in the coupling of his very personal supplication, "quem fugis?" (466) with his final invocation of *fatum* as the higher power that places constraints on their encounter even in the underworld. The tension between the public and the private which suffuses these lines dramatizes Aeneas' imperative to follow his epic quest, albeit at enormous personal cost.

Aeneas' speech to Dido in the underworld serves as a palinode to their exchange in Book 4, not only in that Aeneas is enabled to show compassion toward Dido which he could not earlier but also in the reversal of roles between the two lovers. Aeneas, by echoing Dido's earlier "mene fugis?" (4.314) in "quem fugis?" now becomes the supplicant, and Dido, like Aeneas on that former occasion, remains unmoved:

Aeneas with such pleas tried to placate
The burning soul, savagely glaring back,
And tears came to his eyes. But she had turned
With gaze fixed on the ground as he spoke on,
Her face no more affected than if she were
Immobile granite or Marpesian stone.
At length she flung away from him and fled,
His enemy still, into the shadowy grove
Where he whose bride she once had been, Sychaeus,

Joined in her sorrows and returned her love.
Aeneas still gazed after her in tears,
Shaken by her ill fate and pitying her.

[6.467–76 (F:628–39)]

Now it is Aeneas who implores Dido in tearful supplication. Yet the
Dido he addresses is hardly one to be moved to tears; she is fiery, as
she was both figuratively and literally in Book 4, but the fire is no
longer that of a passionate woman but that of a disembodied and
implacable wrath. She now trades her earlier eloquence that served no
purpose for a silence that nevertheless powerfully expresses her resentment and her intransigence against Aeneas' *fatum*. Her steady
gaze ("fixos oculos" [469]), which bespeaks her intransigence, recalls
how Aeneas held steady his gaze, "immota tenebat / lumina" (4.331–
32), when Dido pleaded with him to stay. Moreover, the poet's
comparison of her to immobile granite or Marpesian stone echoes
Dido's earlier indictment of Aeneas' lack of compassion: "No goddess was your mother. Dardanus / Was not the founder of your
family. / Liar and cheat! Some rough Caucasian cliff / Begot you on
flint" (4.365–67 [F:503–506]). But here, it is Dido who parts from
Aeneas in the company of her "coniunx pristinus," Sychaeus, who
answers her cares and equals her love ("respondet curis aequatque . . .
amorem" [474]), as Aeneas was unable to do. In recapitulating Odysseus' encounter with the silent and intransigent Ajax, who committed
suicide because Odysseus defeated him in the contest over Achilles'
armor, Virgil represents Dido as an epic hero in her own right, while
affirming Aeneas' "victory" over Dido and relieving him of responsibility in her suicide.

Nevertheless, Virgil's final vision of Dido and Aeneas is profoundly ambivalent: he vindicates Dido by Aeneas' compassion toward her unjust fate; at the same time, he underscores Aeneas' pain in
confronting Dido's implacability, which leaves him to go forward
without recognition or words of forgiveness. Dido's presence in the
shady grove ("nemus umbriferum" [473]) points to the ambiguity of
her fate: she was sacrificed to Aeneas' epic mission and relegated to
such shadows, but by taking refuge there with Sychaeus she chooses
to live with "natural" though "untamed" passions, against which
Aeneas must defend himself. Virgil justifies Aeneas' actions by representing Dido as *inimica* (472) to Aeneas not only in her resentment for
his earlier desertion but, more fundamentally, because her exaltation
of private passion over Aeneas' and her own public obligations can-

not be reconciled with Aeneas' epic vocation. By reuniting her with her former husband, Sychaeus, Virgil relegates her to the past. His epic hero, Aeneas, however, must leave his love affair with Dido behind—as he left the shade of Creusa on the night of Troy's fall—in order to toil toward ("molitur" [477]) his future fate in Elysium and, later, on the Lavinian shores.

Lavinia and Amata: *Regia Coniunx*

Near the very beginning of Book 7, in an invocation for the entire second half of the poem, Virgil calls on Erato, the Muse of love poetry, in announcing the Italian wars to follow:

> Be with me, Muse of all Desire, Erato,
> While I call up the kings, the early times,
> How matters stood in the old land of Latium
> That day when the foreign soldiers beached
> Upon Ausonia's shore, and the events
> That led to the first fight. Immortal one,
> Bring all in memory to the singer's mind,
> For I must tell of wars to chill the blood,
> Ranked men in battle, kings by their own valor
> Driven to death, Etruria's cavalry,
> And all Hesperia mobilized in arms.
> A greater history opens before my eyes,
> A greater task awaits me.
>
> [7.37–44 (F:47–59)]

Here Virgil refers explicitly to the strife ("pugnae" [40]) between the Trojans and Latins, but the conflict is also between his Muse and his stated subject matter; this invocation enacts the disjunction between the private and public that will concern him for the remainder of the poem.[27] This unsettling invocation of Erato prefigures the similar invocation of Lavinia as the Muse of the Italian wars in the books to follow. It is perhaps because of this tension that Virgil calls attention to his greater task, his "maius opus" (44), signaling that there can be no happy reconciliation between the private and the public. Just as the Greek Acron, having left behind an uncompleted wedding, is slaugh-

---

[27]See Michael C. J. Putnam, "*Aeneid* VII and the *Aeneid*," *AJP*, 91 (1970), 417–18, on the irony of this invocation.

tered on the battlefield by Mezentius (10.719–31), so Aeneas leaves behind Dido, whose love was inimical to his epic mission and who was thus sacrificed for its sake. Instead, he will wed Lavinia, whom he never even sees within the poem.

For Turnus, who will lose not only his claim to Lavinia but also his life, his promised bride appears more important than solely political considerations.[28] For Aeneas, however, winning Lavinia is merely a necessary condition for the establishment of his dynasty in Italy. In the final book of the poem, Aeneas refers to Lavinia for the first and last time only to predict how she will give her name to the city: "urbique dabit Lavinia nomen" (12.194). Jupiter (1.258, 270; 4.236), the Sibyl (6.84), and even Virgil himself (1.2) refer to Lavinium as the land Aeneas must win, without mentioning the woman who will give it her name. Anchises speaks of "Lavinia coniunx" (6.764) during his prophecy to Aeneas in the underworld, but only as the mother of Silvius, the founder of the Italian dynasty. Even the shade of Creusa speaks of a future "regia coniunx" (2.783) in connection with his future kingship in Hesperia. Thus for Aeneas and for his epic mission, Lavinia's significance is coextensive with the city he must found.

These references to Lavinia confirm the status of woman described by M. I. Finley in an article appropriately titled "The Silent Woman in Rome." Finley notes that Roman women lacked individual names but were given family names with a feminine ending: "It is as if the Romans wished to suggest very pointedly that women were not, or ought not to be, genuine individuals but only fractions of a family. Anonymous and passive fractions at that, for the virtues which were stressed were decorum, chastity, gracefulness, even temper and childbearing."[29] Although Sarah Pomeroy believes that Roman matrons had a range of choices in their roles, as well as a demonstrable influence on the cultural and political life of their times, and Eva Cantarella points out that Roman women were granted new liberties, both nevertheless concede that the authority of the *pater familias* remained absolute.[30] Under Augustus' national program, new codes

---

[28]See, for example, 12.79–80: "Nostro dirimamus sanguine bellum; illo quaeratur coniunx Lavinia campo." Note also that in begging Aeneas for mercy, it is Lavinia he gives up: "Tua est Lavinia coniunx" (12.937). Putnam suggests, however, that Turnus' love for Lavinia becomes transformed into destructive warlust (*Poetry of the Aeneid*, pp. 226–27n).

[29]M. I. Finley, *Aspects of Antiquity, Discoveries and Controversies* (New York: Viking, 1968), p. 131.

[30]Sarah B. Pomeroy, *Goddesses, Whores, Wives, and Slaves: Women in Classical Antiq-

sought to bring the family under the protection of the state by tightening the matrimonial bond;[31] to strengthen the stability of marriage, the power of husbands over wives, supposedly prevalent in early Rome, was idealized and became an element in the marriage propaganda of Augustan authors. As in the example of Augustus' own betrothing of his sister Octavia to Mark Antony, these marriages were often convenient means for men to achieve political alliances—though this particular alliance, of course, proved to be rather short-lived.[32]

Despite references to Lavinia that, at least from Aeneas' point of view, confirm her suitability as a perfect Roman wife, the other participants in the Italian wars choose to see Lavinia as a second Helen and Aeneas as a second Paris.[33] Juno, angry at Aeneas' successful landing in Italy, utters an ominous curse, superimposing the Trojan war upon the Italian war to come:

> "In blood,
> Trojan and Latin, comes your dowry, girl;
> Bridesmaid Bellona waits now to attend you.
> Hecuba's not the only one who carried
> A burning brand within her and bore a son
> Whose marriage fired a city. So it is
> With Venus' child, a Paris once again,
> A funeral torch again for Troy reborn!"
>
> [7:318–22 (F:434–441)]

We are not meant to take Juno's assessment of the situation at face value, since throughout the epic she acts as the embodiment of the irrational and the violent, as a force that seeks always to subvert the unfolding of *fatum*. But almost immediately following Juno's outburst, Lavinia's mother, Amata, invokes the same analogy in opposing her husband Latinus' proposal to give their daughter to Aeneas

---

uity (New York: Schocken, 1975), pp. 149–52, 189. Eva Cantarella, *Pandora's Daughters: The Role and Status of Women in Greek and Roman Antiquity* (Baltimore: Johns Hopkins Univ. Press, 1986), pp. 135, 140–41.

[31]Ronald Syme, *The Roman Revolution* (London: Oxford Univ. Press, 1939; rpt. 1960), pp. 444–45, discusses the institution of *Lex Julia*, which converted adultery into a crime with severe penalties.

[32]Pomeroy, pp.154–57, also points out, "It is unlikely that girls of twelve (the minimum age for marriage determined by Augustus) were in fact able to resist a proposed marriage."

[33]Anderson, *Art of the Aeneid*, pp. 66–67, considers this analogy to be completely invidious and fallacious.

instead of Turnus: "Was that not the way / The Phrygian shepherd entered Lacedaemon / And carried Helen off to Troy's far city?" (7.363–64 [F:501–503]). Although Amata makes a cogent case for Turnus' claim as her daughter's betrothed, asserting that he fulfills the role of the stranger that the oracles demand, Virgil discredits her passionate objection to Aeneas by ascribing it to her misplaced desire for Turnus. Finally, Turnus appeals to this same analogy while rousing his troops for battle:

> I have my fate as well, to combat theirs,
> To cut this criminal people down, my bride
> Being stolen. Pain over such a loss is not
> For the Atridae only, nor may only
> Mycenae justly have recourse to arms.
> Enough that Trojans perished once? Their sin
> That once had been enough, were they not still
> Given to hatred of all womankind.
>
> [9.136–42 (F:190–97)]

Turnus' grievance against Aeneas as the interloper between himself and Lavinia demands to be taken seriously, especially since he echoes Achilles' expression of indignation when Agamemnon robbed him of Briseis (*Iliad*, 9.337–45);[34] he thereby fulfills the Sibyl's prophecy that Aeneas will meet another ("alius") Achilles in Italy (6.89).

The Sibyl had also prophesied the eventual marriage of Aeneas to Lavinia and the war in Italy as reenactments of the abduction of Helen and the Trojan war: "causa mali tanti coniunx iterum hospita Teucris / externique iterum thalami" (6.93–94), "The cause of suffering here again will be / A bride foreign to Teucrians, a marriage / Made with a stranger" (F:140–42). There is no denying the strong sense of *déjà vu* that pervades the Italian section of the epic, and the Sybil's prophecy perhaps gives sanction to Amata's and Turnus' indignation that they are being victimized by yet another Paris. Lavinia had been promised to Turnus, and the war fought in her name in some ways repeats the earlier war fought over another woman. Yet Virgil emphasizes the difference between the pleasure-loving Paris, who launched his nation into a fatal war by his abduction of Helen, and *pius* Aeneas, who steadfastly follows his epic mission to found a new home for his displaced countrymen and gods. Moreover, the

---

[34]Matters are complicated, however, by Putnam's suggestion (*Poetry of the Aeneid*, pp. 225–26n) of a link between Virgil's Turnus (12.9) and Lucretius' Paris (1.474–75).

Sibyl, unlike Aeneas' adversaries, simply states the fact of repetition ("iterum") without assigning blame to Aeneas.

Virgil thus consistently sets up parallels between the *Iliad* and his poem, only to shift them. The Sibyl announced Turnus as the *alius* Achilles, but it is Aeneas who takes on the role of the second Achilles in his grief over the death of Pallas (another Patroclus), which leads him to kill Turnus. In this final confrontation between the two warriors, Turnus actually becomes an *alius* Hector. These shifting parallels function to destabilize our judgments of Virgil's characters.

Lavinia, in addition to being a second Helen, takes on the role of a second Dido when she replaces the queen of Carthage as the preeminent woman in the second half of the poem. Like Helen, Penelope, and Dido before her, Lavinia has been wooed by many suitors (7.54–55). Just as Iarbas, Dido's principal suitor, became Aeneas' enemy in Carthage, so Turnus, Lavinia's betrothed, becomes Aeneas' chief adversary. Moreover, in a repetition that is significant and ironic, Aeneas' emissary, Ilioneus, comes to Latinus offering peace (7.213ff.), just as he had earlier come to Dido (1.520ff.). Both Carthage and Italy unwittingly accept Aeneas and the Trojans, who bring not peace but devastation. Yet the fact that Ilioneus addresses Dido in the first instance and Latinus in the second points to an important difference between Dido and Lavinia: whereas queen Dido disposed of her own fate, Lavinia is a princess to be given in marriage by her father, the king. Virgil's representations of the two women carry this difference yet further: whereas Dido dominated the episode in Carthage, in the Italian section of the poem Lavinia appears only twice.

Furthermore, unlike Dido, who when alive passionately pleaded with Aeneas not to leave her, Lavinia, like Dido's shade in the underworld, never speaks. Although the outcome of the Italian wars will decide her fate, she never reveals her feelings about either of her two suitors, except obliquely in her enigmatic blush.[35] When Amata pleads passionately with Turnus to desist from fighting Aeneas,[36]

> Lavinia, listening to her mother, streamed
> With tears on burning cheeks; a deepening blush
> Brought out a fiery glow on her hot face.

[35]The Old French *Eneas* supplies this romance motif that is missing in the *Aeneid:* as Lavinia stands on her father's towers, she falls in love with Aeneas (8047ff.)

[36]Divergent readings of this blush give testimony to its ambiguity. See Putnam, *Poetry of the Aeneid*, p. 159; Anderson, *Art of the Aeneid*, p. 116n; and Johnson, pp. 56–57.

As when one puts a stain of crimson dye
On ivory of India, or when
White lilies blush, infused with crimson roses,
So rich the contrast in her coloring seemed.

[12:64–69) (F:92–98)]

Lavinia's tears answer her mother's invocation of her own tears ("per has ego te lacrimas" [56]), and her blush perhaps signals her agreement with Amata's vow to share Turnus' fate should he meet his death rather than see Aeneas her son (61–63). In fact, when Amata commits suicide later in the same book, Lavinia's blush, here compared to fire ("ignem" [65])—for Virgil an image that always suggests dangerous passion—will transform itself to devastating grief. This blush is appropriately compared to a work of art, for Lavinia is not an agent of her own fate but an embodiment of beauty to be contemplated from a distance, fought over, and won. Moreover, the Iliadic subtext of this simile, in which Menelaus' bloody thigh is compared to stained ivory (*Iliad,* 4.141–47), calls attention to the blood shed over her prototype Helen and over possession of Lavinia herself in the *Aeneid.*

Thus Lavinia occupies one pole of a binary opposition and Dido occupies another; Virgil divides the two Helens—passive in Book 2 and active in Book 6—and embodies them separately in his two female characters. Dido passionately attempted to thwart Aeneas' epic mission, whereas Lavinia in her passive silence apparently makes for a perfect vessel. The absence of Dido's male relatives (she fled to Carthage from her brother, murderer of her husband) underscores Dido's status as a subject rather than an object of exchange; she jealously guards her sexual and political independence by refusing Iarbas, but she gives herself to Aeneas with disastrous results. By contrast, Lavinia is never represented as a subject but always as an object to be exchanged between males—a daughter to be given in marriage by Latinus, whose possession is fought over by Turnus and Aeneas, and whose eventual marriage to Aeneas will unite the Trojan and Latin peoples. This difference between the two women is evident in their names as well: Dido's name is her own (Servius attributes it to her chastity in rejecting her numerous suitors) whereas Lavinia's coincides with her land.

Despite this apparent opposition between Dido and Lavinia, however, Lavinia's silence is already prepared for by Dido's silence in

Book 6 which expressed her implacable enmity toward Aeneas and his *fatum*. Moreover, the silent Helen in Book 2 was far from innocuous. Lavinia's insistent and enigmatic silence could in fact be read as more subversive than innocuous, in tension with *fatum*, Jupiter's speech. Her portentous silence also recalls that of Aeschylus' Cassandra in *Agamemnon:* like Cassandra who eventually bursts into speech, Lavinia will cast off her silence to mourn for her mother, Amata.

Perhaps even more disquieting are references to Lavinia's descent from the sorceress Circe and Italy's close ties with Circe. With Neptune's help, Aeneas has succeeded in avoiding Circe on his way to Italy (7.10–24). Yet the Laurentian palace contains a depiction of Picus, the founder of the Italian line, who was changed into a bird by his bride Circe (7.187–91), and Latinus bestows Circe's horses on Aeneas (7.280–83).[37]

These disquieting references culminate in the description of the double-edged omen, when Lavinia caught fire as Latinus sacrificed at his altars. The figurative fire in Lavinia's blush becomes quite literal and, again, is ambiguous in import: "mirabile" and "horrendum" (78), wonderful and terrible. On the one hand, it recalls another "mirabile monstrum" (2.680), the flames that played on Ascanius' forehead on the night of Troy's fall, which signaled the divine sanction for the future destiny of Aeneas' son. Lavinia, too, will play a part in the same destiny, as the interpretation of the omen suggests: "inlustrem fama fatisque canebant" (79), "it was read by seers to mean the girl / Would have renown and glorious days to come" (F:102–3). Whereas Ascanius' flames were harmless ("innoxia" [2.683]) and merely grazed about his hair and temples, Lavinia's flames actually burn her hair and headdress as she scatters them through the palace. This difference is an important one, for it points to the darker, more sinister ("horrendum") aspect of the omen and its interpretation: "sed populo magnum portendere bellum" (80), "But

---

[37]Putnam, "*Aeneid* VII and the *Aeneid*," sees Aeneas' passing by the shores of Circe as a "precursorial symbol for the whole book" (pp. 412–14). Circe signifies the power of metamorphosis as embodied most notably in Allecto's transforming poisons (pp. 415–16). See also Charles Segal, "Circean Temptations: Homer, Vergil, Ovid," *TAPA*, 99 (1968) 428–36, who shows that Virgil eliminates the positive, human side of Homer's Circe and makes her "a type of demonic, seductive power" (p. 436). He also notices the connection between Circe and Allecto, and sees Circe as "the threat of human brutalization [that] hang[s] over both Aeneas' victory and Turnus' defeat" (p. 431).

that she brought a great war on her people" (F:104). The fires cannot be contained within the palace but will become flames of war, engulfing her country as they did Troy on the night of its fall. The double-edged interpretation of the omen, in fact, applies equally to Helen and Dido as well as to Lavinia, for the fame of these women are linked to the disasters they supposedly brought to their peoples. In fact, the detailed description of the flames enveloping Lavinia's regalia suggests that they are a rekindling of the fire on Dido's funeral pyre, especially in: "her head-dress caught / In crackling flame, her queenly tresses blazed, / Her jewelled crown blazed" (75–76) (F:96–98). Unlike Dido, Lavinia cannot actually be sacrificed, since she is necessary for Aeneas' establishment of Rome. But this omen dramatizes Lavinia's position as a sacrificial victim: she is sacrificed as a person in order to become a vessel of Aeneas' *fatum*.

Having portrayed Lavinia as the vessel of omens but not as an agent that fulfills them, Virgil exorcizes Dido's fiery sexuality and passion from Lavinia by transposing it onto her mother, Amata, as sacrificial substitute. The flames that literally engulfed first Dido, then Lavinia, will figuratively invade Amata and even Turnus, and eventually will gather force to become the fires of war on the Italian countryside. Amata is already burning with "feminine" anger ("femineae ardentem curaeque iraeque coquebant" [7.345] over Aeneas' disruption of her daughter's planned marriage with Turnus, when Juno sends the chthonic Fury Allecto to her.[38] Juno's intervention signals that Amata's madness seeks to disrupt the unfolding of Jupiter's *fatum;* Allecto intervenes only in the sense that her victimization of Amata dramatizes a process of increasing fury which has already begun. Virgil insists upon the sexual nature of Amata's madness in the graphic description of Allecto's snake slithering down her robes:

> And the serpent
> Slipping between her gown and her smooth breasts
> Went writhing on, though imperceptible
> To the fevered woman's touch or sight, and breathed
> Viper's breath into her.
>   .   .   .
> While the infection first, like dew of poison
> Fallen on her, pervaded all her senses,

[38]See Pöschl's discussion of the Allecto scenes as the initial symbol of the Iliadic half of the poem (pp. 24–33).

Netting her bones in fire—though still her soul
Had not responded fully to the flame—
[7.349–51, 354–56 (F:480–84, 488–91)]

The sinister and violent influence of the serpent on Amata recalls
Virgil's use of the same image in Aeneas' narrative of Troy's fall. As
in Book 2, these images of serpents are closely associated with those
of fire: the serpent's venom transforms itself into "ignem" and "flammam" (355–56)—placed in the prominent final position of consecutive lines. The conjunction of flames and poison, moreover, associates the hysteria of *infelix* (376) Amata with the passion injected into
Dido by Cupid. According to Virgil, both women suffer from misplaced and frustrated desire: Amata's frenzy on behalf of her daughter's betrothed corresponds to Dido's seduction by Cupid disguised
as Ascanius.

Just as Dido was unable to persuade Aeneas, so Amata attempts to
sway Latinus in vain. Amata then literally reenacts Dido's figurative
Bacchic frenzy: "quin etiam in silvas simulato numine Bacchi / maius
adorta nefas maioremque orsa furorem" (7.385–86), "she feigned /
Bacchic possession, daring a greater sin / And greater madness"
(F:530–32). Here Amata's feigning of Bacchic rites ("simulato") re-
calls that of Helen ("simulans" [6.517]) around the Wooden Horse.
Like Helen, Amata carries a Bacchic firebrand ("flagrantem . . .
pinum" [397]) that literalizes the figurative fire injected in her by
Allecto. Just as Helen sought to subvert masculine order by feigning
Bacchic madness, so here Amata seeks to obstruct Latinus' plans by
hiding Lavinia in the mountains and claiming to dedicate her to Bacchus (387–91).[39] Amata's action reveals that her power struggle with
Latinus centers on Lavinia: she protests against patriarchy's decree
that the daughter properly belongs to the father so that, through her,
he can enter into exchange and form an alliance with another man. In
taking refuge in the forest and the mountains, and roaming amid
woods and wild beasts' coverts (404), Amata becomes beastlike, possessed by untamed passions. Her madness proves to be contagious, as
"fama volat" (392), and the Italian matrons leave their homes to don
fawn skins and take up thyrsi (392–96). Through her leadership of the
Bacchic matrons, Virgil underscores Amata's emblematic role as

---

[39]Finley, p. 141, points out that a great wave of Dionysiac religion spread in Italy
after the wars with Hannibal and were suppressed by the Senate in 186 B.C.

destructive mother in the *Aeneid*. As in Euripides' *Bacchae*, the women—closer to "nature" and hence to the "irrational"—set themselves apart from masculine modes of civilizing and build a rival feminine disorder separate from and opposed to masculine order.[40] In an analogous moment, the Trojan women were instigated by Iris, another messenger of Juno, to set fire to their ships in their desire— irrational from the point of view of the Roman Empire—to settle rather than move on (5.659ff.).[41]

After the skirmish following the killing of Sylvia's stag by Ascanius' hunting dogs, Amata's Bacchae clamor for war:

> The kin, then, of those mothers in ecstasy
> Who danced for Bacchus in the wilderness—
> Amata's name no light encouragement—
> Came in from everywhere with cries for Mars.
> Nothing would do but that, against the omens,
> Against the oracles, by a power malign
> They pled for frightful war. And they all thronged,
> Outshouting one another, round the palace.
>
> [7.580–85 (F:797–804)]

Just as Aeneas was likened to a rooted oak buffeted by winds in his resistance to Dido's pleas (4.441–46), so Latinus is compared in this confrontation to a steadfast ocean cliff (7.586). Since the Bacchae are more violent than Dido, Latinus is less successful than Aeneas was in withstanding the storm of female influence and is eventually swept away (7.594). Thus Virgil represents female aggression and male passivity to be in inverse proportion to one another: as the female becomes more aggressive, the male becomes more weak and helpless. Significantly, Virgil does not report the women's words, as he did Dido's; but the women nevertheless prove to be an ominous force in their indomitable opposition to all order, exemplified by *fatum*. They thus succeed in bringing "infandum . . . bellum," (583), the war both

---

[40]In an important study for the inquiry into "sexual meanings," Sherry Ortner argues that there is a universal tendency in cultural thought to align male with culture and to see female as closer to nature. "Is Female to Male as Nature Is to Culture?" in *Woman, Culture, and Society*, ed. M. Z. Rosaldo and L. Lamphere (Stanford: Stanford Univ. Press, 1974), pp. 67–87. On "nature and culture" in the *Bacchae*, see Segal, *Dionysiac Poetics*, pp. 162–63.

[41]Yet this abandonment of Trojan women in fact promotes the foundation of the Roman Empire, for like Aeneas' marriage to Lavinia, the Trojans' marriages to Italian women will serve to unite the two peoples.

unspeakable and against fate. But just as Jupiter's *fatum* ultimately cannot be subverted by Juno's manipulations, so Aeneas' *fatum* will be fulfilled despite, or perhaps because of, the opposition of Amata and her Bacchae.

Turnus is therefore naive in asserting to Allecto, who attempts to rouse him in the guise of an old priestess of Juno, that the business of war and peace should be left to men: "bella viri pacemque gerent quis bella gerenda" (444). Turnus echoes Hector's admonition to Andromache on Troy's walls, but Virgil calls attention to the difference between his world and Homer's. Allecto proves Turnus' error by announcing that she carries "bella . . . letumque" (455), death and war, while hurling at him a firebrand that succeeds in maddening him with warlust: "saevit amor ferri et scelerata insania belli" (461), "Lust of steel / Raged in him, brute insanity of war" (F:634–35). Here, madness, though primarily associated with Bacchic women, affects Turnus; Virgil thus appears to question Hector's separation of and opposition between masculine and feminine spheres. Yet in this questioning, Virgil diverges from the *Odyssey,* which celebrated Penelope and Odysseus' likemindedness through their shared *metis.* For Virgil considers passion, sexuality, and madness—qualities he considers inimical to social order as embodied in the Roman Empire—to be feminine; when males are affected by these qualities, they cede their masculine position of superiority to take on the feminine. Thus Virgil follows the Iliadic warriors in considering as feminine males who are weak or are defeated in battle (such as Turnus, Nisus, and Euryalus). Many critics have noticed links between Dido and Turnus;[42] Turnus' contamination with feminine qualities, as well as the need of Roman *fatum* to defeat him, seems to justify, or even necessitate, his sacrifice.

Lavinia is typically silent while Allecto in Book 7 enrages those close to her. She does not even appear in this book, except in the description of the fiery omen, sent before Aeneas' arrival. But when Amata commits suicide as a culmination of her frustrated passion and in a reenactment of Dido's suicide, Lavinia no longer remains passive and silent:

> When Latin women heard of this disaster,
> Doubling their sorrow, princess Lavinia first
> Tore her flowerlike hair and scored her cheeks,

[42]For example, see Pöschl, pp. 109ff., 136ff.; and Putnam, *Poetry of the Aeneid,* pp. 151ff.

> Then all the rest crowded about her, mad
> With horror and grief. The palace rang with wailing.
>
> [12.604–607 (F:823–27)]

Assuming Amata's role in leading the Latin women, Lavinia acts as
the chief mourner for her mother and expresses her grief in lamentations. The mother, when alive, seemed to have taken on the emotions
that her daughter was not allowed to express; and so it is fitting that
Amata be sacrificed in Lavinia's place.[43] Although in Lavinia's silence
Virgil seems to have exorcized feminine passion that proved so dangerous to Aeneas' epic quest, our final vision of her does not bode
well for the future of the Roman Empire. Lavinia will also eventually
lose Turnus, although the epic ends with his death, before he can be
mourned by those close to him.

Camilla *Bellatrix,* Juturna *Virago*

If Amata embodied the passion that Lavinia was not allowed to
express, Camilla, the maiden warrior, acts as a surrogate for Lavinia
in yet another sense by fighting side by side with Turnus. Camilla,
like Amata, first appears in Book 7; in fact, Virgil marks her prominence by introducing her immediately after Turnus, at the very end
of the catalogue of Italian allies. This passage, as Erich Auerbach
pointed out, is not a systematic description detailing Camilla's personal characteristics.[44] In the catalogue, Virgil gives the genealogies
of the allies, but he recounts Camilla's upbringing in more detail in
Book 11. Here in Book 7, Virgil gives a portrait of her instead:

> Beside all these
> Camilla of the Volscian people came,
> Riding ahead of cavalry, her squadrons
> Gallant in bronze. A warrior girl whose hands
> Were never deft at distaff or wool basket,
> Skills of Minerva, she was hard and trained

---

[43]Amata's stated reason for committing suicide ("se causam clamat crimenque
caputque malorum [12.600]) could have been Lavinia's, for she is called "causa mali
tanti" (11.480).

[44]Erich Auerbach, "Camilla or the Rebirth of the Sublime," in *Literary Language and
its Public in Late Latin Antiquity and in the Middle Ages,* trans. Ralph Manheim (New
York: Pantheon, 1965), pp. 183–234.

To take the shock of war, or to outrace
The winds in running. If she ran full speed
Over the tips of grain unharvested
She would not ever have bruised an ear, or else
She might have sprinted on the deep sea swell
And never dipped her flying feet. To see her,
Men and women pouring from the fields,
From houses, thronged her passage way and stared
Wide-eyed with admiration at the style
Of royal purple, robing her smooth shoulders,
Then at the brooch that bound her hair in gold,
Then at the Lycian quiver that she bore
And the shepherd's myrtle staff, pointed with steel.

[7.803–17 (F:1104–22)]

According to Auerbach, Virgil relates only "what enhances the power and lightness of her movement," but even this statement already hints at Camilla's sexual ambiguity.[45] As *bellatrix* (805), Camilla is like Minerva, but she has never cultivated the feminine art of spinning also sacred to that warrior goddess. Her military prowess and freedom of movement, which this passage dramatizes, seem to depend on the suppression of traditionally feminine traits and on her virginity ("virgo" [806]).

In Book 11, Diana, mourning over Camilla's imminent death, relates how the warrior maiden was dedicated to the virgin goddess by her father, Metabus. The exiled tyrant, in flight from his pursuing countrymen, bound his infant daughter to his lance and hurled her over the river, entrusting her safety to Diana:

Daughter of Latona,
Diana, kindly virgin of the groves,
I, her father, swear this child shall be
Thy servant—the first weapon she embraces
Thine, as by thy mercy through the air
She escapes the enemy. I beg thee, goddess,
Take her as thine own, this girl committed
Now to the veering wind.

[11.557–60 (F:758–65)]

[45]Auerbach, p. 185. For a discussion of the "motif of duality" in Camilla's portrait. See Mario A. Di Cesare, *The Altar and the City: A Reading of Vergil's Aeneid* (New York: Columbia Univ. Press, 1974), p. 133.

Just as this first weapon, *primum tellum* (558–59), finds its fulfillment in the lance she holds as she rides by with the Italian allies, so Camilla's oft-noted fleetness of movement seems to originate in this primal flight over the waters: "rapidum super amnem / infelix fugit in iaculo stridente Camilla" (11.562–63), "over the rushing stream / Small and forlorn Camilla soared across / Upon the whistling spearshaft" (F:768–70). Giving Camilla the same epithet, *infelix,* that he had given Dido and Amata, Virgil suggests the problematic aspect of her extraordinary upbringing. Camilla attains her maidenhood in the wilderness without the benefit of civilizing influences, for Metabus, like Mezentius, was forced into exile for his tyranny and lived among shepherds on lonely mountains (11.567–69). Barbarous Metabus, though a loving father as was Mezentius, reared Camilla as if she were a wild animal, nursing her on the milk of a wild mare and dressing her in tiger skin instead of providing her with normal adornments for girls, such as gold hairclasps and trailing robes (11.576–77). Virgil reveals his psychological astuteness in relating that Metabus named his daughter after his deceased wife: "matrisque vocavit / nomine Casmillae mutata parte Camillam" (11.542–43). Camilla's jealously guarded virginity seems to stem from this close relationship with her father, who effectively placed a limit on her sexuality and trained her exclusively in masculine pursuits. As Lillian Robinson points out, Virgil deliberately removes Camilla, if not from the fact of gender, from the realm of sexuality; she succeeds as a warrior because she is not a woman.[46] This requisite conjunction of her virginity and prowess can best be seen when the Italian matrons wish her for their sons, and she chooses instead to wed herself to war: "All her contentment being with Diana, / The girl remained untouched and ever cherished / Passion for arms and for virginity" (11.582–84 [F:794–96]). These matrons, together with the boys not yet old enough to fight, admire Camilla as she rides by; the women, whose frustrated impotence could find an outlet only in Bacchic subversion, seem drawn to Camilla for her prowess which is denied to them. Yet Camilla's association with the matrons links her to Amata, who disrupted masculine order with her Bacchae, and prepares the way for the male warriors' (and Virgil's) disquiet concerning her ascendancy.

Virgil's portrait of Camilla concludes with an image that sums up the uneasy balance within her between the feminine and the masculine. Camilla glories in precisely those "feminine" ornaments de-

[46]Robinson, pp. 70, 72.

nied her as a child, a purple robe and a gold clasp, which prefigure her death in pursuit of glamorous booty. Her "masculine" weapon, the shepherd's staff with metal point, encapsulates the movement from her pastoral childhood to martial maidenhood, as well as the more general transformation of shepherds' staffs into weapons that marked the onset of the Italian wars.

Camilla's *aristeia* occurs in Italy's hour of need, against the invading Trojan forces. Her admirers, the matrons and the boys, gather to the call for the final struggle, and prayers are offered to Minerva by the women, including Amata and Lavinia:

> The queen as well
> Rode in her carriage with a company
> Of mothers to the shrine of Pallas, high
> Above the town, with gifts, and close beside her
> The young princess, Lavinia, rode—the cause
> Of so much suffering, lovely eyes downcast.
> The women, entering, beclouded all
> That shrine with smoke of incense, and sad voices
> Rose from the portal in a tide of prayer:
> "O power over battle, our protectress,
> Virgin, Tritonia, shatter in thy hand
> The spearhaft of the Phrygian corsair!
> Throw him headlong to earth, let him lie dead
> Below our high gates!"
>
> [11.477–85 (F:648–61)]

Camilla, both a *virgo* like Lavinia and a *regina* (11.499) like Amata, appears as if in answer to the women's prayers to the virgin warrior, Minerva. She nobly offers to take Turnus' place in meeting Aeneas in combat while he defends the city; Turnus, however, suggests that she guard the walls while he sets an ambush for Aeneas.

Thus Camilla's *aristeia* and her at once tragic and pathetic death are far from "episodic," as some maintain, but come at a critical juncture in the Italian wars.[47] In the midst of her uncurbed militance, Virgil likens Camilla to an Amazon:

> Amid the carnage, like an Amazon,
> Camilla rode exultant, one breast bared

---

[47]For example, see J. William Hunt, *Forms of Glory: Structure and Sense in Virgil's Aeneid* (Carbondale: Southern Illinois Univ. Press, 1973), p. 8.

For fighting ease, her quiver at her back.
At times she flung slim javelins thick and fast,
At times, tireless, caught up her two-edged axe.
The golden bow, Diana's weapon, rang
Upon her shoulders. . . .
                    . . .
So ride the hardened Amazons of Thrace,
With drumming hooves on frozen Thermodon,
Warring in winter, in their painted gear,
Sometimes around Hippolyta, the chieftain,
Or when the daughter of Mars, Penthesilea,
Drives her chariot back victorious
And women warriors bearing crescent shields
Exult, riding in tumult with wild cries.

    [11.648–52, 659–63 (F:881–87, 895–902)]

Camilla's movement from the aggression of masculine weapons to
the grace of Diana's bow again points to her sexual ambiguity. But
these weapons themselves are double-edged, as the battle axe ("bi-
pennem" [651]) actually is: "lenta . . . hastilia" (650), like the shepherd's staff with the metal point, could be either a pliant branch or a
rigid javelin, and "aureus . . . arcus" (652) conjoins the ornamental
and the martial and prefigures Chloreus' golden armor that will soon
lead to her death. "Exsultat" (648) brings together Camilla's freedom
and joy of movement, on the one hand, and her primitive ferocity on
the other; this hint of grotesque barbarism is made more explicit in
the actual Amazons who "exsultant" (663). This simile links Camilla
and her maiden comrades to Penthesilea and her women warriors
("feminea . . . agmina" [663]); both bear embellished weapons ("pic-
tis . . . armis" [660]) and combine masculine militance ("Martia . . .
Penthesilea" [661–62]) with feminine frenzy ("ululante" [662])—
recalling the Bacchic shrieks ("ululatibus" [7.395]) of the women who
rallied around Amata.[48]

    The routed men will not long abide the ascendancy of Camilla's
womanly weapons, "mulieribus armis" (11.687), and male Jupiter
initiates a counter-offensive by moving Tarchon to taunt his troop's

[48]Page duBois, *Centaurs and Amazons: Women in the Prehistory of the Great Chain of
Being* (Ann Arbor: Univ. of Michigan Press, 1982), discusses the Amazons as an
embodiment of the Athenian Greek's view of woman as Other, a view which also
connected her with animals and barbarians. See also William Blake Tyrell, *Amazons:
A Study in Athenian Mythmaking* (Baltimore: Johns Hopkins Univ. Press, 1984).

impotence—on the battlefield if not elsewhere—against the women. Arruns, "fatis debitus" (759), marked by fate, stalks Camilla and cunningly awaits the opportunity for ambush. Camilla's death, therefore, comes not in a face-to-face confrontation with a warrior worthy of her but in a moment of blind and furious desire for the glamorous spoils of Chloreus:

> By chance, Chloreus, Mount Cybelus' votary,
> Once a priest, came shining from far off
> In Phrygian gear. He spurred a foaming mount
> In a saddle-cloth of hide with scales of bronze
> As thick as plumage, interlinked with gold.
> The man himself, splendid in rust and purple
> Out of the strange East, drew a Lycian bow
> To shoot Gortynian arrows: at his shoulder
> Golden was the bow and golden too
> The helmet of the seer, and tawny gold
> The brooch that pinned his cloak as it belled out
> And snapped in wind, a chlamys, crocus-yellow.
> Tunic and trousers, too, both Eastern style,
> Were brilliant with embroidery.
>
> [11.768–77 (F:1045–58)]

The detailed description of the former priest's ornate and un-Roman accoutrements, reminiscent of Dido's Tyrian purple, stands as the culmination of previous images of ornamental armor. The insistence on gold throughout the passage mirrors Camilla's obsessive and fatal attraction to its glitter. The gold is fatal also in the sense that it promotes *fatum:* the bronze scales ("aenis . . . squamis" [770–71]) hark back not only to Pyrrhus in his snake-like splendor, but more immediately to the simile comparing Tarchon's victory over Turnus' messenger, Venulus, to that of an eagle over a snake ("squamis" [754]). Here again, the image of the serpent resurfaces as a signal of the unfolding of *fatum,* for this Trojan rally foreshadows not only the death of Camilla but the eventual defeat of the Latins. The conjunction, moreover, of Arruns' snake-like stealth ("furtim celeris" [765]) in encircling Camilla ("circuit" [761], "circuitum" [767]) and Chloreus' serpentine scales signals the inexorability of Camilla's consequent death under *fatum.*

Virgil, however, also gives a complex double motive behind Camilla's apparently single-minded pursuit of armor:

> her heart's desire
> Either to fit luxurious Trojan gear
> On a temple door, or else herself to flaunt
> That golden plunder. Blindly, as a huntress,
> Following him, and him alone, of all
> Who took part in the battle, she rode on
> Through a whole scattered squadron, recklessly,
> In a girl's love of finery.
>
> [11.778–82 (F:1059–66)]

Virgil equivocates ("sive ut . . . sive ut" [778–79]) between Camilla's piety, which recalls Aeneas' dedication of Greek arms to Apollo's temple (3.268–88) and her vain desire to deck herself in splendor, like Chloreus, on the other. The ambiguity in the final line between the traditionally masculine "praedae et spoliorum" (782)—which recalls Euryalus' also fatal cupidity for armor—and the "femineo . . . amore" enclosing it crystallizes Camilla's tragic doubleness as *virago*.

In the successive deaths of Camilla and Arruns, the conflict between the sexes finds expression on the divine level as well, in the interventions by Apollo and Diana, male and female gods of the hunt. Apollo grants Arruns' prayer to guide his arrow against Camilla, though his refusal to hear the accompanying request for homecoming allows Diana's delegate, Opis, to draw an avenging arrow at the slayer of the goddess' favorite. Although Camilla's upbringing by Metabus as a huntress resurfaces in her pursuit of Chloreus ("venatrix" [780]), she ironically meets her death as Arruns' prey: his arrow fatally wounds her below her bared breast, that paradoxical sign of her Amazon ferocity (11.649) and female vulnerability.

Arruns' cravenness in his subsequent flight and taking cover heightens by contrast Camilla's heroism as she meets her death:

> Until now, sister, I was able.
> Now this wound galls me and finishes me.
> Everything around is growing dark.
> Make your escape and take my last command
> To Turnus: that he join the battle here
> To keep the Trojans from the town. Farewell.
>
> [11.823–27 (F:1119–24)]

In these words to Acca that bespeak her overriding concern for Turnus and her sense of responsibility as his ally, Camilla goes beyond the opposition between the sexes which marked her final moments. The loyalty of "Acca soror" and Opis' elegiac tribute, "Nor will your end be unrenowned / Among earth's peoples, nor will it be known / As unavenged" (846–47 [F:1152–54]), vindicate Camilla's death; by stark contrast, Arruns meets his death, alone and forgotten: "As he moaned and died / His fellow troopers rode off, unaware, / And left him in the dust, a spot unknown / On the wide terrain" (865–66 [F:1175–78]).

Camilla's death turns the tide of battle, and the Italian forces are thrown into a confusion reminiscent of the Night of Troy. This time, however, it is the Trojans who penetrate the gates of the city to slaughter the enemy. The desperate Italian situation compels the matrons, who so admired Camilla, to imitate her in their city's defense, despite their pathetic impotence (891–95). Turnus must therefore return to Laurentum, although Aeneas was about to fall into his trap. Camilla's death, in effect, spells the defeat of the Latins and sets the scene for the final confrontation between Aeneas and Turnus as they both march toward the city.

In addition to strategic importance, Virgil gives Camilla's death a figural prominence near the end of the penultimate book, thus linking it to Turnus' death, which closes the final book. In fact, the lines relating the moment of the two warriors' deaths are identical: "vitaque cum gemitu fugit indignata sub umbras" (11.831 = 12.952). Through their joint entry into the poem and, more important, through their noble friendship, Camilla becomes Turnus' female counterpart and precedes him as a victim on the altar of Aeneas' epic mission. Although as *bellatrix,* Camilla is the unique female among the warriors fallen in the course of the Italian wars eulogized by Virgil—Pallas, Lausus, Nisus and Euryalus, for example—as *regina* she also shares important traits with Amata and Dido. Virgil links Camilla's Amazonian ferocity with Amata's Bacchic madness; the affinity between the two apparently different women is made explicit in the Latin matrons who follow Amata in her Bacchic rites and who are also the most ardent admirers of Camilla's prowess. Virgil's more sympathetic representation of Camilla can be explained by her insistent denial of female sexuality; his ambivalence toward her arises from her superior military ability that threatens to make male warriors "feminine." Camilla is associated with Dido through Penthesilea, who figures in the introduction of Dido into the poem and to whom Camilla is compared in her militancy. Unlike Camilla, Dido succumbs to passion in her love for Aeneas and fails in her duty as ruler of Carthage, but Camilla's arguably successful suppression of

her female sexuality—displaced onto a desire for golden ornament—
nevertheless leads to her tragic death. As *virgo*, finally, Camilla seems
to fight in the stead of the passive maiden Lavinia; upon her death,
another *virago*, Turnus' sister Juturna, takes her place..

Like Camilla, Juturna straddles two realms, not only as a *virago*
(12.468) but also as a mortal woman granted immortality. In return
for ravishing her virginity, Jupiter made her a river nymph (12.140–
41), but she retains mortal ties, most notably in her brother Turnus.
Juno exploits Juturna's sisterly love in order to avert Aeneas' victory
and Turnus' death by sending her to break the pact dictating a duel
between the two warriors. After Aeneas and Latinus solemnly take
oaths to uphold the treaty—"talibus inter se firmabant foedera dictis"
(212), "By these spoken vows / They sealed the pact between them"
(F:291–92)—Juturna, in the shape of Camers, succeeds in inflaming
the Latin warriors against it: "Talibus incensa est iuvenum sententia
dictis" (238), "[These words] fueled the fire of what the soldiers
thought" (F:328). The repetition of "talibus . . . dictis," which enclose both lines, reveals a problematic disjunction between words and
deeds, a disjunction that marked Achilles' tragic predicament in the
Iliad. The gap between the sign and its referent is dramatized yet
again in the misleading "signum" (245) that Juturna then sends.
Tolumnius duly misinterprets the omen and not only instigates the
troops to battle but hurls the first spear that effectively breaks the
peace treaty. The by now familiar scene of warlust ("One passion
took possession of them all: / To make the sword their arbiter" [282
(F:387–88)] and accompanying sacrilege ensue, as the soldiers strip
the altar for firebrands.[49] Unlike the *Odyssey*, which moved to its
conclusion through a series of omens and signs that were indeed
fulfilled in Odysseus' return, the *Aeneid* moves towards its tragic
conclusion by dramatizing the gap between omen and event.

Juturna thus assumes a pivotal role in the breaking of the pact
between the Trojans and Latins, though her intervention here, and
later, when she attempts to avert the confrontation between her
brother and Aeneas, ultimately proves to be in vain. Jupiter sends
Juturna an omen (854), one of the "geminae pestes . . . Dirae"
(845)—his own chthonic messenger, like Juno's Allecto, with serpen-

---

[49]William S. Anderson, "Two Passages from Book Twelve of the Aeneid," *CSCA*,
4 (1971), 49–58, gives a detailed analysis of this false omen and the Italian irrationality
that makes for its effectiveness.

tine associations ("serpentum spiris" [848]).[50] The Dira, which serves as a frightful sign to Turnus of his own impending death, causes Juturna to mourn for her brother and leave the field:

> she tore her hair,
> Despairing, then she fell upon her cheeks
> With nails, upon her breast with clenched hands.
> "Turnus, how can your sister help you now?
> What action is still open to me, soldierly
> Though I have been?
>
> . . .
>
> Whip-lash of your wings
> I recognize, that ghastly sound, and guess
> Great-hearted Jupiter's high cruel commands.
> Returns for my virginity, are they?
> He gave me life eternal—to what end?
>
> . . .
>
> Never to die? Will any brook of mine
> Without you, brother, still be sweet to me?
> If only earth's abyss were wide enough
> To take me downward, goddess though I am,
> To join the shades below!"
>
> [12.870–86 (F:1177–99)]

Infelix (870) she is indeed, for the gift of immortality granted her by Jupiter can be nothing but a curse; no death will end her acute grief for her mortal brother.[51] Juturna, like Thetis in the *Iliad* an immortal woman mourning for a mortal man, represents more generally woman's fate in the *Iliad* and Lavinia's in the *Aeneid*: as we learned from Briseis' lament for Patroclus and the lament of Hecuba, Andromache, and Helen for Hector, a typical woman's fate in these poems of war is to survive the male warrior slain in battle. Yet the *Aeneid*'s inclusion and sacrifice of "masculine" women tends to subvert this Iliadic paradigm, as Allecto's attack on Turnus called into question Hector's assertion of war as a male prerogative.

Unlike Thetis, however, whom Jupiter honored by intervening in the war on her son's behalf, Juturna is a victim of Jupiter's patriarchal prerogatives; first by his rape and then by his grant of her immortal-

---

[50]See Johnson, p. 14, on this problematic link between Dira and Jupiter.
[51]Di Cesare, pp. 214–15, compares Juturna's bitter reward to Cassandra's: "Juturna cannot die, but remains human enough to taste the bitterness of that ultimate violence."

ity, which brings only mourning unrelieved by her own death. Juturna's mourning for Turnus' imminent death—she tears her hair,
scratches her cheeks, and beats her breast—recalls Lavinia's mourning for Amata and enacts proleptically Lavinia's sorrow upon Turnus'
death. Unlike the *Iliad,* which closed with the laments of Hector's
kinswomen, however, the *Aeneid* ends abruptly with Turnus' death,
which remains unhonored by funeral and mourning.

Fatum, Sacrifice, and Scapegoating

The final woman to appear in the poem, Juturna, embodies cru-
cially problematic disjunctions between word and deed, and between
the divine and the human, disjunctions that mark the tragic gap between divine *fatum* and the human understanding and fulfillment of it.
As he unrolls *fatum*'s scrolls, Jupiter makes clear its etymology from
the verb *fari,* meaning "what is spoken": "fabor enim, quando haec te
cura remordet, / longius, et volvens fatorum arcana movebo" (1.261–
62), "now let me speak of him, / In view of your consuming care, at
length, / Unfolding secret fated things to come—" (F:352–54).[52]
Juno, as the presiding female deity, exemplifies the force that ob-
structs the unfolding of male Jupiter's *fatum,* and, accordingly, all the
female characters or figures associated with her—Dido, Iris, Allecto,
Amata, and Juturna—temporarily thwart Aeneas' following of his
fatum. The female characters exemplify the personal impulse that opposes public imperatives: Juno's hatred of Aeneas and the Trojans
stems from Paris' slighting her in choosing Venus; Dido's love for
Aeneas is inimical to his duty as a leader of a people as well as to her
own; the Trojan women's weariness leads them to set fire to the ships
necessary to reach Italy; Amata's misplaced love for Turnus sets off
her Bacchic opposition to Latinus and Aeneas; Juturna's love for her
brother compels her to attempt to avert his inevitable death.

Aeneas, unlike these women, follows his *fatum,* despite the attendant losses he must suffer—the separation from Creusa, then Dido,
and the loss of Pallas—and despite his lack of understanding of it.
When he leaves the underworld after Anchises has shown him the
fulfillment of *fatum* in the future Rome, it is through the gate of ivory
from which issue false dreams.[53] Similarly, he gazes uncomprehend-

---

[52]Bailey, p. 205. See also Steele Commager, "Fateful Words: Some Conversations
in *Aeneid* 4," *Arethusa,* 14 (1981), 101–13, on the implications of this etymology.
[53]Anderson, *Art of the Aeneid,* pp. 61–62, gives all the possible meanings of this crux
without deciding among them.

ingly ("rerumque ignarus" [8.730]) at the future depicted on Vulcan's
shield, though he is nonetheless willing to bear the shield and his
fatum that it depicts: "attollens umero famamque et fata nepotum"
(731), "taking up / Upon his shoulder all the destined acts / And fame
of his descendants" (F:990–992).

Aeneas' following of *fatum*, however, has its problematic as well as
its heroic aspect, for it increasingly precludes his listening to human
words. He must heed the words of Mercury, Jupiter's messenger, and
consequently remain unmoved by those of Dido. In the latter part of
the epic, Aeneas, like Achilles in the *Iliad*, becomes more and more
merciless, unheeding of supplicants' pleas for mercy, especially after
Pallas has been killed by Turnus. Aeneas' increasing rage culminates
in his confrontation with Turnus, who evokes Anchises in pleading
for his life. Aeneas hesitates, but the sight of Pallas' belt on Turnus'
shoulder decides his fate. This final act of Aeneas is profoundly ambiguous: was it necessary to kill Turnus in order to fulfill his *fatum*, or
did he purely sate his desire for revenge? Turnus in his plea acknowledges his defeat and gives up his claim to Lavinia, but Aeneas might
well be skeptical, for as we have seen, the previous pact was broken,
though through no fault of Turnus. Even though his act may coincide
with the dictates of *fatum*, Aeneas' final words to Turnus show that
avenging Pallas is his primary motive:

> Blazing up
> And terrible in his anger, he called out:
> "You in your plunder, torn from one of mine,
> Shall I be robbed of you? This wound will come
> From Pallas: Pallas makes this offering
> And from your criminal blood exacts his due."
> He sank his blade in fury in Turnus' chest.
>
> [12.946–51 (F:1289–95)]

The language that describes Aeneas in this passage ("furiis accensus et
ira / terribilis" [946–47]; "fervidus" [951]) links him to those characters whose furious passion consistently served as foils to his *pietas*. It
also recalls the previous instance in which he lusted for vengeance
("poenam" [949]), when he rushed forth to slay Helen, only to be
stopped by Venus. These echoes suggest that Aeneas has been contaminated by passionate fury during the course of the Italian wars,
that he no longer differs from the vengeful hero Achilles in the *Iliad*,
from whom Virgil took such pains to separate him. He seems to have
forgotten Venus' lesson to lay aside personal desires and Anchises'

command to spare the defeated (6.851–53). Yet it could also be argued that Aeneas has finally regained his humanity by allowing his emotion to resurface after so much repression in the service of *fatum*. It is difficult to decide.[54] The import of Pallas' belt is also ambiguous: while for Aeneas it recalls Pallas' death, the slaughter of the bridegrooms depicted on it also mirrors Aeneas' slaying of Turnus.[55] The radical ambiguity of this final scene and of the final ecphrasis leads to a consideration of the doubleness of *fatum* itself and of Virgil's poem that relates and imitates its unfolding.

The doubleness of *fatum* is perhaps best exemplified in the image of serpents that pervade the poem, which signals at once the obstruction of *fatum* and its fulfillment: Juno sends Allecto to serve her purposes against *fatum*, but Jupiter has his own Fury, the Dira, indicate his wishes to Juturna. Prophecies, which foretell the events to be unfolded on *fatum*'s scroll, are similarly problematic: Aeneas, told to return by Apollo to the land of his ancestors, discovers that Troy has a double origin; the golden bough hesitates;[56] the Harpies' terrible prophecy is fulfilled in an unexpectedly benign manner; according to Amata, Turnus as well as Aeneas fulfills the role of foreigner that the oracles demand.

Virgil does not exempt his own poetry from the doubleness that marks prophecy, for he links poetry and prophecy by the verb *canere*. The Sibyl's prophecies are "ambages" (6.99) and wrap truth in darkness ("obscuris vera involvens" [100]), thereby calling for interpretation. The scattering of the Sybil's verses written on leaves further associates prophecy to poetry but also serves to link both to ephemeral and unreliable *Fama*. The poet, like Jupiter, enjoys a privileged point of view, since he sings of unfolded *fatum*. Virgil repeatedly calls attention to the double perspective of "then" and "now," especially toward the end of his poem:

> What god can help me tell so dread a story?
> Who could describe that carnage in a song—

---

[54] On this crux, see Anderson, *Art of the Aeneid* p. 100; Putnam, *Poetry of the Aeneid*, pp. 200–201; and Johnson, pp. 13, 134.

[55] Conte, "The Baldric of Pallas: Cultural Models and Literary Rhetoric," in *The Rhetoric of Imitation*, pp. 185–95, suggests that the baldric, depicting the slaughter of bridegrooms, serves as a synecdoche for the pervasive motif of "mors immatura," relevant for both Pallas and Turnus. See also Hunt, pp. 25–26, on the doubleness of the significance of the belt.

[56] On the doubleness of the golden bough, see Robert A. Brooks, "Discolor Aura: Reflections on the Golden Bough," *AJP*, 74 (1953), 260–80.

The captains driven over the plain and killed
By Turnus or in turn by Troy's great hero?
Was it thy pleasure, Jupiter, that peoples
Afterward to live in lasting peace
Should rend each other in so black a storm?

[12.500–504 (F:680–86)]

Here the knowledge of the end does little to mitigate the destruction
that was necessary to reach it; in fact, Virgil questions the necessity of
such enormous sacrifice. Unlike Homer's Zeus who wept tears of
blood over the death of Sarpedon, Virgil's Jupiter is unmoved by the
numerous lives wasted in the service of *fatum*. While Virgil's poem
retrospectively imitates the unfolding of *fatum*, it also commemorates
those who have been sacrificed to *fatum*:[57]

Fortunate, both! If in the least my songs
Avail, no future day will ever take you
Out of the record of remembering Time,
While children of Aeneas make their home
Around the Capitol's unshaken rock,
And still the Roman Father governs all.

[9.446–49 (F:633–38)]

In this eulogy to Nisus and Euryalus, Virgil builds a poetic monument to their memory that actually proves more enduring than the
house of Aeneas, "domus Aeneae" (448), the embodiment of *fatum* to
which they were both sacrificed. The seemingly irrelevant detail that
Virgil includes in these lines, that the Roman people built their dwellings around "the Capitol's unshaken rock," "Capitoli immobile sax-
um" (448), reveals the crucial fact that at the heart of the empire lies
the Tarpeian rock on the Capitol hill from which criminals were

[57]See Adam Parry, "The Two Voices of Virgil's *Aeneid*," *Arion* 2.4 (Winter 1963),
66–80, for an analysis of the "Virgilian note of melancholy and nostalgia, a note
produced by the personal accents of sorrow over human and heroic values lost" set in
continual opposition to "the public voice of Roman success." See also Conte, "Virgil's
Aeneid: Toward an Interpretation," in *The Rhetoric of Imitation*, p. 163n.: "It is possible
that Virgil disapproved of the unilateral, exclusive passion of these figures [such as
Dido], enclosed in their splendid isolation. But one cannot appreciate the greatness of
the *Aeneid* without becoming fully aware of the humanity of that individual passion,
its possible value, and the sacrifice involved in rejecting it. In fact, just because every
great literary work has its own unified world view . . . we must—if this work is truly
great—be able to find in it an awareness of the other values that this unified vision
rejects or represses or that it fails to incorporate in its own system."

pushed to their deaths. Walter Burkert has discussed the Tarpeian rock as a site of sacrifices for the sake of the community.[58] Virgil understands that the Roman Empire was built on the sacrifice— decreed by the "Father"—of those such as Nisus and Euryalus. His poem, however, contains both the divine *fatum* and the human word, and includes their opposing claims, while dramatizing the tragic disjunction between them.

The function and significance of female characters in the *Aeneid* can be explained in terms of this disjunction: their sacrifice is seemingly justified because they passionately oppose the "rational" ordering of masculine *fatum*. Yet Virgil's palpable attraction to and sympathy for most of these victims express his own ambivalence about the cost of empire whose prerogative his poem seeks to justify.[59] For this reason, I find the *Aeneid* the most divided and self-contradictory text among those studied here. On the one hand, Virgil's allegiance to patriarchy finds expression in his projection of undesirable qualities on the female so that they may be exorcized: he represents Juno, "regina deum" (1.9), as the irrational and violent principle opposing Jupiter's and Aeneas' *fatum,* and he represents Amata as the destructive mother who, with her Bacchae, threatens masculine order and male prerogative. Yet in Dido, Lavinia, Camilla and Juturna, Virgil takes pains to represent the female victim's point of view; even so, Dido and Camilla are contaminated with some of the disquieting qualities that Amata exhibits.

Shadowy Helen is no longer a character within the poem but already a myth, an emblem for the doubleness of the necessity and destructiveness of *fatum*. Although Virgil has Venus demystify Helen as *casus belli,* she nevertheless serves as a scapegoat—as she did in the *Odyssey*—for the poet's own ambivalence toward the authority of the Homeric epics. Thus her two appearances mark Virgil's assertion of

---

[58]Walter Burkert, *Structure and History in Greek Mythology and Ritual* (Berkeley: Univ. of California Press, 1979), pp. 76–77.

[59]For another perspective on sacrifice in the *Aeneid,* see Cesareo Bandera, "Sacrificial Levels in Virgil's *Aeneid,*" *Arethusa,* 14 (1981), 217–39. In an essentially Girardian reading, Bandera argues that sacrifice is "a law of history": "By making the Roman order the representative of this [sacrificial] principle, Virgil is making Rome the representative of order for all mankind" (pp. 223–24). He therefore "read[s] the poem as a sacrificial process of victimization," claiming that "without such a process of victimization, the poem itself, like the violent circularity it portrays, would find no issue, it would remain literally meaningless, *inanis*" (p. 234). He concludes: "The social order emerges from the victim, and not the victim from the social order" (p. 237).

his hero's superiority over mystified versions of Homeric heros: vengeful Achilles in the *Iliad* and guileful Odysseus in the *Odyssey*. Yet Virgil, like Aeneas, finds that he cannot simply exorcize the specter of Helen by either sacrificing her or banishing her from his narrative. Rather the threat of the female Other that Helen embodies resurfaces in various surrogates—Dido, Amata, Camilla, Juturna, and even Lavinia, who is almost sacrificed on Latinus' altars and is indeed sacrificed to Aeneas' *fatum*. Through the sequential sacrifice or scapegoating of these surrogates, Virgil dramatizes at once his need and the need of Augustus' empire to destroy or exorcize woman as Other and the ineffectiveness of these attempts to keep intact masculine order and the male self. Even though Virgil expresses sympathy toward the victims, the number and the clarity of the sacrifices and scapegoatings in the *Aeneid* testify to the severity of Roman patriarchy, which sought to separate absolutely the public and the private, and to punish especially such women as Cleopatra—the foreign queen, the "fatale monstrum," and the historical type for Dido—who transgressed the boundary of their womanly, domestic sphere.[60]

[60]Syme, p. 299, notes that the death of Cleopatra occasioned greater jubilation from the partisans of Octavian than the defeat at Actium of Antony, the greatest soldier of the day.

4 Spenser's *Faerie Queene*

Where is the Antique glory now become,
  That whilome wont in women to appeare?
Where be the brave atchievements doen by some?
Where be the battels, where the shield and speare,
And all the conquests, which them high did reare,
That matter made for famous Poets verse,
And boastfull men so oft abasht to heare?
Bene they all dead, and laid in dolefull herse?
Or doen they onely sleepe, and shall again reverse?
                                    —*Faerie Queene* 3.4.1

Spenser was praised by his contemporary Nashe as the "Virgil of England."[1] Choosing self-consciously to style his poetic career after Virgil's—"For trumpets sterne to chaunge mine Oaten reeds" (1.Pr.1)—Spenser himself announced his *Faerie Queene* as the English descendant of the *Aeneid* in the Renaissance.[2] The *Aeneid* informs the epic structures of both Books 1 and 2, especially Guyon's Book 2, which concerns itself with the classical virtue of temperance; but the importance for Spenser of the Virgilian model becomes even more pressing when he undertakes in Book 3 to praise Elizabeth through Britomart, as Virgil had praised Augustus through Aeneas.

In fashioning the maiden warrior Britomart as his sovereign's ancestor, however, Spenser diverges from Virgil, for whom female rulers such as Dido and Camilla were problematic obstacles to his

[1] *The Works of Thomas Nashe,* ed. R. B. McKerrow (1904; rpt. Oxford: Basil Blackwell, 1958), 1:299. According to Nashe, Chaucer is the English Homer.
[2] All quotations from Spenser are from *Poetical Works,* ed. J. C. Smith and E. de Selincourt (Oxford: Oxford Univ. Press, 1912). Spenser also translated the Virgilian *Culex* as *Virgils Gnat.* On the relationship between the two poets, see Merritt Y. Hughes, *Virgil and Spenser* (1929; rpt. London: Kennikat Press, 1969), esp. pp. 317ff.; William Stanford Webb, "Vergil in Spenser's Epic Theory," *ELH,* 4 (1937), 62–84. For a more recent discussion, see Andrew Fichter, *Poets Historical: The Dynastic Epic in the Renaissance* (New Haven: Yale Univ. Press, 1982), pp. 156ff.

hero's epic mission.[3] Yet Spenser also took his heroine's name from the Virgilian *Ciris,* in which Britomartis, a chaste Cretan nymph, is apotheosized as Diana-Dictyna. This subtext answers Spenser's needs perfectly, for Diana as the virgin goddess was one of the most prevalent mythological representations of Elizabeth, and Britomart's Book 3 is "Of Chastity."[4]

Like Virgil's Aeneas, Spenser's Britomart pursues an epic quest to found an imperial dynasty, a quest that extends beyond her own Book 3 into Books 4 and 5. Britomart's promised union with Artegall, however, is not merely a prerequisite for her epic mission, as was Aeneas' marriage to Lavinia. In fact, Britomart's education in her epic destiny comes about as a consequence of her falling in love with Artegall's image in the "wondrous mirrhour" (3.2.38): her old nurse Glauce takes Britomart to consult Merlin because "she shortly like a pyned ghost became, / Which long hath waited by the Stygian strond" (3.2.52). Thus Britomart's visit to Merlin recapitulates metaphorically Aeneas' descent to the underworld, a crucial step in the education of an epic hero. Accordingly, Spenser signals his epic intentions by prefacing this episode with an invocation to Clio, the muse of epic poetry:

> Begin then, O my dearest sacred Dame,
>   Daughter of *Phoebus* and of *Memorie,*
>   That doest ennoble with immortall name
>   The warlike Worthies, from antiquitie,
>   In thy great volume of Eternitie:
>   Begin, O *Clio,* and recount from hence
>   My glorious Soveraines goodly auncestrie,
>   Till that by dew degrees and long protense,
> Thou have it lastly brought unto her Excellence.
>
>   [3.3.4]

In a reenactment of Anchises' prophetic display to Aeneas of his descendants, Merlin "shewes the famous Progeny / which from

---

[3]Fichter argues that Spenser uses Ariosto as an instrument for overgoing Virgil (pp. 157–58). On Spenser and Ariosto, see Paul J. Alpers, *The Poetry of the Faerie Queene* (Princeton: Princeton Univ. Press, 1967), pp. 160–99.

[4]On the *Faerie Queene* as an epideictic poem, see Thomas H. Cain, *Praise in The Faerie Queene* (Lincoln: Univ. of Nebraska Press, 1978), pp. 1–6 and *passim;* and Robin Headlam Wells, *Spenser's Faerie Queene and the Cult of Elizabeth* (London: Croom Helm, 1983), pp. 1–21 and *passim.* On the many epideictic representations of Elizabeth as Diana, see Elkin Calhoun Wilson, *England's Eliza* (Cambridge: Harvard Univ. Press, 1939), pp. 167–229.

them springen shall" (3.3.Argument). Merlin here acts as a surrogate for Britomart's absent father, who never appears in the poem,
though it is in his closet that she finds the fateful mirror (3.2.22) that
"the great Magitian *Merlin* had deviz'd" (3.2.18).[5]

Although Britomart is the epic hero of Book 3, as Redcrosse was of
Book 1 and Guyon was of Book 2, Spenser includes in Britomart's
book various other female figures: Malecasta, Florimell (and False
Florimell), Belphoebe and Amoret, Hellenore. In fact, Britomart is
absent from the central four cantos of the book. These figures, however, are not merely surrogates for Britomart, in the sense that the
female characters in the second half of the *Aeneid* were surrogates for
the Iliadic Helen and for Virgil's Dido. Rather, the Spenserian figures
stand in a complex relation to the book's heroine Britomart—and to
her prototype Elizabeth—either by presenting aspects of her self (Florimell, Amoret, Belphoebe) or by serving as negative examples to be
repudiated (Malecasta, Hellenore). Spenser's juxtaposition of Britomart to these alternative figures can be best explained by Angus
Fletcher's definition of character in allegory: "A systematically complicated character will generate a large number of other protagonists
who react against him or with him in a syllogistic manner. . . . By
splitting off these chips of composite character, the author is able to
treat them as pure, isolated, personified ideas.[6] In the same way,
Spenser represents the complexity of his heroine Britomart by setting
her against these more simple female figures. Spenser anticipates this
representation of Britomart's complex and multifaceted self in the
Proem to Book 3, where he couches his praise of his sovereign Elizabeth in terms of similar multiplicity:

> Ne let his fairest *Cynthia* refuse,
> In mirrours more then one her selfe to see,
> But either *Gloriana* let her chuse,
> Or in *Belphoebe* fashioned to bee:
> In th'one her rule, in th'other her rare chastitee.
>
> [3.Pr.5]

---

[5]See Susanne Lindgren Wofford, "Gendering Allegory: Spenser's Bold Reader and
the Emergence of Character in *The Faerie Queene* III," *Criticism*, 30 (1988), 7–9, on the
multiple meanings of "closet" as private room, womb, heart, mind, and Spenser's use
of the word here to suggest interiority in Britomart's character.

[6]Angus Fletcher, *Allegory: The Theory of a Symbolic Mode* (Ithaca: Cornell Univ.
Press, 1964), p. 35. On Renaissance notions of the multiplicity of the self, see Thomas
M. Greene, "The Flexibility of the Self in Renaissance Literature," in *Disciplines of
Criticism,* ed. Peter Demetz, Thomas Greene, Lowry Nelson, Jr. (New Haven: Yale
Univ. Press, 1968), pp. 241–64.

Spenser refrains from positing a restrictive correspondence between his sovereign and one of his characters; moreover, his comparison of Elizabeth to the Faery Queen Gloriana, who never appears in the poem except in Arthur's vision of her, emphasizes his refusal to fix Elizabeth's self by representing it. Spenser thus succeeds in according her the respect due to an enigmatic (and powerful) Other. Britomart, like her descendant Elizabeth, then, will see "in mirrours more then one her selfe."

In praising Elizabeth and in fashioning Britomart, Spenser insists upon his divergence from his predecessors and claims to recover from antiquity the fame of women which has been obscured by male invidiousness:

> Here have I cause, in men just blame to find,
>   That in their proper prayse too partiall bee,
>   And not indifferent to woman kind,
>   To whom no share in armes and chevalrie
>   They do impart, ne maken memorie
>   Of their brave gestes and prowesse martiall;
>   Scarse do they spare to one or two or three,
>   Rowme in their writs; yet the same writing small
> Does all their deeds deface, and dims their glories all.
>
>   [3.2.1]

Although Boccaccio's *De Claris Mulieribus,* Chaucer's *The Legend of Good Women,* and Ariosto's *Orlando Furioso* may belie this assertion, Spenser envisions for Britomart a heroic role usually reserved for men and thus claims to portray a woman for the first time as a subject from her own perspective and not as an object from a male perspective.[7] He had earlier presented this ideal of self-sufficiency in a sonnet addressed to his future wife, another Elizabeth:

> Such selfe assurance need not feare the spight
>   of grudging foes, ne favour seek of friends:

[7]See Maureen Quilligan, *Milton's Spenser: The Politics of Reading* (Ithaca: Cornell Univ. Press, 1983), pp. 185–99, for a discussion of "Book 3 and the gender of the reader." She shows that Book 3, addressed to Elizabeth and to "overtly inscribed female readers," is governed by female perspectives. Lillian S. Robinson, *Monstrous Regiment: The Lady Knight in Sixteenth-Century Epic* (New York: Garland, 1985), p. 316, similarly states that "Spenser attempts . . . to compensate for a prevalent literary and political model of society that is based on an unexamined masculine norm." See also Wofford, "Gendering Allegory," pp. 10–16, for a discussion of Britomart as a figure for an "oppositional" female reader, who "search[es] for the countertext, and read[s] against as well as with the allegory" (p. 16).

> but in the stay of her owne stedfast might,
> nether to one her selfe nor other bends.
>
> [*Amoretti*, 59.10–13]

In the *Faerie Queene*, Spenser applies this notion of self-assurance—reliance on internally generated values—to his representation of his epic heroine.

As the primary vehicle of this self-sufficiency, Spenser emphasizes Britomart's androgyny—her embodiment of power and grace—that belies conventional separation of these characteristics according to gender:

> For she was full of amiable grace,
>   And manly terrour mixed therewithall,
>   That as the one stird up affections bace,
>   So th'other did mens rash desires apall,
>   And hold them backe, that would in errour fall.
>
> [3.1.46]

Like Helen, Penelope, and Dido, Britomart participates in the traditionally masculine world of epic. But unlike these anterior heroines and her more conventionally feminine counterparts Florimell and Amoret, Britomart successfully defends against male victimizations of her as female Other by military prowess and knightly armor that masks her gender. Yet Britomart, though androgynous, is not self-contained to the point of narcissism; unlike Virgil's Camilla, who suppressed her sexuality in order to wed herself to war, Britomart seeks Artegall to achieve that ideal union between the sexes which Spenser figures in the emblem of the Hermaphrodite.[8]

Britomart's androgyny allows her to be compared to male figures as well as female ones. She subsumes the heroes of Books 1 and 2 in her encounters with them early in Book 3.[9] First, she unhorses Guyon, "so furious and fell" (3.1.6), to his "great shame and sorrow"

---

[8]C. S. Lewis suggested that the Hermaphrodite captures in an emblem the Biblical metaphor of man and wife as one flesh. *The Allegory of Love: A Study in Medieval Tradition* (1936; rpt. Oxford: Oxford Univ. Press, 1975), p. 344. On the emblem of the Hermaphrodite, see also Thomas P. Roche, *The Kindly Flame: A Study of the Third and Fourth Books Of Spenser's Faerie Queene* (Princeton: Princeton Univ. Press, 1964), pp. 134–36; Donald Cheney, "Spenser's Hermaphrodite and the 1590 *Faerie Queene*," *PMLA*, 87 (1972), 192–200; and Lauren Silberman, "The Hermaphrodite and the Metamorphosis of Spenserian Allegory," *ELR*, 17 (1987), 207–23.

[9]Jonathan Goldberg, *Endlesse Worke: Spenser and the Structures of Discourse* (Baltimore: Johns Hopkins Univ. Press, 1981), p. 4, holds that compared to Guyon and Redcrosse, Britomart is undermined as a hero by "the weakening of the quest as a

(3.1.7) and leaves him and Arthur to pursue Florimell: "faire *Britomart*, whose constant mind, / Would not so lightly follow beauties chace, / Ne reckt of Ladies Love, did stay behind" (3.1.19). She then rescues Redcrosse, beset and wounded by Malecasta's six knights, who demand that he forsake Una to serve Malecasta (3.1.27). Britomart more generally assumes the roles of both Una and Redcrosse. Redcrosse's reference to Una as the *"Errant Damzell"* (3.1.24) links the heroine of Book 1 and Britomart; and Britomart will undergo many trials for the sake of her beloved, as Redcrosse had already done for Una. Yet Britomart, unlike Redcrosse who left Una for Duessa, will keep her promise of steadfastness; she asserts to Malecasta's knights: "Yet will I not fro mine owne love remove" (3.1.28). Finally, her quest to realize her vision of Artegall reenacts Arthur's similar quest for Gloriana: "From that day forth I lov'd that face divine; / From that day forth I cast in carefull mind, / To seek her out with labour, and long tyne" (1.9.15).

In the same way that Britomart can be compared to male heroes such as Redcrosse and Arthur, her vision of Artegall in her father's mirror evinces a complex interplay of sameness and otherness that cuts across the boundary between the sexes. Her need for Artegall points to another aspect of her ambiguity: although Spenser took her name from the nymph in *Ciris* who martyred herself to chastity, Britomart's dialogue with Glauce depends upon Scylla's complaint in the same poem to her nurse about her illicit love for Minos, her father's enemy.[10] Thus Spenser combines in Britomart the seemingly antithetical qualities of chastity and passion, and thereby redefines chastity to mean chaste generation. Unlike her namesake, Britomart will gain immortality not through absolute chastity but through generation, and unlike Scylla, her passion will create a nation, not destroy one.

Britomart's Two Wounds

Britomart's own perception of self-division arises precisely from this ambiguous tension between chastity and passion; Spenser repre-

---

principle of narrative structure." He considers Britomart's armor to be a "mask of power . . . [that] attempt[s] to affirm a self that has been rendered impotent by desire" (p. 85).

[10]Hughes, pp. 348–54, gives a detailed comparison of the Spenserian passage and its subtext. See also Roche, pp. 53–54.

sents this self-division through the physical wounds that she receives first from Gardante in Malecasta's castle and later from Busirane. At the close of the opening canto of Book 3, immediately after Britomart has repulsed the advances of Malecasta who stole upon her in her sleep, Gardante wounds her:

> The mortall steele stayd not, till it was seene
> To gore her side, yet was the wound not deepe,
> But lightly rased her soft silken skin,
> That drops of purple bloud thereout did weepe,
> Which did her lilly smock with stanes of vermeil steepe.
>
> [3.1.65]

Gardante, the chief of Malecasta's six knights, represents "Daunger" of the courtly love tradition;[11] his inflicting on Britomart a "wound not deepe" represents Malecasta's assault on her chastity from which she ultimately defends herself successfully. Accordingly, Spenser alludes to the *Roman de la Rose* by likening Britomart in her knightly disguise to a rose with protective thorns: "As he, that hath espide a vermeill Rose, / To which sharpe thornes and breres the way forstall" (3.1.46).

In the midst of the "lascivious disport" at Castle Joyeous and the "loose demeanure of that wanton sort" (3.1.40), Redcrosse disarms, but "the brave Mayd would not disarmed bee" (3.1.42). Yet in defensively refusing to reveal her identity even after Malecasta makes explicit her "fleshly flame" (3.1.50), Britomart paradoxically encourages Malecasta's lust toward the knight she assumes to be male. Because Britomart herself suffers from love for Artegall, she mistakenly and naively empathizes with Malecasta's "faire semblaunce" (3.1.54) of love and so refrains from explicitly repulsing her advances: "For great rebuke it is, love to despise, / Or rudely sdeigne a gentle harts request; / But with faire countenaunce, as beseemed best, / Her entertaynd" (3.1.55). Thus in her wrongheaded defensiveness and in misinterpreting Malecasta's lust for love, she leaves herself vulnerable to Malecasta's nocturnal visit.

If in Malecasta's castle, at the beginning of Book 3, Britomart's

---

[11] *Variorum,* ed. Edwin Greenlaw, Charles G. Osgood, and Frederick M. Padelford (Baltimore: Johns Hopkins Univ. Press, 1932–49), 3:211. See Lewis, pp. 364–65, for a discussion of the medieval usage of *daunger.* Mark Rose, *Heroic Love: Studies in Sidney and Spenser* (Cambridge: Harvard Univ. Press, 1968), p. 91, states, however, that Gardante means "seeing."

traditionally "feminine" defense of chastity was at stake, at the end of Book 3, in Busirane's castle, she takes on a traditionally "masculine" role in her passionate attack to rescue Amoret. To Scudamour who is unable to rescue his beloved, Britomart counsels: "Daunger without discretion to attempt, / Inglorious and beastlike is" (3.11.23). Britomart, however, persists in her attempt to brave the flames that enclose Busirane's castle, "for shamefull thing / It were t'abandon noble chevisaunce, / For shew of perill, without venturing" (3.11.24). Scudamour demonstrates anew his inability to rescue Amoret when he attempts to follow Britomart's lead "with greedy will, and envious desire," and is "pitifully brent" (3.11.26). Once in the castle, Britomart is repeatedly enjoined by mysterious signs to "*Be bold*," but also to "*Be not too bold*" (3.11.54). Although she does not understand "what sence [they] figured" (3.11.50), Spenser nevertheless repeatedly describes her as "bold" (3.11.50; 12.2) for pressing forward, despite the sinister and bizarre Masque of Cupid she witnesses. When she is about to rescue Amoret from Busirane who "figur[es] straunge characters" from Amoret's "living bloud" (3.12.31), she receives the knife wound that Busirane intended for Amoret:

> Unwares it strooke into her snowie chest,
> That little drops empurpled her faire brest.
> Exceeding wroth therewith the virgin grew,
> Albe the wound were nothing deepe imprest,
> And fiercely forth her mortall blade she drew,
> To give him the reward for such vile outrage dew.
>
> [3.12.33]

In her anger Britomart almost kills Busirane, but Amoret restrains her, since only he can "reverse" (3.12.36) the charms he wrought on Amoret. Although the wound precedes and indeed motivates Britomart's strike against Busirane, it nevertheless bespeaks the difficulty to "be bold" but "not too bold," and to temper passionate attack with discretion. Britomart succeeds where Scudamour failed in rescuing his beloved, for as A. Kent Hieatt has suggested, Scudamour was overly "bold" (4.10.4) in abducting her from the Temple of Venus.[12]

---

[12]A. Kent Hieatt, "Scudamour's Practice of *Maistry* upon Amoret," *PMLA*, 77 (1962), 509–10. See also Roche, pp. 72–88, who stresses the boldness of Britomart and sees the significance of the episode to lie in "the boldness of love conquered by the boldness of chastity." Hieatt's discussion is a rejoinder to Roche's. On the Busirane episode as a dramatization of male aggression against and appropriation of the female

Britomart's two wounds thus represent the tension between "feminine" defense and "masculine" attack, which also corresponds to the difficulty of reconciling chastity and passion already noted. This anxiety-producing difficulty is dramatized in Britomart's dialogue with Glauce after she has fallen in love with Artegall's "shade and semblant" (3.2.38). There she speaks of her passion as a "wound" (3.2.36) that threatens to engulf her whole being:

> For no no usuall fire, no usuall rage
> It is, O Nurse, which on my life doth feed,
> And suckes the bloud, which from my hart doth bleed.
>
>   .   .   .
>
> Sithens it hath infixed faster hold
> Within my bleeding bowels, and so sore
> Now ranckleth in this same fraile fleshly mould,
> That all mine entrailes flow with poysnous gore,
> And th'ulcer groweth daily more and more.
>
>   [3.2.37, 39]

Glauce reassures Britomart that her love is "affection nothing straunge" and not "filthy lust, contrarie unto kind" (3.2.40), like that of Myrrhe who loved her father (3.2.41). But because Britomart loves the image in her father's mirror, her anxiety understandably results from the conflict between chastity and passion as well as one between incest or narcissism and other-directed love.

Spenser thus presents "the tyranny of love" (3.2.40) as an onset of acute self-consciousness, which Britomart perceives as an external assault on the independence and integrity of the self: "no powre / Nor guidance of her selfe in her did dwell" (3.2.49). Britomart's two wounds therefore are physical signs of her metaphorical wounds of love: her armored prowess proves ineffectual in defending her against this vulnerability that arises from her love for Artegall. Spenser takes this figure of a wounded heart from a conventional conceit of love poetry but accords the self-division to a woman—usually the beloved

---

psyche, see Harry Berger, Jr., "Busirane and the War Between the Sexes: An Interpretation of *The Faerie Queene*, III.xi–xii," *ELR*, 1 (1971), 99–121. See also the recent discussions by Wofford, "Gendering Allegory," pp. 9–16, and Lauren Silberman, "Singing Unsung Heroines: Androgynous Discourse in Book III of the *Faerie Queene*," in *Rewriting the Renaissance: The Discourses of Sexual Difference in Early Modern Europe*, ed. Margaret Ferguson, Maureen Quilligan, and Nancy J. Vickers (Chicago: Univ. of Chicago Press, 1986), pp. 259–71.

who is merely addressed in such poems—thereby fulfilling his promise to diverge from male-centered conceptions of the self.

Britomart, Paridell, and Hellenore

When Britomart reenters the poem in canto 8 at Malbecco's castle, she encounters Paridell and Hellenore, latter-day versions of Trojan Paris and Helen, and learns of her descent from Trojan Brutus—an important step in her education as an epic heroine, founder of Troynovant. Accordingly, the Malbecco episode becomes a locus also for Spenser's meditation on his own classical genealogy, his descent from Virgil and Ovid.[13]

Malbecco, "old, and withered like hay" (3.9.5), and Hellenore, his young wife who "joy[es] to play emongst her peares" (3.9.4), are "unfitly yokt together in one teeme" (3.9.6).[14] In concluding the 1590 *Faerie Queene*, Spenser returns to this image of harnessing a ploughing team—an image that suggests the mastery of his medium resulting in fertile generation—to figure his activity as a narrating poet: "But now my teme begins to faint and fayle . . . / Therefore I will their sweatie yokes assoyle" (3.12.47).[15] In the Malbecco episode, Spenser's chosen mode seems to be that of "unfitly yok[ing] together" various antithetical pairs, for at the very beginning of the canto he signals this mode of dialectical definition: "But never let th'ensample of the bad / Offend the good: for good by paragone / Of evil, may more notably be rad, / As white seems fairer, macht with

---

[13]Fletcher, in *The Prophetic Moment: An Essay on Spenser* (Chicago: Univ. of Chicago Press, 1971), maps out what he calls "typological matrices" of the poem, but his discussion of Virgil focuses on Book 2 and its hero, Guyon. He does, however, note Ovid's influence on the Malbecco episode as that of "the creative use of parody" (p. 98). Hughes, pp. 339–40, does not see Virgil as a prominent subtext in this episode: "These stanzas do not ring as if they had been forged from the metal of the *Aeneid*." Although he does not discuss specific subtexts, Harry Berger, Jr., comes closest to my concerns in focusing on what he calls Spenser's "technique of conspicuous allusion," of "presenting stock literary motifs, characters and genres in such a way as to emphasize their conventionality." "The Discarding of Malbecco: Conspicuous Allusion and Cultural Exhaustion in *The Faerie Queene* III, ix–x," *SP*, 66 (1969), 135.

[14]The quoted line comes after Spenser has repeatedly called attention to the misalliance: the couple are of "unequall yeares," "unlike conditions" (3.9.4), and Malbecco is "unfit faire Ladies service to supply" (3.9.5).

[15]Spenser opens Book 6, canto 9, using this same figure: "Now turne againe my teme thou jolly swayne, / Back to the furrow which I lately left."

blacke attone" (3.9.2). In addition to the mismatched couple, Spenser juxtaposes Britomart and Paridell, two competing heirs of Troy who actually engage in combat; Britomart and Hellenore, whose conceptions of themselves as women and readers are diametrically opposed; and finally, Virgil and Ovid, the classical exponents of epic and courtly love, or public and private imperatives.[16]

To this canto which contains explicit references by Paridell to Virgil's hero and his epic career, Spenser introduces Aeneas' descendant Britomart amid a tempest like the one that beset her ancestor at the beginning of the *Aeneid*. The storm that brings Britomart to seek shelter in Malbecco's castle and then in the swine shed occupied by Paridell and Satyrane is not simply a narrative device but an allusion to the tempest in *Aeneid* 1, which brought Aeneas to Dido's shores and which signifies the unleashing of passions that generate disorder. In her passionate anger directed against the Trojans for Paris' Judgment, Juno enticed Aeolus, king of the winds, to forgo his control over his subjects by promising him the sexual possession of a beautiful nymph (1.65–75). In the simile describing Paridell's attack on Britomart, Spenser alludes to Virgil's description of Aeolus' winds shut up in a cave:[17]

> Tho hastily remounting to his steed,
>   He forth issew'd; like as a boistrous wind,
>   Which in th'earthes hollow caves hath long bin hid,
>   And shut up fast within her prisons blind,
>   Makes the huge element against her kind
>   To move, and tremble as it were agast,
>   Untill that it an issew forth may find;
>   Then forth it breakes, and with his furious blast
> Confounds both land and seas, and skyes doth overcast.
>
> [3.9.15]

> Talia flammato secum dea corde volutans
> nimborum in patriam, loca feta furentibus Austris,
> Aeoliam venit. hic vasto rex Aeolus antro

---

[16]See Roche, pp. 62ff., for a discussion of the Malbecco episode as "the interplay of the themes of love perverted and society destroyed."

[17]Berger discusses this simile as a description of an earthquake or volcanic eruption, though he, too, sees its function as locating Paridell in "a world of primal forces." "Discarding of Malbecco," pp. 140–41.

luctantis ventos tempestatesque sonoras
imperio premit ac vinclis et carcere frenat.
illi indignantes magno cum murmure montis
circum claustra fremunt; celsa sedet Aeolus arce
sceptra tenens, mollitque animos et temperat iras;
ni faciat, maria ac terras caelumque profundum
quippe ferant rapidi secum verrantque per auras.
sed pater omnipotens speluncis abdidit atris,
hoc metuens, molemque et montis insuper altos
imposuit regemque dedit, qui foedere certo
et premere et laxas sciret dare iussus habenas.

[*Aeneid*, 1.50–63]

Thus inwardly pondering with an inflamed heart, the goddess came to
Aeolia, the country of storm clouds, regions that breed raging south
winds. Here, in his vast cave, King Aeolus holds rule over the strug-
gling winds and resounding tempests; he bridles them with chains and
imprisons them. They roar in indignation around their bands to the
loud rumbling of the mountains. In his high citadel sits Aeolus, holding
a scepter, and restrains their passions and tempers their rage; if he had
not done so, they would surely seize and bear off with them the sea, the
land, and the vast sky, sweeping them through the air. But fearing this,
the omnipotent father hid them in dark caverns and placed over them
high mountains and gave them a king, who, by fixed covenant, should
know when to tighten and loosen the reigns of command.[18]

Spenser's verbal echo of the Virgilian passage becomes apparent in
phrases such as "hollow caves," "prisons blind," and "land and seas,
and skyes," which translate corresponding phrases in the subtext. By
revealing the internal and metaphorical source of the actual storm,
Spenser already presents Paridell as subject to passions that will prove
destructive not only of private order but of public and epic order.

In Virgil, Neptune's quelling of the tempest was likened to the
calming of a mob by a man respected for civic service (1.142–56). In
Spenser's poem, Britomart, as Paridell's adversary in her concern for
"countries cause" (3.9.40), not only jousts with him and unhorses
him but fittingly brings out the sun after the storm, in a second simile
which describes the effect of her unvizarding.[19]

[18]Quotations from Virgil and Ovid in this chapter are from the edition of Loeb
Classical Library. I have occasionally modified the translations.
[19]See A. Bartlett Giamatti, "Spenser: From Magic to Miracle," in *Exile and Change
in Renaissance Literature* (New Haven: Yale Univ. Press, 1984), pp. 76–88, for a

Tho whenas vailed was her loftie crest,
Her golden locks, that were in tramels gay
Upbounden, did them selves adowne display,
And raught unto her heeles; like sunny beames,
That in a cloud their light did long time stay,
Their vapour vaded, shew their golden gleames,
And through the persant aire shoote forth their azure streames.

[3.9.20]

This passage takes as its subtext Ovid's description in the *Metamorphoses* of how the god Vertumnus, disguised as an old woman, revealed himself to Pomona in order to win her love:

in iuvenem rediit et anilia demit
instrumenta sibi talisque apparuit illi,
qualis ubi oppositas nitidissima solis imago
evicit nubes nullaque obstante reluxit,
vimque parat.

[*Metamorphoses, 14.766–70*]

He returned to his youthful form, put off the old woman's trappings, and stood revealed to the girl as when the sun's most beaming face has conquered the opposing clouds and shines out with nothing to dim his radiance.

Britomart's introduction to the episode as "another knight" (3.9.12) and Spenser's repeated references to her by the masculine pronoun before she reveals herself to the company parallel Vertumnus' successful concealment of his gender. The Ovidian subtext calls attention to the redemptive power that both the male god and the female warrior derive from their androgyny. Upon Britomart's unveiling, the company marvels at her "in contemplation of divinitie" (3.9.24).

Spenser further links Britomart to the divine in comparing her to another androgynous god, Minerva:

Like as *Minerva,* being late returnd
    From slaughter of the Giaunts conquered;
    Where proud *Encelade,* whose wide nosethrils burnd
    With breathed flames, like to a furnace red,

---

discussion of this recurring moment of vision resulting from raising a visor or helmet in Spenser and his predecessors.

> Transfixed with the speare, downe tombled ded
> From top of *Hemus,* by him heaped hye;
> Hath loosd her helmet from her lofty hed,
> And her *Gorgonian* shield gins to untye
> From her left arme, to rest glorious victorye.
>
> [3.9.22]

In the 1590 version, the comparison was to Bellona;[20] the revision to Minerva suggests that Spenser wished to insist upon his heroine's wisdom rather than her physical might. Spenser's singling out of Minerva's victory over the giants further points to this opposition between wisdom and elemental force, set forth in this and the previous simile describing Paridell. Finally, the reference to the site of Minerva's victory, Mount Hemus, where Achilles' parents, Thetis and Peleus, were wed (*Metamorphoses,* 11.229), points to the fruitful conjugal love that will produce progeny of epic importance.[21] Through these similes and through his allusions to Virgil's critique of uncontrolled passion and Ovid's celebration of love, Spenser already establishes the fundamental opposition between Paridell's destructive passion and Britomart's redemptive power.[22] These similes that open the Malbecco episode, then, signal Spenser's creative use of the interplay between Virgil and Ovid throughout the episode.

Spenser, however, criticizes Ovid's exaltation of the private over the public when he has Paridell seduce Hellenore in a reenactment of Paris' wooing of Helen in *Heroides* 16. Ovid opposed Virgil and undercut empire building in the *Heroides,* through the laments of women such as Dido and Medea who were sacrificed to empires, and in the *Metamorphoses* he criticized the hollowness of Augustanism.[23]

---

[20] *Variorum,* 3:279.

[21] See also *Metamorphoses,* 11.266: "Felix et nato, felix et coniuge Peleus" (Pelius was blessed in his son, blessed in his wife). Spenser again alludes to this Ovidian episode in the *Mutabilitie Cantos:* "Was never so great joyance since the day, / That all the gods whylome assembled were, / On *Haemus* hill in their divine array, / To celebrate the solemne bridall cheare, / Twixt *Peleus,* and dame *Thetis* pointed there" (7.7.12).

[22] In canto 4, Britomart had already overcome within herself the forces exemplified by Paridell (expressed there in Petrarchan terms: "Huge sea of sorrow, and tempestuous griefe" [3.4.8]) before she jousted with Marinell on the "rich strond"; thus she is now prepared to defeat Paridell. On Spenser's critique of Petrarch in this episode, see Susanne Lindgren Wofford, "Britomart's Petrarchan Lament: Allegory and Narrative in *The Faerie Queene* III, iv," *CL,* 39 (1987), 28–57.

[23] See W. R. Johnson, "The Problem of the Counter-classical Sensibility and its Critics", *CSCA,* 3 (1970), 148: "Augustus apparently detected something more in the *Metamorphoses* and in the *Ars Amatoria* than the work of an irresponsible spokesman for *la dolce vita.* What Augustus heard was a clear and resonant voice that spoke of love

Spenser translates Ovid's "tecta . . . signa" (17.81–82), the secret
signs sent by Paris to Helen, in the phrase "close messages"
(3.9.27).[24] Paridell, a "learned lover" (3.10.6), knows his Ovid well
and seems to almost "go by the book" when he repeats his ancestor's
writing of a love message on the spilt wine. Spenser criticizes from a
Christian perspective Paridell's anachronistic imitation and his blas-
phemous perversion of Holy Communion by calling it a "sacrament
prophane in mistery of wine" (3.9.30).[25]

Spenser quarrels with Paridell's reductive use of Ovid as the advo-
cate of adultery and the progenitor of courtly love, not only by
affirming the Christian sacrament of marriage but also by insisting
upon public and social responsibilities. The repetition of the words
"close," "secret," and "privy" in the description of the two eventual
adulterers' dealings with one another paradoxically links them to the
wronged husband Malbecco, whose "privitie" (3.9.3) compelled him
to hoard selfishly his "mucky pelfe" (3.9.4) and to lock Hellenore

---

that would not be codified, of divinity that could not respond to artificial respiration,
of the continuance of the age of iron, and of the crumbling of empires. Augustus was
not amused." On Ovid's anti-Augustanism and his parody of Virgilian epic, see also
Brooks Otis, *Ovid as an Epic Poet* (1966; 2d ed. Cambridge: Cambridge Univ. Press,
1970), pp. 350–51, 361–62.

[24]Compare also with Ovid's lines: "Iuppiter his gaudet, gaudet Venus aurea *furtis;* /
haec tibi nempe patrem *furta* dedere Iovem (16.291–92; emphasis added). Spenser
consistently links lust with secrecy; Malecasta sent "secret darts" (3.1.51) to Britomart, but she, unlike Hellenore here, "dissembled . . . with ignoraunce" (3.1.50).

[25]In Castiglione's *The Book of the Courtier* (1528), during the discussion of how to
fashion a perfect court lady, one of the interlocuters refers to Ovid's counsel that "a
good way to make your love known to a lady at a banquet [is to] dip a finger in the
wine and write it on the table." Another speaker, however, points out the anachronism: "There was nothing wrong with that in those days." Trans. Charles S. Sin-
gleton (Garden City, N.J.: Anchor, 1959), p. 277. John Harrington, in the Preface to
his translation of Ariosto (1591), perhaps following Castiglione, makes a similar
point: "*Ovid* gave precepts of making love, and one was that one should spill wine on
the boord & write his mistresse name therewith. This was a quaynt cast in that age;
but he that should make love so now, his love would mocke him for his labour, and
count him but a slovenly sutor." *Elizabethan Critical Essays*, ed. G. Gregory Smith
(Oxford: Clarendon Press, 1904; rpt. 1937), 2:215. Spenser has Paridell repeat from
Ovid Paris' seduction of Helen by writing "amo" in the spilt wine (*Heroides*, 17.87–
88). Helen Cheney Gilde points out other passages in Ovid where similar techniques
of seduction are presented (*Ars Amatoria*, 1.569–72, *Amores*, 1.4.17–20), but she does
not discuss the crucial passages in the *Heroides*. Gilde, moreover, sees Spenser's imitation of Ovid to be straightforward and uncritical; she concludes that Spenser is sympathetic toward Hellenore. "Spenser's Hellenore and Some Ovidian Associations,"
CL, 23 (1971), 233–39. But see Rosemond Tuve's discussion of the passage as a
deliberately "shocking blasphemy" of Communion which perverts "heavenly Passion
into self-seeking lust." *Elizabethan and Metaphysical Imagery* (Chicago: Univ. of
Chicago Press, 1947), p. 221.

from "all mens sight" (3.9.5). The consequences of Malbecco's solipsism are laid bare when his "privy griefe" (3.10.60) in having lost both his gold and his wife ultimately leads to his solitary transformation into *Gealosie* that "feed[s] it selfe with selfe-consuming smart" (3.11.1). Just as Malbecco's pathological selfishness made him a "cancred crabbed Carle" with "no skill of Court nor courtesie" (3.9.3), so Paridell and Hellenore turn away from the public to the private, by appropriating public signs and, as we shall see, epic history for private and self-serving ends. By calling attention to the etymology of "courtesie," Spenser defines that public virtue as stemming from life at court.[26] Although adept at exploiting courtly forms, "Sir" Paridell fails to understand that these forms arise from, and are grounded in, civic life.

Spenser's relationship to Virgil is somewhat more problematic. In presenting Britomart's founding of a second Rome, he knew the dangers of merely repeating Virgil, which Petrarch's and Ronsard's less than successful attempts at rewriting the *Aeneid* amply demonstrate.[27] Virgil himself had dramatized the consequences of literal and diminished imitation: in the wrongheaded and pathetic replicas of once magnificent Troy that Aeneas founds after leaving the ashes of his fallen city, such as Aeneadae (3.18) and Pergamum (3.133); and in Hellenus and Andromache's "parva Troia" (3.349) with its dried-up counterfeit of Xanthus. Heeding Virgil's lesson, Spenser exorcizes the specter of servile repetition through the figure of Paridell, whose recounting of his genealogy to the company that includes Hellenore and Britomart is styled after Aeneas' narrative to Dido in Books 2 and 3 of the *Aeneid*. Against Paridell, who trivializes Virgil's hero through iteration, Spenser sets his own heroine Britomart, who corrects and supplements Paridell's narrative.

[26]On Spenser's use of etymology, see Martha Craig, "The Secret Wit of Spenser's Language," in *Essential Articles for the Study of Edmund Spenser,* ed. A. C. Hamilton (Hamden: Archon, 1972), pp. 313–33; and A. C. Hamilton, "Our New Poet: Spenser, Well of English Undefyled," in *Essential Articles,* pp. 488–506. But Maureen Quilligan notes the problematic etymology of "courtesy" in Book 6: "Is the metaphor inherent in the etymology of "courtesy" a thrust at truth or a lie?" *The Language of Allegory: Defining the Genre* (Ithaca: Cornell Univ. Press, 1979), p. 47. C. S. Lewis made a similar point: "Courtesy . . . for the poet, has very little connexion with the court." But his definition of courtesy as "charity and humility in so far as these are *social,* not theological virtues" (p. 350; emphasis added) is pertinent to my discussion of the absence of these public virtues in both Paridell and Malbecco.

[27]See Thomas M. Greene, *The Descent from Heaven: A Study in Epic Continuity* (New Haven: Yale Univ. Press, 1963), pp. 1–7, on how Petrarch's *Africa* and Ronsard's *Françiade* mistakenly sought to capture the spirit of Virgil by copying the letter of the text.

Aeneas unwittingly seduced Dido by his anguished tale of the fall of his city. Paridell follows Aeneas' example, but, exploiting his knowledge of the consequences of Aeneas' narration, he quite consciously sets out to seduce Hellenore. Moreover, unlike Aeneas, Paridell speaks unfeelingly of Troy as "but an idle name, [that] in thine ashes buried low dost lie" (3.9.33).[28] Yet Troy is not an "idle name" for Paridell, who repeats in this very canto the seduction of another Helen, or for Britomart, the future ruler of Troynovant. Paridell, moreover, blames the "angry Gods, and cruell skye" for Troy's "direfull destinie" (3.9.33), preferring to disregard the individual's responsibility in forging history.[29] Britomart had already learned from Merlin that:

> Indeed the fates are firme,
> And may not shrinck, though all the world do shake:
> Yet ought mens good endevours them confirme,
> And guide the heavenly causes to their constant terme.
>
> [3.3.25]

Britomart was exhorted by Merlin to fulfill her destiny, as Aeneas was enjoined by his father Anchises before her, but Paridell has withdrawn from the historical process. Accordingly, his apostrophe to Troy concludes with these lines:

> What boots it boast thy glorious descent,
> And fetch from heaven thy great Genealogie,
> Sith all thy worthy prayses being blent,
> Their of-spring hath embaste, and later glory shent.
>
> [3.9.33]

His insistence that Troy's "glorious descent" is now "blent" and "shent" reveals his conception of history as an inevitable decline, although it is pale imitations of prior heroes like himself who have "embaste" Troy by their decadence. As Harry Berger, Jr., has pointed out, Paridell sees the sole significance of the Trojan war that caused "many Ladies deare lament / The heavie losse of their brave Paramours" (3.9.35) to reside in its generation of courtly love.[30] Literary convention thus mediates Paridell's experience and deadens his imagination

---

[28]See Roche, pp. 63–65, and Berger, "Discarding of Malbecco," pp. 138–39, for discussions of the inadequacies of Paridell's narrative.

[29]In Ovid, Paris compels Helen by invoking the fates as having ordained their love (*Heroides*, 16.41), much in the same way that Paridell speaks of history here.

[30]Berger, "Discarding of Malbecco," p. 138.

to such an extent that he is only capable of stock responses that reveal his callousness toward suffering.

Hellenore, too, uses history and texts reductively when she allows herself to be seduced by Paridell's tale. If Paridell is the figure for the reductive poet, Hellenore represents the reductive reader. Spenser repeatedly calls attention to her role as reader: "But in his eye his meaning wisely red" (3.9.28); "well she red out of the learned line" (3.9.30). She is eager to put to practice her reading in the "lewd lore" (3.9.28) of courtly love and follows Paridell's lead by spilling the wine on her lap (3.9.31). As the modern Helen (ore = now) and Dido, she appears determined, in both senses of the word, to repeat her literary models without any interesting differences; hence she trivializes them. Consequently, the fires that consumed Troy and the flames on Dido's pyre diminish with iteration into those set by Hellenore on her miser husband's hoard:

> The rest she fyr'd for sport, or for despight;
> As *Hellene,* when she saw aloft appeare
> The *Trojane* flames, and reach to heavens hight
> Did clap her hands, and joyed at that dolefull sight.

> This second *Hellene,* faire Dame *Hellenore,*
> The whiles her husband ranne with sory haste,
> To quench the flames, which she had tyn'd before,
> Laught at his foolish labour spent in waste;
> And ranne into her lovers armes right fast.
> [3.10.12–13]

Thus Hellenore's imprisonment by Malbecco may be read as an allegory for her self-inflicted subjugation to both texts and patriarchal attitudes, the latter exemplified by Satyrane's misogynistic *sententiae* about "womans will, which is disposd to go astray" and their "wilfull wandring feet" (3.9.6–7). Although Hellenore, with her "fraile wit" (3.9.52) may confirm Satyrane's contemptuous generalization about women, his words are belied by Britomart's appearance as soon as he has uttered them. Hellenore escapes the tyranny of Malbecco by eloping with Paridell, but after he casts her off, she chooses her ultimate fate to be handled by the satyrs in democratic ownership as "commune good" (3.10.36)—a debased repetition of Una's sojourn with the same satyrs who worshipped her in Book 1.[31] Britomart, by

---

[31]Critics who focus on the pastoral in canto 10 tend to approve of Hellenore's sojourn with the satyrs. James Nohrnberg sees her ultimate fate as an "innocent self-

contrast, leaves Malbecco's castle to pursue her traditionally masculine quest for Artegall and, as we have already seen, in canto 12
rescues Amoret, another woman imprisoned by literary convention
that has been made horribly literal by Busirane. As Spenser has already informed us, everything is known by its contrary, and so Britomart's errancy, set against Hellenore's subjugation, emerges as a
sign of her independence and freedom that derive from her androgyny. Just as the *Odyssey* and the *Aeneid* made Helen static in
order to generate and replace her with other female characters (Penelope, Dido, Camilla) who embodied the energies and ambiguities of
the Iliadic Helen, so here Spenser supersedes Hellenore through his
new heroine Britomart.

Britomart's visionary response to Paridell's narrative offers a corrective both to his cavalier attitude toward history and to Hellenore's
unimaginative reading of his tale:

> Whenas the noble *Britomart* heard tell
>   Of *Trojan* warres, and *Priams* Citie sackt,
>   The ruefull story of Sir *Paridell,*
>   She was empassiond at that piteous act.
>   · · ·
>   O lamentable fall of famous towne,
>   Which raignd so many yeares victorious,
>   And of all *Asie* bore the soueraigne crowne,
>   In one sad night consumd, and throwen downe:
>   What stony hart, that heares thy haplesse fate,
>   Is not empierst with deepe compassiowne,
>   And makes ensample of mans wretched state,
> That floures so fresh at morne, and fades at euening late?
>   [3.9.38–39]

Unlike Paridell, who neglects his public duty and chooses instead to
lead a life endlessly pursuing "faire Ladies love" (3.9.37), Britomart

---

realization." *The Analogy of the Faerie Queene* (Princeton: Princeton Univ. Press,
1976), p. 31. Alpers, p. 388, similarly considers the pastoral setting to give sanction to
the lustful satyrs. More recently, John D. Bernard characterizes it as "the pastoral of
erotic fulfillment . . . an idyllic view of eroticism as essentially innocent, untram-
meled by the constraints of conventional morality." "Pastoral and Comedy in Book
III of *The Faerie Queene*," *SEL,* 23 (1983), 8. Roche, p. 202, however, sees Hellenore's
transformation, as well as Malbecco's, as "not a vision or an instruction except in the
negative sense."

constructively yokes the public to the private; in stating that her heart is "empierst" by compassion for fallen Troy, Spenser employs the same figure that he appropriated from love poetry to represent her love for Artegall. Paridell's heart was also wounded by "firie dart[s]" sent by Hellenore, but for the seasoned reader of love poetry the wound was "nothing new" and caused "ne paine at all" (3.9.28,29). Thus Britomart, like Paridell and Hellenore, is seduced, but her seduction results not in a trivial repetition of adulterous courtly love but in a renewal of her purpose to wed herself to her people, just as her descendant Elizabeth claimed that she considered herself wed to her British subjects. It is also worth noting in this context that in the well-known 1569 portrait of Elizabeth at Hampton Court, she was represented as another Paris who gives the apple to herself rather than to one of the competing goddesses.[32]

Britomart's superior imagination is also revealed in these visionary lines, for Troy is not merely an "idle name" to be addressed in empty apostrophes but a city to which she feels a personal tie, because she knows that from its "race of old / . . . she was lineally extract: / For noble *Britons* sprong from *Trojans* bold, / And *Troynovant* was built of old *Troyes* ashes cold" (3.9.38). Similarly, when Merlin foretold the fate of her progeny, she was "full deepe empassioned, / . . . for her peoples sake, / Whose future woes so plaine he fashioned" (3.3.43).[33] Her interpretation of Troy's fall as "ensample of mans wretched state" evinces her dynamic relationship to history: not only is she imaginatively engaged with her past, she is willing to heed its lessons. Moreover, by having Britomart take this line from the Psalms, Spenser reveals that she harmonizes the sacred and the secular, unlike Paridell who appropriated the sacred for his own ends.[34] By acknowledging her shared origin with Paridell, Britomart paradoxically calls attention to and sums up her radical opposition to Par-

---

[32]On the Hampton Court painting and Peele's slightly different use of the same myth to praise Elizabeth, see Louis A. Montrose, "Gifts and Reasons: The Contexts of Peele's *Arraignement of Paris*," *ELH*, 47 (1980), 433–61.

[33]Isabel G. MacCaffrey's comment is pertinent here: "Britomart's story is, among other things, the story of the vicissitudes of imagination. Two contrary impulses of the imagining power are called in question: the impulse to seal off the psyche in a self-created world of love, a dark glass; and the impulse to serve a wonder-working natural providence." *Spenser's Allegory: The Anatomy of Imagination* (Princeton: Princeton Univ. Press, 1976), p. 312.

[34]*Variorum*, 3:281, cites Psalm 90.5–6: "In the morning they are like grass which groweth up. . . . / in the evening it is cut down and withereth."

idell's nonchalance toward "countries cause": "Behold, Sir, how your pitifull complaint / Hath found another partner of your payne" (3.9.40).

Although Britomart places herself in the service of history, Paridell seeks to promote himself by appropriating history for his own ends. He speaks of his ancestor Paris as the "most famous Worthy of the world" (3.9.34) and effaces such Trojan heroes as Hector and Aeneas from his narrative.[35] Falsely claiming that Helen was given to Paris by Venus as "meed of worthinesse" (3.9.34), he suppresses the fact that the goddess rewarded him for choosing her over Juno and Athena. His own description of Paris' career, however, makes apparent that his ancestor's "noble fame" stems from his abduction of Helen that "brought [Ilion] unto balefull ruine" (3.9.34).

Britomart restores Aeneas to his rightful place when she requests to hear his story, thus implicitly criticizing Paridell's self-aggrandizement in narrating his own genealogy as if it were the only and most important line descending from Troy. Yet even then he omits the Dido episode.[36] Thomas Roche considers Aeneas' repudiation of Dido to be the exemplum that Paridell should have heeded;[37] but in playing second Aeneas to Hellenore's second Dido, Paridell perhaps intentionally excludes Dido from his narrative to cover his tracks. In fact, Spenser paradoxically calls attention to that well-known episode by its very absence. Moreover, Spenser subtly links Paridell to Aeneas by having him echo Juno's disparagement of Aeneas as the second Paris (7.318): "Wedlock contract in bloud, and eke in blood / Accomplished, that many deare complaind" (3.9.42). Berger is surely right in seeing Paridell's insistent repetition of "wedlock" as revealing his aversion to marriage;[38] yet Spenser in addition sets Britomart's eventual marriage to Artegall as a corrective not only to Paridell's iterative philandering but also to Aeneas' abandonment of Dido in favor of a "wedlock" with Lavinia that he "hardly praisd . . . good" (3.9.42).

Although Britomart tactfully refrains from speaking of Dido, she calls attention to another gap in Paridell's narrative by telling of Brutus' line, descending from Aeneas' son, Sylvius. Paridell excuses the

---

[35]Compare with Ovid, where Paris' self-aggrandizement as a great warrior (*Heroides*, 16.353–70), is deflated by Helen (17.251–56).

[36]Hughes, pp. 339–40, cites this omission by Spenser as evidence for his view that Virgil does not figure prominently in the Malbecco episode.

[37]Roche, p. 65.

[38]Berger, "Discarding of Malbecco," p. 139.

omission by claiming to have forgotten the story he heard from Mnemon—the Greek word for "memory." Spenser had invoked Clio, the daughter of Memory to good purpose before recounting Merlin's prophecy of Britomart's progeny in canto 3, but Paridell here reveals himself to be an epic poet *manqué*.[39] Memory is as essential for the epic hero in the service of history as it is for the epic poet. In Books 1 and 2 Spenser had used the image of a nautical voyage to figure the epic careers of Redcrosse and Guyon as well as his own poetic project; here, Spenser signals the convergence of the poet and the hero in the name, Nausa, that he gives to the first settlement of Paridell's ancestors.[40] Although Paridell as epic hero and poet is revealed to be less than adequate, Spenser has Britomart supplement and correct Paridell, and thus his heroine emerges as the rightful heir to the epic line extending from Troy.

Paridell, however, casts a shadow on the origins of Britomart's line by alluding to Brutus' slaying of his father, Sylvius, in a hunting accident, which led to his self-exile and eventually to his founding of Britain. By including this incident in Paridell's narrative, Spenser reveals that in the beginning of even this idealized line there was a transgression, a parricide. Although Isabel MacCaffrey considers Britomart's virtue to ensure her nation against the fate of Troy, in the end, just as the original Troy and Rome, the second Troy, fell, so the third Troy will fall if it is to "equalise" (3.9.44) its predecessors.[41] It is worth noting in this context that Spenser had translated Du Bellay's *Les Antiquités de Rome* as *Ruines of Rome*. Britomart's elegiac likening of the life of a city to that of a man in speaking of Troy's fall also makes the coming of evening and death to Troynovant inevitable.

If the relationships between fathers and sons and between poets and their predecessors lie at the heart of epic, then just as Brutus' parricide was a prerequisite for his founding of Troynovant, so is Spenser's divergence from his epic sources essential to his conception of a new epic heroine and her mission. Spenser depends upon, but diverges from, both Virgil and Ovid. Like Ovid's Paris, Britomart journeys to

---

[39]See Quilligan, *Milton's Spenser*, pp. 132–34, for the importance of remembering. She discusses Malbecco's transformation as an interpretation of "the final effects of the loss of memory, of that consciousness of a developing history that ensures the only real change."

[40]See 1.2.1; 2.7.1; 1.12.42. *Variorum*, 3:281, gives Nausa as an invention of Spenser's. For another discussion of the significance of the nautical image and the pervasive references to oceans in Book 3, see Berger, "Discarding of Malbecco," p. 143.

[41]MacCaffrey, p. 311.

match the vision of the beloved to its reality (*Heroides*, 16.36–37, 103), but as a result she will create a nation, not bring about its destruction. Moreover, by combining the seemingly antithetical qualities of chastity and passion in Britomart—and thereby redefining "chastity" as chaste generation—Spenser criticizes Paris' assertion in Ovid that beauty and chastity are at odds (*Heroides*, 16.290). Although Britomart traces her ancestry from Aeneas and follows his example in founding another Troy, Spenser questions Virgil's subordination of private happiness to the public good, through Paridell's reference to Aeneas' "wedlock" that he "hardly praisd . . . good" (3.9.42). In Britomart, Spenser manages to have it both ways by wedding Virgil to Ovid and "unfitly yok[ing them] together" (3.9.6): her marriage to Artegall will yoke her union with her beloved to her epic imperative to found Troynovant.

Britomart had recounted how Brutus, in founding London, fixed as its boundaries two gates and two rivers:

> The *Trojan Brute* did first that Citie found,
>   And Hygate made the meare therof by West,
>   And *Overt* gate by North: that is the bound
>   Toward the land; two rivers bound the rest.
>   So huge a scope at first him seemed best,
>   To be the compasse of his kingdomes seat:
>   So huge a mind could not in lesser rest,
>   Ne in small meares containe his glory great,
> That *Albion* had conquered first by warlike feat.
>
> [3.9.46]

In these lines, the interplay of confinement and liberation—especially notable in "Overt" or open gate—sums up Spenser's insistence on balancing constraint and freedom in fashioning both his new epic and its heroine. Both character and poet are guided in their self-definitiòns by the boundaries set by Virgil and Ovid, but unlike Paridell and Hellenore, who restrict and reduce themselves in merely repeating literary tradition, Spenser and Britomart assert their visionary freedom in "so huge a scope"—the dialectical space he clears between the two classical poets.

In the following canto 10, Britomart leaves Malbecco's castle without witnessing how Paridell achieves his seduction of Hellenore in typical courtly fashion, by "singing sweetly" and "making layes of love" (3.10.8). In Paridell and Hellenore, Britomart has confronted without much danger the negative examples for her quest as both an epic hero and a woman, and so she hardly needs to follow them further. Moreover, canto 10 merely delineates the logical consequences of what Britomart has already seen in canto 9: Paridell, true to his name that implies all women are equal to him, wins Hellenore only to cast her off as his ancestor, Paris, had left Oenone; and Hellenore chooses the satyrs as her lovers, as we have seen. Malbecco similarly undergoes a process of fulfilling the tendencies already noted. In his attempt to win back his wife by mingling with the satyrs' flocks to avoid detection, he "counterfeite[s]" (3.10.47) a goat, but his disguise is facilitated by the cuckold's horns he has actually sprung; he has already taken steps toward becoming an allegorical figure, *Gealosie*.[42] His objectification of Hellenore ultimately finds its Dantesque *contrappasso* in his own reification.

Florimell and False Florimell

If in the Malbecco episode Spenser explicitly refers to the Helen myth, then the Florimell episode is his "allusive adaptation" of the same myth.[43] According to the dwarf from the Faery court, Florimell is, as Helen once was, the "fairest wight alive" (3.5.5). Moreover, in an apostrophe to the knights, Spenser speaks of her in terms that recall the Greek mission to reclaim Helen:

> How soone would yee assemble many a fleete,
> To fetch from sea, that ye at land lost late;
> Towres, Cities, Kingdomes ye would ruinate,
> In your avengement and dispiteous rage,
> Ne ought your burning fury mote abate.
>
> [3.8.28]

In fact, Paridell comes upon Hellenore during his quest for Florimell and thus substitutes one descendant of Helen for another.

Spenser compares Florimell's sudden entry in Book 3 to the appearance of a baleful comet:

[42]See Fletcher, *Allegory*, pp. 49–50, for a discussion of the movement from realism and mimesis to allegory in the transformation of Malbecco. See also Alpers, p. 218: "The poet's act of renaming [Malbecco] . . . produces the awesome recognition that the name of a passion has become the name of a creature."

[43]I take the term from Kathleen Williams, who distinguishes these two uses of myth in Spenser. "Venus and Diana: Some Uses of Myth in the *Faerie Queene, ELH*, 28 (1961), rpt. in *Spenser: A Collection of Critical Essays*, ed. Harry Berger, Jr. (Englewood Cliffs: Prentice Hall, 1968), p. 98.

Still as she fled, her eye she backward threw,
  As fearing evill, that pursewd her fast;
And her faire yellow locks behind her flew,
Loosely disperst with puffe of every blast:
All as a blazing starre doth farre outcast
His hearie beames, and flaming lockes dispred
At sight whereof the people stand aghast:
But the sage wisard telles, as he has red,
That it importunes death and dolefull drerihed.

[3.1.16]

In her fearful flight from the "beastly lust" of the "griesly Foster" (3.1.17), Florimell is compared to a comet that signals bane, not because she is sinister in herself but because men project on Florimell ambivalence about their own desires that make them forget all else to pursue her. Thus her male pursuers project their own disequilibrium on her and read her as a sign of "death and dolefull drerihed," much as the men in the *Iliad* projected their ambivalence toward the heroic code on Helen.

Even Arthur and Guyon pursue her as "most goodly meede, the fairest Dame alive" (3.1.18). However, the cooperative spirit evidenced during their encounter with Britomart—Guyon asked "the Prince of grace, to let him runne that turne. / He graunted" (3.1.5)—gives way to emulation and rivalry: "Full of great envie and fell gealosy, / They stayd not to avise, who first should bee" (3.1.18). Accordingly, when they come to a "double way, / . . . they did dispart, each to assay, / Whether more happie were, to win so goodly pray" (3.4.46). Their pursuit of Florimell has "dis-paired" them, and it has also transformed them from knights to hunters—of a woman. The punning antithesis "dispair"/"pair" recalls the division between Achilles and Agamemnon over Briseis. Just as Patroclus refrained from participating in the warriors' objectification of Briseis, so Timias refuses to join in the hunt after Florimell. He alone pursues the offending Forster rather than Florimell, casting an unfavorable light on the knights and their feverish chase. Four cantos later, Arthur will "greatly . . . complaine / The want of his good Squire late left behind . . . / For doubt of daunger, which mote him betide" (3.5.12).

Arthur's pursuit of Florimell is especially problematic, because it diverts him from his quest for Gloriana, his "first poursuit" (3.5.2), to which he returns after he has lost sight of Florimell. Spenser's comparison of Arthur to a "ship, whose Lodestarre suddenly / Covered with cloudes, her Pilot hath dismayd" (3.4.53) calls attention to his losing sight not only of Florimell but, more important, of his true "Lodestarre," Gloriana. His rest on "grassie ground" (3.4.53) recalls Gloriana's appearance to him as he lay on "verdant gras" (1.9.13). In his "restlesse anguish and unquiet paine" (3.4.61), he wishes that Florimell were Gloriana: "Oft did he wish, that Lady faire mote bee / His Faery Queene, for whom he did complaine: / Or that his Faery Queene were such, as shee" (3.4.54). Although Florimell is clearly mistaken in being "no lesse affrayd" (3.4.51) of Arthur than of the Forster, Arthur's perception of her alternately as "pray" and as substitute for Gloriana renders her "needelesse dreed" perhaps not so unjustified.

But against these variously reductive objectifications of Florimell as either a sinister beauty to be possessed or food for a Hyena that "feeds on womens flesh" (3.7.22), Spenser sets his own more complex representation that accords her selfhood and subjectivity. Although most readers of Spenser remember Florimell simply as a beautiful and skittish woman constantly running away from some danger, real or imagined—a view perhaps best encapsulated in the couplet, "Whose face did seeme as cleare as Christall stone, / And eke through feare as white as whales bone" (3.1.15)—she also demonstrates a "boldness" much like Britomart's in her "wandring for to seeke her lover deare, / . . . her dearest *Marinell*" (3.6.54). Like Britomart, she persists in the quest for her beloved, who does not know of her existence, and her "boldness" in setting out from her own element, the Faery court, to verify the rumors that Marinell is "yslaine" by a "forreine foe" (3.5.9) leads her to venture into Marinell's element, where she will eventually be united with her love. Her quest takes her through many perils, but the greatest comes when she is "compeld to *chaunge* / The land for sea" (3.8.20; emphasis added). In Proteus' realm, under his protean attempts to woo her and then threaten her "unto his wished end" (3.8.41), Florimell bravely withstands "change," the dissolution of "her selfe" (3.8.20):[44]

---

[44]A. Bartlett Giamatti, "Proteus Unbound: Some Versions of the Sea God in the Renaissance," in *Exile and Change,* p. 115 and *passim,* notes that Proteus was a *deus ambiguus.* In the *Faerie Queene,* he is indeed ambiguous in his relations with Florimell: he saves her from the Fisher's lust and comforts her, only to subject her to his own lust and throw her into his "Dongeon deepe" (3.8.41). In addition, his ambiguous prophecy that "play[s] / With double senses" (3.4.28) causes Marinell to shun women, but Proteus' imprisonment of Florimell and his hosting of the Marriage of the Rivers brings them together.

> Eternall thraldome was to her more liefe,
>   Then losse of chastitie, or chaunge of love:
>   Die had she rather in tormenting griefe,
>   Then any should of falsenesse her reprove,
>   Or loosenesse, that she lightly did remove.
>   Most vertuous virgin, glory be thy meed,
>   And crowne of heavenly praise with Saints above,
>   Where most sweet hymmes of this thy famous deed
> Are still emongst them song, that far my rymes exceed.
>
> [3.8.42]

Spenser's apostrophe to Florimell, that her "vertuous deedes" will bring her "endlesse fame" (3.8.43), reveals that the poet does not conceive of her as merely a fearful maid who "flyes away of her owne feet affeard" (3.7.1). There is no denying that Florimell is compelled by male lust and her own fears to a degree that Britomart is not, but her "stedfast chastitie and vertue rare" (3.5.8) give her a measure of self-determination. Although the two female figures never meet—Britomart refuses to join Guyon and Arthur in pursuit of Florimell, as has already been noted—Spenser nevertheless has Britomart play a redemptive role for Florimell: by wounding Marinell, she exposes the error in his mother's interpretation of Proteus' prophecy which had caused him to shun woman's love and, in addition, leads Florimell on her quest to verify the rumor that he is dead.

Florimell's sojourn with Proteus alludes to the tradition of the two Helens, in which a phantom Helen went to Troy while the true (and chaste) Helen stayed with Proteus in Egypt. In the creation of False Florimell, Spenser recalls Hera's successful creation of a decoy to mislead the warriors. False Florimell takes the predominant male attitude toward Florimell as an object to be possessed to its logical conclusion: in order to satisfy her son's lust for unavailable Florimell, the witch creates an amalgamation of literalized Petrarchan conceits:

> In stead of eyes two burning lampes she set
>   In silver sockets, shyning like the skyes,
>   And a quicke moving Spirit did arret
>   To stirre and roll them, like a womans eyes;
>   In stead of yellow lockes she did devise,
>   With golden wyre to weave her curled head;
>   Yet golden wyre was not so yellow thrise
>   As *Florimells* faire haire: and in the stead
> Of life, she put a Spright to rule the carkasse dead.
>
> [3.8.7]

Through this creation of a counterfeit doll by joining various artificial body parts, Spenser exposes the violent appropriation of woman implicit in the *blason*.[45] The witch's son is completely satisfied with this "carkasse dead" (3.8.7), for False Florimell is the perfect "Idole faire" (3.8.11) that answers to male fantasies. Furthermore, as far as her male pursuers are concerned, Florimell might as well be a doll, for the "counterfet . . . shame[s] / The thing it selfe" (3.8.5). Spenser had described his own art as "living art" (3.Pr.1) that only "shadow[ed]" (3.Pr.3), unlike the witch's art that counterfeits and hence reifies. The real Florimell was threatened by "chaunge" and dissolution, but False Florimell proves quite willing, like Hellenore, to be treated as a prized object by men who seek to possess her: Blandamour, Paridell, and Braggadocchio. It is appropriate that Braggadocchio, who "in vaunting vaine / His glory did repose, and credit did maintaine (3.8.11), takes her from the witch's son, for his "glozing speaches frame[d] / To such vaine uses" (3.8.14) mirror exactly the process through which False Florimell came into being. In fact, False Florimell in Book 4 will choose Braggadocchio as her knight from among the many who joust for her.

Scapegoating Radigund

In the 1596 *Faerie Queene*, Spenser diverges from his earlier mode of allegory by introducing in Book 5 the Amazon queen Radigund, with whom Britomart shares her androgyny as a "martiall Mayd" (3.4.18). Britomart's distinction from the Amazon queen becomes of necessity more problematic than in the previous instances, where her knightly armor and prowess distinguished her quite clearly from more conventionally feminine figures such as Hellenore and Florimell. At the same time, Spenser diverges from his use of the Virgilian model: Artegall displaces Britomart as "Aeneas" in this episode, thus making Radigund a Dido figure and Britomart, surprisingly, a Lavinia. Both the difficulty of maintaining distinctions between Radigund and Britomart and the displacement of Britomart as an epic hero announce Spenser's departure from his earlier poetry of praise.

[45]Nancy Vickers has shown that the Petrarchan *blason* finds its source in the myth of Diana and Actaeon; to defend against his own dismemberment and dispersal and to affirm the unity of his self, the male poet fragments the body of the beloved. "Diana Described: Scattered Woman and Scattered Rhyme," in *Writing and Sexual Difference*, ed. Elizabeth Abel (Chicago: Univ. of Chicago Press, 1982), pp. 95–110.

This subversion of Britomart, I suggest, expresses Spenser's disillusionment with the Elizabethan order. Several recent critics have observed this disillusionment in the latter part of Spenser's poetic career. For example, Richard Helgerson locates this disillusionment in the split between heroic action and love that marks Books 5 and 6: "The optimistic faith that had animated the early books, the faith that history was going the right way, seems to have left Spenser in the 1590s. Heroic poetry requires, as Cuddie argued in the October eclogue, an heroic age. By the time he wrote Books V and VI, that age seemed to have passed."[46] David L. Miller also sees in Spenser's late work signs of withdrawal from "his engagement *as a poet* with the cultural and political institutions of late sixteenth-century England," manifested in his questioning of the humanist faith in literature as a mode of persuasion.[47] Recent social historians of this period also see the closing years of Elizabeth's reign as a time of economic crisis, political disintegration, and burgeoning corruption, an age in which things turned horribly sour.[48] Since Spenser's praise of Elizabeth's order in Book 3 focused on her special status as a woman ruler, which allowed him to represent her as both the object of desire, on the one hand, and the ruler and patron to be praised on the other, it is not surprising that Spenser's later expression of ambivalence centers also upon the gender of his sovereign, especially in Book 5's Radigund episode.[49]

The confrontation between Britomart and Radigund has traditionally been read as Spenser's heroine's triumph over "the mas-

[46]Richard Helgerson, *Self-Crowned Laureates: Spenser, Jonson, Milton and the Literary System* (Berkeley: Univ. of California Press, 1983), pp. 55, 91.

[47]David L. Miller, "Spenser's Vocation, Spenser's Career," *ELH*, 50 (1983), 215–16. For similar views, see also Cain, pp. 131–32; Michael O'Connell, *Mirror and Veil: The Historical Dimension of Spenser's Faerie Queene* (Chapel Hill: Univ. of North Carolina Press, 1977), p. 13; and Jonathan Goldberg, *Endlesse Worke*, pp. 166–74.

[48]Robert Ashton, *Reformation and Revolution: 1558–1660* (London: Paladin, 1984), p. 180.

[49]O'Connell maintains, specifically in reference to the Radigund episode, that the mythic power of Spenser's fiction "enable[d] him to respond to the pressure of history without endangering his moral allegory" (pp. 139–40). But see Judith H. Anderson, "'In liuing colours and right hew': The Queen of Spenser's Central Books," in *Poetic Traditions of the English Renaissance*, ed. Maynard Mack and George deForest Lord (New Haven: Yale Univ. Press, 1982), pp. 47–66, who argues that Spenser's representation of Elizabeth is already complexly shaded in Book 3, and in Book 4 is even more critical. The vehicle of such criticism is the distinction and distance between "life and antiquity, historical present and mythic past, current truth and Faerie image" (p. 51).

culine, violent, inequitable aspect of her own Amazonian nature."[50]
Simply put, Radigund, according to this interpretation, represents
the "bad Amazon," over whom Britomart, the "good Amazon," will
inevitably prevail.[51] Critics have also argued that from this episode
can be deduced Spenser's so-called moderate Puritan position regard-
ing women in power: that women in general (including Mary Tudor
and Mary Stuart) are not equipped to exercise political authority, but
God sometimes sees fit to endow certain exceptional women (such as
Elizabeth) with the necessary qualifications.[52] According to this reading, then, Radigund functions as a convenient scapegoat for Spenser
and his heroine Britomart: Radigund's destruction allows Spenser to
dissociate Britomart from anxiety-producing qualities traditionally
associated with Amazons and to assert her prerogative to found the
Tudor line.

Yet Spenser complicates this apparently simple allegorical conflict,
and his artistic choice expresses ambivalence toward Elizabeth's rule.
Spenser forgoes his control over Radigund's meaning by quite deliberately swerving from his representation of her as an allegorical figure
signifying belligerence and tyranny.[53] At the heart of Book 5, which
has been noted for its conspicuous political and historical allegory,
Spenser develops and complicates Radigund beyond a personified

[50]Fletcher, *Prophetic Moment*, p. 279. See also the fuller statement on p. 248: "The
allegory must show her relation to her own violence, namely the potential Radigund
in her, so that she may experience this violence and reject it for her ultimate marriage
to [Artegall]." Similarly, A. C. Hamilton, *The Structure of Allegory in the Faerie Queene*
(London: Oxford Univ. Press, 1961) observes: "Radigund expresses Britomart's
womanly pride to which Artegall submits" (p. 185); "In terms of the allegory [Brit-
omart] changes from her role as Radigund—one who occasions Artegall's fall—to
one who restores his power" (p. 189).

[51]For example, T. K. Dunseath, *Spenser's Allegory of Justice in Book Five of the Faerie
Queene* (Princeton: Princeton Univ. Press, 1968), p. 177, states: "The only physical
clash between two women in the poem . . . pits upholders of different principles
against one another—love against lust. In the logic of the poem's structure, it is
Britomart's final confontation of the forces of Malecasta. . . . The outcome of the
battle is never in doubt." See also *Variorum* 5:221: "[Britomart's] victory is the vin-
dication of social justice against a revolutionary polity."

[52]James E. Phillips, Jr., "The Woman Ruler in Spenser's *Faerie Queene*," *HLQ*, 5
(1942), 217–18, 233–34. See also his "The Background of Spenser's Attitude Toward
Women Rulers," *HLQ*, 5 (1942), 5–32; and Constance Jordan, "Woman's Rule in
Sixteenth-Century British Political Thought," *Renaissance Quarterly*, 40 (1987), 421–
51.

[53]See Fletcher, *Allegory*, p. 38. Fletcher considers the essence of allegory to be its
abstraction, its "omission of human detail," which neither the mimetic nor the mythic
mode omits (p.29n).

abstraction into something closer to a dramatic or novelistic character, thereby creating tensions in his chosen allegorical mode which
result in its eventual breakdown. Spenser's departure from allegory in
representing Radigund as a complex character who appeals to the
reader's sympathy recapitulates Virgil's depiction of Dido not simply
as an obstacle for Aeneas' epic mission but as a tragic heroine in her
own right.

Spenser need not motivate the Amazon Radigund's animosity toward men, but he nevertheless explains it as resulting from anger
and humiliation arising from unrequited love. Having been rejected
by Bellodant (a characteristically allegorical name meaning "war-
giver"), Radigund "turn'd her love to hatred manifold" (5.4.30).
Radigund's conception of love, like Malecasta's, does not respect the
integrity and difference of the Other: in her failure to possess Bellodant, to "w[i]nne [him] unto her will," (5.4.30), her love turns to
angry spite. She reacts to this disappointment by dressing men in
"womens weedes" (5.4.31) and compelling them to perform domestic chores. Like Virgil, Spenser dramatizes his anxiety concerning
what is perceived as the necessary correlation between female ascendancy and male humiliation; here Radigund follows the hallowed
tradition of domineering and emasculating queens such as Omphale,
who bought Hercules as a slave and put him to woman's work. But at
the same time, by explaining Radigund's motives for her actions,
Spenser already departs from his treatment of previous allegorical
figures such as Lucifera in Book 1 and Malecasta in Book 3, whose
motivations were irrelevant and thus never explained. Moreover,
unlike Bellodant's transparently allegorical name, Radigund's name,
derived from St. Radegunde—who was known for piety, meekness,
virginity, and special charity to prisoners—stands in tension with the
character Spenser gives her;[54] through this ironic discrepancy between Radigund and her name, Spenser again signals his divergence
from allegory.

Spenser complicates Radigund further by having her fall in love
with Artegall, whom she has vanquished. Initially, she persists in
speaking of her love as bondage, revealing yet again her conception of
love only in terms of domination and submission: "It is so hapned,
that the heavens unjust, / Spighting my happie freedome, have

[54]Cain, p. 153.

agreed, / To thrall my looser life, or my last bale to breed" (5.5.29).[55]
Yet her love allows her to see herself and her relationship with Artegall in a new perspective. Her transformation by the "kindly flame"
(4.Pr.2) is made evident in her new-found humility: she admits that it
was not her "valour" but Artegall's "owne brave mind" that led to his
subjection, and she voices remorse over her unjust treatment of him
although he had saved her life (5.5.32). She also appears to abandon
her conception of love as possession; she no longer is satisfied to have
Artegall under "bondage" but instead desires his "free goodwill"
(5.5.32). Radigund's self-consciousness arising from her love for Artegall recalls Britomart's similar awakening when she saw his image
in her father's mirror. Unlike Virgil, who makes Dido less sympathetic after she falls in love with Aeneas, Spenser makes evident his
intention to win the reader's sympathy for Radigund by transposing
Radigund's duplicity, manifested during her combat with Artegall, to
her handmaid Clarinda (a confidante like Virgil's Anna), who deceives
her mistress in order to further her own love toward Artegall.[56]

As well as displaying affinities with Britomart, Radigund's development from cruelty to humility parallels Artegall's similar transformation in this episode. The moment that encapsulates the old and
new Artegall occurs when he spares Radigund's life upon unvizarding
her.[57]

[55]Hamilton, *Structure of Allegory*, p. 183, sees the central issue of the Radigund
episode to be that of "maisterie" between Britomart and Artegall.

[56]Rosemond Tuve, "Spenser's Reading: The *De Claris Mulieribus*," in *Essays by
Rosemond Tuve: Spenser, Herbert, Milton*, ed. Thomas P. Roche (Princeton: Princeton
Univ. Press, 1970), pp. 87–90, explains the "enlargement and deepening of the action," Radigund's development beyond "merely a martial Acrasia," by reference to
Spenser's use of Boccaccio's Iole, who was somewhat justified in her humiliation of
Hercules because he had caused her father's death. Radigund, whom Spenser compares to Iole, begins to elicit a "sympathy . . . which we ought to feel only for a tragic
heroine." But Fletcher sees Radigund as an allegorical figure conforming to his theory
of allegory and so interprets this same process differently: "Sometimes, indeed an
allegorist will go out of his way to create the monuments of evil and the rationality of
madness as when Spenser does . . . when he shows that Radigund, *the absolute antago-
nist of the good*, has her own laws, her own rights, her own feelings, and her own
ideals" (*Allegory*, p. 361; emphasis added).

[57]Judith Anderson also sees a change in Artegall "from a principle to a person" in his
battle with Radigund and notes in this passage "Artegall's fall into a human context, a
human condition." She goes on to remark, "Once Artegall sees a human reality
outside himself, he becomes aware of his own feelings and, at least to this degree, of
himself." "'Nor Man it is': The Knight of Justice in Book V of Spenser's *Faerie
Queene*" *PMLA*, 85 (1970), rpt. in *Essential Articles*, p. 455.

But when as he discovered had her face,
  He saw his senses straunge astonishment,
  A miracle of natures goodly grace,
  In her faire visage voide of ornament.
              .   .   .

At sight thereof his cruell minded hart
  Empierced was with pittifull regard,
  That his sharpe sword he threw from him apart,
  Cursing his hand that had that visage mard:
  No hand so cruell, nor no hart so hard,
  But ruth of beautie will it mollifie.

                                    [5.5.12,13]

Artegall's pity for Radigund is clearly the cause of his later woes, but his pity, which was absent from his justice up to this point, is also a "ruth of beautie." The erotic overtone of this moment is underlined not only by the reference to Achilles' falling in love with Amazon Penthesilea as he was about to slay her but also by the close verbal echo of Artegall's earlier unvizarding of Britomart—a repetition that again serves to link the two women.[58]

With that her angels face, unseene afore,
  Like to the ruddie morne appeard in sight,
              .   .   .

His powrelesse arme benumbd with secret feare
  From his revengefull purpose shronke abacke,
  And cruell sword out of his fingers slacke
  Fell downe to ground, as if the steele had sence,
  And felt some ruth, or sence his hand did lacke.

                                    [4.6.19,21]

Although some may criticize Artegall for sparing the Amazon (or for abandoning his "sharpe sword"), if he were to destroy Radigund at this point, he would be no different from the ruthless and inflexible Talus. More difficult and perhaps even more crucial than maintaining the distinction between Artegall and Talus is telling apart Britomart and Radigund. For Artegall, and even for the reader, the similarity between the two moments of unvizarding prefigures the conflation of

---

[58]Alpers, pp. 127–31, argues that although we note the basic parallel between Artegall's two battles with Britomart and Radigund, critical tact advises against seeking out detailed remembrances.

Britomart and Radigund and the consequent breakdown of allegory in this episode.

Just as Artegall's attraction to Britomart was predicated on their resemblance to one another—Artegall, after all, is Britomart's mirror image—so his attraction to Radigund bespeaks his resemblance to the Amazon queen. In Book 3, Spenser signaled Britomart's imaginative affinity with her British progeny and Trojan forebears by stating that her heart was "empierst" with pity by the story of their misfortunes (3.9.39). Artegall's similar figurative wound, therefore, links him to Radigund, for it is his "cruell hart" that is "empierst" by the sight of Radigund's face. Spenser had figured Artegall's cruelty in his companion Talus, "that great yron groome, his gard and government" (5.4.3). Moreover, at the end of canto 3, which immediately precedes Radigund's introduction to the poem, Guyon restrained Artegall's "choler" from exacting excessive punishment on Braggadocchio (5.3.36). Finally, at Isis Church, where Britomart arrives while Artegall is imprisoned by Radigund, the priest interprets Britomart's dream thus:

> For that same Crocodile doth represent
> The righteous Knight, that is thy faithfull lover,
> Like to *Osyris* in all just endever.
> For that same Crocodile *Osyris* is,
> That under *Isis* feete doth sleepe for ever:
> To shew that clemence oft in things amis,
> Restraines those sterne behests, and cruell doomes of his.
>
> [5.7.22]

Artegall is susceptible to Radigund precisely because he shares with her the propensity toward "cruell doomes." In a simile comparing Artegall's subjugation by Radigund to Hercules' choice of pleasure with Iole (5.5.24), Spenser highlights the willfulness of Artegall's choice and his attraction for Radigund.[59] As Kathleen Williams shrewdly notes, Artegall's tyrannous and ruthless character paradoxically implies a "capacity for submission," what we might less

---

[59]Jane Aptekar has noted the paradigm of the "choice of Hercules" between pleasure and virtue as governing Artegall's mistaken "choice" of Radigund. She thus sees Britomart and Radigund, representing virtue and pleasure, as diametrically opposed "choices" for Artegall. *Icons of Justice: Iconography and Thematic Imagery in Book V of the Faerie Queene* (New York: Columbia Univ. Press, 1969), pp. 172–200.

charitably call a sado-masochistic tendency that he shares with Hercules.[60] But once vanquished, Artegall diverges from the Herculean model. Unlike Hercules who "with his mistresse toyed" (5.5.24), Artegall deflects the advances of both Radigund and Clarinda. In addition, he accepts the consequences of his "choice" with a humility uncharacteristic of him up to this point. Through his subjection by Radigund and his consequent taking on of "feminine" roles, Artegall seems to learn to incorporate those characteristics necessary to temper his excessively "masculine" justice. Just as Britomart's heroism is predicated upon her combination of both traditionally feminine and masculine characteristics, so Artegall must accept the feminine in order to be her equal.

Although Spenser may appear to affirm this exchange of gender roles, the text moves to restore sexual difference and hierarchy at a crucial moment, in the simile likening Britomart's reunion with Artegall to Penelope's recognition of Odysseus:

> Not so great wonder and astonishment,
>   Did the most chast *Penelope* possesse,
>   To see her Lord, that was reported drent,
>   And dead long since in dolorous distresse,
>   Come home to her in piteous wretchednesse,
>   After long travell of full twenty yeares,
>   That she knew not his favours likelynesse,
>   For many scarres and many hoary heares,
> But stood long staring on him, mongst uncertaine feares.
>
> [5.7.39]

Unlike the similes in the *Odyssey* which affirmed the exchange of gender roles, this simile insists upon strict correspondence along gender lines: between Britomart and Penelope, Artegall and Odysseus. Yet because Artegall has been emasculated, it is Britomart who has been acting as a second Odysseus in completing a journey of her own to rescue Artegall. In hyperbolically likening Artegall's appearance in "womens weedes" to Odysseus' "piteous wretchednesse" after twenty years of wandering, Spenser seems to project his own anxiety concerning Artegall's identity onto Penelope's (and Britomart's) "uncertaine feares." Spenser stresses the temporary nature of this anxiety-producing exchange of gender roles by likening it to carnival

---

[60]Kathleen Williams, *Spenser's World of Glass: A Reading of the Faerie Queene* (Berkeley: Univ. of California Press, 1966), p. 134.

inversion—Britomart asks Artegall, "What May-game hath misfortune made of you? (5.7.40)—a reference that serves to reestablish more securely the patriarchal order, as we shall see.[61] Indeed, Spenser's desire in this simile to differentiate his protagonists clearly by gender signals his unease with Elizabeth's rule, for, as Joan Kelly has pointed out, the strict separation of domestic and public spheres along gender lines characterizes patriarchies.[62]

When Britomart slays Radigund in order to rescue Artegall, these analogies between Radigund and herself, on the one hand, and between Radigund and Artegall, on the other, do not allow Radigund's destruction to be read simply as an allegory for the victory of true justice over false. In a "wrothfull" (5.7.34) fury, Britomart "empierce[s]" (5.7.33) her enemy and "with one stroke both head and helmet cleft" (5.7.34). The verb, as in the previous instances in which Spenser used it, underscores the similarity of rather than the difference between the two women. Moreover, Radigund's fatal wound which cleaves her in two finds its reflection in Britomart's own wound, much graver than the flesh wounds she has received up to this point: "it bit / Unto the bone, and made a griesly wound, / That she her shield through raging smart of it / Could scarse uphold" (5.7.33). The two lighter grazes she received in the opening and closing cantos of Book 3 signaled Britomart's vulnerability to the threats posed by Malecasta and Busirane; here the more serious wound implies that her violent slaying of Radigund constitutes a partial self-destruction. Although Britomart had been enjoined to "clemence" in "restrain[ing] . . . sterne behests, and cruell doomes" (5.7.22) at the Temple of Isis, she seems to have forgotten the lesson

---

[61]On the reversal of gender roles in the Radigund episode, see Robinson's discussion, pp. 337–41, especially her observation that "Spenser explicitly equates the female sex and people who work for wages," placing both in opposition to the aristocratic soldier (p. 341). Natalie Zemon Davis, "Women on Top," in *Society and Culture in Early Modern France* (Stanford: Stanford Univ. Press, 1975), pp. 124–51, argues that transvestism and sexual reversal associated with the carnival were multivalent images that at once affirmed and undermined the status quo. Concerning Radigund, however, she suggests: "Some portraits of [the disorderly woman] are so ferocious (such as Spenser's cruel Radagunde and other vicious viragoes) that they preclude the possibility of fanciful release from, or criticism of, hierarchy" (p. 133). See also Quilligan, "The Comedy of Female Authority in *The Faerie Queene*," *ELR*, 17 (1987), 167–72, on the Radigund episode's "transgression [of gender roles] deserving the text's violent laughter" (p. 168). Concerning Britomart's restoration of male rule, she writes, "Female authority here is not funny, because it is real" (p. 171).

[62]Joan Kelly, "The Social Relation of the Sexes," in *Women, History, and Theory: The Essays of Joan Kelly* (Chicago: Univ. of Chicago Press, 1984), p. 14.

she was taught there. This moment recalls the similarly problematic final lines of the *Faerie Queene*'s prototype, Virgil's *Aeneid:* like Britomart, Aeneas seems to forget Anchises' instruction to exercise the arts of peace and law by sparing the vanquished (6.851–53), when, overcome by *furia* and *ira,* he slays his enemy Turnus. Spenser underscores Britomart's lack of "clemence" by having Talus follow her lead to engage in a "piteous slaughter" of the Amazons (5.7.35); Talus, earlier the agent of Artegall's violence, becomes Britomart's agent. Britomart here takes on Artegall's earlier cruelty just as she had, in the preceding scene of Radigund's slaughter, assimilated her victim's fury.

In the allegory of previous books, Spenser either maintained a clear distinction between apparently similar figures by keeping them apart (Una and Duessa, Florimell and False Florimell) or by dramatizing a confrontation between antagonists whereby one triumphed over the other (Redcrosse and the dragon, Britomart and Busirane). If allegory is predicated upon the separation of moral qualities and the dialectical resolution of the conflict between them through the victory of one over the other, then in this confrontation between Britomart and Radigund the allegory breaks down, for the opposition between the two poles can no longer be maintained. In the course of the episode, Radigund has gone beyond a simple negation of Britomart, and at its climax, Britomart takes on Radigund's former ferocity. This final encounter between the two viragos dramatizes an ironic doubling rather than an allegorical opposition. Britomart's slaying of her double Radigund, then, does not allow Spenser's heroine simply to exorcize from herself the troubling qualities of tyranny and violence; she annihilates what is vital in herself as well as what is problematic, for the two are inextricably linked.

It is altogether fitting, then, that after slaying Radigund, Britomart gives up her prerogative by instituting male rule in Radegone:

> During which space she there as Princess rained,
> And changing all that forme of common weale,
> The liberty of women did repeale,
> Which they had long usurpt; and them restoring
> To mens subjection, did true Justice deale:
> That all they as Goddesse her adoring,
> Her wisdome did admire, and hearkned to her loring.
>
> [5.7.42]

The final couplet does little to mitigate Britomart's acceptance of patriarchal assumptions that woman's sovereignty can result only from the usurpation of originary and rightful male rule. This act of self-destruction in repealing woman's liberty repeats and confirms the self-destruction implicit in her slaying of Radigund. As if in recognition of her own contamination by Radigund's violence, Britomart cedes her power to Artegall. Thus the distinction between women in general who are unfit to rule and the exceptional woman who receives divine sanction to rule cannot be maintained, for Britomart undermines her own prerogative and power in destroying Radigund and abolishing woman's rule in Radegone, in the end becoming a shadowy figure like Virgil's Lavinia.

In keeping with the poem's tendency to diminish Britomart, her repeal of women's liberty is followed by her sudden and hitherto unexplained disappearance from the poem at the conclusion of the Radigund episode. Artegall goes forth to pursue his quest of rescuing Irena, leaving behind Britomart, who fades away from the poem in "paine," "sorrow," and "anguish" (5.7.45) over the deferral of her union with him. In Book 3, Britomart's errancy, set off against the imprisonment and subjugation of Hellenore, Amoret, and Florimell, signaled her independence and freedom. Left behind in Radegone, where she herself has instituted male rule, Britomart cedes her role as epic hero to Artegall; this final vision of Britomart presents a much reduced version of her self-sufficient and energetic former self.

Yet the prevailing reading of this episode insists upon affirming Britomart and hence the allegory: it maintains the distinctions between the two Amazons by loading Radigund with negative attributes and Britomart with positive ones. Despite the evidence to the contrary, then, most critics give affirmative readings of the conclusion of Britomart's plot:

> Now she *becomes* Isis ruling Radigund's kingdom with true justice. . . .
> This final appearance of Britomart in the poem—like Una restored to her kingdom—fulfils that vision of herself as Isis.[63]

> Britomart now has the attributes of a perfect wife. To all intents and purposes, her long journey in the *Faerie Queene* is over. . . . It has led from darkness into the light, from love in nature to love in grace.[64]

[63]Hamilton, *Structure of Allegory*, p. 185.
[64]Dunseath, pp. 181–82. Some critics, however, express misgivings about the conclusion of Britomart's plot: Tuve remarks that "there is something oversuccessful

I argue rather that the breakdown of allegory, transforming Radigund from a simple negation of Britomart to a complex counterpart or alter-ego, works to diminish and ultimately erase Britomart through her own destruction of Radigund. Britomart cleaves Radigund in two just as the poem itself splits the Amazonian warrior in two parts and has one destroy the other; the half that remains can only be an extremely diminished representation of the militant woman.

The simultaneous conclusion of both the Radigund episode and Britomart's plot dramatizes the disquieting but irreducible fact that the scapegoating of Radigund works ultimately to destroy Britomart as well. For previous readers this scapegoating succeeds (as does the allegory): the "bad" Amazon is purged so that the "good" Amazon can survive. Yet as we have seen, Britomart, the putative "good" Amazon, also disappears from the poem. Victor Turner's description and analysis of ritual sacrifice carries particular significance for our understanding of the workings of the scapegoating of Radigund *and* Britomart:

> A [social or ritual] drama has a kind of circularity of form and intention. There is an intention of restoring an antecedent condition, in this case a condition of dynamic equilibrium between the parts of a society. But any process that involves conflict has its "victims," and any process that reaffirms norms implies condemnation of norm-breakers. It also implies punishment of the innovator as well as the lawbreaker, since the introduction of radical novelty would prevent the ultimate closure of the circle. This "victimizing" and punitive tendency of a cyclical system is reflected in its ritual dramas, for most of them contain a sacrifice. A sacrifice may be regarded as restorative, regenerative; at the moment when the wheel has come a full circle, it sets the cycle going again, the victim is held to be at once innocent and guilty: innocent because the conflicts that have gone before are not the victim's fault, but guilty because a scapegoat is required to atone for those conflicts. In the victim extremes meet.[65]

Just as the reversal of gender roles between Artegall and Radigund

---

about Britomart despite the sop in vii, 36" (p. 90), and Alpers finds unconvincing the contradictions in Britomart's role—"the princess who restores women to men's subjection and then is adored as a goddess" (p. 304).

[65]Victor Turner, *The Drums of Affliction: A Study of Religious Processes among the Ndembu of Zambia* (Oxford: Clarendon Press, 1968), p. 276.

follows the ritual of carnival (the "May-game" that Britomart alludes to), so here the slaughter of Radigund corresponds to the ritual of sacrifice of which Turner speaks, for both rituals function to affirm the social order by exorcizing elements that threaten it. The sacrifice of Radigund clearly intends to restore the antecedent condition of patriarchal rule. We have already seen that Britomart's destruction of Radigund allows the victor's restoration of patriarchy or, indeed, makes it all but inevitable. Yet this reaffirmation of norms also entails the condemnation of Britomart as a woman ruler—in Turner's terms, "innovator," if not "norm-breaker" (like Radigund): the poem accomplishes this punishment by having Britomart restore patriarchal rule, and ultimately by erasing her from the poem, despite her "innocence" and her seeming antagonism to the sacrificial victim.

Thus Spenser's blurring of crucial distinctions between Britomart and Radigund leads him to destroy Britomart as well as Radigund. According to René Girard, such a contamination of categories bespeaks a failure of sacrifice:

> All victims, even the animal ones, bear a certain *resemblance* to the object they replace; otherwise the violent impulse would remain unsatisfied. But this resemblance must not be carried to the extreme of complete assimilation, or it would lead to disastrous confusion. . . . In order for a species or category of living creature, human or animal, to appear suitable for sacrifice, it must bear a sharp resemblance to the *human* categories excluded from the ranks of the "sacrificeable," while still maintaining a degree of difference that forbids all possible confusion.[66]

This "confusion" between Radigund and Britomart, the victim and the character whom she replaces, exposes the inefficacy of scapegoating to resolve the problem of the woman ruler, for this scapegoating is supposedly motivated by the overt ideological desire to legitimize one woman ruler over another (or others)—Spenser's so-called "moderate Puritan position" concerning women rulers. But Spenser represents both Amazons as unacceptable rulers. Hence the antecedent condition to which the poem returns after the Radigund episode is not, as most readers have assumed, the legitimate rule of one exceptional woman; rather, through conflating Britomart and Radigund, the text moves to restore the legitimacy of patriarchal rule.

In Spenser's refusal to affirm Britomart, not only by contaminating

[66]René Girard, *Violence and the Sacred*, trans. Patrick Gregory (Baltimore: Johns Hopkins Univ. Press, 1979), pp. 11–12.

her with the violence of her enemy but by ultimately effacing her from his poem, we may discern a divergence from his earlier motives, in the sense that Kenneth Burke uses that term.[67] From Book 3 on, Britomart as founder of the Tudor line and ancestor of Elizabeth was the primary vehicle for Spenser's praise of his queen. In the Radigund episode, however, Spenser's changed motive—his faith now turned to disillusionment—finds expression in his subversion of the allegorical mode that he had sustained successfully in the earlier books. This crisis of allegory converges with the failure of sacrifice, for both allegory and sacrifice have in common the need to hold categories apart, and what marks the Radigund episode is the blurring of crucial distinctions; Spenser thereby transgresses the limits of the poetry of praise.

Unwilling to blame Elizabeth overtly, Spenser disguises his criticism of his queen, and his success in doing so is attested to by critics who have interpreted this episode as Spenser's affirmation of Elizabeth's prerogative over that of Mary Stuart.[68] Yet as we have seen, the distinctions between Britomart and Radigund, and hence between Elizabeth and Mary, are difficult to maintain. In fact, Radigund exhibits disquieting similarities with Elizabeth: for example, after the defeat of the Armada, representations both literary and pictoral of Elizabeth as Amazon became commonplace.[69] Radigund's emasculation of her male prisoners recalls Elizabeth's strict control over even the private lives of her male courtiers. In a speech addressed to Parliament during Mary's trial, Elizabeth referred to her reputation for tyranny, a characteristic that links her with the Amazon Radigund:

[67]See, for example, Kenneth Burke, *The Philosophy of Literary Form* (Berkeley: Univ. of California Press, 1973), p. 20.

[68]James Emerson Phillips, however, does not discuss the Radigund episode as an example of literary representations of Mary Stuart in his *Images of a Queen: Mary Stuart in Sixteenth-Century Literature* (Berkeley: Univ. of California Press, 1964). But O'Connell sees the Radigund episode as the first allusion to Mary in Book 5, one generous in its portrayal of her, and the combat between Britomart and Radigund as the twenty-year struggle between the two queens (p. 140). Cain thinks that the episode recalls the project of marrying Leicester to Mary (p. 154).

[69]Winfried Schleiner, "*Divina virago:* Queen Elizabeth as an Amazon," *SP,* 75 (1978), 164. He discusses Belphoebe's association with Penthesilea (pp. 176–79). See also Celeste Turner Wright, "The Amazons in Elizabethan Literature," *SP,* 37 (1940), 433–56. Louis Adrian Montrose, "Shaping Fantasies: Figurations of Gender and Power in Elizabethan Culture," *Representations* 1:2 (Spring 1983), 65–68, discusses the Amazonian myth as the culture's "collective anxiety about the power of the female not only to dominate or to reject the male but to create and destroy him." Shakespeare's *A Midsummer Night's Dream,* he argues, "eventually restores the inverted Amazonian system of gender and nurture to a patriarchal norm."

I have besides, during my reigne, seene and heard many opprobrious bookes and Pamphlets against me, my Realme and State, accusing me to be a Tyrant: I thanke them for their almes: I beleeve, therein their meaning was to tell me newes, and newes it is to me indeede: I would it were as strange to heare of their impietie. What will they not now say, when it shalbe spread, That for the safety of her life, a Mayden Queene could be content to spill the blood, even of her owne kinsewoman? . . .

I am not so voide of judgement, as not to see mine owne perill: nor yet so ignorant, as not to knowe it were in nature a foolish course, to cherish a sworde to cutte mine owene throate: nor so carelesse, as not to weigh that my life dayly is in hazard . . . but I pray you thinke, that I have thought upon it.[70]

Elizabeth repeatedly calls attention to the danger to her own prerogative and life implied in the execution of another queen, her relative. She thus stresses her similarity to Mary rather than the differences between them—as I have suggested that Spenser does also in representing the conflict between the two queens in Radegone. It is well known that Elizabeth avoided signing Mary's warrant until the last possible minute. Despite Elizabeth's obsession for her reputation as a woman of clemency (and here we may recall Britomart's lesson at Isis Church), she eventually acquiesced to Mary's execution.

Spenser's disquiet over his inability (or refusal) to resolve contradictions in the Radigund episode finds yet another expression in cantos 9 and 10, where Duessa is judged and executed at Mercilla's castle. This episode has traditionally been read as a straightforward and uncritical allegory of Elizabeth's execution of Mary;[71] yet it is Zele

---

[70]"The Copie of a Letter to the Right Honourable the Earle of Leycester," in *Elizabethan Backgrounds*, ed. Arthur F. Kinney (Hamden, Ct: Archon, 1975), p. 234.

[71]For example, Frank Kermode, "*The Faerie Queene*, I and V," in *Shakespeare, Spenser, Donne* (London: Routledge and Kegan Paul, 1971), p. 58: "*Being herself Justice incarnate as Equity*, [Mercilla] proceeds, as Britomart proceeded to the suppression of Radigund, to the trial of Duessa" (emphasis added). More recent critics note tensions in the episode, though without necessarily concluding that Spenser was critical of Elizabeth. O'Connell sees a Spenser co-opted by Elizabethan policy: "His own vision of mercy . . . becomes no better than the mercy finally afforded Mary. . . . His devotion to his queen and her cause is evident, even touching, but . . . the Legend of Justice falters" (p. 154). Cain considers the problem to lie in the discrepancy between "the harmony of justice and mercy praised in the icon" and the necessary insufficiency of political action (p. 145). Goldberg sees Mercilla passing judgment as "an exemplary figure of contradiction." See his discussion of the Mercilla episode as the site of a "fiction of sovereign power" in *James I and the Politics of Literature: Jonson, Shakespeare, Donne, and their Contemporaries* (Baltimore: Johns Hopkins Univ. Press, 1983), pp. 1–17. On the correspondences of Duessa and Mary Stuart in Books 1 and 5, see Richard A. MacCabe, "The Masks of Duessa: Spenser, Mary Queen of Scots, and James VI,"

who advocates her execution and persuades the reluctant Mercilla, who let fall a "few perling drops" (5.9.50), "ruing [Duessa's] wilfull fall" (5.10.4). It is worth noting, too, that the jury, as it were, renders a split verdict: Artegall characteristically takes Zele's side, but Arthur is for sparing Duessa. Moreover, Spenser states baldly that "it is greater prayse to save, then spill / And better to reforme, then to cut off the ill" (5.10.2). Here again, Spenser's criticism of Mary's execution is attenuated, but present nonetheless.

As in the Radigund episode, Spenser avoids blatant criticism of Elizabeth as Mercilla, and so the prevailing reading of this episode assumes that Spenser endorsed Mercilla's judgment. For example, T. K. Dunseath asserts that "Mercilla has no choice but to condemn Duessa." Yet his repeated insistence that Mercilla's actions fulfill her name reveals a suspicion that they do not: "She cannot mitigate the punishment, which is to exercise that part of mercy called clemency. The greatest mercy she can show is through the virtue of meekness, or the suppression of wrath. That this is the meaning of Mercilla's judgment and the tears she sheds is obvious from the beginning of Canto X when Arthur and Artegall praise her mercy."[72] Other critics simply read an accepted view of history back into the text: assuming that Elizabeth's execution of Mary met with public approval and that the intent of Spenser's poem was to praise his queen, they conclude that Spenser represents with approbation Elizabeth as Mercilla.[73] Such a reading ignores important elements in the poem which contradict or undermine it; in addition it precludes the possibility that Spenser came to diverge from the dominant ideology.

As Paul Alpers points out, the conflict between justice and mercy remains unresolved at the end of canto 9, and the condemnation of Duessa is deferred to the next canto, "where its context is not the single process of judgment, but a general account of mercy and praise

---

ELR, 17 (1987), 224–42. He holds that Spenser's Mercilla episode is favorable to Elizabeth but also points out that in altering the details of the trial, Spenser makes Elizabeth directly responsible for Mary's execution and actively courts political reaction by representing a subject that had become complex and dangerous: "Those who wished to avoid controversy either left it untouched or attempted to dissociate both Elizabeth and James from the whole affair" (p. 241).

[72]Dunseath, p. 218.

[73]For example, René Graziani, "Elizabeth at Isis Church," *PMLA*, 79 (1964), 376–89; and James E. Phillips, "Renaissance Concepts of Justice and the Structure of *The Faerie Queene*, Book V," *HLQ*, 33 (1970), rpt. in *Essential Articles*, pp. 471–87. Both argue that contemporaries justified the execution of Mary on the grounds that Elizabeth showed mercy toward her subjects.

of Mercilla for possessing this virtue."[74] I suggest that Mercilla does not act in accordance with her allegorical name, because the pressures of history do not allow Spenser to sustain the allegory implied in her name. Significantly, Douglas Northrop, though arguing that Spenser defended Elizabeth in his poem, points out that she was coming under attack generally as a woman ruler, as a tyrant, and, specifically, for the execution of Mary:[75]

> The numbers and the vehemence of Elizabeth's defenders reveal the importance of the controversy. Shortly after the death of Mary there appeared *A Defence of the Honorable Sentence and execution of the Queene of Scots* (London n.d.). In 1587 appeared Richard Crompton's *A Short Declaration of the ende of Traytors,* and George Whetstone's *The Censure of a loyall Subject.* The burden of them all is the same: the execution of Mary was justified; the Queen is just; the Queen is merciful.

Only serious attacks can prompt such strong defenses. Northrop's account paradoxically makes veiled criticism of Elizabeth by Spenser no longer unthinkable. Even if we were to forgo a strictly topical reading of the Mercilla episode, we might still notice Spenser's peculiar obsession with the destruction of female rulers, Radigund and Duessa, who may well function as monstrous doubles or surrogates for Elizabeth herself.

If allegory resolves ambivalence by categorizing and codifying opposing forces, Spenser's departures from allegory in the Radigund and Mercilla episodes expose his ambivalence toward his queen.[76] The unresolved ambivalence, however, generates anxiety concerning his vocation as laureate, his divergence from his earlier poetry of praise. In Mercilla's castle, Spenser describes a self-proclaimed poet whose tongue is nailed to a post for "blasphem[ing] that Queene"; above his head

> There written was the purport of his sin,
> In cyphers strange, that few could rightly read,
> BON FONT: but *bon* that once had written bin,

[74]Alpers, p. 287.

[75]Douglas A. Northrop, "Spenser's Defense of Elizabeth," *University of Toronto Quarterly,* 38 (1969), 277–94. The quoted passage is on pp. 280–81.

[76]On "Spenserian ambivalence," see Fletcher, *Allegory,* pp. 269–73, who sees personal but not social ambivalence in Spenser, "because his poem is a largely idealized defense of the establishment." He does, however, consider the "taboo of the ruler" (Gloriana) to be at the center of the poem.

> Was raced out, and *Mal* was now put in.
> So now *Malfont* was plainely to be red;
> Eyther for th'evill, which he did therein,
> Or that he likened was to a welhed
> Of evill words, and wicked sclaunders by him shed.
>
> [5.9.26]

In the earlier books of the poem Spenser was confident in his ability to make distinctions between himself and false artists such as Archimago. Here, he can no longer affirm his difference from Bonfont turned Malfont, since he has abandoned unqualified praise for his queen not only in Britomart's slaying of Radigund but also in Mercilla's execution of Duessa. Moreover, by introducing the Mercilla episode with this striking figure of Bon/ Malfont, Spenser appears at once to announce that the disgraced poet could very well be himself and to deflect criticism by anticipating it and dramatizing it. Yet Spenser also subtly calls into question the justice of the punishment itself, since underneath the newly inscribed "Mal," the originary "Bon" can still be read; the self-interested and capricious power of the sovereign to rename the poet cannot completely efface his former name. The other emblem of the poet's transgression, his nailed tongue, is also ambiguous: as Michel Foucault has suggested, such punishment marks the victim's body as the vehicle of display for the sovereign's power, although its excessive violence can subvert sovereignty by eliciting solidarity between the people and the victim.[77] The nailed tongue and its superscription thus raise many questions: Is the poet in fact Bonfont or Malfont? According to whose standard? Does Spenser accept the queen's power to rename which rivals or supersedes his own? Does he acquiesce to her power to rename *him* as Malfont?[78]

---

[77]Michel Foucault, *Discipline and Punish: The Birth of the Prison,* trans. Alan Sheridan (New York: Pantheon, 1977), pp. 3–131, *passim.* Foucault's important study traces the disappearance of public execution and its displacement by private incarceration in late eighteenth- and early nineteenth-century Europe. He argues that in this process, punishment becomes the most hidden part of the penal process, and publicity shifts to the trial and the sentence. Although Spenser describes Duessa's trial at great length, he does not represent her execution; the juxtaposition of the public punishment of Bon/Malfont and the secret execution of Duessa appears to encapsulate the transitional stage that Foucault describes.

[78]See Goldberg, *James I,* pp. 2–3, for another interpretation of "Spenser's representation of the relationship of his text . . . to the royal word." He suggests that Spenser submits to Elizabeth's truth in Book 5 generally and specifically in the representation of Bon/Malfont: "The poet . . . authorizes a view of society that denies him authority and makes his text simply a transcription of the social text."

In the Proem to Book 5, Spenser lamented the degeneration of the world, which has "runne quite out of square, / From the first point of his appointed sourse, / And being once amisse growes daily wourse and wourse" (5.Pr.1). The ultimate consequence of this degeneration is the confusion of opposites:

> For that which all men then did vertue call,
>   Is now cald vice; and that which vice was hight,
>   Is now hight vertue, and so us'd of all:
>   Right now is wrong, and wrong that was is right,
>   As all things else in time are chaunged quight.
>   Ne wonder; for the heavens revolution
>   Is wandred farre from where it first was pight,
>   And so doe make contrarie constitution
> Of all this lower world, toward his dissolution.
>
> [5.Pr.4]

If, as Helgerson suggests, Spenser's eminence over the other poets of his age resided in his ability to make and maintain distinctions (for example, between Una and Duessa, Florimell and False Florimell), then the blurring of distinctions in the later books (between Britomart and Radigund, Bonfont and Malfont), which subverts his allegory, can be seen as symptoms of Spenser's loss of faith in the course of contemporary history.[79]

It is fitting, then, that as the ultimate breakdown of the distinction between self and Other, at the end of Book 5 Spenser's poem generates the Blatant Beast, a monstrous reincarnation of Slander—and of Malfont. Yet unlike Malfont, who could be silenced by nailing his tongue to a post, this monster threatens, with a multiplicity of uncontrollable tongues, to backbite and destroy Spenser's poem at the end of Book 6.

Monsters of Language: From Errour to the Blatant Beast

I have been arguing that the Radigund and Mercilla episodes are veiled expressions of Spenser's ambivalence toward woman's power, especially in Artegall's emasculation by Radigund and the more literal mutilation of Bonfont's tongue by Mercilla, bearer of the rusty sword. More explicit expressions of the horror of female sexuality

---

[79]Helgerson, p. 65.

can be found throughout the poem. Spenser consistently figures linguistic duplicity through female monsters, who seduce by concealing their hideous deformity under an attractive appearance. The emphasis on the monstrosity of their female sexuality focuses and exorcizes Spenser's anxiety about the duplicity of his linguistic medium and the necessary doubleness of his own poetry. Spenser creates these monsters in order to destroy them; the destruction of female monsters enables Spenser to affirm clarity and unity as masculine traits, through their opposition to ambiguity and multiplicity as feminine and monstrous ones. Yet the *Faerie Queene* complicates this dichotomy, for Spenser's poem depends on the female and monstrous Other in order to define itself as masculine and unified; hence as soon as one monster is destroyed, the poem must generate another, to take its place. These substitutions dramatize the process whereby the double legacy of female monstrosity and linguistic duplicity can never be completely exorcized but on the contrary resurfaces in ever more problematic forms. Moreover, not only do the female monsters exert an undeniable fascination for Spenser, but his own narrative begins to display unmistakable affinities with them. The replacement of one monster by another also parallels a similar process we noted in Virgil, whereby the legacy of the monstrous female Helen resurfaces in Dido in the first half of the poem and in Amata and Camilla in the second half. Yet Spenser, unlike Virgil, finally accepts the monstrous Other as part of the self, in his creation of the male Blatant Beast, the final monster of language.

The convergence of ambivalence about language and about the female is not unique to Spenser, as we have seen. Spenser follows his epic predecessors in his figuration of linguistic duplicity in demonized female figures. The poet of the *Odyssey* scapegoats Helen in Sparta as his negative counterpart—a duplicitous and dangerously seductive storyteller. The Sirens compete with the poet of the *Odyssey* in offering to sing to Odysseus of his exploits at Troy. These beautiful but deadly figures threaten the hero's homecoming and hence the making of the *Odyssey* itself. In the *Aeneid,* Virgil figures *Fama* with her thousand tongues as a demonized double for the fame he will bestow on Aeneas. The monstrous and disorderly female *Fama* spreads the rumor of Aeneas' dalliance with Dido, while Virgil, allying himself with male Jupiter's orderly *fatum,* sings the fame of the Roman Empire. Yet not only does the *Aeneid* include *Fama* and her antics, but the unfolding of Virgil's narrative actually depends upon the mediation of *Fama*'s narrative, just as it includes and depends upon Juno and her Gorgon Allecto's obstruction of Jupiter's masterplot. Although the scattering of the Cumaean Sibyl's verses, written on leaves, associates her prophecy with Virgil's poetry, it also links both to ephemeral and unreliable *Fama*. Like Homer and Virgil, Spenser deploys female monsters as demonized doubles essential for his dialectical allegory, monsters who serve to generate and propel his narrative. In their multiplicity and in their confounding of categories, the monsters represent figures of perversion and error; but Spenser's own literary form, in its dependence on a similar multiplicity of plot as well as of literary models and subtexts, displays inescapable affinities with the monstrous.

In the opening canto of Book 1, Spenser represents linguistic duplicity in the female monster, Errour, who "Halfe like a serpent horribly displaide, / But th'other halfe did womans shape retaine" (1.1.14), metonymically juxtaposing the beguiling serpent and the beguiled Eve. In addition to the biblical subtext, Spenser here alludes to a classical subtext, Hesiod's description of Echidna: "half fair-cheeked and bright-eyed nymph / and half huge and monstrous snake inside the holy earth" (*Theogony*, 297–99).[80] In the *Theogony*, Echidna eats men raw and is a mother of many monsters including Cerberus, the Hydra, the Chimera, the Sphinx, and Orthrus, Geryon's two-headed dog; and in Spenser's Book 6 she is the mother of the Blatant Beast: "her face and former parts professe / A faire young Mayden, full of comely glee; / But all her hinder parts did plaine expresse / A monstrous Dragon, full of fearfull uglinesse" (6.6.10). Through Echidna, Spenser establishes a genealogical link between Errour and the Blatant Beast.

The better to deceive, Errour shuns light and thrives in darkness: "Where *plaine* none might see, nor she see any *plaine*" (1.1.16; emphasis added). In her avoidance of "plaine," readily perceptible, meaning, Errour stands as the first figure for the duplicity of language in the poem, as Una ironically signals in her punning warning to Redcrosse: "I read beware" (1.1.13).[81] Accordingly, Spenser describes Errour through images of textuality: "Her vomit full of bookes and papers

[80]Hesiod, *Theogony, Works and Days, Shield*, trans. Apostolos N. Athanassakis (Baltimore: Johns Hopkins Univ. Press, 1983), p. 20. John Steadman, "Spenser's Errour and the Renaissance Allegorical Tradition," *Neuphilologische Mitteilungen*, 62 (1961), 23–27, notes that Renaissance commentators associated Hesiod's Echidna with erudition and rhetorical subtlety.

[81]Quilligan, *Language of Allegory*, p. 258, sees this pun as "the specific signal for the parallel between the Redcrosse Knight's reading and the reader's reading. . . . The reader, of course, reads 'beware' at just the moment Una counsels it." On Errour, see also Patricia A. Parker, *Inescapable Romance: Studies in the Poetics of a Mode* (Princeton: Princeton Univ. Press, 1979), pp. 64–71: "Along with the demand to 'read' goes the

was" (1.1.20), and her offspring are "blacke as inke" (1.1.22). Redcrosse allies himself with virginal Una to combat Errour, whose grotesqueness Spenser links to her processes of generation. Since the difference between Errour and Una is readily discernible, Redcrosse easily passes this, his "first adventure" (1.1.27).

Yet matters are more complicated than they seem, for although Errour's actual offspring burst after feeding on their dead mother, the destruction of Errour unleashes energies that generate the narrative and that the poem then seeks to contain. Like Echidna's sister, Medusa, another snake-woman whose blood also produced a swarm of venomous serpents, Errour is perhaps more powerful and dangerous dead than alive. Appearing at the very beginning of the narrative, Errour functions as a parodic version of the Muse: her destruction does not bring closure to the narrative but instead works to generate not only the narrative of Book I (which concludes with the destruction of the dragon, a more formidable reincarnation of Errour), but also the narrative of the rest of the *Faerie Queene,* which is animated by monsters of language that appear to issue from Errour's dead body.

Upon destroying Errour, however, Redcrosse meets Archimago, the seemingly virtuous hermit, "simple in shew" (1.1.29), who will create false Una to cause him to doubt Una's faithfulness. In this doubling of Una, Spenser recapitulates (as he will do so again in the doubling of Florimell and False Florimell) the myth of two Helens: the phantom Helen who eloped with Paris and the true Helen who remained chaste. Just as the false Helen led the Trojans and Greeks to war, so the false Una leads Redcrosse to leave the true Una, only to fall into the hands of Errour's reincarnation, Duessa. In Duessa, Spenser actually conjoins Errour and Una: like Errour, Duessa combines the forms of a human female and a monster, but unlike Errour, whose monstrosity was readily discernible, Duessa successfully conceals her monstrous nether parts under a fair female form that resembles Una's. Fradubio tells Redcrosse:

> Her neather partes misshapen, monstruous,
> Were hidd in water, that I could not see,

---

danger of a false or premature reading. . . . For Red Cross as for the reader, objectification, as a distancing from the self, may be both victory and delusion " (p. 68). She concludes that the "Body of Errour . . . 'dilates' to fill out the remainder of the narrative" (p. 69).

But they did seeme more foule and hideous,
Then womans shape man would beleeve to bee.

[1.2.41]

Fradubio's insinuation that "womans shape" is "foule and hideous"
and Duessa's only more so, stresses the link between the female and
the monstrous. Spenser himself later states that "her neather parts, *the
shame of all her kind,* / My chaster Muse for shame doth blush to
write" (1.8.48; emphasis added). By setting his "chaster Muse" in
opposition to "foule" Duessa, Spenser makes Duessa exemplify the
false Muse. In refusing to describe Duessa's nether parts, Spenser
declines to lift the veil of allegory; Fradubio, who transgresses by
partially lifting the veil—the passage I quoted oscillates between a
covering and an uncovering—himself is transformed into a monstrous hybrid of a tree and a man. In this moment of meta-allegory,
Spenser likens the fascination of allegory to that of a seductive woman; for allegory promises to unveil a fuller meaning while constantly
withholding that meaning. Thus the unfolding of Spenser's allegorical narrative depends on the continued mediation of meaning and the
postponement of ultimate reckoning; woman veiled (Una) becomes a
figure for that allegory, and her unveiling (as Duessa) arouses fascination and dread. (Britomart's unvizarding, as we have seen, belongs to
a different tradition—the redemptive revelation of a goddess). In
being mastered by Duessa, Fradubio functions here as the negative
counterpart of Redcrosse, who overcame Errour; more importantly,
Fradubio acts as the poet's surrogate in dramatizing the frightening
consequences of seeing Duessa's Medusa-like nether parts.[82] Spenser
deflects the anxiety that such an unmediated vision holds by attribut-
ing a foulness to every *other* part of Duessa's body:

Her craftie head was altogether bald,
    And as in hate of honorable eld,
    Was overgrowne with scurfe and filthy scald;
    Her teeth out of her rotten gummes were feld,
    And her sowre breath abhominably smeld;
    Her dried dugs, like bladders lacking wind,
    Hong downe, and filthy matter from them weld;

[82]Freud argues that "the terror of Medusa is . . . a terror of castration that is linked
to the sight of . . . the female genitals." "Medusa's Head" (1922), in *Collected Papers*,
ed. James Strachey (New York: Basic Books, 1959), 5:105–6.

Her wrizled skin as rough, as maple rind,
So scabby was, that would have loathed all womankind.

[1.8.47]

Moreover, by soiling Duessa "with dong all fowly dight" (1.8.48), Spenser ritually debases her.[83]

In the Fradubio episode, as in the case of Errour, Spenser signals the multiplicity of his literary models: in Duessa he conflates the *Odyssey*'s Circe, the seductive witch with transformative powers, and Virgil's Dido, the initially attractive woman who later becomes grotesque, because sexual. In addition, he alludes to the Harpies and Scylla as they appear in Aeneas' narrative to Dido: both combine beautiful virginal faces and disgusting nether parts (3.216–18, 426–28). Fradubio himself, of course, recapitulates Virgil's Polydorus (3.19–68), and Dante's Pier delle Vigne (*Inferno*, 13.22–108). This multiplicity of models parallels Duessa's monstrous amalgamation of body parts from various animals—"foxes taile," "Eagles claw," and "Beares uneven paw" (1.8.48)—as well as her ability to take on "manie shapes . . . / As ever could Cameleon colours new" (4.1.18).

During the festivities celebrating Redcrosse's victory over the dragon and his betrothal to Una, Duessa sends a slanderous letter— an unauthorized text that underlines Duessa's significance as duplicitous textuality—accusing Redcrosse of having already been betrothed to her. Although her fraud is exposed, this incident, coming after the hero's slaying of the dragon, serves as a reminder that Duessa, a more pernicious monster than the dragon in that she hides her monstrosity under a fair appearance, is still at large. Spenser contains Una within Book 1, but Duessa, her monstrous counterpart, moves beyond Book 1 as does the hero of the book, Redcrosse. In fact, although Duessa acted in Book 1 as an adversary of Redcrosse, she exceeds that role and her career beyond Book 1 no longer depends on Redcrosse. Although Spenser's allegory appears to define itself by writing against Duessa and other opponents of his heroes, Duessa, and hence his own allegory, prove to contravene fixed categories of meaning.

Duessa is absent from Britomart's Book 3, for in that book Spenser criticizes the male literary language of Paridell and Busirane, which

---

[83]On ritual debasement, see Mikhail Bakhtin, *Rabelais and His World*, trans. Helene Iswolsky (Cambridge: MIT Press, 1968), pp. 21, 197–208. See also Bakhtin's discussion of the body and its products, chap. 6, "The Material Bodily Lower Stratum."

objectifies and fragments women. But in Book 4, Duessa reappears in the company of *Ate,* "mother of debate, / And all dissention" (4.1.19), who generates an "infinite increase" from "seedes of evill wordes, and factious deedes" (4.1.25). Duessa and *Ate* both counterfeit a "Ladie's" appearance:

> But Ladies none they were, albee in face
> And outward shew faire semblance they did beare;
> For under maske of beautie and good grace,
> Vile treason and fowle falshood hidden were,
> That mote to none but to the warie wise appeare.
>
> [4.1.17]

The doubleness of exterior and interior finds expression also in the doubleness of *Ate*'s speech—"Her lying tongue was in two parts divided, / And both the parts did speake, and both contended" (4.1.27)—and its divisive effects:

> And all within the riven walls were hung
>   With ragged monuments of times forepast,
>   All which the sad effects of discord sung:
>   There were rent robes, and broken scepters plast,
>   Altars defyl'd, and holy things defast,
>   Disshivered speares, and shields ytorne in twaine,
>   Great cities ransackt, and strong castles rast,
>   Nations captived, and huge armies slaine:
> Of all which ruines there some relicks did remaine.
>
> [4.1.21]

Spenser presents the fall of cities—such as Babylon, Thebes, Rome, and Troy—as *Ate*'s work (4.1.22). The reference to the Judgment of Paris, "the golden Apple, cause of all their wrong" (4.1.22), is particularly appropriate, since Paridell accompanies *Ate;* in fact, *Ate* functions here as a monstrous type of Helen. In addition, Spenser alludes to the *Iliad*'s *Ate* who Agamemnon claimed caused the strife between himself and Achilles (19.86–94), thus creating the material for the *Iliad.* Seen in this light, Spenser's Duessa and *Ate* recapitulate the *Iliad*'s Helen and *Ate* (and here we may recall Helen blaming *ate* for her coming with Paris to Troy); these figures of division function as generative principles of narrative, for the unfolding of both the *Iliad* and the *Faerie Queene* depends on oppositions and conflict.

Duessa is finally executed at the court of Mercilla, in Book 5, canto

10. As if to compensate for her disappearance, however, in the following canto there appears Geryoneo's unnamed monster, like Duessa, a hybrid of various beasts—a "body of a dog," "Lions clawes,"
"Dragons taile," and "Eagles wings" (5.11.24)—and a woman: "For
of a Mayde she had the outward face, / To hide the horrour, which
did lurke behinde, / The better to beguile, whom she so fond did
finde" (5.11.23). This description also underlines the monster's affinities with Errour; significantly, Geryon's two-headed watchdog,
Orthrus, was born of Typhaon and Echidna—Errour's prototype, as
we have seen. But the monster is more perniciously human and thus
more closely approximates Duessa in that she can speak "fowle blas-
phemous speaches" and "bitter curses, horrible to tell" (5.11.28).
Through the simile comparing Geryoneo's monster to the Sphinx—
another daughter of Echidna and Typhaon—Spenser reveals how the
two hybrid monsters figure the duplicity of language and specifically
of poetry:

> Much like in foulnesse and deformity
>   Unto that Monster, whom the Theban Knight,
>   The father of that fatall progeny,
>   Made kill her selfe for very hearts despight,
>   That he had red her Riddle, which no wight
>   Could ever loose, but suffred deadly doole.
>   So also did this Monster use like slight
>   To many a one, which came unto her schoole,
> Whom she did put to death, deceived like a foole.
>   [5.11.25]

The Sphinx's riddle, like poetry, must be "red," and the monster's
"schoole" where she "use[s] like slight" recalls Spenser's avocation, as
stated in the Letter to Raleigh, to "fashion a gentleman or noble
person in vertuous and gentle discipline." Moreover, allegories, like
riddles, call attention to their otherness and the need for interpretation. The figure of the Sphinx also serves to emphasize the link between sexual and linguistic seduction. The Sphinx was said to allure
men with her beautiful face in order to molest sexually and kill them.
Oedipus, who "red" her riddle correctly, nevertheless produced "fa-
tall progeny," a hybrid generation—daughters and sisters, sons and
brothers—by his misinterpretation of Apollo's oracle. These concerns with language and interpretation culminate in the simile comparing the monster's destruction by Arthur to the destruction of a
ship (5.11.29)—an image Spenser had used to figure poetic activity

(1.12.42). Through this simile, Spenser links his own poetry with the monstrous.

In the penultimate canto of Book 5, Geryoneo's monster is slain, but in the final canto, Spenser already introduces the Blatant Beast, the monster of Book 6, and the final exemplum of the monstrosity of language, to take her place. Following Virgil's *Fama*, Spenser's Blatant Beast with a "hundred tongues" (5.12.41) embodies the destructive aggression of misspeaking—*blatant* derives from the Latin *blatire* and the Italian *blaterare*, meaning to babble.[84] The Blatant Beast, in addition, focuses Spenser's concern with the destructive aggression of misreading. If the previous monsters of language—Errour, Duessa, Ate, Geryoneo's monster—embodied producers of language who exploited double senses, then the Blatant Beast represents as well the faulty reader who violates texts by misinterpreting them. The beast does not respect the otherness of either texts or people, seeking to appropriate them and destroy their integrity. Seen in this light, the virtue of the book, Courtesy, consists essentially of respect for others and for otherness.

The Blatant Beast enters the poem under the direction of "two old ill favour'd Hags" (5.12.28), Envy and Detraction. The beast is also a male reincarnation of female Slander, who "with leasings lewdly did miscall, / And wickedly backbite" (4.8.24).[85] Slander's "backbiting," which "pierce[s] the hart, / And wound the soule it selfe with griefe unkind" (4.8.26), becomes literalized in the beast's actual biting which results in festering physical wounds. Although Spenser links the beast to his own allegorical figures, Slander, Envy, and Detraction, he also gives the beast a double classical genealogy: the beast is at once the offspring of Cerberus and Chimera (6.1.8) and of Echidna and Typhaon (6.6.9–11). Furthermore, the beast has yet another prototype in Malory's Questing Beast, whose "quest"—meaning "yelp" or "bark"—punningly links him to Sir Palomides, whose quest is to capture him. As in the case of Duessa and the other monsters, the beast's multiple genealogy—from Hesiod, Virgil, Malory, and Spenser himself—is a measure of his monstrosity.

[84] *Variorum*, 5:267. The *OED* gives Spenser's beast as the first instance of "blatant." On the specifically linguistic and verbal nature of the Blatant Beast, see Fletcher, *Prophetic Moment*, pp. 289–94. See also Kenneth Gross's discussion of the Blatant Beast as a "demonic iconoclast." *Spenserian Poetics: Idolatry, Iconoclasm, and Magic* (Ithaca: Cornell Univ. Press, 1985), pp. 224–34.

[85] Anderson, "In liuing colours," pp. 62–63, observes that Spenser's unique use of the word "quean" in reference to Slander allows for "the possibility that for one awful moment the image of the bitter old woman glances at the living Queen."

Yet the Blatant Beast diverges in the crucial fact of gender from Spenser's earlier female monsters: in fact, the Blatant Beast with his multiplicity of tongues can be seen as parodically reincarnating Malfont, made monstrous by his tongue nailed to a post. Malfont is certainly an ambivalent figure for Spenser, as we have seen. Malfont may represent a version of Fradubio who dared to lift the veil of a political allegory Spenser desists from unveiling. If so, then Spenser ultimately suggests an affinity between Duessa and Mercilla, powerful women who can make monsters of men, and hence are themselves monstrous. Although Mercilla succeeds in silencing Malfont, Spenser cannot so easily contain the Blatant Beast.

Just as the figure of the Hermaphrodite ended the first part of the poem, so the Blatant Beast closes Book 6 and hence the poem itself as we have it.[86] In the 1590 ending of Book 3, Amoret and Scudamour's embrace, which Spenser compares to a Hermaphrodite, served as an antidote to Busirane's murderous "penning" of Amoret. But at the end of Book 6, the Blatant Beast, having bitten and wounded Spenser's characters, threatens to destroy even his poem. Spenser's androgynous, if contrived, solution has been replaced by a monstrous problem.

At the end of Book 6, Calidore captures the beast, albeit for a time, and leads him through Faeryland. The people of Faery, many of whom had been victimized by the beast, "wondred at the sight" (6.12.37) and thus reveal their strong fascination with the "Monster" (6.12.38). In fact, in the line "And much *admyr'd* the Beast, but more *admyr'd* the Knight" (6.12.37; in which "admyre" means "wonder at"; emphasis added), the people seem barely to distinguish hero from monster. The people's failure to distinguish here mirrors the beast's indiscriminate backbiting; thus the beast, perhaps gathering strength from the "fault of men," breaks his chains to roam the world.[87] This time, however, he works even greater damage and can no longer be

[86]On the unity of the six books of the poem, see Richard Neuse, "Book VI as Conclusion to the *Faerie Queene*," *ELH*, 35 (1968), rpt. in Hamilton, *Essential Articles*, pp. 329–53; and Northrop Frye, "The Structure of Imagery in the *Faerie Queene*," in *Fables of Identity* (New York: Harcourt Brace, 1963), p. 70.

[87]For another perspective on the beast's liberation, see Harry Berger, Jr., "A Secret Discipline: *The Faerie Queene* Book VI," in *Form and Convention in the Poetry of Edmund Spenser,* ed. William Nelson (New York: Columbia Univ. Press, 1961), p. 43. Berger sees Calidore's binding of the beast as a wish-fulfillment, a "ticker-tape parade through Faerie, exposed a moment later when the beast roars into the present and threatens the poet." Of interest also is his related discussion of the beast as "an artificial and ideographic fable . . . which permits evil to be expressed in physical terms so that chivalric action is possible" (p. 41).

restrained by either Calidore or the other knights: "Yet none of them could ever bring him into band" (6.12.39). In the penultimate stanza of the book, Spenser catalogues the beast's present activity:

> So now he raungeth through the world againe,
>> And rageth sore in each degree and state;
>> Ne any is, that may him now restraine,
>> He growen is so great and strong of late,
>> Barking and biting all that him doe bate,
>> Albe they worthy blame, or cleare of crime:
>> Ne spareth he most learned wits to rate,
>> Ne spareth he the gentle Poets rime,
> But rends without regard of person or of time.
>
> [6.12.40]

Just as Spenser called into question the difference between Calidore and the Blatant Beast, so here he calls into question the distinction between the backbiting beast and its creator *and* victim, "the gentle Poets rime":[88]

> Ne may this homely verse, of many meanest,
>> Hope to escape his venemous despite,
>> More then my former writs, all were they clearest
>> From blamefull blot, and free from all that wite,
>> With which some wicked tongues did it backebite,
>> And bring into a mighty Peres displeasure,
>> That never so deserved to endite.
>> Therefore do you my rimes keep better measure,
> And seeke to please, that now is counted wisemens threasure.
>
> [6.12.41]

Not only does the poem generate the beast, but, with the pun on "endite," Spenser collapses the distinction between the "indictment" by his backbiters (figured in the Blatant Beast) and his own "enditing" of the poem.[89] Although Spenser had insisted on distinguishing his own poetry from duplicitous language by figuring the latter through female monsters, doubly Other, in the end he demystifies his

---

[88]Humphrey Tonkin, *Spenser's Courteous Pastoral: Book VI of the Faerie Queene* (Oxford: Oxford Univ. Press, 1972), p. 154, sees this passage "either as a plaintive request for better consideration or as a dare to find fault." See also his discussion, pp. 206ff., of Spenser's "defense of poetry" in the context of Renaissance defenses and, in particular, of Sidney's *Apology*.

[89]The *OED* gives "endite" as obsolete forms for both "indict" and "indite."

own practice of demonizing the Other and accepts the monstrous and destructive Other as part of the self. In Book 6 the Blatant Beast generates the narrative as Errour had done, but unlike female Errour, he cannot be readily contained or destroyed. Indeed his trajectory through Book 6 necessarily parallels that of Calidore, Spenser's knight whose quest it is to capture him. And at the end of Book 6, Spenser allows the beast to escape and survive the ending of his own narrative, acknowledging once again the impossibility of destroying the anxiety-producing monstrosity of language once and for all.

Dame Nature and the Sabaoths Sight

In the redemptive palinode of the *Mutabilitie Cantos,* which have been compared to Chaucer's Retraction in the *Canterbury Tales,* Spenser replaces the Blatant Beast with Dame Nature, which he represents as Venus Hermaphrodite.[90] She is neither a human character like Britomart nor an emblem like the female monsters, but like them, she combines contraries:

> Whether she man or woman inly were,
> That could not any creature well descry:
> For, with a veile that wimpled every where,
> Her head and face was hid, that mote to none appeare.
>
> That some doe say was so by skill devized,
> To hide the terror of her uncouth hew,
> From mortall eyes that should be sore agrized;
> For that her face did like a Lion shew,
> That eye of wight could not indure to view:
> But others tell that it so beautious was,
> And round about such beames of splendor threw,
> That it the Sunne a thousand times did pass,
> Ne could be seene, but like an image in a glass.
>
> [7.7.5,6]

Nature combines these oppositions—male and female, young and

---

[90]See Neuse, 631n: "On the analogy of the Retraction one is tempted to take 'canto vnperfite' as Spenser's own superscription and to see in the concluding prayer an acknowledgement that every design of the poet's must remain 'vnperfite' here in this realm which itself awaits the 'perfection' or completion of God's eternal realm."

old—in dynamic and mysterious suspension, unlike the monsters whose doubleness was static and emblematic. Instead of fixing and thereby domesticating the terrifying otherness of Nature, or ridiculing and thereby deflecting his fascination with female powers of generation as he did in debasing Duessa, Spenser conveys Nature's enigmatic numinosity and accords it respect.

Nature renders judgment against the claims of the Titaness Mutabilitie, asserting that Change is ultimately subsumed in "[all things'] owne perfection" (7.7.58); nevertheless, in the final "canto unperfite," Spenser acknowledges that even though Mutabilitie might be denied "Heav'ns Rule; yet very sooth to say, / In all things else she beares the greatest sway" (7.8.1), and closes his poem with a prayer for "that . . . time when no more *Change* shall be":[91]

> But stedfast rest of all things firmely stayd
> Upon the pillours of Eternity,
> That is contrayr to *Mutabilitie,*
> For all that moveth, doth in *Change* delight:
> But thence-forth all shall rest eternally
> With Him that is the God of Sabbaoth hight:
> O that great Sabbaoth God, graunt me that Sabaoths sight.
>
> [7.8.2]

Losing faith in his ability to negotiate politics and history without being "raced" as a Malfont or incurring "a mighty Peres displeasure," Spenser leaves the public arena for his private vision at Arlo Hill and this final prayer for apocalypse. It is significant for my argument that the pun on "Sabbaoth" (hosts or armies) and "Sabaoth" (the seventh day of rest) has led the *OED* to state that Spenser confused the two words, although the *Variorum* notes the importance of the two meanings and of maintaining the different spellings.[92] The question of whether Spenser intended to maintain or collapse distinctions is thus encapsulated in these two readings. "Sabaoth" is, in addition, etymologically related to "Elizabeth," derived from Hebrew "Elisheba," "God is my oath."[93] If a verbal allusion to Elizabeth can be discerned

---

[91]See Greene, *Descent from Heaven,* pp. 322–23: "The metaphysical reply of Nature is little consolation to the individual in the existential desolation of his *contemptus mundi.* . . . If faith is indeed a refuge here, it is a lonely and bitter one. . . .[Spenser] invokes and he waits, but he affirms only the reality of the Titaness."

[92]*Variorum,* 6:315–16. See also Miller, pp. 224, 231n, on the pun and its critical history.

[93]See Hamilton, "Our New Poet," p. 496: "Since Spenser would know that 'Sab-

here, I suggest that the Elizabeth Spenser invokes is not exclusively the sovereign whom he set out to praise in his poem, written in Ireland, exiled from her court, but a composite figure of female authority with more personal than political significance. For in *Amoretti* 74, Spenser praised his three Elizabeths—his mother, his queen, and his wife: "Ye three Elizabeths for ever live, / that three such graces did unto me give." By bringing together the male God of the apocalypse and this female authoring principle, Spenser gives final expression to his personal mythology of the ineffable terror of and desire for Venus Hermaphrodite. In the *Mutabilitie Cantos,* which explicitly departs from the structure and mode of the preceding books of the *Faerie Queene,* and especially in these final fragmentary cantos, Spenser not only gives over historical allegory but indeed turns away from representation itself, to express his desire for an unmediated vision.

Spenser's giving over of representation can perhaps be explained by his changed relationship to female authority, both in the political realm and in his artistic practice. In Book 3, Spenser set out to write the English *Aeneid* praising his "Augustus," Elizabeth Tudor; in writing for a female patron and reader, he fully engages the implications of a woman hero's pursuit of an epic destiny, attempting to represent female subjectivity without violating it. Unlike Hellenore, Florimell, and Amoret—versions of "Helen" and victims of male reification—Britomart recapitulates Aeneas' career in her mission to found Troynovant; in her simultaneous quest for Artegall, the androgynous heroine also combines the literal and metaphorical journeys of Odysseus and Penelope toward one another.

In the 1596 *Faerie Queene,* however, Spenser's faith now turned to disillusionment with the Elizabethan order entails a shift in his conception of female sovereignty and the relationship between the sexes. In Book 5, Artegall displaces Britomart as the epic hero, and recapitulating Aeneas' dalliance with Dido, he becomes ensnared by the Amazon Radigund. Radigund's emasculation of Artegall also recalls the threat posed by Camilla's military prowess to Virgil's male warriors. Although Britomart rescues Artegall from Radigund's thrall,

---

bath' signifies 'rest' . . . [and] that Elizabeth signifies 'Peace of the Lord, or quiet rest of the Lord,' his final prayer as an exile in war-ravaged Ireland is for sight of the Queen and the rest which she signifies." Nohrnberg, p. 83, etymologizes Elizabeth as Eli-sabbath, which can mean sabbath God. He notes, further, that the forms *shabua,* week; *sheba, shibah,* seven; and *shabbath,* cessation, sabbath are all related.

she appears to sap her own energies by slaying her counterpart and instituting male rule in Radegone; she fades away from the poem and, in acceding epic initiative to Artegall, becomes a shadowy figure resembling Virgil's Lavinia. In the Radigund episode Spenser demonstrates the inefficacy of sacrificing a demonized double to preserve the self and the consequent untenability of "the moderate Puritan position" that affirms one exceptional woman ruler over all other women unfit to rule. Spenser, then, moves from an elaboration of the *Odyssey*'s interest in the possibility of female heroism to a Virgilian anxiety about female power and dominance. Although critics often consider Spenser to be protofeminist, this ambivalence concerning female sovereignty and female sexuality deserves attention.

Spenser's ambivalence, especially concerning female sexuality, is already present in Book 1, in figures such as Errour and Duessa; the monstrous doubleness of female sexuality represents for Spenser negative versions of his own artistic practice and recalls at once the *Odyssey*'s duplicitous Helen and Virgil's monstrous *Fama*. His attempt to exorcize the problematics of language and representation by projecting it on a sequence of female monsters, doubly Other, recalls the *Aeneid*'s sequential scapegoating of female characters opposed to Jupiter's *fatum*. Even so, at the end of Book 6 and in the *Mutabilitie Cantos,* Spenser demystifies his own practice of demonizing the Other: in allowing the Blatant Beast to close Book 6, Spenser acknowledges the monstrous and destructive Other as a part of the self; and in the *Mutabilitie Cantos,* he represents Venus Hermaphrodite not as a monster that can be dismissed or destroyed but as a numinous Other that demands respect.

5 Shakespeare's *Troilus and Cressida*

"Was this fair face the cause," quoth she,
"Why the Grecians sacked Troy?
Fond done, done fond,
    Was this King Priam's joy?"
        —*All's Well That Ends Well*, 1.3.67–70

Shakespeare wrote *Troilus and Cressida* in 1601–2, during the final years of Elizabeth's reign. The play's dark disillusion, often said to address the sophistication of its intended audience, the lawyers of Inns of Court, perhaps reflects more generally the temper of the times, when the aging queen lingered on the throne without naming a heir and the Elizabethan Settlement had disintegrated.[1] Leah Marcus has suggested that Shakespeare's comic heroines played by boy actors (who called attention to their androgyny by taking on male disguises) found their historical analogue in the queen who called herself a Prince.[2] But Elizabeth also made political use of her female gender when convenient, claiming that she was wedded to her nation and that she was the virgin mother of her people.[3] It is peculiarly appropriate, then, that at the close of Elizabeth's reign Shakespeare turns to an oft-told tale of a woman's betrayal, significantly couched in terms

---

[1]Robert Ashton, *Reformation and Revolution: 1558–1660* (London: Paladin, 1985), pp. 180–219. The Elizabethan Settlement usually refers to the settlement of religion, but Ashton takes it as a set of comprehensive solutions pertaining to domestic policy, foreign affairs, the economy, and social life (pp. 70–107).

[2]Leah Marcus, "Shakespeare's Comic Heroines, Elizabeth I, and the Political Uses of Androgyny," in *Women in the Middle Ages and the Renaissance,* ed. Mary Beth Rose (Syracuse: Syracuse Univ. Press, 1986), pp. 135–53. Marcus also points out that Elizabeth, in addition to the well-known instance of remarking that *she* was Shakespeare's Richard II, took the inevitable marriage of the heroine at the end of the comedies as an implied criticism of her single state, and concludes, "her unwillingness to separate dramatic texts from the political milieu of their performance suggests how strongly she perceived the drama as a figuration of public life" (p. 144).

[3]Marcus, pp. 141–42.

210

of a mother's betrayal ("Think we had mothers" [5.2.128], Troilus exclaims, upon his disillusionment with Cressida). Although queens and mothers hold power over their subjects and sons, Shakespeare dramatizes the "persistence of patriarchy" even during Elizabeth's reign in the buying and selling of Helen, and then Cressida, as merchandise.[4] The play's representation of woman thus supports Joan Kelly's assertion that women did not, in fact, have a Renaissance.[5] Indeed, *Troilus and Cressida* dramatizes Kelly's observation that the emergence of private property led to the commodification of both men and women, but especially of women.

In this atmosphere of cash and carry, Shakespeare directly engages the tradition of classical epic for the first time in his dramatic career. Significantly, in 1598, several years before the composition of *Troilus and Cressida*, the first parts of Chapman's translation of the *Iliad* (*Seaven Bookes of the Iliades* and *Achilles Shield*) were published. By the time Shakespeare came to this tradition, however, the world of Homer's *Iliad* had been mediated not only by Chaucer's poem, whose title he borrows, but also by the medieval legends of Troy and Henryson's completion (and interpretation) of Chaucer.[6] Thus in *Troilus and Cressida*, Shakespeare foregrounds the problem of telling a tale that had already been told many times over, his predicament of writing in a tradition already overcrowded and overdetermined.[7] In fact, one of

---

[4]I take the phrase from Allison Heisch's "Queen Elizabeth and the Persistence of Patriarchy," *Feminist Review*, 4 (Feb. 1980), 45–56.

[5]Joan Kelly, "Did Women Have a Renaissance?" in *Women, History, and Theory: The Essays of Joan Kelly* (Chicago: Univ. of Chicago Press, 1984), pp. 19–50.

[6]On the sources of the play, see Robert Kimbrough, *Shakespeare's Troilus and Cressida and its Setting* (Cambridge: Harvard Univ. Press, 1964), pp. 25–46; Kenneth Muir, *The Sources of Shakespeare's Plays* (New Haven: Yale Univ. Press, 1978), pp. 141–57; and the *Variorum*, ed. Harold N. Hillebrand and T. W. Baldwin (Philadelphia: J. P. Lippincott, 1953), pp. 419–49. For a review of critical opinions on Shakespeare's knowledge of Homer, see the *Variorum*, pp. 421–24, and Robert K. Presson, *Shakespeare's Troilus and Cressida and the Legends of Troy* (Madison: Univ. of Wisconsin Press, 1953), pp. 5–9, 137–41. Presson argues that Shakespeare's play shows closer affinities to Chapman's Homer than to the medieval matter of Troy, in both characterization and narrative technique. E. M. W. Tillyard, *Shakespeare's Problem Plays* (Toronto: Univ. of Toronto Press, 1949), pp. 41–49, stresses the importance of Lydgate's *Troy Book* and Caxton's *Recuyell of the Historyes of Troye* over the classical sources. On Shakespeare's relationship to Chaucer, see Hyder E. Rollins, "The Troilus-Cressida Story from Chaucer to Shakespeare," *PMLA*, 32 (1917), 383–429; and M. C. Bradbrook, "What Shakespeare Did to Chaucer's *Troilus and Criseyde*," *Shakespeare Quarterly*, 9 (1958), 311–19.

[7]See Thomas M. Greene, *The Light in Troy: Imitation and Discovery in Renaissance Poetry* (New Haven: Yale Univ. Press, 1982), chapter 3, "Imitation and Anachronism" (pp. 28–53). My departures from his theory will become apparent in what

Shakespeare's major concerns in this play seems to be precisely the question of the overdetermining power of tradition—both for himself as a writer who is in danger of being mastered by tradition and for his characters around whom tradition has authorized certain meanings. By Shakespeare's time, Cressida had become, as Pistol's casual reference to the "lazar kite of Cressid's kind" (*Henry V*, 2.1.77) suggests, the prototype of false woman. Shakespeare frees himself from the fate of merely repeating, by demystifying and radically revising the myth of Cressida through his own fiction. He constructs a cardboard representation of Helen as a synedoche for mystified tradition, which he criticizes through his newly conceived fiction of Cressida.

From Epic to Drama

The play is introduced by "A Prologue armed . . . / . . . suited / in like condition as [his] argument" (Pr. 23–25), whose speech serves as the dramatic equivalent of an epic argument.[8] Just as in the Prologue to *Henry V*, where Shakespeare had presented the transformation— by his and the audience's dramatic imagination—of a stage into a kingdom, the "wooden O" into a battlefield, so here, in *Troilus and Cressida*, he sets forth to transform the epic material of the Trojan war into dramatic form:

> To tell you, fair beholders, that our play
> Leaps o'er the vaunt and firstlings of those broils,
> Beginning in the middle; starting thence away
> To what may be digested in a play.
>
> [Pr. 26–29]

---

follows. Unlike Harold Bloom, whose "anxiety of influence" posits a paternal precursor poet/text to be wrestled with by the "belated" poet, I am concerned here with Shakespeare's relationship to tradition, not in T.S. Eliot's sense of a single line of "monuments" that form an "ideal order" but as a complex accretion of a body of texts from which Shakespeare chooses to juxtapose competing subtexts in order to create his own meaning through such a competition. Bloom, *Anxiety of Influence* (New York: Oxford Univ. Press, 1973); Eliot, "Tradition and the Individual Talent" (1919), in *Selected Prose of T. S. Eliot*, ed. Frank Kermode (New York: Harcourt, 1975), pp. 37–44.

[8]All quotations from *Troilus and Cressida* are taken from Kenneth Muir's edition in the Oxford Shakespeare (1984). References to other Shakespeare plays are to David Bevington's *The Complete Works* (Glenview, Ill.: Scott Foresman, 1980).

Shakespeare places his play in epic tradition by reference to a feature Horace greatly admired in the *Odyssey:* Homer starts *in medias res,* "beginning in the middle," a choice which became a necessity for later epics. Yet an important difference between this Prologue and that of *Henry V* must not be overlooked. In *Henry V,* though the choric Prologue disclaims the "Muse of fire, that would ascend / The brightest fire of invention" (Pr. 1–2), Shakespeare presents dramatic imagination as a liberating and creative force, an effective vehicle for epic. But in *Troilus,* the "digestion" of epic material into the dramatic mode implies not a dignified transition from the epic to the dramatic, as is underscored by the Prologue's repeated use of the image of vomiting in describing the two armies' entrance into combat: "And the deep-drawing barks do there *disgorge* / Their [the Greeks'] warlike fraughtage" (Pr. 12–13), and "Priam's six gated city— / . . .with massy staples / And corresponsive and fulfilling bolts, / *Sperr up* the sons of Troy (Pr. 15–19; emphasis added).⁹ These lines introduce the imagery of destructive feeding that pervades the play, of which Ulysses' comment on "appetite, an universal wolf" (1.3.120) is perhaps the best known example.¹⁰ In these images of interrupted or incomplete digestion, the play reveals its uneasy relationship to its epic sources. Harry Berger, Jr., has suggested the dramatic exigencies of such a falling off: Shakespeare's characters "have been deported from the wide and open epic spaces to the more crabbed and exposed confines imposed by the visual context and physical stage of the play."¹¹

This reduction of epic grandeur, the cutting down to size of the matter of legend, is also evident in the rhetorical movement of the Prologue itself:

> In Troy there lies the scene. From isles of Greece
> The princes orgulous, their high blood chafed,

---

⁹Muir and the *Variorum* editors gloss "sperr up" to mean "shut up," but the *OED* gives "sper" as an obsolete variation of "speowen," "to spew," which is often constructed with the adverbs "up," "out," "forth." Muir notes that the accepted definition derives from "sper," an obsolete variant of "spar," meaning "to shut." The *OED* gives "sperel," as "a means of closing or fastening." The gates may just as well "spew up" as "shut up" the warriors, especially since several lines earlier, the Greeks have been "disgorged" from their ships to engage in war.

¹⁰Many critics have noted the imagery of eating and food in the play. See especially Caroline Spurgeon, *Shakespeare's Imagery and What It Tells Us* (Cambridge: Cambridge Univ. Press, 1935), pp. 320–24, who notes that these images are as pervasive in this play (she counts 44 instances) as are those of disease in *Hamlet*.

¹¹Harry Berger, Jr., "*Troilus and Cressida:* The Observer as Basilisk," *Comparative Drama,* 2 (1968), 131.

Have to the port of Athens sent their ships,
Fraught with the ministers and instruments
Of cruel war. Sixty and nine that wore
Their crownets regal, from th'Athenian bay
Put forth toward Phrygia, and their vow is made
To ransack Troy, within whose strong immures
The ravished Helen, Menelaus' queen,
With wanton Paris sleeps—and that's the quarrel.
[Pr. 1–10]

The highly Latinate, elevated, and hence, epic, style of the opening
lines is suddenly deflated by the intrusion of the colloquial, "and
that's the quarrel." This deflation by juxtaposition will be Shakespeare's strategy throughout the play; it anticipates how the "tortive
and errant" (1.3.8) rhetoric of Agamemnon and Nestor will be de-
molished by Thersites' colloquial and mocking "all the argument is a
whore and a cuckold" (2.3.68) and how the agreement among the
Trojans that Helen is a "theme of honour and renown" (2.2.198) is
undercut by Shakespeare's representation of her in the low style.[12]
The moment of deflation occurs in all three instances when the subject turns to Helen: the supposedly epic struggle is nothing more than
a "quarrel" over a woman, and as Thersites repeatedly puts it, it is
only "lechery" that brings about the war and keeps it going. In this
scene, the Prologue is indeed suited to the argument, for his rhetoric
enacts that disjunction between the war and its supposed cause, as
well as between the play and its epic sources.

Although the armed Prologue speaks of armies and promises
battles—his parting line is "'tis but the chance of war" (Pr. 31)—it
will not be until well into Act 5 that we are presented with scenes of
combat, and by then our view of them will have been severely
qualified not only by the anticlimactic ingloriousness of the battles
themselves but by the seemingly endless discussions that have intervened and have proven so unavailing. Unlike the choric Prologue
in *Henry V* that introduces each act and speaks the Epilogue as well,
this "epic" Prologue never reappears; in fact, diseased Pandarus, a
character most unsuited to the decorum of epic, will have the final
word.

---

[12]See Tillyard, p. 58, for a discussion of the rhetorical deflation in the Greek council
scene: "the inflated style contains, through its excess, its own deflatory self-criticism."

Women Are Angels, Wooing

More immediately, the armed Prologue is followed and replaced in Act 1, scene 1, by Troilus, who is about to "unarm again" (1.1.1). Troilus repudiates Helen as "too starved a subject for [his] sword" (1.1.91) and asks, "Why should I war without the walls of Troy / That find such cruel battle here within? (1.1.2–3). By invoking the commonplace opposition between wars "without" and "within," Troilus intends to dramatize the apparent irreconcilability between his public duty to fight for his besieged city and his private preoccupation with Cressida; but, in fact, the apparent opposition masks an essential analogy between Troilus' two wars.

Troilus' obsession with Cressida is set off against his disavowal of Helen as an inadequate "argument" for the war: "Fools on both sides: Helen must needs be fair, / When with your blood you daily paint her thus" (1.1.88–89). Troilus here gives explicit voice to the Prologue's insinuation that the supposedly epic war is merely a "quarrel," and hence its object, Helen, trivial. Helen is merely an ornamental surface, a "painted" icon whose value the warriors affirm through the sacrifice made daily to win or keep her. The discrepancy between Helen and her value will be elaborated in the debate among the Trojans, although, there, Troilus will be the chief proponent of continuing the fight to keep her, for her abstract significance as the "theme of honour and renown" (2.2.198).

The language Troilus employs here to repudiate Helen suggests, however, that she is "too starved" (1.1.91) because she will not satisfy Troilus' hunger; it is telling that he will later speak of her as "remainder viands" (2.2.69), picked over by Paris. If Helen is Paris' dish, then Cressida will be Troilus': he hopes Cressida will satisfy him, as his ready acceptance of Pandarus' homely analogy of winning Cressida to baking and eating cake suggests:

PANDARUS.   He that will have a
   cake out of the wheat must tarry the grinding.
TROILUS.   Have I not tarried?
PANDARUS.   Ay, the grinding; but you must tarry the boulting.
                  .   .   .
TROILUS.   Still have I tarried.
PANDARUS.   Ay, to the leavening; but here's yet in the word hereafter,
   the kneading, the making of the cake, the heating of the oven, and the

baking. Nay, you must stay the cooling too, or you may chance to
burn your lips. [1.1.14–26]

It is perhaps no accident that Troilus' thoughts wander to Cressida
when he sits at Priam's table (1.1.29–30), especially since he will later
denounce Cressida by using images of leftover food: "orts of her
love, / The fragments, scraps, the bits and greasy relics / Of her o'er-
eaten faith" (5.2.156–58).

   In fact, despite Troilus' contemptuous dismissal of Helen and those
who fight over her, his own conception of Cressida differs not at all
from the two armies' superficial and arbitrary valuation of Helen.

> I tell thee I am mad
> In Cressid's love. Thou answer'st she is fair,
> Pourest in the open ulcer of my heart
> Her eyes, her hair, her cheek, her gait, her voice;
> Handlest in thy discourse—O that her hand,
> In whose comparison all whites are ink
> Writing their own reproach, to whose soft seizure
> The cygnet's down is harsh, and spirit of sense
> Hard as the palm of ploughman! This thou tell'st me—
> As true thou tell'st me—when I say I love her.
>
> [1.1.50–59]

Troilus speaks of Cressida as if he were writing a Petrarchan sonnet.
While intending to praise her, however, his use of conventional conceits makes her indistinguishable from any other lady; individuality
or uniqueness becomes obliterated when Troilus' description of her
is, true to the convention, so fragmented. Troilus in his verse, as
much as Pandarus in his prose, "handle[s] in [his] discourse"
Cressida, and his essentially sensual view of her becomes apparent in
"soft seizure" and "spirit of sense"—prominent alliterating phrases
closing consecutive lines—which reveal Troilus' melodramatic sensualism whereby he seeks to lose himself. Although Troilus disclaims
Helen, his sonnet-writing about Cressida barely masks an objectification of her and thus reenacts the process through which the two
nations have reified Helen as the object of the war.

   Troilus' acquisitiveness of Cressida is made even more explicit in
the extended metaphor comparing his wooing of Cressida to a mercantile voyage:

Tell me, Apollo, for thy Daphne's love,
What Cressid is, what Pandar, and what we?
Her bed is India; there she lies, a pearl;
Between our Ilium and where she resides
Let it be called the wild and wand'ring flood;
Ourself the merchant, and this sailing Pandar
Our doubtful hope, our convoy and our bark.

[1.1.96–102]

Troilus asks the right questions about identity, questions he will be forced to confront later in the play. His invocation of Apollo and Daphne recalls the predatory love of the male god for the mortal woman, who could only escape from divine lust by transforming herself into a laurel tree—which Apollo nevertheless appropriated as his emblem. Daphne's Ovidian metamorphosis also raises the issue of identity as difference, foreshadowing Cressida's supposed betrayal of Troilus. But here Troilus is satisfied with easy answers that only pertain to his desire to acquire and possess Cressida, and hence he affirms the notion of stable (and static) identity by reducing his beloved to a pearl and Pandarus to a vessel, the means by which Troilus the merchant will obtain the coveted merchandise.[13]

Many critics have noted how the juxtaposition of Troilus' verse and Pandarus' prose serves to criticize the other.[14] I suggest, however, that Troilus' conceit of Cressida as pearl is in fact only a lyrical version of Pandarus' more prosaic objectification of Cressida as cake to be baked and eaten; indeed, their seemingly divergent views of Cressida amount to much the same thing. Moreover, Pandarus' repeated comparison of Cressida to Helen, who sets the standard for beauty, reveals his intention to inflate the price of his wares by comparison and thus corresponds to Troilus' mercantile metaphor of Cressida as pearl:

An her hair were not somewhat darker than Helen's—well, go to—
there were no more comparison between the women. But, for my part,

[13]A. P. Rossiter, *Angel with Horns* (New York: Theatre Arts Books, 1971), pp. 142–43, considers the image of the pearl to be an idealization. But see Raymond Southall's discussion of Troilus' "transformation into a merchant for whom Cressida is a desirable commodity" as a symptom of emergent capitalism. "*Troilus and Cressida* and the Spirit of Capitalism," in *Shakespeare in a Changing World,* ed. Arnold Kettle (New York: International Publishers, 1964), p. 222.

[14]For example, Tillyard, p. 56; Rossiter, p. 132; and Lawrence Danson, *Tragic Alphabet: Shakespeare's Drama of Language* (New Haven: Yale Univ. Press, 1974), p. 70.

she is my kinswoman: I would not, as they term it, praise her. . . .
Because she's kin to me, therefore she's not so fair as Helen; an she were
not kin to me, she would be as fair o' Friday as Helen is on Sunday.
[1.1.41–44,73–75]

The justness of Pandarus' comparison of Cressida to Helen lies beyond his narrowly self-regarding awareness. His insistence on
Cressida's kinship to him suggests that he considers her to be disposed of at will—a perception of her which allows him to aggrandize
his own importance in his mediation between Troilus and his niece.
Troilus correctly assesses Pandarus when he describes Cressida's uncle "as tetchy to be wooed to woo" (1.1.94), but he is blind about his
own version of Pandarus' narcissism. Just as Pandarus is solely interested in his own activity of meddling, so Troilus is preoccupied exclusively with his own forming fancy. The idea of Cressida allows
both men to indulge in their respective activities of pandering and
sonnet writing.

While Troilus believes he loves Cressida, and exalts her after a
fashion, his latent misogyny becomes apparent in his disdain of his
own love-induced indolence as feminine:

> The Greeks are strong, and skilful to their strength,
> Fierce to their skill, and to their fierceness valiant;
> But I am weaker than a woman's tear,
> Tamer than sleep, fonder than ignorance,
> Less valiant than the virgin in the night,
> And skilless as unpracticed infancy.
>
> [1.1.7–12]

Troilus' lament exemplifies the ways in which masculinity in a society at war is defined in contradistinction to what is perceived as the
feminine, as we have already seen in the *Iliad*. If prowess is masculine,
its lack—impotence or cowardice—is feminine or childlike. Troilus'
latent misogyny again surfaces at the end of the scene, when to
Aeneas' question, "Wherefore not afield?" he answers, "Because not
there. This woman's answer sorts, / For womanish it is to be from
thence" (1.1.103–5). Like cowardice, tautology is supposedly feminine. Although the war here is fought in the name of a woman, it
paradoxically fosters misogyny, which allows the warriors to disavow what they fear to be the feminine in themselves. A similar
ambivalence characterizes Hector: while challenging the Greeks on
the worth of his "lady" (1.3.271) and stressing the sanctity of conjugal

ties in his proposal to return Helen to Menelaus (2.2.173–85), he chides Andromache in his peeve at having been defeated by Ajax (1.2.6) and turns a deaf ear to his wife's pleas to desist from entering battle (5.3).

Although the entire first scene has dramatized Troilus' obsession with Cressida, it closes with an abrupt and surprising reversal: Troilus cheerfully accepts Aeneas' invitation to join the "good sport" (1.1.111) on the battlefield. This will not be the only instance in which Troilus will reverse himself. The "war within" that Troilus had so conventionally invoked at the beginning of the scene—"As wedged with a sigh, would rive in twain" (1.1.35)—is, in fact, an apposite description of a self-division and contradiction of which he is yet unaware. The real and frightening consequences of such a division will become clear later in the play.

At this point Troilus is still free to indulge his fantasies about his beloved, without having to match his abstraction of her to her own reality. But in the following scene, upon Cressida's first appearance in the play, the disjunction between Troilus' conventional sonnet writing about Cressida and the actuality of his beloved becomes apparent to the audience, if not to Troilus. Cressida shows herself to be quite adept at acting as the situation requires; here she suits her conversation to the prosaic low style of her uncle, as later she will allow herself to be kissed "in general" by the Greeks, answering to their expectation of her (4.5). Unlike Troilus, so completely self-absorbed that he hardly took heed of Pandarus' presence except as an audience for his lyrical outbursts, Cressida fully engages her uncle. As a woman, and especially as a traitor's daughter, she cannot afford to act indifferently toward those men who might protect her. Later in the scene, she jokes to Pandarus about the defensive strategy dictated by her circumstances:

> Upon my back, to defend my belly; upon my wit, to defend my wiles; upon my secrecy, to defend mine honesty; my mask, to defend my beauty; and you, to defend all these: and at all these wards I lie, at a thousand watches. [1.2.247–51]

She does not know, however, that in the preceding scene, Pandarus had commented nonchalantly, "She's a fool to stay behind her father. Let her to the Greeks" (1.1.78–79); nor does she know that both her uncle and Troilus will acquiesce quite readily to the Trojan decision to send her to the Greek camp.

While humoring Pandarus, however, Cressida successfully parries with her superior wit her uncle's vapid attempts to inflate Troilus' value. Pandarus compares Troilus to Hector, the worthiest Trojan warrior, and to Paris, the most handsome Trojan prince, as he had earlier compared Cressida to Helen, the paragon of female beauty. Cressida subtly criticizes Pandarus' repeated assertion that Troilus is a "better man" (1.2.58) than Hector:

CRESSIDA.   O Jupiter! There's no comparison.
                          . . .

PANDARUS.   Well, I say Troilus is Troilus.
CRESSIDA.   Then you say as I say; for I am sure
                   He is not Hector.
PANDARUS.   No, nor Hector is not Troilus in some degrees.
CRESSIDA.   'Tis just to each of them: he is himself.
                          . . .

CRESSIDA.   He is not Hector.

                                                                      [1.2.60–72]

Cressida's response to the trivial anecdote Pandarus tells to illustrate how "Helen loves [Troilus] better than Paris" (1.2.102–3) also shows that she considers the comparison to be beside the point. Her uncle's concluding remark that "it passed" (1.2.159) allows Cressida to dismiss it: "So let it now; for it has been a great while going by" (1.2.160–61). When Pandarus praises Troilus' "birth, beauty, good shape, discourse, manhood, learning, gentleness, virtue, youth, liberality, and such like" (1.2.239–41), Cressida again undercuts his fragmentation of Troilus with her ironic riposte, "a minced man" (1.2.243). Earlier in the scene, she had aptly stated the same point: "Indeed, a tapster's arithmetic may soon bring his particulars therein to a total" (1.2.108–9).

During an inverted and debased reenactment of the *Iliad's* teichoskopia where Helen identified the Greek warriors for Priam, Pandarus and Cressida watch the Trojan warriors pass by. Pandarus reveals his pathetic adulation of the warriors and his lack of judgment in praising Antenor, who will eventually betray Troy. But even more striking is his inability to recognize Troilus when he had praised him so extravagantly and had asked Cressida, "Do you know a man if you see him?" (1.2.61–62). He mistakes his man to be Deiphobus, Helen's husband after Paris' death—a telling detail that subtly links Cressida to Helen. Cressida, who clearly recognizes Troilus, sets her uncle up for a fall by disingenuously asking, "What sneaking fellow comes yonder?" (1.2.214).

In her soliloquy that closes the scene and complements Troilus' soliloquy in the preceding scene, Cressida reveals her strategy, dictated by the male prerogative to take possession of and to discard (or exchange) women at will. Cressida's admission of her love for Troilus, stated in simple terms, stands in stark contrast to Troilus' overblown rhetoric: "But more in Troilus thousandfold I see / Than in the glass of Pander's praise may be" (1.2.270–71).[15] She explains her wariness despite her admitted love for Troilus:

> Yet hold I off: women are angels, wooing;
> Things won are done—joy's soul lies in the doing.
> That she beloved knows nought that knows not this:
> Men prize the thing ungained more than it is.
> That she was never yet that ever knew
> Love got so sweet as when desire did sue.
> Therefore this maxim out of love I teach:
> 'Achievement is command; ungained, beseech'.
> Then though my heart's content firm love doth bear,
> Nothing of that shall from mine eyes appear.
>
> [1.2.272–81]

Cressida's defensive strategy of dissimulation is thus dictated by the value placed on women as "thing"; for women are angels only in the wooing. Even so, the pun on "angel" as a gold coin ("They have in England / A coin that bears the figure of an angel / stamp'd in gold" [*Merchant of Venice*, 2.7.55–57]) foreshadows Cressida's fate to become a medium of exchange between the Trojans and the Greeks. Although she has not heard Troilus speak of her, she shrewdly knows that her price will decline with possession, as is sadly borne out by Troilus' willingness to hand her over to the enemy after one night of love. In fact, Shakespeare confirms the authority of Cressida's maxim by having her echo Ariadne's lament *after* her abandonment by Theseus in Catullus 64:

> In future no woman should believe any man's assurances
> Or hope that anything a man says will come true.
> When they want something and are keen to get it

---

[15]Rossiter, p. 132, however, sees Cressida in this scene as "a chatty, vulgar little piece" and considers her rhyming soliloquy to reveal a cannily selfish woman who uses sexual attraction for power. But R. A. Foakes considers Cressida's couplets to be a mark of seriousness; both Helena in *All's Well* and Beatrice in *Much Ado* make their confessions of love in rhyme. He adds, however: "It is, nevertheless, cool verse, too full of commonplaces and sententiae . . . to be convincing." "*Troilus and Cressida* Reconsidered," *Univ. of Toronto Quarterly*, 32 (1963), 144.

Men will swear anything, and promise anything you like
But as soon as desire is satisfied
It doesn't matter what they've said, they don't mind perjury.[16]

Cressida will indeed share Ariadne's fate as an abandoned woman; in fact, Shakespeare will signal this parallel in the phrase Troilus uses to describe what he perceives to be his betrayal by Cressida, "Ariachne's broken woof" (5.2.150). If Catullus' Ariadne is Cressida's precursor in lyric, Cressida also follows the fate of another woman in epic, Virgil's Dido, who was able to control her destiny as long as she practiced defensive chastity; but like Dido, Cressida will not able to "hold off" indefinitely and will succumb to her emotions for Troilus. She will lose what little control she had over her life when she is sent, despite her desperate protests, to the Greek camp.

In the discrepancy between her feigned nonchalance concerning Troilus and her unadorned expression of her love for him, Shakespeare already depicts Cressida as divided. Her "maxim," "Achievement is command," will indeed be borne out, but her inability to be true to her feelings by declaring them will exact its price. In the preceding scene, Troilus had unwittingly encapsulated Cressida's dilemma: "But sorrow that is couched in seeming gladness / Is like that mirth fate turns to sudden sadness" (1.1.39–40). Indeed, dissimulation—a division between surface and essence—will lead to a more problematic split between Cressida's "a kind of self" and "an unkind self" (3.2.139–40) and ultimately, for Troilus, to that between his and "Diomed's Cressida" (5.2.135).

Helen: A Theme of Honor and Renown?

The disjunction in the love plot between Troilus' and Shakespeare's representations of Cressida is recapitulated in the war plot in the analogous gap between the Trojans' and Shakespeare's representations of Helen. Priam opens the debate in the Trojan camp by reporting Nestor's proposal that they return Helen to the Greeks in order to end the "hot digestion of this cormorant war" (2.2.6). Hector and Troilus immediately present themselves as the advocates for and against, in Hector's words, "Let[ting] Helen go" (2.2.16). Picking up

16 *The Poetry of Catullus*, trans. C. H. Sisson (New York: Viking, 1966), pp. 115–17.

the image of destruction in Nestor's proposal, Hector invokes the death of many Trojans that keeping Helen has caused: "Every tithe soul 'mongst many thousand dismes / Hath been as dear as Helen—I mean, of ours" (2.2.18–19). Troilus, however, dismisses Hector's statement as motivated by "fears and reasons" (2.2.31) and claims that "the worth and honour" of Priam cannot be weighed "in a scale / Of common ounces" (2.2.26–28)—of dead soldiers.

In the opening scene of the play, Troilus had expressed scorn for Helen as too "starved" an "argument" to fight upon; in the council scene, however, he advances two seemingly opposed reasons—which, in fact, prove to be corollaries of one another—for continuing the fight to keep her. First, he speaks of Helen as silk soiled by use and as leftover food:

> We turn not back the silks upon the merchant
> When we have soiled them; nor the remainder viands
> We do not throw in unrespective sieve
> Because we now are full.
>
> [2.2.68–71]

Here the consequences of the objectification of Helen as merchandise become evident: her price has fallen through use, but the Trojans cannot return her just because they have consumed her. If Cressida appeared cynical in "holding off" in order to maintain her value, Troilus' devaluation of Helen here confirms the justness of Cressida's maxim. For preceding this comparison of Helen to soiled silks and half-eaten food, Troilus had posited a hypothetical situation whereby he "take[s] today a wife" (2.2.60). Although it is not necessary to assume that he consciously refers to Cressida here, his hypothetical wife could stand for Cressida as well as for Helen, the subject under discussion:

> How may I avoid,
> Although my will distaste what it elected,
> The wife I chose? There can be no evasion
> To blench from this and to stand firm by honour.
>
> [2.2.64–67]

Troilus here postulates a change in his "will"—a synonym for "lust" as made evident in sonnet 135—a division between the initial election based on desire and the subsequent "distaste" of it. Yet "honour" binds him not to "avoid"—to eject by voiding or excreting—his "wife."

Troilus then discards the images of consumed goods, perhaps realizing how they degrade the consumer as well as the consumed, and proceeds to speak of Helen in seemingly more dignified terms, as a "pearl." Yet this repetition of the conceit, "woman as pearl," a conceit he had used earlier in speaking of Cressida, implies that the two women are for him interchangeable. Shakespeare underlines the clichéd bankruptcy of Troilus' imagination by having Troilus parrot lines from Marlowe's *Doctor Faustus:* "Why she is a pearl / Whose price hath launched above a thousand ships / And turned crowned kings to merchants" (2.2.80–82). Although presented in seemingly idealizing terms, Helen is still a commodity, a piece of merchandise. Unlike the soiled silks and leftover food, however, the pearl will not depreciate through use, and its constant value allows Troilus to speak of it as a "worthy prize" (2.2.85) and to reproach his countrymen for not continuing to value it:

> why do you now
> . . .
> Beggar the estimation which you prized
> Richer than sea or land? O theft most base,
> That we have stolen what we do fear to keep!
> [2.2.87,90–92]

Here the "merchants" have degenerated into "thieves"; the objectification of Helen ultimately contaminates those who price her as well as she who is priced. As Terry Eagleton suggests, in talking about Helen, the Trojans talk about themselves: "she mediates their own sense of themselves to them, she is their living reflection."[17] Yet the value of the "worthy prize" ultimately allows Troilus to abstract her into a "theme of honour and renown, / A spur to valiant and magnanimous deeds" (2.2.198–99), much as the Iliadic warriors abstracted Helen as the goal of the war and the embodiment of the *kleos* promised by the heroic code. In fact, this debate concerning Helen's value among Shakespeare's Trojans recapitulates and demystifies a similar debate among Homer's Greeks concerning the war effort: the male warriors confer value upon Helen as either an object with a price

[17]Terry Eagleton, *Shakespeare and Society: Cultural Studies in Shakespearean Drama* (New York: Schocken, 1967), p. 19.

or an abstract "theme" that serves to reflect and confirm male honor and glory.

Hector disagrees with Troilus by persuasively invoking the inviolability of the conjugal bond between Helen and Menelaus—the actual marriage set against Troilus' hypothetical marriage:

> What nearer debt in all humanity
> Than wife is to the husband? . . .
> If Helen then be wife to Sparta's king,
> As it is known she is, these moral laws
> Of nature and of nations speak aloud
> To have her back returned. Thus to persist
> In doing wrong extenuates not wrong,
> But makes it much more heavy. Hector's opinion
> Is this in way of truth. Yet ne'ertheless,
> My sprightly brethren, I propend to you
> In resolution to keep Helen still;
> For 'tis a cause that hath no mean dependence
> Upon our joint and several dignities.
>
> [2.2.174–5,182–92]

Yet this passage also dramatizes Hector's abrupt and surprising reversal in giving in to Troilus' "resolution to keep Helen still." Moreover, Hector's reference to the "roisting challenge" (2.2.208) that Aeneas has already brought to the Greeks on his behalf (1.3) reveals at its conclusion that the entire debate has been a pointless rhetorical exercise. The futile debate also makes manifest in the Trojan camp the absence of "degree" that Ulysses had spoken of among the Greeks: Hector invokes the "law in each well-ordered nation" (2.2.179) which guards conjugal ties only to set it aside.

When Shakespeare actually introduces Helen into the play in Act 3, scene 1, she speaks in the same low style as Cressida did in her banter with Pandarus. But while Cressida suited herself by necessity and in self-defense to her uncle's trivial talk, here it is Helen, together with Paris, who directs the scene and sets the less than dignified tone. Helen passes the time by ridiculing Pandarus' Polonius-like officiousness toward his superiors: "Dear Lord, you are full of fair words" (3.1.45). Shakespeare represents "the mortal Venus, the heart-blood of beauty, love's invisible soul" (3.1.30–32) as a trivial and decadent woman obsessed with love, much like Spenser's Hellenore. Helen prompts Pandarus: "Let thy song be love. 'This love will undo us all'.

O Cupid, Cupid, Cupid!" (3.1.102–103). But the vulgarity of "this love" is quickly enough revealed by Pandarus' song:

> Love, love, nothing but love, still love, still more!
>   For, O, love's bow
>   Shoots buck and doe;
>   The shaft confounds
>   Not that it wounds,
> But tickles still the sore.
> These lovers cry, 'O, O, they die!'
>   Yet that which seems the wound to kill
> Doth turn O! O! to ha! ha! he!
>   So dying love lives still.
>   'O! O!' a while, but 'ha! ha! ha!'
>   'O! O!' groans out for 'ha, ha, ha!'
> Heigh ho!
>
> [3.1.107–19]

Pandarus' first departure from his characteristic mode in prose dramatizes, in the grotesque insistence on the sexual pun on "dying," his poetic incompetence and trivial vulgarity.[18] Yet Paris reveals the similarity of his own conception of love to Pandarus' when he explains: "hot blood begets hot thoughts, and hot thoughts beget hot deeds, and hot deeds is love" (3.1.122–23). This reductively sensual definition of love—though Paris does not speak in poetic conceits and calls a spade a spade—carries Troilus' notion of love to its logical reduction and strips it of its idealizing veneer. Pandarus, however, seems shocked at this cynical genealogy of love and its equation with "hot deeds" and asks, "Is love a generation of vipers?" (3.1.125–26).

During this colloquy on love, Paris and Helen appear barely aware of the war outside their comfortable palace. When Pandarus finally turns the conversation to the battlefield, Paris, after enumerating the "gallantry of Troy" who are fighting his war, explains that he is not afield because "[his] Nell would not have it so" (3.1.128–29). Helen as "Nell" has been entirely stripped of her epic stature and appears callous and selfish, so unlike her former incarnation in the *Iliad,* where she lamented her part in bringing about the war and scorned Paris' cowardice in shirking combat.

---

[18]G. Wilson Knight makes the surprising observation that Pandarus' humor is "always kindly and sympathetic," and that it is like "health-bringing sunshine." His general idealization of the Trojans similarly leads him to call Helen a "queen of romance." *The Wheel of Fire: Interpretations of Shakespearean Tragedy* (1930; enl. ed.

Although Shakespeare allows Cressida to give voice to her private self in her soliloquy, he does not reveal any depth in Helen's character below the frivolous surface dramatized in this scene. Cressida's subjectivity, therefore, is set off against Helen's lack of it. Cardboard Helen, as a synecdoche of the entire trajectory of the legend of Troy, allows Shakespeare to set off Cressida, his own complex and nuanced representation, just as he juxtaposed Hamlet to Fortinbras and Laertes, simpler heroes of an earlier age. We can also explain the triviality of Helen, in terms of her own character, as the consequence of her objectification as "remainder viands" and abstraction as "the theme of honour and renown" by the Trojan warriors. Just as Cressida will eventually submit to Troilus' conception of her as "false," so it seems likely that Helen has already been affected by the Trojans' reification of her, carried to its logical reduction in Diomed's brutal dismissal of her as "a flat tamed piece" (4.1.63) and "contaminated carrion weight" (4.1.72). Speaking of Helen in terms of spoiled food, "sodeyn" Diomed reveals himself to be Troilus' Greek counterpart, who merely carries to an extreme Troilus' and the Trojans' commodification of Helen—Paris accuses Diomed of "disprais[ing] the thing that [he] desire[s] to buy" (4.1.77). The difference between the two men is not in kind but in degree, as will become evident in their analogous treatment of Cressida.

A Kind of Self and an Unkind Self

Troilus and Cressida meet for the first time in the following scene, but their impending union is already severely qualified by the problematic portrayal of "love" between Helen and Paris. In these two consecutive and complementary scenes, Pandarus appears in the company of both sets of lovers as he mediates between them, just as in the opening scenes, he served to introduce Troilus and Cressida to the play, true to his role as pander. The love affair is foreshortened from Chaucer's three years to a single night: the two lovers meet near the middle of the play, in Act 3, scene 2, and by the following morning, in Act 4, scene 2, already Cressida is to be sent to the Greek camp.

1949; rpt. London: Methuen, 1961), pp. 60–62. Foakes, pp. 145–46, voices the majority opinion in characterizing the atmosphere of the scene as that of a "high-class brothel," but he also notes that Helen shares a security of affection with Paris that allows them to tease Pandarus into parodying himself.

Upon their meeting, both lovers express fears concerning the dissolution of identity, albeit in different ways appropriate to their self-perception according to gender roles. Troilus is afraid of losing "distinction" (3.2.25), as he had earlier lamented his failure to be "master of his heart" (1.1.4) in love. His language bespeaks his desire to hold himself separate and in control. Thus he does not see Cressida as a partner but as a vehicle for sexual experience which he simultaneously desires and fears. In a moment of epic self-dramatization, Troilus likens himself to "a strange soul upon the Stygian banks / Staying for waftage" (3.2.8–9) and addresses Pandarus as "my Charon" (3.2.9). Again Troilus has Pandarus play the role of his conveyance, this time for his descent to the underworld. But Troilus pictures this inferno as "lily beds / Proposed for the deserver" where he may "wallow" (3.2.11–12); the descent to the underworld, a crucial rite of passage for the epic hero, has degenerated into a sensualist's self-indulgent fantasy:

> I am giddy. Expectation whirls me round.
> Th'imaginary relish is so sweet
> That it enchants my sense. What will it be
> When that the watr'y palate tastes indeed
> Love's thrice repured nectar?—death, I fear me,
> Swooning destruction, or some joy too fine,
> Too subtle-potent, tuned too sharp in sweetness,
> For the capacity of my ruder powers.
> I fear it much, and I do fear besides
> That I shall lose distinction in my joys,
> As doth a battle, when they charge on heaps
> The enemy flying.
>
> [3.2.16–27]

These lines recast, albeit in a poetic key, Paris' definition of love as "hot deeds" and exemplify Troilus' infantile and narcissistic sensualism—what Raymond Southall has somewhat unmercifully called his "inherent capacity for pig-like defilement."[19] Cressida has completely disappeared, even as a vehicle, as Troilus focuses exclusively on "th'imaginary relish," the tasting of the "thrice repured nectar."

---

[19]Southall, p. 228. On Troilus' sensualism, see also Rossiter, p. 143. Many critics, however, see Troilus in a different light. Knight, pp. 63–64, characterizes him as a "metaphysical lover," and his love as a "spiritual and delicate thing" destined to disaster in the world of the flesh. Similarly, Tillyard, p. 67, considers him "a romantic and unfortunate lover."

Moreover, his likening of their sexual union to annihilation in death is undercut by Pandarus' vulgar punning on "dying" in the preceding scene.

Cressida is also concerned with preserving her integrity, but her concern is of a very different sort from Troilus'. She is afraid of betraying her true and vulnerable self by revealing her love through her previous mask of indifferent nonchalance:

> Hard to seem won; but I was won, my lord,
> With the first glance that ever—pardon me;
> If I confess much, you will play the tyrant.
> I love you now; but not, till now, so much
> But I might master it. In faith, I lie!
> My thoughts were like unbridled children, grown
> Too headstrong for their mother. See, we fools!
> Why have I blabbed? Who shall be true to us,
> When we are so unsecret to ourselves?
>
> [3.2.110–18]

Cressida's savoir-faire has abandoned her, and consequently the division between surface and essence has broken down even as she repeatedly refers to that division while confessing her love.[20] Her language bespeaks her concern with mastery and subjugation ("you will play the tyrant"; "I might master it"; "unbridled children grown / Too headstrong"), thereby dramatizing her awareness of her vulnerable position vis-à-vis Troilus.

Her awareness of a self-betrayal that she speaks of here with much anxiety leads to a prophetic statement concerning another self-betrayal: "I have a kind of self resides with you, / But an unkind self that itself will leave / To be another's fool" (3.2.138–40).[21] The earlier discrepancy between her love and her feigned nonchalance here leads to a more problematic division *within* her self. Even the self she affirms, "a kind of self," is incomplete and indefinite, whereas the "unkind self," though more definite in its negation, is also unstable in

---

[20]For a reading of this scene as an extension of Cressida's dissimulation earlier in the play, see Juliet Dusinberre, *Shakespeare and the Nature of Women* (London: Macmillan, 1975), p. 64. She thinks that Cressida in this scene "counterfeits the confusion of a lovesick girl, baffling Troilus who really feels that confusion."

[21]Rossiter, pp. 132–33, sees Cressida here to be "still clinging to her mean ideal—and fearing to give herself." For discussions of the ambiguities of this passage, see S. L. Bethell, *Shakespeare and the Popular Dramatic Tradition* (London: Staples Press, 1944), pp. 135–36, and William Empson, *Seven Types of Ambiguity* (1930; rev. ed. 1947; rpt. New York: New Directions, 1966), pp. 178–79.

that it is capable of dividing yet again. Cressida thus gives voice to her awareness and fear of the indeterminacy of the self, an awareness that derives from her shifting relationships with the men who claim her in turn and thereby control her value and destiny—Pandarus, Troilus, Calchas, and finally Diomed. In this play, where virtually all the characters suffer a split between "intention" and "action," Cressida is the only character who is aware of the fact that women—and even men—cannot claim to be autonomous subjects.

The essential divergence behind the apparently parallel view of the self held by the two lovers is exemplified in their seeming agreement on the "monstruosity" of love. Troilus laments over the "monstruosity in love . . . that the will is infinite and the execution confined; that the desire is boundless and the act a slave to limit" (3.2.75–78). Troilus here speaks of the impossibility of matching poetic hyperboles—"to weep seas, live in fire, eat rocks, tame tigers (3.2.73)—and actual deeds. Yet Cressida reinterprets his statement; for her the "monstruosity" resides in lovers not fulfilling vows even within the limit of their ability: "They that have the voice of lions and the act of hares, are they not monsters?" (3.2.82–84). Cressida's restatement of Troilus' conventional lament will prove to be an accurate indictment of Troilus' inaction when Cressida is to be sent to the Greek camp.

Truth Tired with Iteration

As Troilus and Cressida are about to spend their first and last night together, Pandarus presides over a mock betrothal between the two lovers. Yet the characters swear not to a marriage but appear to proclaim their literary fates: that Troilus will be the exemplar of truth, Cressida will be that of falsehood, and Pandarus' name will become a common noun. Here, when the characters step forth to speak as if they were in a morality play, Shakespeare pauses to include in his text the reifying judgments that have been passed on by tradition. But his acknowledgement of tradition cuts two ways. On the one hand, the myth of the characters gives Shakespeare a point of departure for his dramatic, dynamic, and ultimately ambiguous fiction of his characters. Yet it also serves to demonstrate yet again the overdetermining force of tradition, for the myth can be made to confine the meaning of these characters, as has been amply demonstrated by the majority of critics who take the characters' self-definitions at face value and fit the entire play into the paradigm presented in this scene.

For example, John Bayley maintains that "Troilus [is a charade] of fidelity, Cressida of faithlessness," and concludes that they "must, are, and cannot but be voices imprisoned in role and argument, figures condemned to tread the mill of time without ever being made free of it."[22] R. A. Foakes argues a similar point, albeit in more affirmative terms: "Here is implied an idea of time as sifting deeds and values, and registering finally what is true and worthwhile. . . . the truth of Troilus is rescued from his faults . . . Cressida's curse on herself has been fulfilled—her falsehood has become proverbial."[23] Yet Shakespeare, I suggest, calls attention to the very fixing of identities that these speeches exemplify: he includes within his play the myth—"truth tired with iteration," to borrow Troilus' self-characterization—but questions the validity of that myth by the juxtaposition to it of his own fiction—his dramatic representation of the lovers.[24] Shakespeare's characters are not those of a morality play: Troilus is not as true and Cressida is not as false as they declare themselves to be, and Pandarus is an ineffectual mediator at best.[25]

Troilus and Cressida's declarations are nevertheless masterful in allowing the two lovers to characterize themselves. Troilus proclaims:

> True swains in love shall in the world to come
> Approve their truth by Troilus. When their rhymes,
> Full of protest, of oath, and big compare,
> Wants similes, truth tired with iteration—
> "As true as steel, as plantage to the moon,
> As sun to day, as turtle to her mate,
> As iron to adamant, as earth to th'centre"—
> Yet, after all comparisons of truth,
> As truth's authentic author to be cited,
> "As true as Troilus" shall crown up the verse
> And sanctify the numbers.
>
> [3.2.163–73]

22John Bayley, *The Uses of Division: Unity and Disharmony in Literature* (London: Chatto and Windus, 1976), p. 191.

23Foakes, p. 150.

24Jacques Derrida has argued that all writing, due to its "iterative structure cut off from all absolute responsibility," shares the fate of an "essential drifting." *Margins of Philosophy*, trans. Alan Bass (Chicago: Univ. of Chicago Press, 1982), p. 316. In my use of the word, however, rather than wandering or errancy, "iteration" involves reification that delimits and circumscribes meaning.

25See Howard Felperin's discussion, in *Shakespearean Representation: Mimesis and Modernity in Elizabethan Tragedy* (Princeton: Princeton Univ. Press, 1977), of Shakespeare's complex relationship to his native dramatic tradition. For example, he discusses Hamlet's speech to the players as "a plea for the new doctrine of dramatic

Troilus envisions himself as "truth's authentic author" and his speech as a model for future love poems. Yet this appropriation of authority, together with his self-dramatization as the vehicle of future similes, undercuts his pledge of truth, especially since he had earlier lamented the impossibility of the "monstruosity of love," of matching poetic figures with actual deeds. In that earlier moment, Troilus had appeared to wish away the slippage between language and action, but the conventionality of his lament is underscored by the fact that his later pledges of "truth" are untroubled by the awareness of such a slippage. Moreover, he unwittingly discredits himself by calling attention to his naiveté and the reductiveness of his "simple truth": "I am as true as truth's simplicity, / And simpler than the infancy of truth" (3.2.159–60). The chiastic structure of these two lines points to the tautology of Troilus' definition of his "truth"; Troilus' self-enclosed, self-referential, and ultimately narcissistic identification with "truth" ("as true as Troilus") denies the dynamic movement inherent in metaphoric language. Although Troilus considers himself an authority on poetic language, his conception of both himself and "truth" are antithetical to poetry.[26]

When Cressida is about to be led off to the Greek camp in exchange for Antenor, Troilus, though quite eager to envision himself as a sacrificing priest "off'ring . . . his own heart" (4.3.9), repeatedly enjoins her to be "true" and again repeats his pledge of "truth"—indeed, a "truth tired with iteration":

> Alas, it is my vice, my fault!
> Whiles others fish with craft for great opinion,
> I with great truth catch mere simplicity;
> Whilst some with cunning gild their copper crowns,
> With truth and plainness I do wear mine bare.
> Fear not my truth: the moral of my wit
> Is plain and true; there's all the reach of it.
> [4.4.100–106]

---

illusionism" which rejects "the medieval conception of drama as a timeless moral vision," though he argues that this archaic conception survives in the play *Hamlet* itself (p. 46). Bethell, p. 99, discusses characters with "something of a 'morality' flavor"— Thersites as Vice, Ulysses as Worldly Wisdom, etc.

[26]See Rosalie Colie, *Shakespeare's Living Art* (Princeton: Princeton Univ. Press, 1974), pp. 330–31, on Troilus' versifying: "Again and again, sonnet-language sounds, just discordant, just out of tune: matching, of course, a plot in which high sonnet-love cannot be accommodated. . . .[Troilus] cannot stop to realize what language, or what a woman, can mean to a man."

What Troilus has to offer Cressida in these parting words are just that—empty words unmatched by deeds. He betrays Cressida by his complicity with the Trojans in treating her as chattel but still persists in his identification with "truth"—in the abstract and in her absence. Although these lines are addressed to Cressida, she is already absent from them. His eternal pledge of abstract "truth" is unwittingly subverted by the language he uses: although he intends to oppose his singular singleness to the rest of the world's doubleness by claiming to "wear" his "truth," he shares with those others who "gild" their crowns the split between surface and essence. Moreover, in ironically calling his "truth" a "vice" and a "fault," his use of a trope that calls attention to its doubleness undermines his insistence on unity.

Terry Eagleton, however, sees Troilus the lyrical lover as truly different from, and a victim of, his prosaic society:

> [Troilus] creates, within society, an area of personal freedom where he can find himself fully. . . . The love-relationship with Cressida contains his authentic self, it is the way he defines himself; when Cressida is snatched away, he is alienated from himself. And it is society which snatches her away: his real self is destroyed by the pressures of a society which is seen as external, hostile to self-expression.[27]

Here Eagleton locates the fundamental opposition between Troilus and his society, thus accepting Troilus' mystified self-portrait as well as his view of Cressida as an instrument of achieving his "authentic self." But in his more recent study of Samuel Richardson's *Clarissa,* Eagleton identifies the male lover with the patriarchal society of which he is a part; this departure from his earlier position stems from his new interest in the subjecthood of woman and the position of woman in patriarchy: "How are women to live by truth and justice in a society where the very criteria for defining what counts as such are already in the hands of the patriarchy? . . . Can truth and power be compatible? . . . Can those who are stripped of power from the outset, excluded by the rules of discourse from full subjecthood, enter the power game at all without being instantly falsified?"[28] Eagleton's analysis of Clarissa's predicament accurately describes that of Cressida, who can only pledge her faithfulness in negative terms, since Troilus has appropriated "truth" for himself:

[27]Eagleton, *Shakespeare and Society*, p. 32.
[28]Eagleton, *The Rape of Clarissa: Writing, Sexuality and Class Struggle in Samuel Richardson* (Minneapolis: Univ. of Minnesota Press, 1982), p. 79.

> If I be false, or swerve a hair from truth,
> When time is old and hath forgot itself,
> When waterdrops have worn the stones of Troy,
> And blind oblivion swallowed cities up,
> And mighty states characterless are grated
> To dusty nothing, yet let memory,
> From false to false, among false maids in love,
> Upbraid my falsehood! When they've said, "as false
> As air, as water, wind or sandy earth,
> As fox to lamb, as wolf to heifer's calf,
> Pard to the hind, or stepdame to her son,"
> Yea, let them say, to stick the heart of falsehood,
> "As false as Cressid."
>
> [3.2.174–86]

These lines suggest Cressida's greater awareness of her situation in society, of the contingency of her love on the larger epic background that impinges upon it. She refers to the fall of Troy in a vision that recalls Homer's description in the *Iliad* (12.10–23) of the leveling of Troy's walls by the overwhelming force of the rivers. In Sonnet 55, Shakespeare had affirmed the power of poetry to outlast the "gilded monuments of Princes"; here, Cressida gives voice to her awareness of the same power of poetry to bestow everlasting blame: despite the inevitable fall of civilizations—"mighty states characterless are grated / To dusty nothing"—Cressida's "character" will survive as the "heart of falsehood." Although Troilus explicitly presented himself as an authority on poetic tradition, here it is Cressida who shares with her creator not only the larger perspective that encompasses the trajectory of the epic narrative and its literary afterlife but also the poet's vocation, since classical antiquity, to praise *and* to blame. In her vatic mode—which she shares with Cassandra whose fate it is to speak and never be believed—Cressida also emerges as a figure who approximates the poet's consciousness more closely than does Troilus, whose limited and self-regarding awareness leads him to prophecies that are belied by his own later actions. Indeed, the fulfillment of Cressida's prophecy seems inescapable, since she compares herself to air, water, wind, and earth, the elemental forces that destroy man's monuments. In fact, Troilus treats Cressida's love as his monument, in speaking of her as his "achievement" (4.2.68) after she has been won.

Cressida also hypothetically compares herself and Troilus to various pairs of natural enemies—"as fox to lamb, as wolf to heifer's calf

. . ."—in lines that recall Achilles' expression of how alien Hector is to him (*Iliad*, 22.262–67). The similes Troilus wrote were intended to define his absolute and abstract "truth" independent of Cressida, but Cressida's similes reveal her interest in describing her relationship to Troilus. Yet in her similes, it is impossible to decide which of the lovers is the predator and which the prey. Unlike Troilus' language which seeks to define, Cressida's language is more indeterminate and ambiguous, and hence like Shakespeare's, more open-ended. Cressida sees difference between herself and Troilus—here heightened to that between adversaries—whereas Troilus seeks to efface differences by appropriating her as his "achievement," as "his own heart," and ultimately as "his" Cressida as opposed to "Diomed's." This distinction between the two lovers' modes of perceiving their relationship had been dramatized earlier when Cressida had spoken of how she would "war" with Troilus for the honor of who will be more true, prompting his reply, "O virtuous fight, / When *right* with *right* wars who shall be most *right!*" (3.2.161–62; emphasis added). Critics have often discussed this play in terms of the "war plot" and the "love plot," but here we see that from Cressida's perspective, the "love plot" is yet another "war plot."[29] The final simile, "stepdame to her son," sums up that adversary relationship between the sexes and anticipates Troilus' perception of Cressida's betrayal as tantamount to an indictment of his own mother.

Although at first Cressida appears to follow Troilus' lead in speaking lines that would befit a morality play, upon closer examination her utterance stands in tension to the hypostatization of "truth" and "falsehood" congenial to the morality tradition. Indeed, she does more than "swerve a hair from truth": Cressida's allusions to the *Iliad* which dramatize historicity and indeterminacy serve to criticize Troilus' abstract and supposedly timeless identification with "truth." Significantly, it is through "false" Cressida, a woman marginal both in her society and in her relationship to Troilus, that Shakespeare inscribes in his text the newly translated and available *Iliad*. With Cressida's echoes of the originary Homeric world, Shakespeare ques-

---

[29]For discussions of the double plot, see William Empson, *Some Versions of Pastoral* (New York: New Directions, 1974), pp. 34–42; and Norman Rabkin, *Shakespeare and the Common Understanding* (New York: The Free Press, 1971), pp. 30–57. Tillyard, p. 55, states that the "two themes [Trojan war and loves of the title characters] are approximated through having as motives a woman, *each bad in her own way*" (emphasis added). But see Rossiter, p. 143, who notes "Helen is to Troy as Cressida is to Troilus; but the whole Trojan destruction is not women, but *will*."

tions the oversimplified if comforting mystification of the morality plays, which he presents as the patriarchal and dominant mode of sense-making in his play. Catherine Belsey argues that in *The Castle of Perseverance*, a fifteenth-century morality play, the protagonist Mankind does not constitute a subject but rather "a fragmented and fragmentary figure," a battlefield that World, Flesh, Devil—on their scaffolds, commanding authority—struggle to possess.[30] I would suggest here that Troilus, by identifying himself with Truth, denies his status as an uncertain and unstable human protagonist, and identifies himself with a simple allegorical figure from a psychomachia, in order to appropriate its univocal authority. Thus to Troilus' "truth," criticized as anachronistic through its identification with the morality tradition, Shakespeare opposes Cressida's complex and revisionary notion of identity as historically determined and hence unstable. Stephen Greenblatt has argued that Renaissance self-fashioning was inseparably intertwined with the pressure exerted by cultural institutions—family, religion, state: "indeed, the human subject itself [is] remarkably unfree, the ideological product of the relations of power in a particular society. . . . If there remained traces of free choice, the choice was among possibilities whose range was strictly delineated by the social and ideological system in force." Significantly, it is Cressida who is in possession of this realization; Troilus, like the sixteenth-century Englishmen in Greenblatt's study, "cling[s] to the human subject," and to "selfhood, even selfhood conceived as a fiction."[31] Shakespeare points to the modernity of Cressida's conception of shifting identity—in opposition also to the medieval belief in "humors"—through references to the humanist recovery of texts from classical antiquity, lost during the middle ages.

The juxtaposition of Troilus and Cressida's two speeches exemplifies the absolute and unambiguous distinction between the two sexes which has informed the language of the play from its beginnings. As we have seen, Troilus not only calls "womanish" (1.1.105) his love-induced indolence, which absents him from the battlefield, but also his tautological answer to Aeneas, "This woman's answer sorts" (1:1.104). The opposition between masculine and feminine thus becomes a paradigm for other binary oppositions in the play: prowess and logic are masculine, cowardice and tautology are femi-

[30]Catherine Belsey, *The Subject of Tragedy: Identity and Difference in Renaissance Drama* (New York: Methuen, 1985), pp. 13–19.

[31]Stephen Greenblatt, *Renaissance Self-Fashioning: From More to Shakespeare* (Chicago: Univ. of Chicago Press, 1980), pp. 256–57.

nine.[32] And of course, it is Troilus and the other male warriors in the play who assign desirable qualities to themselves and their opposites to women.

It is because of this paradigm that Cressida defines herself in opposition to Troilus and pledges her love in negative terms, as Cordelia defines her rhetoric of "nothing" in opposition to the hyperbole of Goneril and Regan. Yet unlike Cordelia, who asserts her own somewhat stiff-necked integrity, Cressida's definition of her difference from Troilus is not affirmative but complies with Troilus' appropriation of truth for himself: since Troilus proclaims himself to be true, Cressida can only pledge her faith in terms of its negation.

More important, perhaps, is Cressida's awareness of her possibility to be false, underscored by the conditional "if" that opens her speech. She had been aware since the beginning of the play that she cannot be "plain and true" as Troilus insists he is.[33] In her soliloquy in Act 1, scene 2, Cressida had announced her defensive strategy of dissimulation, dictated by the value placed on women by men. Having been placed in the role of merchandise, Cressida is acutely aware of the laws of supply and demand, whereas Troilus the consumer can afford to believe that he has autonomy, that he can choose to be "plain and true."

In the following Act 4, when Cressida and Troilus rise from their first—and last—night together, we are given a parody of an *aubade*. Instead of lingering and lamenting over the arrival of dawn as Romeo had done, Troilus is quite ready to leave Cressida for more important matters of the "busy day" (4.2.8). Cressida regrets that she failed to adhere to her maxim: "You men will never tarry. / O foolish Cressid! I might have still held off, / And then you would have tarried" (4.2.16–18).

In a repetition of a similar moment at the end of the first scene, the

---

[32]On gender and sexuality as a culturally determined system of symbols invested with culturally variable meanings, see the collection of essays edited by Sherry Ortner and Harriet Whitehead, *Sexual Meanings: The Cultural Construction of Gender and Sexuality* (Cambridge: Cambridge Univ. Press, 1981). For a discussion of the Renaissance inheritance of the Aristotelian taxonomy of oppositions and of Pythagorean dualities that linked woman with imperfection—left, dark, evil, etc.—see Ian Maclean, *The Renaissance Notion of Woman: A Study in the Fortunes of Scholasticism and Medical Science in European Intellectual Life* (Cambridge: Cambridge Univ. Press, 1980), pp. 86–88.

[33]Belsey, p. 149, argues that a discursive instability characterizes the texts about women in sixteenth- and seventeenth-century England, and "a corresponding instability is evident in the utterances attributed to women: they speak with equal conviction from incompatible subject-positions, displaying a discontinuity of being, an 'inconstancy' which is seen as characteristically feminine."

appearance of Aeneas, who brings Troilus the news that Cressida must go to the Greeks, signals Troilus' turning from Cressida to his "public" concerns.[34] This exchange between Troilus and Aeneas shows how quickly Troilus shifts his ground:

AENEAS.   Ere the first sacrifice, within this hour,
            We must give up to Diomedes' hand
            The Lady Cressida.
TROILUS.   Is it so concluded?
AENEAS.   By Priam and the general state of Troy.
            They are at hand and ready to effect it.
TROILUS.   How my achievements mock me!
            I will go meet them; and, my Lord Aeneas,
            We met by chance: you did not find me here.
                                              [4.1.63–70]

Troilus' first reaction to the news is in keeping with his earlier speech outlining his expectation of their union, for it makes quite apparent that his concern is only for himself and not for Cressida, who has become for him an "achievement." Moreover, instead of going to Cressida after this conversation, he leaves the stage with Aeneas and leaves Pandarus, who had overheard this conversation, to bring the unwelcome news to Cressida.

Just as Troilus, in asking Aeneas to keep this meeting a secret, seems most concerned with his own reputation, so Pandarus is exclusively preoccupied with Troilus' situation and not with the more serious plight of his niece: "Is't possible? No sooner got but lost? / The devil take Antenor! The young prince will go mad" (4.2.73–74). To Cressida who anxiously inquires what has happened, he replies, "Would thou hadst ne'er been born! I knew thou wouldst be his death. O, poor gentleman!" (4.2.83–85). Again, Pandarus makes explicit Troilus' male-centered assumption implicit in his complaint of "how my achievements mock me!" In addition, his use of Cressida to enhance his own bond with Troilus becomes even more apparent.

---

[34]Richard C. Harrier, "Troilus Divided," in *Studies in the English Renaissance Drama,* ed. Josephine W. Bennett, Oscar Cargill, and Vernon Hall, Jr., (New York: New York Univ. Press, 1959), pp. 146–47, also sees Aeneas as Troilus' guide away from his personal concerns to public ones. Harrier argues that Aeneas, "the single Trojan figure whose virtue and magnificence were unquestionable to an Elizabethan audience . . . moves through the play in chivalric perfection, while Hector and Achilles are defaced and blemished" (p. 144). Aeneas' appropriateness for this role lies, however, in that he himself will turn away from the private to the public by sacrificing another woman, Dido.

To Cressida's great sorrow, Troilus' achievement does in fact turn out to be command. I do not believe it has been noticed that Shakespeare has Cressida speak of her grief using language that describes mourning in the *Iliad* and the *Aeneid:*

> Tear my bright hair and scratch my praised cheeks,
> Crack my clear voice with sobs, and break my heart
> With sounding 'Troilus'. I will not go from Troy.
>
> [4.2.105–7]

Although Troilus has not actually died, he has died to Cressida; she conceives of their separation as tantamount to his death. In speaking of disfiguring herself, moreover, Cressida mourns also for her former self as a prized commodity. Would Troilus have allowed Cressida to be exchanged without resistance if she had "held off" for one more night? Although Troilus was so adamant in advocating the keeping of Helen even in the face of Priam and Hector's opposition, he gives up Cressida quite readily:

> I'll bring her to the Grecian presently:
> And to his hand when I deliver her,
> Think it an altar, and thy brother Troilus
> A priest, there off'ring to it his own heart.
>
> [4.3.6–9]

Again, Troilus' self-dramatization as a sacrificing priest throws a disquieting light on his perception and treatment of Cressida: the sacrifice of Cressida is couched in terms of a self-sacrifice, an offering of "his own heart." Moreover, the prominent role played by Paris in the transaction suggests that Cressida is being sacrificed as a substitute for Helen: although the Trojans decide to keep Helen, albeit after lengthy debate, they send off Cressida without even the debate accorded her by Chaucer's Trojans. Paris himself unwittingly calls attention to the irony of his own role in the proceedings: "I know what 'tis to love, / And would, as I shall pity, I could help" (4.3.6–9). The Trojans, as well as the tradition of Troilus and Cressida before Shakespeare, substitute Cressida for Helen and scapegoat her, whereas, as we have already seen, Shakespeare reverses this process, and scapegoats Helen in place of "false Cressida."

When Troilus and Cressida finally meet to discuss their eventual separation, Troilus explains it only in terms of his own "truth":

> Cressid, I love thee in so strained a purity,
> That the blest gods, as angry with my fancy,
> More bright in zeal than the devotion which
> Cold lips blow to their deities, take thee from me.
>
> [4.4.23–26]

Like Agamemnon, who chose to see the Greeks' inability to take Troy as "the protractive trials of great Jove / To find persistive constancy in men" (1.3.19–20), Troilus aggrandizes himself by considering Cressida's plight as proof of his own "truth" and as punishment by the jealous gods. Cassandra, the only character with a link to the divine in this play, criticizes Hector, and implicitly Troilus, for their selfish invocation of the gods to justify their wilful actions: "The gods are deaf to hot and peevish vows" (5.3.16). Troilus' unequivocal answer to Cressida's question, "And is it true that I must go from Troy? / . . . What, and from Troilus too?" (4.4.29–30) is a dismissive and unwittingly prophetic "From Troy and Troilus" (4.4.31). Indeed, Cressida's being exchanged for Antenor will lead her to exchange Troilus for Diomed; her abandonment by "Troy and Troilus" will lead her to seek protection from Diomed among the Greeks.

Troilus' speech about their parting reveals why he is so resigned, or perhaps even willing, to see Cressida go:

> We two, that with so many thousand sighs
> Did buy each other, must poorly sell ourselves
> With the rude brevity and discharge of one.
> Injurious Time now with a robber's haste
> Crams his rich thiev'ry up, he knows not how.
> As many farewells as be stars in heaven,
> With distinct breath and consigned kisses to them,
> He fumbles up into a loose adieu,
> And scants us with a single famished kiss,
> Distasted with the salt of broken tears.
>
> [4.4.38–47]

The imagery of eating, commerce, and theft recalls Troilus' similar language in speaking of Helen and suggests that the parting comes at just the right time for him: Cressida is now devalued, just as Helen was "soiled" through use. Because he conceives of Cressida as consumed goods, Troilus would prefer to be "true" in the abstract, to the "theme" of Cressida, than to her actuality. Moreover, the "Time" he melodramatically speaks of here only amounts to one night, and thus it is not "Time" but Troilus who has done the consuming of Cressida. Finally, Troilus' depersonalization of Cressida in her sorrow becomes evident in his speaking of her departure as "discharge of one" and calling his kiss "distasted with the salt of broken tears."

But as soon as Cressida bemoans her future plight, "A woeful Cressid 'mongst the merry Greeks!" (4.4.55), Troilus' jealousy is aroused: "be thou but true of heart" (4.4.57). Cressida understandably reacts with outrage—"I true! How now! What wicked deem is this?" (4.4.58)—for she must surely perceive Troilus' cavalier attitude toward her plight: "O heavens! you love me not" (4.4.81). Although their separation comes through no fault of Cressida's, and though Troilus can hardly be said to have lived up to his extravagant protestations of "truth," he repeatedly demands her pledge of "truth" as a precondition to their reunion: "be thou true, / And I will see thee" (4.4.65–66). The insistence with which Troilus repeats this injunction reveals his expectation, or perhaps even perverse desire, for her to be "false"; if he appropriates for himself and identifies himself with "truth," she cannot but be "false." Troilus finally manages to arouse Cressida's fears about her "unkind self":

TROILUS.   But be not tempted.
CRESSIDA.   Do you think I will?

[4.4.90–91]

Troilus has revealed his lack of sympathy and affection for her, and her emphatic "I will not go from Troy" (4.2.107) makes glaringly clear her impotence when she is commanded to go and yet be "true." The hollowness of Troilus' poetry in his final pledge of "truth"— indeed, a "truth tired with iteration"—is immediately followed by his use of Cressida as a pawn in an adolescent rivalry with Diomed: "I charge thee use her well, even for my charge" (4.4.124). Although Diomed announces that "To her own worth / She shall be prized" (4.4.131–32), he answers Troilus' rivalry in kind: "but that you say 'Be't so,' / I'll speak it in my spirit and honour 'No!'" (4.4.132–33). Especially since Diomed will later reveal his persistent interest in the identity of Cressida's previous lover and his intention to "grieve his spirit" (5.2.93) by wearing Troilus' sleeve on his helm, perhaps Troilus' boasting only served to whet his rival's appetite.

Daughter of the Game

When Cressida enters the Greek camp, she is kissed "in general" (4.5.21), a game devised by Ulysses. In her witty and cutting ripostes to the Greek generals, especially to Menelaus, whom she may perceive as ultimately responsible for her plight, Cressida shows herself to be "a woman of quick sense" (4.5.54); while answering to male expectations, she attempts to preserve a modicum of independence, as she had done in her scene with Pandarus. Here she is less successful, however, than in that earlier scene: for playing Ulysses' game, she is condemned by the same Ulysses, who transforms the meaning of "sense" from "wit" to "lust," in calling her the "sluttish spoil of opportunity" and "daughter of the game" (4.5.62–63). Critics who accept Ulysses' judgment of her do not notice that before this exaggerated outburst, Ulysses had, in fact, "beg[ged] a kiss of [her]" (4.5.47). In light of his characterization of Troilus which immediately follows, "Speaking in deeds and deedless in his tongue" (4.5.98)—an assessment that diverges from Shakespeare's portrayal of him—the accepted view of Ulysses as the standard of disinterested judgment becomes difficult to maintain.

Cressida's transferance to the Greek camp reunites her with her father, Calchas. The conversation between Calchas and Diomed implies that they have already reached an understanding concerning Diomed's wooing of Cressida:

CALCHAS.   [within] Who calls?
DIOMEDES.   Diomed. Calchas, I think. Where's your daughter?
CALCHAS.   [within] She comes to you.

[5.2.2–4]

Selling Cressida to Diomed may have been Calchas' intention in calling for Cressida's exchange with Antenor:

> Now, princes, for the service I have done,
> Th'advantage of the time prompts me aloud
> To call for recompense. Appear it to your mind
> That, through the sight I bear in things to come,
> I have abandoned Troy, left my possessions,
> Incurred a traitor's name, exposed myself
> From certain and possessed conveniences,
> To doubtful fortunes; sequest'ring from me all
> That time, acquaintance, custom and condition

Made tame and most familiar to my nature;
And here, to do you service, am become
As new into the world, strange, unacquainted.
I do beseech you, as in way of taste,
To give me now a little benefit
Out of those many registered in promise,
Which, you say, live to come in my behalf.

[3.3.1–16]

Calchas must know that Antenor will betray Troy and that the exchange will profit the Greeks (and himself) by fulfilling his prophecy concerning Troy's fall. Yet the predominance of the language of commerce in Calchas' speech, his insistence on "possession," "recompense," and "benefit," suggests that Calchas would not be above suspicion of selling his daughter to Diomed after he has had the Greeks buy her with Antenor. Dryden confirms Shakespeare's suggestion by having Cressida pretend to give in to Diomed in order to please her father.

Calchas abandoned his daughter in the city he betrayed; he refers to the opprobrium he incurred as a traitor and his consequent "doubtful fortunes," but he does not even mention his daughter, though these lines are a prelude to his request for her exchange. Although Cressida is reunited with Calchas, she is not more secure under her father's protection, for he treats her only as a pawn of his political manipulations. Ulysses' epithet for Cressida, "daughter of the game," is truer than he knows, for Shakespeare makes evident that her own father Calchas replaces Pandarus as her procurer in the Greek camp.

Ariachne's Broken Woof

The dénouement of the love plot, where Cressida becomes "another's fool," as she herself had predicted, comes in Act 5, scene 2. Contrary to the judgment of Cressida as a "wanton" by Troilus, Ulysses, and Thersites—a judgment echoed by many critics—Cressida's acceptance of Diomed is by no means unequivocal.[35] As in the

---

[35]Theodore Spencer, for example, unquestioningly accepts the judgment of the observers of this scene as "three emotional mirrors which reflect the demonstration of the evil reality, Cressida's whorishness, under what had seemed so fair an appearance." Accordingly, he sympathizes with Troilus' "outburst of what can only be called metaphysical anguish." *Shakespeare and the Nature of Man* (1942; 2d ed. London:

opening scene of *Antony and Cleopatra,* where Shakespeare places Philo and Demetrius' evaluations of the title characters against his own portrayal of them, here the commentary on Cressida by the audience on stage stands in tension with her actual words and actions.[36]

Even after taking the seemingly decisive step of bestowing Troilus' sleeve on Diomed, Cressida remembers Troilus and attempts to take it back: "You look upon that sleeve; behold it well. / He loved me— O false wench!—Give't me again. . . . I prithee, Diomed, visit me no more" (5.2.68–69,73). Moreover, Cressida repeatedly refuses to disclose the identity of the owner of the sleeve, as if she wished to safeguard her memories of Troilus from Diomed: "By all Diana's waiting-women yond, / And by herself, I will not tell you whose" (5.2.90–91). It is noteworthy that Cressida refrains from blaming Troilus for her plight and instead directs bitter irony against herself in the allusion to Diana, the goddess of chastity. These expressions of ambivalence and self-blame are tersely summed up in her final relenting, "Ay, come. O Jove! Do come. I shall be plagued" (5.2.103), and in her parting lines:

> Troilus, farewell! One eye yet looks on thee,
> But with my heart the other eye doth see.
> Ah, poor our sex! This fault in us I find,
> What error leads must err—O, then conclude
> Minds swayed by eyes are full of turpitude.
>
> 　　　　　　　　　　[5.2.105–110]

Thersites' commentary on these lines, "A proof of strength she could not publish more, / Unless she said 'My mind is now turned whore'"

Macmillan, 1955), pp. 118–19. Similarly, W. W. Lawrence characterizes Troilus as "an ardent, high-spirited boy who gives all the fervor of his idealistic young love to a false and shallow woman, and tastes the bitterest dregs in the cup of disillusion." *Shakespeare's Problem Comedies* (New York: Macmillan, 1931), p. 142.

[36]Janet Adelman sees one of the central issues raised in *Antony and Cleopatra* to be the question of motive and the validity of emotions, and states that "the whole play can be seen as a series of attempts on the parts of the characters to understand and judge each other and themselves." *The Common Liar: An Essay on Antony and Cleopatra* (New Haven: Yale Univ. Press, 1973), p. 20. But in her recent study of *Troilus,* Adelman sees no disjunction between the judgments of the characters and the audience in this scene: "Cressida seems to betray us at the same time that she betrays Troilus; our relationship with her is broken off as sharply as hers with Troilus." "'This is and is not Cressid': The Characterization of Cressida," in *The (M)other Tongue: Essays in Feminist Psychoanalytic Interpretation,* ed. Shirley Nelson Garner, Claire Kahane, and Madelon Sprengnether (Ithaca: Cornell Univ. Press, 1985), p. 128.

(5.2.111–12) is so obviously reductive and inadequate that it paradoxically serves to call attention to the pathos of Cressida's speech. What marks her lines is her unmitigated sense of passivity and impotence ("What error leads must err . . . / Minds swayed by eyes . . ."); but perhaps more important, her aphoristic self-chastisement in the concluding couplet reveals that Cressida's experiences have succeeded in subjugating even her self-perception and the language she uses to express it. Although in earlier scenes Cressida was adept at preserving her own private language while humoring the men with whom she came into contact, in this private moment Cressida no longer acknowledges the exigencies that led her to forsake Troilus and acquiesces to the dominant language of mystification that would forever mark her as the epitome of "false" women.

Unlike Juliet and Cleopatra, who both committed suicide to transcend their circumstances, Cressida is unable to renounce or avoid the role that others expect her to play as the "daughter of the game" (4.5.63). Pandarus had also characterized her accurately as a "burr" that will "stick where [it is] thrown" (3.2.103–4). Although Thersites, Ulysses, and critics who echo this "chorus" see Cressida giving in to Diomed through "lechery," it is her desire for protection that overrides any other concern: she repeatedly addresses Diomed as "guardian," and he calls her his "charge." As we have seen, Troilus had handed Cressida over to Diomed proclaiming, "I charge thee use her well, even for my charge" (4.4.124). From Troilus' "charge," Cressida has become Diomed's: her brutal treatment at the hands of her new "guardian" only carries to its logical reduction Troilus' appropriation of her, now laid bare in the absence of mystifying poetic conceits.

Although Troilus hears the conversation between Cressida and Diomed—he stays behind "to make a recordation . . . / Of every syllable that here was spoke" (5.2.114–15)—he bases his judgment of her only on the "dumb show" and does not seem to take in the import of Cressida's words. Instead of combining "th'attest of eyes and ears" (5.2.120), thereby making an accurate "recordation" and "publishing a truth" (5.2.117), Troilus' judgment is swayed by his "esperance" (5.2.119), which blinds him to his own responsibility for her plight and leads him to see an unequivocal betrayal. Therefore, he characteristically reduces the ambiguity of Cressida before his eyes to a doubleness between his "truth" and her "falsehood":

> Never did young man fancy
> With so eternal and so fixed a soul.
>   · · ·

> O Cressid! O false Cressid! False, false, false!
> Let all untruths stand by thy stained name,
> And they'll seem glorious.
>
> [5.2.163–64,176–78]

Troilus persists in appropriating for himself "truth"—"eternal" and "fixed"—while he proposes to "fix" Cressida as the epitome of its negation, "untruth." Yet before he falls back on this reductive but comforting dichotomy, he attempts to deny what he has seen before him.

> Was Cressid here? . . .
> She was not, sure. . . .
> Why, my negation hath no taste of madness.
>   .   .   .
> Let it not be believed for womanhood!
> Think we had mothers. Do not give advantage
> To stubborn critics, apt without a theme
> For deprivation, to square the general sex
> By Cressid's rule; rather think this not Cressid.
>
> [5.2.123–31]

The opposition between "truth" and "untruth" spawns other binary oppositions: presence and absence, Cressida and not Cressida, and finally, male and female. Generalizing what he perceives to be Cressida's betrayal as contaminating all women leads him to question the purity of his own mother and even his own paternity.

Yet Troilus' crisis of identity arises more immediately because Cressida's exchange of him for Diomed implies that he is interchangeable with his rival. René Girard has characterized Ulysses' famous speech on "degree" as a presentation of the importance of differences, the loss of which gives rise to violence and chaos.[37] Troilus' perhaps equally famous speech that opens with "This she? No; this is Diomed's Cressida" (5.2.135–58) enacts a parallel dissolution of meaning and identity when "degree," or difference—in this case between himself and Diomed—collapses.[38] Troilus must reassert

---

[37]René Girard, *Violence and the Sacred* (Baltimore: Johns Hopkins Univ. Press, 1977), p. 51. Girard has elaborated his reading of *Troilus and Cressida* in terms of his theory of mimetic desire in a recent essay, "The Politics of Desire in *Troilus and Cressida*," in *Shakespeare and the Question of Theory*, ed. Patricia Parker and Geoffrey Hartman (New York: Methuen, 1985), pp. 188–209.

[38]For another discussion of "Difference and No Difference," see Joel Fineman,

his distinction from Diomed by positing two Cressidas, his and Diomed's. I. A. Richards has given a cogent explanation of Troilus'
mental process at work: "When the valuations become irreconcilable
and insuperable, the thing splits and the thinker (or thinger) then has
to remain *one* (if he can) himself."[39] Richards' parenthetical equation of "thinker" and "thinger" and his substitution of "thing" for
Cressida should give us pause, however. Both Troilus and Richards,
the "thinkers," have made Cressida a projection of their thoughts, a
"thing" that can be split with impunity in order to maintain the
indispensable unity of the male self. Since Troilus can no longer
maintain his "plain and simple" self, he projects the destruction of the
"rule in unity" (5.2.139) that results in "bifold authority" (5.2.142) on
Cressida, who has become "strange [in] nature" (5.2.146) because she
no longer belongs to him nor does she reflect back what he wishes to
see of himself. Troilus fails to see that in fact he *is* interchangeable
with Diomed since he had treated her no differently: his "bond" with
Cressida is more like that between Diomed and Cressida, "five-finger
tied," than like those of heaven. He is quite unself-conscious in the
grandiose leap he makes from the chaos of his mind to the dissolution
of cosmic order. What he needs to respect is *Cressida*'s difference from
him; instead, he can only see her as either belonging to himself or to
Diomed.

But rather than acknowledge her difference as an individual,
Troilus claims to "square the general sex / By Cressid's rule," to
conclude that all women are unfaithful. This attempt, however, is
undercut not only by Shakespeare's dramatic representation of
Cressida which resists such mystification but also by a peculiar phrase
in Troilus' own speech, "Ariachne's broken woof" (5.2.150). Richards has suggested that "Ariachne" is a meaningful conflation of
Ariadne and Arachne.[40] The "woof," moreover, parallels the merg-

"Fratricide and Cuckoldry: Shakespeare's Doubles," in *Representing Shakespeare: New
Psychoanalytic Essays,* ed. Murray M. Schwartz and Coppélia Kahn (Baltimore: Johns
Hopkins Univ. Press, 1980), pp. 70–109. He argues that the misogyny in *Troilus* and
other Shakespearean plays allow the men to mature: "The men become men by being
poised against, opposed to, a femininity that is disgusting because it so grotesquely
partakes of its opposite. . . . the perfidy of women is the condition of male exaltation"
(p. 101).

[39]I. A. Richards, "*Troilus and Cressida* and Plato," in *Speculative Instruments*
(Chicago: Univ. of Chicago Press, 1955), p. 209.

[40]In "Ariachne's Broken Woof," *Georgia Review,* 31 (1977), 44–60, J. Hillis Miller
sees the "two simultaneous contradictory sign systems centered on Cressida" as an
instance in which Western logocentrism is called into question. Miller's positing of
duplicitous Cressida as an archetypal text, however, leads Fineman to ask: "Does this

ing of the two proper names in that Ariadne's thread and Arachne's web are conflated in that word. Although Richards claims that the "'broken woof' accurately mirrors the destruction of whatever held him to Cressid—some fabric of gossamer texture," I suggest that Troilus' unwitting conflation of the two mythological women into one serves as a corollary to his avowed desire to see a unique Cressida whose faithfulness will reflect for him the unity of his self.[41] To defend himself against self-division, he splits Cressida in two but conjoins two women, albeit mythological, who are indistinguishable to him. Although Troilus insists upon his difference from Diomed, he is unable to tell the difference between the two women, as he had earlier conflated Helen and Cressida by using the same conceit of "woman as pearl" in speaking of them.

Moreover, the two myths themselves stand in tension to the subject of Troilus' outburst, female infidelity. Ariadne's thread was broken because Theseus betrayed and abandoned her, as he did other women. It is clear from what Oberon says of Theseus in *A Midsummer Night's Dream* that Shakespeare followed the tradition, set forth in North's Plutarch, that conceived of the mythological hero as a man of many loves:[42]

> Didst not thou [Titania] lead him through the glimmering night
> From Perigenia, whom he ravished?
> And make him with fair Aegles break his faith,
> With Ariadne and Antiopa?
>
> [2.1.77–80]

---

kind of deconstruction undo or merely complete a misogynistic philosophical formula?" (p. 108n). See also Nancy K. Miller's feminist critique, "Arachnologies: The Woman, the Text, and the Critic," in *Poetics of Gender* (New York: Columbia Univ. Press, 1986), pp. 270–95. For a recent discussion that sees this crux as a site of interplay between Miller's deconstruction and Bloom's anxiety of influence, see Elizabeth Freund, "'Ariachne's Broken Woof': The Rhetoric of Citation in *Troilus and Cressida*," in *Shakespeare and the Question of Theory*, pp. 19–36.

[41]Richards, p. 210.

[42]Compare North's *Plutarch*, where Theseus is found wanting in comparison to Romulus for his inconstancy in love: "Furthermore, *Theseus* faults touching women & ravishements, of the twaine, had the lesse shadowe & culler of honestie. Bicause *Theseus* dyd attempt it very often: for he stale awaye *Ariadne, Antiope, & Anaxo* the Troezenian. Againe being stepped in yeres, & at later age, & past marriage: he stale awaye *Helen* in her minoritie, being nothing neere to consent to marye. Then his taking of the daughters of the TROEZENIANS, of the LACEDAEMONIANS, and the AMAZONES (neither contracted to him, nor comparable to the birthe and linadge of his owne countrie which were at ATHENS, and descended of the noble race and progenie of

Also noteworthy in Plutarch is his insistence that "there is no trothe nor certeintie" in the story of Ariadne: "For some saye, that *Ariadne* honge her selfe in sorowe, when she sawe that *Theseus* had caste her of. Other write, that she was transported by mariners into the Ile of NAXOS, where she was maryed unto *OEnarus*, the priest of *Bacchus:* and they thincke that *Theseus* lefte her, bicause he was in love with another."[43] In fact, Plutarch relates the Naxians' claim that there were "two *Ariadnees*": "For they celebrate the feaste of the first with all joye & mirthe: where the sacrifices done in memorie of the seconde, be mingled with mourninge and sorowe."[44] The uncertainty of what actually happened to Ariadne, coupled with her doubling in the Plutarchian subtext, anticipates the ambiguity of Shakespeare's Cressida, which leads Troilus to split her into two.

In Ovid's story of the weaving contest between Arachne and Minerva in *Metamorphoses* 6, Minerva weaves a classically ordered and didactic tapestry in which the gods, including Jupiter, Neptune, and herself, are readily recognizable by definite signs: Jupiter by his "Image . . . Kinglike," Neptune by his "threetyned blade," and Minerva by her shield (6.91–96).[45] Arachne, on the other hand, depicts on her web the various instances in which Jupiter, Neptune, Apollo, and Bacchus took on protean forms in order to rape mortal women (6.127–57). Minerva tears Arachne's web not because the girl's work is inferior to that of the goddess: "Not *Pallas*, no nor spight it selfe could quarrell picke / To this hir worke: and that did touch *Minerva* to the quicke" (161–62). In fact, Ovid praises Arachne's tapestry for its superb realism: "Of all these things she missed not their proper shapes, nor yit / The full and just resemblance of their places for to hit" (150–51). Minerva is angry precisely because she cannot fault Arachne's work and because the girl challenges the goddess' insistence on the essential identity and dignity of the gods. In fact, Arachne's view of fluid identity is borne out by Minerva's having taken on an "oldewives riveled shape" (53) when the goddess first appeared to the girl. Arachne's artistic principles, moreover, parallel

Erichtheus, and of *Cerops*) dyd geve men occasion to suspect that his womannishenes was rather to satisfie lust, then of any great love." *Plutarch's Lives of the Noble Grecians and Romanes,* trans. Sir Thomas North (Oxford: Basil Blackwell, 1928), 1: 103.

[43]North's *Plutarch,* 1: 22.

[44]Ibid., p. 24.

[45]All quotations from Ovid are taken from W. H. D. Rouse, ed. *Shakespeare's Ovid Being Arthur Golding's Translation of the Metamorphoses* (Carbondale: Southern Illinois Univ. Press, 1961).

those of Ovid himself, for in his poem, he, like Arachne, had also told the story of Europa and the bull (2.833ff.), and his poem is concerned with precisely the principle of metamorphosis that Arachne so insistently depicts.

This Ovidian subtext picks up and elaborates the implications of Troilus' earlier reference to the Ovidian story of Apollo and Daphne; they both criticize Troilus' insistence upon a fixed and single self by presenting an alternative, fluid conception of identity. Also questioned is Troilus' equation of inconstancy with women, for both Ovid and Plutarch dramatize male changeability and its consequences for women. In fact, in the majority of Shakespeare's plays, it is women who are victims of male forswearing.[46] Seen in this light, Cressida emerges as a victim of Troilus' inability to live up to his extravagant professions of "truth." Moreover, Troilus' conflation of these exemplary myths enacts the process by which myths—including his own—are transmitted. In the same way that Plutarch's reference to the two Ariadnes points to her ambiguity and the uncertainty of the stories told about her, there exist two Cressidas, not in the sense that Troilus invokes the duality but because she is truly ambiguous. Perhaps following Plutarch's treatment of Ariadne, Shakespeare refrains from relating what finally happened to Cressida. Furthermore, the reductive self-labeling by the characters in Act 3 corresponds to Minerva's tapestry in which the divine portraits might as well have identifying labels attached.[47] Shakespeare's mode of representation, then, follows Arachne's, and hence Ovid's, more fluid and complex portrayal of identity and the self. Through his fragmentary and unacknowledged use of Ovid and Plutarch, Shakespeare criticizes the accepted meaning of his received material, especially its most recent interpretation by Henryson; through this creative use of competing subtexts, Shakespeare accomplishes a radical revision of tradition as myth, thereby freeing himself and his characters, especially Cressida, from the overdetermined meaning dictated by tradition.[48]

---

[46]Frances A. Shirley, *Swearing and Perjury in Shakespeare's Plays* (London: George Allen and Unwin, 1979), p. 90, sees *Troilus* as departing from the norm of male perjury in the Shakespearean canon.

[47]This type of oversimplified imitation is also criticized in Achilles' and Patroclus' "pageants" that caricature the Greek generals: "And with ridiculous and awkward action, / Which, slanderer, he 'imitation' calls, / He pageants us" (1.3.148–50).

[48]Thomas M. Greene, in discussing the distinction between the "acknowledged, pervasive subtext" and the "unconfessed genealogical line," states that the latter "may prove to be as nourishing as the visible" but maintains the privileged status of the former (*Light in Troy*, p. 19). My reading departs from Greene's theory in suggesting

Lazar Kite of Cressid's Kind

Troilus' self-serving mystification of Cressida which does not do justice to her moral complexity finds its corollary in the war plot in Ulysses' oft-discussed speech on degree (1.3.74–136). The concept of ordered hierarchy that Ulysses so authoritatively adumbrates is borne out neither by the world of the play as Shakespeare represents it nor by Ulysses' later actions. Most critics have considered this speech an expression of what E. M. W. Tillyard has called the Elizabethan World Picture, and that the world of the play has fallen from this ideal. Rather, it is unwittingly exposed as a construct by Ulysses himself when he proposes to rig the lottery so that Hector's challenge will be met by Ajax instead of Achilles: "Ajax employed plucks down Achilles' plumes" (1.3.381). The idea of the lottery suggests not a stable and rational hierarchy but random and arbitrary workings of chance. Moreover, Ulysses manipulates the lottery so that the lesser man will be chosen. In the *Iliad,* where warriors competed for the epithet "the best of the Achaeans," each hero's *arete* or worth became evident in his *aristeia,* his moment of glory on the battlefield; but here, Ajax, Thersites' "mongrel beef-witted lord" (2.1.12–13) is chosen to be the champion for the Greeks. Later in the play, Ulysses warns Achilles that

>   beauty, wit,
> High birth, vigour of bone, desert in service,
> Love, friendship, charity, are subjects all
> To envious and calumniating Time.
> One touch of nature makes the whole world kin—
> That all with one consent praise new-born gauds,
> Though they are made and moulded of things past,
> And give to dust that is a little gilt
> More laud than gilt o'er-dusted.
>
>   [3.3.171–79]

Ulysses' evocation of Time who puts "alms for oblivion" (3.3.146) in the wallet he carries on his back does not make for an ordered hierarchy or even an essential identity that he affirms in his speech on degree. Ulysses cynically maintains that a man is only as good as the

---

that the fragmentary or hidden subtext works to qualify—or indeed undermine—the dominant "sources" to which *Troilus and Cressida* is most obviously indebted.

superficial appearance of his most recent action; and only so long as others' "emulation" (1.3.133) has not superseded it.

It is not only the concept of "degree" but also the Trojan war itself that is gradually revealed as a construct, for the many crossings between the Trojan and Greek camps make the distinction between them increasingly difficult to maintain.[49] For example, when Aeneas brings to the Greeks Hector's ridiculously anachronistic challenge that "He hath a lady, wiser, fairer, truer, / Than ever Greek did compass in his arms" (1.3.271–72), Agamemnon and even Nestor comply with enthusiasm: "my lady / Was fairer than his grandam. . . . / I'll prove this truth with my three drops of blood" (1.3.294–97). Moreover, when Ajax and Hector finally meet, the combat is interrupted because "Ajax is half made of Hector's blood" (4.5.83); Ajax's mother is Hector's aunt. Other examples of such crossings can be multiplied: Achilles refuses to fight the Trojans because he is in love with Priam's daughter Polyxena, and he receives a letter from Hecuba imploring him to desist. Ulysses and Thersites accompany Troilus to spy on Cressida; Antenor, exchanged for Cressida, will betray Troy. The conflict between Troy and Greece, then, is exposed as merely a pretext for achieving the "theme of honour and renown" (2.2.198), though this ideal is debunked when Hector chases a soldier for his splendid armor and Achilles ambushes Hector with his Myrmidons. In fact, the characters assert the division between Troy and Greece as well as that between male and female in order to avoid the more difficult task of distinguishing between individuals and respecting the differences between them.

Thus it is not surprising that characters tend to "emulate" or imitate one another, and that they are judged only in comparison with one another. For example, we have seen Pandarus claim, in speaking to Troilus of Cressida, that she is more beautiful than Helen, and in speaking to Cressida of Troilus, that he is a better warrior than Hector and a better lover than Paris. While Pandarus reduces each character to a type representing beauty, prowess, and gallantry, Cressida refuses either to assign a single quality to Troilus or to define him in terms of other characters: "he is himself" (1.2.68). She insists upon

---

[49]Knight, however, stresses the differences between the Trojans and the Greeks: the Trojans stand for "human beauty and worth" and the Greeks for "the bestial and stupid elements of man" (p. 47 and *passim*). Bethell, too, thinks that the Trojans were accorded moral superiority over the Greeks because Tudor historiography traced the royal line from Trojan Brutus (p. 48). But Empson sees the Trojan war to be a civil war by reference to Hector's kinship with Ajax (*Some Versions*, p. 35).

seeing differences rather than resorting to comparisons that result in invidious judgments. Like the originary Helen in the *Iliad*, Cressida is subjugated by being made a figure of difference, but *as* a figure of difference, she possesses the ability, unique in the play, to perceive differences among others.

Although Troilus' horror of doubleness, Ulysses' insistence on degree, and Thersites' reductive leveling appear to represent widely diverging reactions to the world of the play, they in fact share in the pervasive refusal to acknowledge differences. It is not an accident that these three characters come together to witness Cressida's seduction and pass judgment on it. This group of one Trojan and two Greeks, one footsoldier and two aristocratic warriors, nevertheless can affirm their community as men by scapegoating "false Cressida." Cressida as outsider is the only character who shares Shakespeare's perspective in offering an alternative mode of sense-making; but as woman, she is judged and categorized by the male warriors who control the language of love, politics, history, and literary tradition, and by the majority of male critics who have controlled the language of literary criticism.[50] Ulysses condemns her as "daughter of the game" (4.5.63) for complying with his proposal that she be "kissed in general" (4.5.21); similarly, Troilus labels her as "false," when "Troy and Troilus" (4.4.31) have in fact already betrayed her. In both instances, the men act to circumscribe severely her choices, but they nevertheless denounce her for making the best of the impossible situation in which they have placed her. Cressida's only source of power in preserving her integrity lies in her unique capacity for achieving an unsentimental understanding of herself and her predicament, but as she herself says, "to be wise and love / Exceeds man's might" (3.2.146–47)—and we might add, woman's. After she gives in to Troilus despite her better judgment, her self-perception becomes increasingly couched in terms of the language made available to her by those who control it. Unlike Cleopatra, who as Egypt's queen could defy both the values and language of Caesar's Rome, Cressida, as traitor's daughter, acquiesces with the myth of her as "false" and, in effect, adds her signature to it.

---

[50]There are, of course, exceptions to the predominant critical opinion that labels Cressida "false." Tucker Brooke, as early as in 1928, described Cressida as "a more helpless being than Chaucer's Criseyde . . . a little soiled from the first and shrinkingly conscious of her predestined pollution." "Shakespeare's Study in Culture and Anarchy," *Yale Review*, 17 (1928), 573. His uncharacteristic sympathy for Cressida seems to arise from his interest in elucidating "the effect of environment on

As Gretchen Mieszkowski has shown, by the time Shakespeare came to the story, the reputation of Cressida had become fixed as a byword for fickle wantonness.[51] Henryson, who quite literally completed Chaucer's poem (his *Testament of Cresseid* was printed at the end of sixteenth-century editions of Chaucer), punishes Cressida with leprosy—a physical mark of her moral debasement and her difference—which prevents Troilus from even recognizing her. Henryson's attempt to close the accounts was quite successful, for Elizabethan poets such as Turberville and Gascoigne called their faithless mistresses Cressida's heirs; in the preface to his "Cressid's complaint" (1576), Whetstone, rejoicing in her downfall, declared: "The inconstancie of Cressid is so readie in every mans mouth, as it is a needelesse labour to blase at full her abuse towards yong Troilus, her frowning on Syr Diomede, her wanton lures and love."[52] Clearly, Shakespeare did not agree with Whetstone that it would be a "needelesse labour" to recount the story yet again. Indeed, he opens the accounts apparently closed by Henryson and asserts his power over tradition by revivifying the mutilated corpse of Cressida.

Shakespeare's revision is motivated by an impulse opposite to Henryson's desire to judge and punish once and for all: rather, Shakespeare not only withholds judgment but questions the very possiblity of rendering judgment. Accordingly, Shakespeare refuses to provide satisfying points of closure from which retrospective judgments can be made. Troilus remains alive, unlike in Chaucer, where he looked on "this litele spot of erthe" (5.1815) and laughed at his sorrows from

---

character" and "the social forces operative in England at the end of Elizabeth's reign" (p. 572). More recently, E. Talbot Donaldson has suggested that the "preoccupation with establishing Cressida's sluttishness seems itself to reflect a kind of emotional involvement with her [on the part of the critics] that is less literary than personal." "Cressid False, Criseyde Untrue: An Ambiguity Revisited," in *Poetic Traditions of the English Renaissance*, ed. Maynard Mack and George deForest Lord (New Haven: Yale Univ. Press, 1982), p. 73. Feminist critics have contributed to Cressida's recent critical rehabilitation. Gayle Greene, in her study on Cressida and her "relation to the men and society who make her what she is" argues that "the stereotypical in her character occurs in a context that constitutes a critique of stereotyping." "Shakespeare's Cressida: 'A kind of self'," in *The Woman's Part: Feminist Criticism of Shakespeare*, ed. Carolyn Lenz, Gayle Greene, and Carol Neely (Urbana: Univ. of Illinois Press, 1980), p. 145. Janet Adelman, "This is and is not Cressid," focuses her discussion of Cressida on Troilus' need to conceive of her as a maternal figure: Troilus' fantasy of union with a nurturing figure is shattered when it is contaminated by sexuality.

[51] Gretchen Mieszkowski, "The Reputation of Criseyde: 1155–1500," *Transactions of the Connecticut Academy of Arts and Sciences*, 43 (1971), 71–153.

[52] Quoted in Geoffrey Bullough, *Narrative and Dramatic Sources of Shakespeare* (New York: Columbia Univ. Press, 1966), 6: 97.

the eighth sphere. Our final glimpse of Shakespeare's Troilus is in his pursuit of Diomed, which bespeaks an unenlightened displacement of his war within to that without. Nor is Cressida shown to live out her life in leprosy and misery, though Shakespeare alludes to the horrible literalness of her fate at the hands of Henryson in the metaphorical curse on herself, "I shall be plagued." Rather than punish Cressida, Shakespeare literalizes her metaphorical disease in Pandarus' "Neapolitan bone-ache" (2.3.17) which he bequeathes to the audience at the play's end.[53]

The oft-discussed difficulty in classifying the play as either a comedy or tragedy stems from this lack of a closure that would mark its dramatic genre. All comedies, even the problem comedies such as *All's Well That Ends Well* and *Measure for Measure,* end in marriage, and all tragedies, with the death of the hero; *Troilus and Cressida* does not conclude with either. Yet Shakespeare deliberately alludes to a comic ending in Pandarus' epilogue, a parody of Puck's request for applause, and to a tragic ending in Hector's death, though the hero of the title remains alive.[54] Even in Shakespeare's day, the play was assigned to different genres: although in the 1609 quarto it is called the "Famous Historie," the epistle to the reader refers to it as a comedy, and in the 1623 folio the play appears in the section containing the tragedies. Modern critics have yet to agree on its genre, but I suggest that the play's generic ambiguity corresponds to Shakespeare's critique of the codification and classification of Cressida.[55]

[53]Pandarus' references to the brothels at Winchester (5.10.53) mark a sobering moment for the contemporary audience that may have felt detached and superior to the diseased world depicted in the play. The (venereal) disease is revealed as properly affecting not a Cressida or even solely a "trader in the flesh" (5.10.45), such as Pandarus, but rather the entire society that sanctions the selling and buying of women as merchandise. On Pandarus' role as mediator and as a problematic counterpart of Shakespeare as mimetic artist, see Richard Fly, " 'I cannot come to Cressid but by Pandar': Mediation in the Theme and Structure of *Troilus and Cressida,*" *ELR,* 3 (1973), 145–65. Girard, "Politics of Desire," p. 208, considers Pandarus, the play's mediator of desire, to turn the epilogue into "almost . . . an allegory of the contagious power of mimetic desire."

[54]On the two endings of the play, see Foakes, pp. 142–43. He thinks that Shakespeare first intended to end the play with Troilus' couplet, characteristic of concluding lines in Shakespeare: "Strike a free march to Troy! With comfort go; / Hope of revenge shall hide our inward woe" (5.10.30–31). He considers the two endings to be complementary.

[55]Frederick Boas first classified *Troilus* as a "problem play," together with *All's Well, Measure,* and *Hamlet,* in *Shakspere and his Predecessors* (London: John Murray, 1896), pp. 369–84. Knight discusses it as a tragedy (p. 49); Robert Ornstein calls it "dialectical drama" which approaches the issues of tragedy ironically and analytically. *The Moral Vision of Jacobean Tragedy* (Madison: Univ. of Wisconsin Press, 1960), p.

Swinburne captured the uncertainty that lies at the heart of Shakespeare's play by referring to it as "this hybrid and hundred-faced and hydra-headed prodigy, [which] at once defies and derides all definitive comment."[56] Swinburne acknowledges the play's complexity and multiplicity—what I have called Shakespeare's fiction that opposes itself to myths that seek to reduce and simplify. Yet Swinburne's language reveals a palpable anxiety vis-à-vis the monstrosity of indeterminacy that not only eludes but with aggressive hostility "defies" and "derides" attempts to define it. Here Swinburne unwittingly reenacts the impulse to mystify dramatized in *Troilus and Cressida*, his language showing the desire to control and contain the indeterminacy of experience and the impossibility of fully knowing either the self or the other. Thus it is not surprising that most critics have identified either with Troilus—who, rather than acknowledging these troubling uncertainties, insists upon his unitary "truth" that can be maintained only by projecting anxiety-producing internal divisions on Cressida, whose role as scapegoat is to exemplify doubleness and falseness—or with Ulysses, whose exposition on degree affirms that an essential and orderly hierarchy prevails and can be discerned. These critical reactions are contained and anticipated in the play itself, for *Troilus and Cressida* enacts the very process through which characters and writers alike transform complex and ambiguous fictions into tidy and manageable myths.

Although in *Troilus and Cressida* Shakespeare ironically rewrites the story of Troy, he shares with Homer an interest in the process by which dominant males deny subjecthood to women. Systems of commerce in *Troilus and Cressida* differ greatly from the system of exchange in the *Iliad;* even so, in both works, women are exchanged, and that exchange is institutionalized. In Homer, women stand as

---

240. For discussions of the play as comedy, see Lawrence, pp. 122–73; and Alice Walker's introduction to her edition in the New Cambridge Shakespeare (1957), p. xvi. Oscar J. Campbell discusses the play as a Jonsonian "comical satire" in *Comicall Satyre and Shakespeare's Troilus and Cressida* (San Marino: Huntington Library, 1938), pp. 185–234. For a discussion of the problem of genre that parallels mine, see Danson, pp.68–96. He persuasively argues that the play is "a searching ironic parody of tragic form and tragic values" (p. 96). For similar views, see Colie, pp. 317–19. Una Ellis-Fermor, *Frontiers of Drama* (London: Methuen, 1946), pp. 63, 69, 73, considers the play's disjunctive form as corresponding to its central theme of discord.

56Algernon Charles Swinburne, *A Study of Shakespeare* (London: Chatto and Windus, 1880), p. 200. He expresses, however, great enthusiasm for the play, which he calls a "quasi-tragedy": "One of the most admirable among all the works of Shakespeare's immeasurable and unfathomable intelligence" (p. 198).

signifiers and prizes of honor; in Shakespeare, Pandarus calls attention
to prostitution in the brothels at Winchester. Thus Shakespeare models Cressida—reduced by the men around her and by literary tradition to a quasi-allegorical figure of duplicity—after the Iliadic Helen,
a symbol of the doubleness of the war effort. Yet both poets criticize
such objectifications of women by representing their subjecthood,
though Shakespeare extends Homer's critique by dramatizing the
process by which women eventually give up their autonomous subjectivity to confirm their own victimization: Homer's Helen blames
herself for the war, and Shakespeare's Cressida ultimately accepts the
oppressive stereotyping of her as the byword of falsehood. Shakespeare also explores the ultimate consequences of such an acquiescence: like Spenser's Hellenore, locked up by Malbecco with his
"mucky pelfe," Shakespeare's trivial and vulgar Helen has become
nothing but a "daughter of the game," whose rules are set by the
dominant males. Shakespeare offers an alternative to Cressida's (and
Helen's) acquiescence in his representation of Egypt's queen, Cleopatra, who insists upon retaining her independence from Octavian's
efforts to deploy her as a symbol of his patriarchal and imperial
power—though it is only by staging her own death that she is able to
do so.

Epilogue: *Antony and Cleopatra*

A quibble is to Shakespeare, what luminous vapours are to the traveller; he follows it at all adventures; it is sure to lead him out of his way, and sure to engulf him in the mire. . . . A quibble, poor and barren as it is, gave him such delight, that he was content to purchase it, by the sacrifice of reason, propriety and truth. A quibble was to him the fatal Cleopatra for which he lost the world, and was content to lose it.

—Samuel Johnson, "Preface to Shakespeare"

Just as Euripides' story of faithful Helen's sojourn in Egypt revised the legend of adulterous Helen's flight to Troy, so Shakespeare's portrait of Cleopatra in *Antony and Cleopatra* revises the portrait of Helen in *Troilus and Cressida*. In fact, Plutarch, Shakespeare's main source for *Antony and Cleopatra*, explicitly compares Cleopatra to Helen: "In the ende, as Paris fledde from the battell, and went to hide him selfe in Helens armes: even so did he [Antony] in Cleopatraes armes, or to speake more properlie, Paris hidde him selfe in Helens closet, but Antonius to followe Cleopatra, fledde and lost the victorie."[1] Although Plutarch criticizes Cleopatra and her prototype Helen from a Roman perspective, Shakespeare celebrates his Cleopatra from an Egyptian perspective. Shakespeare's Cleopatra recalls Helen in Egypt in yet another manner: both women function as figures of mutability and difference—the sea god Proteus guards Helen in Egypt, and Cleopatra's "infinite variety" (2.2.246) identifies her with the overflowing Nile. In each of these representations, mutability does not preclude a crucial constancy: Helen's loyalty to Menelaus and Cleopatra's to Antony.

Although Cleopatra, the woman of many husbands, and Elizabeth, who refused to marry, may seem more different than alike, several

---

[1] "The Comparison of Demetrius and Antonius," in *Narrative and Dramatic Sources of Shakespeare,* ed. Geoffrey Bullough (New York: Columbia Univ. Press, 1964), 5: 319–20.

critics have pointed out similarities between Cleopatra and Elizabeth.[2] In particular, they cite the parallel between Cleopatra questioning the messenger about the details of Octavia's appearance and
Elizabeth's similar curiosity about Mary Stuart.[3] This parallel points
to another historical analogy between Octavia, the sister of Augustus,
and Mary Stuart, the mother of James I, as female relatives and
instruments of the male monarchs who replaced Cleopatra and Elizabeth. More fundamentally, these two share the predicament of ruling as a woman in a patriarchy. Accordingly, Cleopatra's sexual
ambiguity—she exchanges clothes with Antony and wears his
"sword Philippan" (2.5.23)—recalls Elizabeth's frequent references to
herself as a "Prince" and her famous military review, dressed in armor, at Tillbury. Even if we were to forgo a strict topical identification between the two queens, "it would have been difficult for any
Elizabethan to think of an imperious queen without remembering the
monarch who had reigned so long in England."[4]

Yet critics who have noticed the analogy between Cleopatra and
Elizabeth have not discussed the significance of the historical moment
of the composition of *Antony and Cleopatra,* only several years after
the passing of the English monarchy from Elizabeth to James. At this
juncture, Elizabeth is, indeed, "a great spirit gone" (1.2.126), as
Fulvia, Antony, and Cleopatra are said to be by characters who survive them in Shakespeare's play. I have argued that in *Troilus and
Cressida,* Shakespeare represented the persistence of patriarchy during
Elizabeth's reign; in *Antony and Cleopatra,* I would suggest that he
nostalgically represents Elizabeth, replaced by James, through Cleopatra, a fiercely independent and canny queen, who was ultimately
defeated by the quintessential patriarch, Caesar Augustus.[5]

Antony and Cleopatra's difference from *Troilus and Cressida* is per-

---

[2]Keith Rinehart, "Shakespeare's Cleopatra and England's Elizabeth," *Shakespeare
Quarterly,* 23 (1972), 81–86; Helen Morris, "Queen Elizabeth I 'Shadowed' in
Cleopatra," *HLQ,* 32 (1969), 271–78; and Kenneth Muir, "Elizabeth I, Jodelle, and
Cleopatra," *Renaissance Drama,* n.s. 2 (1969), 197–206.

[3]Muir, p. 199. Morris, p. 272, points out that these are details not in the source,
Plutarch.

[4]Morris, p. 278.

[5]See Jonathan Goldberg, *James I and the Politics of Literature* (Baltimore: Johns
Hopkins Univ. Press, 1983), pp. 85–112, on representations of the family during
James I's reign that emphasized the power of the patriarch. Robert Filmer, in *Pa-
triarcha,* the only defense of the political theory of absolutism written during the Stuart
period, argues that the organization of the ideal state imitates the patriarchalism of the
family (p. 85). See also Gordon J. Schochet, *The Authoritarian Family and Political
Attitudes in Seventeenth-Century England* (Oxford: Basil Blackwell, 1975).

haps most evident in Shakespeare's affirmation of sexuality in *Antony and Cleopatra,* by contrast to his representation of degraded sexuality in *Troilus and Cressida.* Accordingly, Shakespeare has Antony revise the story of Dido and Aeneas:[6]

> Eros!—I come, my queen.—Eros!—Stay for me.
> Where souls do couch on flowers, we'll hand in hand,
> And with our sprightly port make the ghosts gaze.
> Dido and her Aeneas shall want troops,
> And all the haunt be ours.
>
> [4.14.50–54]

Antony swerves from his prototype Aeneas' abandonment of Dido and, more specifically, rewrites Dido's silent rejection of Aeneas in *Aeneid* 6 by imagining how he and Cleopatra will be reunited in the underworld. In Antony's version, troops of lovers will replace troops of soldiers and he and Cleopatra will establish their empire of love in the underworld, in opposition to Octavius' empire of policy above. Shakespeare signals this reversal by emphasizing the significant name of Antony's armorer, Eros, who stands in for Cleopatra here as Antony's partner in his erotic suicide. Moreover, Shakespeare marks a radical revision of his literary model when he reverses the sequence between historical prototype and literary character; the historical Antony and Cleopatra were prototypes for Virgil's Aeneas and Dido. Shakespeare makes his position as literary descendant of Virgil into a source of strength and insight by criticizing Aeneas and Dido as incomplete models for his own Antony and Cleopatra.

This revision of the *Aeneid* allows Cleopatra to escape Dido's fate, to avoid being sacrificed on the altar of the Roman Empire. Octavian intends to parade Cleopatra in the theatrical display of a triumph, in order to represent what he and his empire have successfully conquered and subdued. Cleopatra foils this degradation, speaking explicitly of her refusal to be represented and reduced to Caesar's puppet:

> Saucy lictors
> Will catch at us, like strumpets, and scald rhymers

[6]For the relationship between the *Aeneid* and *Antony and Cleopatra,* see Janet Adelman, *The Common Liar: An Essay on Antony and Cleopatra* (New Haven: Yale Univ. Press, 1973), pp. 68–75; and Barbara J. Bono, *Literary Transvaluation: From Vergilian Epic to Shakespearean Tragicomedy* (Berkeley: Univ. of California Press, 1984), pp. 141–219.

Ballad us out o' tune. The quick comedians
Extemporally will stage us, and present
Our Alexandrian revels; Antony
Shall be brought drunken forth, and I shall see
Some squeaking Cleopatra boy my greatness
I'th' posture of a whore.

[5.2.214–21]

Cleopatra understands the politics of representation. She realizes that by allowing Caesar to caricature her she will lose her fiercely guarded autonomy; since she must be represented in any case, she will be the author, director, and actor of the scene that will define her character.[7] Her extended suicide, therefore, is her own theatrical triumph. By foiling Caesar's plan with her carefully orchestrated suicide, she repeats Dido's suicide, but with a difference: Cleopatra's suicide is a controlled and creative act, unlike Dido's passionate act, which bespoke defeat and desperation.[8] Instead of being appropriated and travestied by a saucy Roman boy, Cleopatra appropriates for her own end the Roman practice of principled suicide, exhorting her maids, "Let's do't after the high Roman fashion" (4.14.87).

By this act, Cleopatra takes representation out of the hands not only of Caesar but also of Enobarbus.[9] For Cleopatra envisions her moment of death as a reenactment of her first meeting with Antony at Cydnus: "Show me, my women, like a queen. Go fetch / My best attires. I am again for Cydnus, / To meet Mark Antony" (5.2.227–29). Enobarbus' striking portrait of her also referred to that moment of meeting at Cydnus. Thus Cleopatra, by attiring herself in her "crown and all" (5.2.232), succeeds in doing "that thing that ends all other deeds, / Which shackles accidents and bolts up change" (5.2.5–6); she makes herself a monument—this scene significantly takes

---

[7]Shakespeare significantly omits Plutarch's description of how Cleopatra disfigured herself, "overcome with sorow and passion of minde": "both for that she had plucked her heare from her head, as also for that she had martired all her face with her nailes, and besides, her voyce was small and trembling, her eyes sonke into her heade with continuall blubbering: and moreover, they might see the most parte of her stomake torne in sunder." Bullough, 5: 313.

[8]Sheila Murnaghan, in a paper given at the 1986 Modern Language Association Convention, "'The high Roman fashion': *Antony and Cleopatra* and the Classical Traditions of Male and Female Suicide," suggests that Cleopatra's suicide simulates Cato's noble Stoic death, and that she is more Cato's heir than was Portia, who swallowed fire.

[9]Bono, p. 219, also suggests that Cleopatra remakes Enobarbus' picture of her at Cydnus.

place in her "monument"—and thus refuses to allow Enobarbus' portrait of her to stand by itself and therefore to define her. She also justifies Antony through her persuasive representation of a larger-than-life Antony after his ambiguous, botched suicide:

> I dreamt there was an Emperor Antony.
> O such another sleep, that I might see
> But such another man! . . .
> His face was as the heav'ns, and therein stuck
> A sun and moon, which kept their course, and lighted
> The little O, th' earth. . . .
> His legs bestrid the ocean, his rear'd arm
> Crested the world, his voice was propertied
> As all the tuned spheres, and that to friends;
> But when he meant to quail and shake the orb,
> He was as rattling thunder. For his bounty,
> There was no winter in't: an autumn it was
> That grew the more by reaping. His delights
> Were dolphin-like; they show'd his back above
> The element they liv'd in. In his livery
> Walk'd crowns and crownets; realms and islands were
> As plates dropp'd from his pocket.
>
> [5.2.75–91]

This portrait is so compelling that it convinces Caesar's man Dol-abella to betray his master and to reveal his plans for her: "Your loss is as yourself, great. . . . / . . . I do feel, / By the rebound of yours, a grief that smites / My very heart at root" (5.2.100–104). Even Octa-vian, who never understood her allure while she was living, gives tribute to her resolve—"Bravest at the last, / She level'd at our pur-poses, and being royal, / Took her own way" (5.2.334–36)—and is moved to speak of her "strong toil of grace" (5.2.347).

Shakespeare thus rewrites Roman history and the literary tradition based on Virgil's authority by rendering the defeated Antony and Cleopatra, and especially Cleopatra, more compelling than the victor Octavian (whom Cleopatra disdainfully calls "Fortune's knave" [5.2.3]) and his empire. Non-Western and nonwhite, she is doubly Other as both woman and racially different;[10] but these differences

---

[10]On "Cleopatra's blackness," see Adelman, pp. 184–88. She points out that al-though for Plutarch and Daniel Cleopatra is Greek, Shakespeare's use of the word "black," the reference to her sunburn, and the association of Egypt and Africa suggest that he imagined her as dark, which contributed to the sense of her ancient and mysterious sexuality.

Cleopatra makes into sources of artistic, if not political, strength. Allowing heroic Cleopatra to take control of her own representation, Shakespeare allies himself with her energies of difference rather than with political hegemony and the literary tradition that justified that hegemony.

Samuel Johnson remarked that a "quibble" was Shakespeare's fatal "Cleopatra," for whose sake he willingly sacrificed "reason, propriety, and truth." (Tellingly, Johnson next faults Shakespeare for neglecting the unities.)[11] Like the other male poets of epic in this study, Shakespeare figures the problem of authority—exemplified by Johnson's "reason, propriety, and truth"—and difference, in his representation of female characters such as Cressida and Cleopatra. His rewriting of epic in the dramatic medium underscores his interest in multiple voices, especially those of women differing from the voice of patriarchial authority. As a writer confronting the authority of the anterior epic tradition, it is fitting, then, that Shakespeare finds compelling (and useful) these feminine voices of difference.

[11]"Preface to Shakespeare," in *Johnson on Shakespeare,* ed. Walter Raleigh (London: Henry Frowde, 1908), p. 23.

Index

Library of Congress Cataloging-in-Publication Data

Suzuki, Mihoko, 1953–
  Metamorphoses of Helen : authority, difference, and the epic / Mihoko
Suzuki.
    p. cm.
  Includes index.
  ISBN 0-8014-2219-1 (alk. paper)
    1. Classical literature—History and criticism. 2. Helen of Troy (Greek
mythology) in literature. 3. Trojan War in literature. 4. Homer—
Knowledge—Folklore, mythology. 5. Virgil—Knowledge—Folklore,
mythology. 6. Spenser, Edmund. 1552?–1599—Knowledge—Folklore,
mythology. 7. Shakespeare, William. 1564–1616—Knowledge—Folklore,
mythology. 8. English literature—Early modern, 1500–1700—History and
criticism. 9. Literature, Comparative—Classical and English. 10. Literature,
Comparative—English and classical. I. Title.
PA3015.R5H377 1989   809'.93351—dc 19   89-764